The Politics of
Nationalism in Canada:
Cultural Conflict since 1760

DAVID CHENNELLS

UTP
1901-2001

UNIVERSITY OF TORONTO PRESS
Toronto Buffalo London

© University of Toronto Press Incorporated 2001
Toronto Buffalo London
Printed in Canada

ISBN 0-8020-4224-4

Printed on acid-free paper

Canadian Cataloguing in Publication Data

Chennells, David
    The politics of nationalism in Canada : cultural conflict since 1760

    Includes bibliographical references and index.
    ISBN 0-8020-4224-4

    1. Nationalism – Canada – History.   2. Canada – Politics and
government.   3. Canada – English-French relations –
History.   I. Title.

    FC97.C534 2001   320.54'0971   C00-932581-6
    F1008.C534 2000

The University of Toronto Press acknowledges the financial assistance
to its publishing program of the Canada Council for the Arts and the
Ontario Arts Council.

University of Toronto Press acknowledges the financial support for its
publishing activites of the Government of Canada through the Book
Publishing Industry Development Program (BPIDP).

The state is not an end, the state is a means to an end. Part of the duties of a state is to protect life, liberty, and intellectual freedom, not less than the general public welfare. It has not the right to undertake to destroy the mental vision of one section of a population with the design of creating it anew.

David Mills, 1890

He held with Burke, that it was not the duty of a member of the Legislature to be a slavish representative of the opinions of his constituents ... He was sent as a representative to protect the interests of the whole community ... What was the object of establishing a government: it was not merely to build a machine as a curiosity, it was to protect the rights of all men, the minority as well as the majority.

Robert Baldwin (Transcribed Speech), 1850

If my readers are satisfied with the form, the colours, the new arrangement which I have given to the labours of my predecessors, they may perhaps consider me not as a contemptible Thief, but as an honest and industrious Manufacturer, who has fairly procured the raw materials, and worked them up with a laudable degree of skill and success.

Edward Gibbon, 1779

Contents

Acknowledgments

As unorthodox as this work is in many respects, it has benefited greatly from the advice and guidance of others. Marissa Quie initially sparked my interest in nationalism and proposed a historical approach   to the Canadian case. Geoffrey Hawthorn painstakingly read the work many times and provided a thorough commentary and helpful advice. Alan Cairns, John Dunn, Anthony Giddens, Murray Greenwood, Noel McLachlan, Kenneth McRoberts, Jeffrey McNairn, Ged Martin, Innes Molinaro, Peter Russell, Michael Twohey, Annis May Timpson, and two anonymous reviewers for the University of Toronto Press all generously commented on this work. Any remaining deficiencies are solely my responsibility.

Virgil Duff, executive editor of University of Toronto Press, has with great patience guided a first-time author through the publishing process. The late Beverley Endersby heroically cast her acute attention to detail upon the manuscript. Anne Laughlin, managing editor, gently but firmly pressed onwards. Babara Schon compiled a comprehensive index with great speed. Silvana Dean, of the Faculty of Social and Political Sciences at Cambridge, patiently dealt with many administrative matters over the years. Excellent research libraries at the University of Toronto and University of British Columbia provided facilities and accommodated my daily presence for more years than I care to admit. The Committee of Vice-Chancellors and Principals of Great Britain, the Cambridge Commonwealth Trust, and the Social Sciences and Humanities Research Council of Canada furnished financial support, the last in the form of a doctoral fellowship. My consulting firm, Bain and Company, most recently permitted a ten-month leave of absence to allow me to expand the work.

My greatest debt of all is to those who have supported me personally and never lost faith: my family, Joanne, Bill, Suzanne, and Alice Chennells; friends Claire Bane, Roger Gillott, Isabelle Lemaire, Douglas Lonsbrough, and Michael Twohey. My wife, Dr Roberta Janzen, has been a constant source of joy and en-couragement to me.

This work is dedicated to my grandmother, D. Alice Chennells.

THE POLITICS OF NATIONALISM IN CANADA

Exclusive Nationalism and Conflict Regulation

Canadian history has often been conceived in terms of some form of nationalism.[1] But seldom has any attempt been made to advance the theory of nationalism by considering Canadian history.[2] This reluctance to abstract from particularity rests uneasily with a core article of faith in Canada: that the great Canadian experiment – of cultural coexistence within an evolving constitutional order – defines the country's main contribution to the global store of experience. Strengthening the dialogue between theory and Canadian history, in both directions, is the purpose of this work. It attempts to organize salient experience within Canadian political history on lines suggested by a novel conceptual framework, and, at the same time, to confront and enrich the framework with a close consideration of that historical experience.

'Nationalism' has become a highly analysed and rather indistinct category; this work focuses specifically on the exclusive variety, that is (roughly), nationalism catering exclusively to a (generally singular) linguistic, cultural, or religious group. My focus on this type arises from concern that it has become all too prevalent, and that it has aggravated civil strife within many diverse societies on numerous occasions.

This work argues that the extent of influence exclusive nationalism has had in the Canadian experience has been related to ebbs and flows in the political elite's capacity to manage conflict, and, further, that such fluctuations have been strongly conditioned by the level of popular mobilization and the form of political representation. I suggest, specifically, that popular mobilization, and procedural shifts to more direct forms of representation have at key points limited the capacity of political elites to treat diverse religious, linguistic, and cultural groups even-handedly, and have opened the door to official, exclusivist efforts at imposing particular national ways of life. Finally, and most significantly, this work argues that the relevant popular mobilization and shifts in the form of political representation have had many causes apart from the intensification of national identity or specifically ethnic grievance. If true, this thesis would imply that the penetration of the state by exclusive nationalism may be less fully explained by variations in the most superficially obvious characteristics – national consciousness and discontent – than generally believed.

In this introduction I define the generic term 'nationalism,' distinguish between its 'exclusive' and 'inclusive' forms, set out my normative assumptions, explain the need for new approaches to the study of exclusive nationalism particularly, formulate hypotheses generated in part from the literature on consociationalism and conflict regulation, and introduce periods of Canadian history exhibiting distinct phases of exclusive nationalism. At the end of this introduction, I touch upon questions of methodology of interest primarily to professional historians and theorists.

0.1 Concepts of Nationalism

Peter Alter suggests that nationalism is 'one of the most ambiguous concepts in the present-day vocabulary of political and analytical thought.'[3] Concepts of nationalism have indeed addressed a wide range of phenomena: a state of mind; concrete political manifestations; and the pursuit of multifarious, often intangible objectives. As a state of mind or consciousness, nationalism embodies loyalty to the way of life and symbols of an existing nation-state or a nation lacking a state of its own.[4] As politics, as a call to action, nationalism seeks to re-create the relationship between state and nation. The relationship sought can be 'congruence' between the two, that is, an independent state for a nation, or a uniform, cohesive nation for an existing state.[5] But nationalists do not seek only, or even necessarily, their own nation-state; in many cases, political objectives of securing cultural succour and official recognition are paramount.[6] So, beyond 'congruence' one should perhaps speak of 'symbiosis' to describe the mutually sustaining relationship between nation and state sought by nationalists.

Nationalism derives its greatest significance from its manifestation as an organized and broadly political force. Its frequent virulence often seems connected with the depth of the underlying consciousness. A challenge in developing a common view of nationalism is to link such consciousness with a consistent and coherent political program. One means of linking the two is to admit under the aegis of nationalism the full array of projects entered into under the influence of national consciousness.[7] But such expansive definitions inflate the topic to the point where it can hardly be coherently discussed in terms of its normative implications or its past causality. A more limited conception would focus on the elements that most obviously reflect the particularist consciousness of nationalism and the direct pursuit of greater 'congruence' or 'symbiosis.' This is the approach adopted here. Nationalism, generically speaking, may then be defined as *political activity seeking to create a more congruent or symbiotic relationship between the state and the nation so as to bind the state to the nation's will and to entrust the state with sustaining the nation's way of life.*

Even so defined, nationalism remains an overstretched category that invites subdivision and academic specialization. To derive the particular form of nationalism that is the focus of this work, it is useful to consider a few of the major taxonomies that have been proposed.

American historian Carlton Hayes set out in 1931 a classification system that proved seminal for later theorists who would also attempt to combine ideological and historical sensitivity.[8] Hayes's categories range from humanitarian nationalism (premised upon the world of equal and distinctive nationalities contemplated in the eighteenth-century Enlightenment) through the Jacobin nationalism of the French Revolution (externally militaristic and internally determined to 'expand a dominant nationality by forcing its language upon all the citizens of France'), through an (anti-imperial and nation-statist) liberal nationalism, to the integral nationalism of Charles Maurras (preaching 'the exclusive pursuit of national policies' and 'hatred of "alien" influences within France').[9] Hans Kohn, following a decade later, proposed a highly generalized geopolitical taxonomy that ignored pernicious side-effects of nationalism in the West (where, by and large, state preceded and delimited nationalism, and universal political liberty was achieved) but discovered them in a more florid, Eastern form (wherein nations and ethnic nationalism take their own boundaries, which often clash with existing polities).[10]

Anthony Smith criticized the typologies of Hayes and Kohn in his influential *Theories of Nationalism.* Kohn's dichotomy had conflated 'too many levels of development, types of structure and cultural situations.' Furthermore, both Hayes's and Kohn's taxonomies, being concerned mainly with doctrines, had failed to grasp the ideological heterogeneity of nationalist movements, which, on Smith's view, should be treated as primary and integral units.[11] Smith argues that taking ideology as primary in classifying nationalism 'risks attaching too much weight to the statements and declarations of a tiny minority of intellectuals,' and that the realm of ideas is too far divorced from the sphere of action.[12]

Smith's response to these perceived shortcomings is to classify nationalist *movements* according to two simple aspects of their sociological circumstances: whether they represent a culturally distinctive group, and whether they have already attained independence or must yet contemplate seeking it through separation.[13] In terms of the first of these, the distinctiveness dimension, *ethnic* nationalist movements are those that 'start from a pre-existent homogeneous entity' and seek independence as a 'means for cultural ends.' *Territorial* nationalist movements, by contrast, often lack a common 'cultural identity' and they seek to institute an internally focused rule by 'wresting' sovereignty from 'alien rulers,' thus fulfilling a 'direct political function.'[14]

Yet it is possible to accept Smith's criticisms of Kohn's oversimplification without adopting Smith's sociological approach. By presuming a correspondence between sociological composition and objectives (in taking objectives as *given* by composition), Smith muddies the waters in a particularly unfortunate way. For Smith's typology would, for example, consign all culturally distinctive movements seeking their own state to the same general category. Yet, for liberals, if there is one fundamental and emphatic distinction to be made concerning nationalism it is between separatist movements (or elements therein) committed to the systematic domination or expulsion of other ethnic communities and preferences present, and those committed to the even-handed treatment and coexistence of all such communities in a prospective state. Unfortunately, this is not a point of narrow, academic interest, for eliding such distinctions at the conceptual level fails to guide enquiry to the types that require systematic analysis as a matter of practical urgency.[15]

A promising alternative is to treat ends sought, rather than sociological profile, as the primary basis for a classification scheme. This means focusing less on the ethnic credentials and progress to statehood of aspiring nations, and more on the *cultural objectives* of the nationalist agenda, aspects that Smith himself has recognized more recently as pivotal.[16] Admittedly, there often *are* relationships among these various facets: the sociological composition of movements may shape its objectives. Nationalists within culturally heterogeneous, *territorial* movements, for example, often *do* emphasize publicly shared *civic* beliefs and values, such as liberalism or democracy. But to presume this sort of correlation is too often misleading. Nationalism that might appear at first glance to be of the *ethnic* variety, as considered from the self-conscious, relative homogeneity and distinctiveness of its constituency (e.g., of the Czechs or Catalonians) might upon closer examination be deemed *civic* from a consideration of the pluralistic institutions implied in their objectives. Conversely, cases of nationalism that might initially be considered *territorial*, such as those arising from a heterogeneous, emergent 'state-nation,' can turn out to be narrow-minded and intolerant of minorities, as has been deemed the case with revolutionary France vis-à-vis its Jewish population.[17]

Some scholars, including Michael Keating, perhaps with this in mind, distinguish between ethnic and civic forms of nationalism on the basis of the place given to the individual within the nation.[18] Civic nationalism 'tends to start from the individual and build to the nation'; ethnic nationalists conceive of the nation in terms of more particularist 'ascriptive criteria.'[19] Overall, this seems useful, except that the retention of the 'ethnic' type might confusingly link it to pre-existing, 'ethnic' uniformity, rather than to 'ethnicity-making' goals. Achieving descriptive and evaluative clarity thus weighs in favour of setting aside the ethnic/territorial/civic distinctions entirely to focus solely upon the cultural objectives of nationalist movements, or fractions thereof, and to ignore their sociological composition altogether.[20]

0.2 Exclusive and Inclusive Nationalism

The distinction that marks the emphasis of this work rests between exclusive and inclusive nationalism. Building upon the generic definition of nationalism proposed above, I define exclusive nationalism as *nationalist political activity (that is, political activity seeking to create a more congruent or symbiotic relationship between state and nation so as to bind the state to the nation's will and to entrust the state with sustaining the nation's way of life) of a kind that seeks to privilege one recognizable way of life over others, in the sense of imposing it and intentionally altering the balance present among adherents of various real communities of religion, language, or culture.* The term 'balance' here refers to the proportions of residents adhering to, or primarily identifying with, various religious, linguistic, or cultural allegiances. In referring to real communities, my intention is not to represent social reality as comprising more finitely bounded entities than it in fact does, but rather to avoid overly expansive definitions of culture, which at the extreme might include sociological artefacts ('criminal culture,' 'civic culture'). An extremely broad concept would take us excessively away from the sense in which mobilized, culturally denominated constituencies are at play in nationalism, in the normal sense of the word.

The reader will observe that I do not use 'exclusive' to refer to exclusivity of membership, in the sense of 'exclusive tennis club.' Although a state that went so far as to deny citizenship to residents on the basis of cultural criteria would presumably be acting on exclusive-nationalist grounds, the converse is not necessarily true. Exclusive nationalism very often does *not* go to the full extent of barring residents from legal membership. As in revolutionary France, it may be officially open to all present, but on steep terms of conformity to the national language or culture being actively privileged. 'Exclusive' is thus used here to refer to the exclusivity of the language(s), culture(s), or religion(s) with which symbiosis is sought by nationalists for the state.

The concept of inclusive nationalism, which arises here mainly as a residual, and somewhat hypothetical category, might be applicable to situations where, although nationalists seek to foster one or more ways of life, they: (1) define the national way of life so broadly (or vaguely) that fostering it does not in practice privilege the way of life of any one recognizable group of individuals over that of others present; or (2) support more specific ways of life present, but equitably, so as to avoid intentionally altering the balance among them, or manipulating individual choice.[21] In either case, inclusive nationalism would grant equal or proportionate respect to the religious, linguistic, or cultural attachments of individuals. This is not, however, a matter taken up here, and I would not vouch that inclusive nationalism represents the best alternative to exclusive nationalism.

A few other preliminary comments: Classifying nationalism on the basis of objectives rather than on the sociological profile of putative nations requires considerably more contextual sensitivity, and also greater subjectivity. Exclusive nationalism is an ideal type, and is often empirically a characteristic of elements or phases of movements, and not, of course, of every constituent member or grouping of a movement.[22] Finally, my assumption is that exclusive nationalism runs seriously afoul of liberalism, which I must confess from the start provides the basic ethical compass of this work.

As this study is almost wholly occupied with causation, rather than with evaluation, I hope that my own normative assumptions will not deprive this work of interest to readers holding ethical commitments differing from my own. But to the extent that my own biases are inescapably embedded in my conceptual and descriptive vocabulary, let me come clean from the start. As the relevant theoretical territory has been extremely well trodden by others, my main effort here is to provide pointers to existing, recent arguments, although I will also attempt one brief extension to this theory at the end. In any case, I cursorily disclose my normative assumptions here about exclusive nationalism with considerable diffidence and certainly not with any expectation of persuading those holding differing assumptions.

Even without resorting to liberal theory, the ethical deficiencies of exclusive nationalism have been apparent to many. As Alter puts it, some nationalists 'are prepared unscrupulously to assert the interests of their own nation at the expense of others.'[23] With this in mind, Thomas Pogge suggests confronting 'ethnic or religious chauvinism with a version of the Golden Rule: Base any claims you make for your own ethnic (religious) group on principles that you would be prepared to extend to any other ethnic (religious) group.'[24] Exclusive nationalism, by construction, almost certainly breaches such a principle. In practical terms, exclusive national-ism often invites serious civil strife. As Donald Horowitz succinctly notes, 'group claims are not necessarily equal. Some groups seek domination, not the mere avoidance of it. Some seek to exclude others from the polity altogether, and some seek merely to be included on equal terms. If all groups merely wanted inclusion, distrust and anxiety would still make ethnic conflict serious, but more tractable than it is.'[25] Thus, even from purely practical, theoretically naive considerations, exclusive nationalism has clear drawbacks.

In assaulting individual cultural preferences, particularly of minorities or cultural dissidents, exclusive nationalism is also illiberal. The basic unit of concern for liberalism is individual preferences, including, of course, the individual preference to enjoy linguistic, religious, or cultural affinities held in common with others (and constitutive of their shared identities, etc.).[26] Liberals most plausibly base their concern for such individual preferences on the substantive moral value of autonomy and choice. Indi-vidual choice – the prerogative, as Will Kymlicka puts it, 'to lead our life from the inside,' – is held to have intrinsic and developmental value in human life.[27] Liberalism also recognizes broad benefits that arise from individual-led creativity; adaptation; and independent, critical reason.[28] Furthermore, powerful prudential, or consequentialist reasons have been recognized for the state to be restrained from overriding individuals' commitments to self-regarding ways of life; these are asserted largely on the basis of a connection discerned between several historical atrocities (e.g., the post-Reformation wars of religion, the Holocaust, the cultural revolution) and a lack of such restraint.[29] Finally, some liberals (including myself) are deeply sceptical of claims that changes over time in individuals' 'constitutive' commitments, particularly where these arise from circum-stances of the individual's own choosing, are typically for the worst.[30] So liberalism accords a higher priority to the procedural norm of individual autonomy than to substantive objectives relating to a deemed optimal level of cultural diversity, homogeneity, or authenticity.[31] Ways of life, in short, are accorded by liberalism no direct political claims; these are bestowed only on individual sentient human beings.[32]

Dilemmas arise where individual autonomy turns against itself. Should the state respect, even facilitate, individuals' preferences to submit to autonomy-restricting, sub-state communities? Responses have variously considered externalities imposed by illiberal groups on others, the circumstances of individuals' original choices, costs of exit, groups' credentials of separateness, and the utility of submitting the 'private' choices in question to rational public engagement.[33] Debate continues. Fortunately we need not resolve these questions here, for a reasonable consensus exists among liberals that tolerance of illiberal preferences does not extend to the realm of public choice, that is, to the *state's* intentional manipulation, even by popular acclaim, of individual, self-regarding choices of culture and religion.[34] Freedom of exit from states is deemed too insubstantial and costly to legitimate such collective 'choices.' Liberals in the tradition of Immanuel Kant have also maintained that the conditions that foster reason and limit dogmatism depend in part on state tolerance of diverse positions.[35]

Conservatives, including communitarians, respond that, with so little to bind them, individuals may go their separate ways, corroding community and even the state.[36] Concern for the individual might also undermine claims by disadvantaged groups for reparations or other resource transfers to reduce inequality. But liberals may reply that honouring self-regarding individual choices does not vitiate differential entitlements to assistance; nor does it presuppose the popularity of divisive choices. They might well suggest, moreover, that few conservative polities over the long term have proved any more capable of furnishing the aspects of cultural isolation and stasis conservatives desire. Most significantly, liberalism does not necessarily deny that culture and ethnicity are collective goods in the economic sense, to be publicly supported.[37] As a self-described liberal scholar, Michael Walzer, puts it, 'as long as ethnicity is experienced as a collective good by large numbers of people it probably makes sense to permit collective money, taxpayers' money, to seep through the state/ethnic group (state/church) barrier. This is especially important when taxes constitute a significant portion of the national wealth and when the state has undertaken, on behalf of all its citizens, to organize education and welfare.'[38] Hypothetically speaking, such measures would assume their most liberal formulation in the equal distribution to individuals of the sort of fungible 'cultural vouchers' conceived by Yael Tamir, a policy that could readily be implemented, for example, by polling census respondents as to their priorities for public cultural support.[39]

If this is the epitome of liberal cultural policy, it will be immediately clear that the vast majority of modern states fall well short. Particularly in education and official language policy, there are few, if any, paragons of virtue in the world that grant individual cultural choice the respect required by liberalism. Yet, one must make no apologies for confronting the inadequacies of modern national states with the full brunt of their own liberal values. Nor should one be blind to shades of inadequacy or excellence. For example, although English and French Canadians take justifiable pride in the fact that Canada (and Quebec) extend greater generosity to individual members of minority cultures and religions than is extended elsewhere, such pride does not vitiate the insights attainable from critical self-examination. In short, if the concept of exclusive nationalism has an embarrassingly wide breadth of application (if variable depth) among modern states, such is reason for concern and analysis, not for jettisoning what the same states affirm as fundamental.

To continue, although the argument has not to my knowledge been put forward, a liberal convinced of the value to individuals' lives of cultural or linguistic continuity might attempt to extend the collective-goods argument from state provision to state regulation. Although I think this argument ultimately fails, it nonetheless bears analysis. For brevity it will be cast here in the language of rational-choice theory. Two basic scenarios may be posed, both arguing for restrictions on cultural dissidents. The first relates to individuals' decisions to divest part of their contribution to their *preferred* cultural space (e.g., by learning a foreign language) on the presumption that their preferred space will be fully maintained by others, a presumption that might prove self-negating if adopted by large numbers of individuals. This scenario is analogous to the 'free rider' problem of public choice. A second scenario might be posed in which all or most individuals 'bail out' of their preferred mode of cultural production or expression for fear that everyone else soon will, a fear that might become self-fulfilling because broadly shared, a variant of the 'prisoner's dilemma.'

I take the deficiencies of the application of the free-rider problem to be that: (a) personal cultural investments are not conjointly limited in many important instances, including even language acquisition, in which investing in learning one's first language at an early age may not limit the acquisition of other languages during the same period[40] (this implies that the concept of divestiture in the scenario has only narrow application);

(b) cultural forms and identity within modern, technological societies are often not discrete or susceptible to boundary enforcement, making syncretistic cultural processes ubiquitous (this suggests that the choice presumed in the scenario between discrete and stable cultural options is seldom available in any event); and, most damagingly, (c) the presumption that actual partial 'divestors' would ultimately prefer the static preservation of an 'authentic' communal home identity generally lacks an empirical basis and, indeed, much face validity, when held up against the broad, and very high contemporary levels of consumption (and presumably personal resonance and local appropriation) of foreign cultural content and idioms[41] (this argues for extreme caution in invoking the free-rider scenario in the first place).

I take the flaws associated with the application of the prisoner's dilemma to be: (1) cultural change is typically sufficiently gradual that individuals will not normally be forced to make choices by the threat of a drastically altered cultural climate within their own lifetimes; (2) cultural choices are not generally one-time, irretractable, or mutually exclusive; left to their own devices, individuals could generally hedge their cultural 'bets' anyway and therefore not be constrained in their daily cultural choices by the risk of being left isolated (in the distant future) within their preferred cultural mode; and (3), therefore individuals' cultural choices may be taken to reflect their ultimate preferences and overall complexion of their own valued personal [and (sub-)group] identities. As such they must be respected (by liberals) as the chosen disposition for their cultural vouchers, as it were.

To summarize, this work addresses the causes of exclusive nationalism, which, incidentally, I take to be unfair, unwise, and illiberal.

0.3 Theoretical Perspectives on Nationalism

Exclusive nationalism, as defined, clearly encompasses a political agenda bearing on the state. Needless to say, it generally lacks universal appeal within plural societies. Indeed, where it embodies deeply held sentiment and is forcefully articulated within the public domain, it typically reflects, even reinforces, sharp ethnic cleavages and conflict. Within some range of vociferousness or violence, it may present challenges to established governing elites that they cannot welcome. As Smith observes, even generic, popular nationalism 'encounters the suspicion, if not hostility, of powerful state elites intent on upholding the prevailing pattern of bureaucratic states linked by networks of economic, diplomatic and military ties.'[42] In so far as the core role of political elites entails maintaining bridges with those beyond the natural constituency of exclusive nationalists, and pursuing prosaic objectives of economic growth and social development, exclusive nationalism can present enormous nuisance.

In this sense, exclusive nationalism is not necessarily much different from a range of issues dreaded by comfortably governing elites (and plausible aspirants) that similarly threaten to cleave their (political, economic, or military) bases of support. Religious education, abortion, capital punishment, and, indeed, sharp class conflict (where parties are not already organized on class lines) are but a few illustrative examples. In such domains, positions taken by the political elite, who may well seek to defend the status quo or otherwise dispose quickly of such issues, can be quite different from those taken by theoretically dominant elements of society.

Theda Skocpol, in her excellent work on social revolution, argues that scholars in her own field have too often conflated state and society. 'Both dominant-class instrumentalism' (construing the state simply as the tool of dominant classes of production), and a more subtle 'class-struggle reductionism' (assuming that the state is 'buffeted by the class struggle between dominant and subordinate classes'), are inadequate according to Skocpol to capture the potential autonomy of the 'logic and interests' of the state.[43] As she puts it,

> State organizations necessarily compete to some extent with the dominant class(es) in appropriating resources from the economy and society. And the objectives to which the resources, once appropriated, are devoted may very well be at variance with existing dominant-class interests ... The state normally performs two basic sets of tasks: It maintains order, and it competes with other actual or potential states ... Although both the state and the dominant class(es) share a broad interest in keeping the subordinate classes in place in society ... the state's own fundamental interest in maintaining sheer physical order and political peace may lead it – especially in periods of crisis – to enforce concessions to subordinate-class demands.[44]

Precisely analogous points, substituting dominant *ethnie* for classes, are arguably appropriate to discussions of exclusive nationalism. Many discussions of nationalism take for granted state penetration as a quasi-automatic outcome of national consciousness and grievance among large ethnic groups. On this view, diffuse nationalist sentiment (or more concentrated exclusive nationalism) comes to inhere within a dominant ethnic group, and presto, the doctrine is absorbed by the state.

Yet, particularly within a historical perspective subsuming old regimes in Europe, the twentieth-century Soviet Union, and, as we will argue, Canada through much of both periods, this assumption is often misleading. Even where a majority of citizens are exercised with exclusive nationalism, such proclivities can, under certain circumstances, be rechannelled or ignored in the interests of peace and order by the political elite nominally representing them.

Before speculating as to some of the key variables affecting this crucial contingency, it is worth digressing for a moment to emphasize that existing theories of nationalism have not sufficiently concerned themselves with the hand-off of exclusive nationalism from civil society to official political discourse and the state. In fairness, theories have typically been more concerned with the infection of civil society by nationalism than with its transmission to politics and the state. But this emphasis arises partly because they have not focused specifically on *exclusive* nationalism, which often generates a heartier immune response, so to speak, within the state than does nationalism generally.

In any case, theories of nationalism generally take one of two major tacks. The first traces and explains the consolidation and differentiation of discrete cultures and national identities; the second addresses the role of various sorts of inequalities in stimulating nationalism. Taking the first of these first, the central idea is that modern subjects, as Ernest Gellner puts it, 'now perceive the cultural atmosphere.'[45] They therefore desire as a matter of course, as John Plamenatz suggests, 'to preserve or enhance ... [their] national or cultural identity when that identity is threatened,' and to privilege it within a state in which sovereignty is entrusted only to those sharing their culture.[46]

Much thought has been given in this context to the evolution of discrete cultural spaces. The modern salience of vernacular language, driven by either the 'lexicographic revolution' wrought by print capitalism, or by the requirements of knowledge-intensive economies, has, according to scholars such as Benedict Anderson and Ernest Gellner, led to distinct national communities differentiated fundamentally on language.[47] Anthony Giddens has also emphasized the role of the modern state, with its ever deeper penetration of the lives of citizens. The growing mutual dependence of subjects and rulers (which Giddens calls the 'dialectic of control'), together with an intensifying, print-mediated political discourse, shaped distinct publics imprinted with such concepts as citizenship and sovereignty. Consciousness of distinct national characteristics followed.[48]

A useful adjunct to these accounts is provided by Walker Connor, who proposes to explain how compact cultures, once formed, have been set in conflict. Connor argues that the modern increase in the density of communications has served not to assimilate diverse cultures into larger unified wholes, but rather to end their long, splendid isolation and to stir xenophobia.[49] 'Improvements in the quality and quantity of communication and transportation media progressively curtail the cultural isolation in which an ethnic group could formerly cloak its cultural chasteness from the perverting influences of other cultures within the same state. The reaction to such curtailment is very likely apt to be one of xenophobic hostility.'[50] Such hostility and associated nationalism arise from the recognition of a 'divergence of basic identity,' and are only indirectly a product of the linguistic, religious, cultural, or economic differences themselves.[51]

Connor's argument holds considerable appeal to practitioners of national self-determination. Vaclav Havel, president of the Czech Republic, argued in a 1994 speech:

> The homogenization and enforced proximity brought about by the integrating nature of civilization in which we all – whether we wish it or not – find ourselves, and from which there is practically no escape, clearly induces a higher awareness of mutual 'difference.' If the autonomy and identity of various cultural spheres is smothered, if these spheres are squeezed together, as it were, by thousands of civilizational pressures and forced to behave in a more or less uniform way, then one understandable response is an increased emphasis in these communities on what is really proper to them, on what is their own, on what makes them different from others. As a result, their antipathy to other communities is augmented as well. The more that diverse cultures have been drawn into the single maelstrom of contemporary civilization, the more aroused seems to be their need to defend their original autonomy, their otherness.[52]

More intensive cultural links among nations are leading to conflict, so he argues, not to understanding or assimilation to a global culture.

Yet, even leaving aside the obvious questions raised by these various approaches when juxtaposed – collectively, they appear to predict *both* steady cultural consolidation *and* isolationist backlash out of linguistic, political, and economic integration – a serious gulf of causality lies between the differentiation of large, culturally exposed populations and the incidence of exclusive nationalism.[53] Breuilly argues, more broadly, that it is 'impossible to produce an independent definition of the nation which can be correlated in any reliable way with the existence or the intensity of nationalism ... Clearly nationalism expresses a sense of national identity among nationalists. That is a tautology ... one is forced to go further and inquire under what conditions will intensified forms of internal communications lead to increases in conflict or solidarity expressed in nationalist terms.'[54] Hobsbawm draws attention to a real clanger from Karl Renner's work, *Staat und Nation*: 'Once a certain degree of European development has been reached, the linguistic and cultural communities of peoples, having silently matured throughout the centuries, emerge from the world of passive existence as peoples ... They become conscious of themselves as a force with a historical destiny. They demand control over the state, as the highest available instrument of power, and strive for their political self-determination.'[55] But such narratives have very limited explanatory power before the highly uneven pattern and evolving nature of nationalism in late modern times, as contrasted with the pervasive and centuries-old contest of culturally, religiously, and even politically variegated identities.

Overall, theories of nationalism emphasizing the projection, mixture, and consolidation of distinct cultural identities help to explain large-scale cultural coalescence, and, by extension, why nationalism should be a feature of modernity. But they are insufficiently subtle to explain why nationalism has been felt by some nations more strongly than by others, and why nationalism has penetrated and shaped the state in some cases much more than in others.

Similar causal links appear to be missing from the second major approach, namely theories of nationalism emphasizing inequality. This approach argues that inequality, be it cultural, economic, or political, is liable to be contested, and that nationalism provides a plausible outlet, specifically for aggrieved national groups.[56] Without engaging in extended exegesis of the variants of this argument, it may be suggested that they all tend to suffer from both empirical and conceptual problems.

Empirically, nationalism has often emerged from what would appear to be positions of strength.[57] Historically, nationalism first arose in the 'core' areas of England, France, and Holland – not in the periphery. More recently, not all nationalist regions have been underdeveloped: there was no great economic difference between Norway and Sweden, and Finland and Russia, when nationalist movements developed in the smaller countries. In Spain, the Basque region and Catalonia are the most developed areas. The Jewish citizens of Israel, moreover, can hardly be construed as being (in aggregate) culturally or economically disadvantaged. Finally, the horrors of the Third Reich make it frighteningly clear that nationalism may be unleashed from the dominant side of political-power inequalities.

Conceptually, the difficulty is that even if one were to grant that many aroused nationalist groups *are* aggrieved over what they at least perceive as inequity (or, at minimum, disproportion), the converse proposition, which is really the acid test of the theory's predictive value, does not seem to present a very powerful relationship: among groups aggrieved over perceived inequities, even taking only those groups sharing plausibly 'national' characteristics, few can be expected to turn to nationalism, and fewer still will successfully thrust it upon official state institutions and discourse.[58] Upon close inspection, indeed, one might well suspect circular logic here too. Our original starting point of the aroused nationalist group would appear to *contain* the notion of grievance over – well, presumably over – some perceived cultural, economic, or political inequity. So, we run the risk with this approach of merely describing that which we seek to explain.

To be sure, a fully comprehensive view of the entire causal chain would be required to explain the original (Babylonian) congealment of distinct national or ethnic groups, and, also, to take into account the impetus given to nationalism by the preference of groups (weak *and* strong) for their own dominance over that of rivals. But for the particular focus of this work on the penetration of exclusive nationalism within official political discourse and the state, there is clearly virtue in expanding the discussion beyond existing theories of nationalism *per se*.

0.4 Exclusive Nationalism and the Relationship between State and Society

Existing theories of nationalism have in effect addressed the question, What is the general context for nationalism in the modern world? Our interest in the exclusive form of nationalism and particularly its impact as an organized political force compels us to move beyond this question to ask, What forms of political agency have historically regulated the impact of exclusive nationalism on the politics and state institutions of nations otherwise predisposed to it? This question, concerned with the evolving relationship between state and society, broaches a broader set of issues than those squarely addressed by studies of nationalism narrowly defined. It invites a brief exploration of existing concepts of ethnic conflict regulation and cross-cultural political relations. In particular, such ideas may help to identify the factors that determine the impact of exclusive nationalism on the state.

Theories of consociationalism represent one important analysis of successful ethnic conflict management by political elites. Briefly, these theories, which arose in the late 1960s, sought to explain the stability of several western European democracies despite their (then) deep cultural cleavages. Arend Lijphart, who analysed politics in the Netherlands, observed several factors that contributed to the stability of the Dutch system: a 'minimum consensus' among the leaders of the self-contained blocs that the polity could and should be preserved by elites' upholding more pragmatic and moderate positions than their mass constituencies; the acceptance of cultural cleavages as permanent 'basic realities'; the tempering of majoritarianism with the 'spirit of concurrent majority'; a substantial degree of elite secrecy in order to transcend mass-level polarization, while avoiding unseemly perceptions of elite flippancy; the maintenance of the legitimacy of the (coalition-based) cabinet, the main forum for accommodation; and a significant degree of deference.[59]

Later theorists have revised consociational theory, but have consistently reinforced the implication of Lijphart's work that populist and direct forms of democracy often do not provide an effective bulwark against ethnic conflict and exclusive nationalism. Based on a review of numerous European cases, Adriano Pappalardo emphasized the salience of 'elite predominance over a politically deferential and organizationally encapsulated following.'[60] In conditions of declining mass deference or unstable political organization, conflict regulation through elite accommodation becomes problematic.

A work by Eric Nordlinger helps to explain these observations. He explains that citizens' 'perceptions of benefits and costs are unlikely to accord with leaders' assessments,' with the result that particular accommodations may give rise to popular dissatisfaction.

> Although the nonelites are very likely to realize some advantages from conflict regulating agreements and the absence of violence and repression, yet they will tend not to view them as especially salient: where violence and repression have not yet appeared, their continued absence would be seen as especially problematic advantages; benefits are likely to be ignored when they are of a collective variety shared equally by the members of both segments; once realized, benefits will be taken for granted; and other advantages will be of an indirect kind or realized only at some future date, making them seem less 'real' than the readily apparent costs to be paid ... (N)onelites maintain a shorter time perspective and greater expectations than elites.[61]

Given these systematic differences of perspective, Nordlinger argues that achieving optimal compromises requires leaders to enjoy and exercise 'extensive independent authority.' This requires 'structured predominance' within strong party organizations. Among the other factors Nordlinger identifies as favouring accommodation are the presence of external threat or danger; the opportunity to acquire or retain political power through the formation or maintenance of coalitions, particularly where there is no clear majority group; and sufficient political security to obviate any incentive for leaders to render themselves indispensable by deepening conflict.[62]

Other works have focused on the consequences of failures of conflict regulation. Ian Lustick has elaborated a 'control model' to describe the government of deeply divided societies in which there is little or no cooperation between the elites of the segments.[63] Regimes governing on the control model – Lustick cites the example of Iraq with respect to the Kurdish minority – do so on the basis of a sort of 'internal colonialism.'[64] Disturbingly, another study suggests that features of the control model sometimes seep beyond undemocratic, imposed rule. Sammy Smooha and Theodor Hanf have coined the term 'ethnic democracy' to describe systems that combine 'real political democracy with explicit ethnic dominance.'[65] While such systems may extend certain political and civil rights to the entire population, they nevertheless accord 'a structured superior status to a particular segment of the population,' sometimes manifested in official preferences favourable to the dominant group given in the realm of symbols, language, religion, or immigration policy.[66] More generally, 'majoritarianism' is generally synonymous in the conflict-regulation literature with systems in which the demands and interests of minorities are consistently set aside in favour of those of the majority.[67]

In summary, a review of the literature on consociationalism and conflict regulation prompts several reflections relative to exclusive nationalism. First, democratic, representative government is not sufficient in itself to inoculate the state against ethnic dominance and exclusive nationalism. Indeed, declining deference to political elites and inflexible majoritarianism can undermine efforts to strike compromises and avert the domination of minorities. Second, systems in which the political power of popular ethnic majorities is unresponsive to minority interests are at risk of conferring official support for an exclusive nationalism of the majority, or of spawning a reactive exclusive nationalism of minorities. Finally, it is apparent that theorists of consociationalism have deployed their models synchronically, in explaining differences among contemporary political systems, and have given little consideration to historical developments in the key variables underlying conflict regulation.[68] In the next section we explore possible historical shifts in a few of the variables that support elite accommodation and in turn regulate exclusive nationalism.

0.5 Historical Shifts in the Underpinnings of Conflict Regulation

If effective conflict regulation can in principle buffer the state from exclusive nationalism, but is susceptible to being undermined by shifts in the underlying pattern of political representation, then gaining greater historical perspective on that relationship is an urgent undertaking for studies of conflict regulation and exclusive nationalism. This emerges even more clearly from the work of James Rosenau in the field of international relations.[69] Rosenau speaks of a period of 'postinternational politics' in which international relations are decreasing in salience as political power is diffused beyond the purview of statesmen.[70] Rosenau argues that decisive shifts in several parameters through the postwar period have resulted in much greater political power being wielded within sub-state systems, particularly since the 1960s.[71]

As citizens have gained in analytic skills, following the spread of improved education, television, and computers, they have become more engaged in public issues, often channelling their involvement via sub-state organizations and collectivities that are 'relatively close in time, space, and function,' collectivities that may shield them somewhat from 'absorption by the [larger] systems of which they are a part.'[72] This affects the nature of political representation, the relationship between government and the governed. Rosenau argues that it shifts the basis of legitimacy from habitual and traditional norms towards performance criteria. As Rosenau puts it, 'as people become more skilled at locating themselves in an ever more complex world, at seeing through the authorities who claim they have answers to the problems of complexity, and at identifying sub-groups that seem to offer greater hope of satisfying their needs and wants, clearly they are less and less likely to accept as legitimate the directives issued by the leaders of whole systems.'[73] Leaders lacking legitimacy, moreover, may find themselves the objects of internationally inspired, sharply focused extra-parliamentary opposition. As Rosenau notes, 'Global media of communication have provided images of authority being successfully challenged elsewhere in the world.'[74] The net result is that governments 'constrained by subgroupism' may have difficulty maintaining 'even well-established policies ... if the global crises of authority continue to intensify and cascade tensions along the many fault lines of cleavage.'[75]

Given the importance, observed from consociational theory, of legitimate and secure authority to manage ethnic conflict, the shifts Rosenau identifies may clearly weaken the regulation of exclusive nationalism and increase its impact on the state. Yet there remains an open, empirical question as to the historical timing of these developments. Indeed, one might usefully recall at this point Elie Kedourie's sweeping analysis of the breakdown of the 1815 Settlement in the mid-nineteenth century decline of the Concert of Europe:

> The Industrial Revolution ... was gradually penetrating everywhere ... New wealth was being created and new social classes were coming to the top who would, sooner or later, claim and obtain their share of political power. To the new classes politics presented themselves in a guise different from that familiar to the absolute monarchs and the nobility in whose hands lay the destiny of Europe in the eighteenth century. To these, the countries they ruled were a personal and family concern; their family relations and combinations extended all over Europe regardless of linguistic and religious differences, or of international frontiers, and they were as powerful a factor as any in deciding the fate of a country or a province. In contrast to them, the new social classes had no such ties to claim their attention and loyalty.[76]

Kedourie argues that as the international concerns of the old aristocratic rulers were eclipsed by a narrower set of allegiances and cultural affinities, the way was cleared for nationalism. Smith further elaborates that the old elite social identities and alliances, which had often extended to other realms, suffered challenges from rival new classes ('notably the intelligentsia and bourgeoisie'), which utilized 'some of the vernacular peasant myths and cultures to create a broader, alternative "national" culture-community.'[77] Whatever the details of this case, it suggests that a retreat to narrower social and political horizons was beaten well before the late twentieth century, with which Rosenau is concerned.

The common thread through these accounts is that a systematically changing balance of political influence is somehow related to this retreat. As mentioned, one uncertainty, particularly given the considerable length of the period in which social change – not least the expansion and empowerment of the middle-class – unfolded, concerns the question of timing. Another, perhaps even more fundamental, issue concerns precisely what elements the relevant balance of power is a balance *between*. The work of Hobsbawm and John Dunn, besides Rosenau, would suggest that, whatever changes have occurred in the balance of power among social classes, one should not neglect the altered distribution of power across the most obvious and visible division within the political system, between governments and subjects. If certain states have become more beholden to the cultural outlook of specific national groups, then perhaps, they argue, this reflects the increasing influence, vis-à-vis government, of civil majorities (or significant minorities), some of which happen to share, and desire to assert, a common language, religion, or culture.

On this last point, Hobsbawm argues that it was the democratization of countries that created a 'populist' and 'Jacobin patriotism' flowing from the greater personal stake in and attachment to the state, generated by the newly acquired ballot.[78] 'For if "this country" is in some way "mine", then it is more readily seen as preferable to those of foreigners, especially if those lack the rights and freedom of the true citizen.' This patriotism born of participation was often re-routed to national movements 'independent of the state'; but the important consequence was that citizens' loyalties, not elites', now acquired overriding political significance.[79] John Dunn makes a similar point, noting that the shift in the basis of sovereignty brought an increasingly national dimension to state agency and an altered concept of legitimacy. He argues,

> since nation states are ... democratic in their own conception of their legitimacy (nervously eager, at least at the ideological level, to ingratiate themselves with their own populations as a whole, or at a minimum, to portray themselves as truly representing the latter), and since nation states today are both organizationally and in terms of social process so much more participant societies in terms of literacy, media, physical communications and public expression than any territorial states of the past, one can see readily enough the complicity between state powers and subject populations in determining the locus of interests which these powers should represent.[80]

Dunn's reference to the evolution of legitimate expectations hints at a shifting context of ideas that influences popular demands on the political system, as well as a powerful ideological motive for elite acquiescence in those demands.

The historical connections offered by Hobsbawm and Dunn among the democratization of politics, changing ideas of sovereignty and legitimacy, and the incidence of nationalism offer a tantalizing avenue of inquiry. They may be fruitfully supplemented by Giddens's analysis of the far-reaching impact of the evolution of the state. His notion of the intensifying dialectic of control (that is, the growing mutual dependence of citizen and state) arguably implies that while the state may penetrate the lives of citizens more deeply, state activities such as the mediation of sectional conflict by political elites may be increasingly constrained by ordinary citizens. These, one might add, have clearly traditionally enjoyed much weaker social, economic, and diplomatic links beyond their local communities than political elites typically have.

Together these observations suggest that national politics, tragically for liberals, may have become more parochial and exclusivist as a result of the participatory nature of modern citizenship.

0.6 Core Hypotheses

Several major hypotheses have guided this work. The first is that the political elite has traditionally exercised a gatekeeping function that has determined the extent to which exclusive nationalism has been admitted within official political discourse, state institutions, and policy. The second hypothesis is that the exercise of this gatekeeping function, that is, the deflection of popular preferences for exclusive nationalism, has been strongly conditioned by the pattern of political representation, and specifically by the extent of direct political influence of ordinary subjects. Systems in which popular influence has been greater, typically by virtue of popular political mobilization, are hypothesized, all other things being equal, to reduce the capacity of political elites to keep the gate closed to exclusive nationalism of their own accord. Third, and perhaps most crucially, I argue that, in relevant cases, popular mobilization and influence has depended upon a much broader array of factors than the intensification of ethnic competition and identity, the factors most emphasized in conventional theories of nationalism.

Besides these formal hypotheses, several supporting assumptions and conceptual building blocks can also be reviewed. One assumption is that securely entrenched political elites have frequently exercised their gatekeeping function in the context of maintaining alliances with the representatives of other national groups; this has generally inclined them against admitting exclusive nationalism. Another assumption is that political elites have better grasped the external exigencies that under many conditions predispose against privileging particular ways of life at the expense of others. (One case, for example, occurs where groups that would particularly be imposed upon by exclusive nationalism arouse the solidarity of states or external interests with which relations of mutual trust are crucial.) A more cosmopolitan outlook among the political elite has in some instances also increased their propensity to strike compromises with other national groups beyond the extent countenanced by their own natural constituencies.

An important operating assumption is that subjects perennially and almost universally desire that their own way of life be granted advantages over others by the state in which they live. This simplification enables us to cast our attention beyond this powerful desire, to focus on the evolving pattern of political representation and the rising assertiveness of sub-state organizations within politics, both of which may limit the extent to which state policy can deviate from the preferences of dominant ethnic constituencies. In limiting our attention in this way, we focus on the factors that cause assertive populations to exert extraordinary influence on the state, and by this means for politics to become a medium for the articulation and dissemination of exclusive nationalism.

Combining these premises, we arrive at a hypothesized pattern to be termed the *political power cleavage*, or in the short form used throughout this work, the power cleavage. This term refers to the tension or division, apparent under many circumstances, between those holding political power and those who do not – that is, between *political* elites and ordinary citizens – associated with *the lower propensity of political elites than ordinary citizens to embrace exclusive nationalism*. The power cleavage, whether or not it overlaps with cultural cleavages or corresponding economic or cultural power differentials, is here taken for the pivot point in exclusive nationalist struggles. The precise position of that point, of course, varies. Occasionally, the elected political elite, virtually as a whole, can be discerned to have a markedly different position relative to exclusive nationalism than the average citizen. Perhaps more commonly, however, the cleavage rests between, on the one hand, the *established governing* political elite, which is often more constrained by alliances and concerns external to the daily life of popular constituencies, and, on the other hand, a portion of the opposition offering to represent, with greater fidelity, the often considerable segment of popular opinion predisposed to exclusive nationalism. Under other circumstances, the power cleavage may collapse altogether.

To fast-forward for a moment, my opening hypothesis in approaching the historical case was to expect exclusive nationalism to succeed and conflict regulation to fail specifically at points where (1) the long-term evolution of forms of political representation lurches ahead towards more direct and popular forms, consequently spurring a purge of the most unpopular policies that had insulated the state from exclusive nationalism; or, (2) has reached a terminal phase of direct, majoritarian democracy. At these stages, I reasoned, the capacity of the political elite might be most constrained in outfacing popular exclusive nationalism. As it turns out, I think the historical record (especially portions covered in chapters 2 and 4) offers considerable evidence that this is a credible reading. I have therefore endeavoured to trace there, further upstream as it were, the various tributaries to the evolution of political representation: norms, the growth of sub-state organizations, the increasing popular capacity for political participation, and, the intensifying codependence of state and society.

At the same time, my reading of the Canadian historical case, which I had not studied prior to embarking on this work, has convinced me that the question of the influence of popular ethnic constituencies on the state extends beyond the issue of political representation. Official exclusive nationalism, I have realized, flows not only from actively pressed popular demands, but also from elite-initiated efforts under certain circumstances to curry popular favour or defuse threats. Locating *these* circumstances, particularly in the range of strategic factors impinging on state and political interests, subsequently became the focus of much effort. Along the way, I have also recognized that my optimism as to the cosmopolitan and pluralist outlook of political elites has in some cases been misplaced, and that through much of the period covered in this work, such personal attributes have often been insufficient in themselves to determine uniform elite resistance to official exclusive nationalism. Particularly in later historical periods, the power cleavage, where it holds, appears to arise not so much from the personal outlook, class, or social attributes of politicians as from the strategic conditions of governing and preparing to govern. Overall, I have been left with a finer appreciation of the complex contingencies underlying conflict regulation at all stages in the evolution of political representation.

In any case, the approach adopted here differs substantially from most other approaches to nationalism in that it does not emphasize the influence of the substantive concerns of nationalism, and in particular, the linguistic, cultural, or religious issues and identities it articulates. This is not, it is crucial to emphasize again, because divisive issues of language, culture, and religion are deemed irrelevant, but, on the contrary, because, in one form or another, they are taken to be so pervasively relevant for subjects in multi-ethnic societies that it becomes useful to consider other, potentially more variable, factors. Based on this priority I will generally treat as exogenous the processes that differentiate religions, languages, and cultures and lead to the rise of group identities, although I take such long-term processes to be *necessary* (if *insufficient*) for exclusive nationalism to penetrate politics.

0.7 Phases of Conflict Regulation and Exclusive Nationalism in Canadian History

The thrust of the case study that constitutes the body of this work is that different historical patterns of political representation and conflict regulation have strongly influenced the prevailing form and impact of exclusive nationalism. Canada provides an ideal case for exploring this historical progression because exclusive nationalism has been a politically significant force there; because the country contains a major cultural cleavage that has persisted from an early through an advanced stage of political and social development; and because historians have already developed solid descriptive accounts of virtually all of the pertinent episodes.

From the Conquest in 1760, conflict regulation between French and English speakers has provided the central political and constitutional challenge for the country. This case study suggests that three phases can be delineated in the dual pattern of legitimate political representation and conflict regulation. These may now be set out formally as *imposed statecraft, affiliative trusteeship,* and *ethnic delegate representation.* Imposed statecraft is defined as *the mediation of conflict based on the idiosyncratic sympathies and strategic calculations of an elite not dependent upon mechanisms of local consent.* Affiliative trusteeship refers to *conflict regulation by elected elites impelled by the practical imperative of forming broad political affiliations and enabled by their perceived role as arm's-length trustees of the public interest.* Ethnic delegate representation describes a *majoritarian system in which the legitimate role of the political elite is confined to executing the preferences of their popular constituents, thereby aligning the political elite strictly with whatever geographically concentrated linguistic, cultural, or religious constituencies are present.*

These phases are argued to have traced a decline in the capacity of the state and of the political elite to regulate conflict. This declining capacity is in turn implicated in the increased potency of exclusive nationalism, that is to say, in its increased influence on political discourse and the formation of state policy. Thus, the three phases of representation and legitimate conflict regulation, and particularly the transition points between them, are asserted to coincide with manifestations of progressively more serious forms of exclusive nationalism, categorized here as *popular chauvinism, demotic exclusive nationalism,* and *official exclusive nationalism.* Popular chauvinism refers to *transient, local, and antagonistic assertions of a distinct identity.* Demotic exclusive nationalism denotes *popular chauvinism grafted onto organized activity generally directed to other political causes, conducing to a temporarily broader pattern of exclusive nationalist activity.* Official exclusive nationalism refers to instances in which *exclusive nationalism is embraced and actively promoted by the political elite of a major political party.*

The first chapter traces the earliest evolution of the British imperial regime in the old province of Quebec. Government was imposed after the Conquest in what became known as the province of Quebec. Conflict regulation – certainly until the Constitutional Act of 1791, and to some extent until the grant of responsible government during the 1840s – emanated from the imperial centre and the governors. The discussion here evaluates whether that regime engaged in official exclusive nationalism by privileging an Anglo-Protestant way of life in the colony. Contrary to the implications of several older histories of the period, it is argued that popular pressures from English Protestants in both Great Britain and the colony were generally resisted, and that a tolerant, inclusive policy developed based upon both the ad hoc accommodations of enlightened governors and the careful deliberation of British policy makers. In effect, the system greatly limited the influence of exclusive nationalism.

A significant power cleavage persisted through this period of imposed statecraft. This was rooted in differences between the main preoccupations and values of the governors and those of their most clamorous subjects, the ambitious British merchants. Whereas the first concern of the governors rested with the security of the colony – which was necessarily bound up with accommodating the French-speaking bulk of the population – the merchants sought a legal and political infrastructure that would provide a stable environment comprehensible to them for trade and commerce. Whereas the values of the governors were imbued with the emerging tolerance of Roman Catholicism characteristic of social and political elites in Britain, the British population of the colony manifested the Protestant enthusiasm and deeply ingrained abhorrence of Papistry prevailing in America and within the lower social orders of England.

For the relatively literate and urban British population, imposed statecraft never enjoyed any legitimacy as a form of political representation. An assembly was demanded very early by their leaders. As the British population subscribed to a relatively advanced concept of representation and organized to press its demands, so it also generated a more advanced form of exclusive nationalism. Coupled with its frequent early appeals for a democratic term in the constitutional equation were proposals to ensure the hegemony of British interests and schemes to privilege a Protestant, English-speaking way of life in the colony.

By contrast, the relative quiescence of the French-Canadian population in the face of imposed statecraft entailed that little effort was devoted among them to political organization. This foreclosed any possibility of their exclusive nationalism immediately progressing beyond the sporadic, popular chauvinism exhibited in riots in 1794 and 1796.

After 1791, political power over the colony was no longer vested exclusively in British parliamentarians and servants of the crown. Chapter 2 describes the new category of French Canadian politicians that emerged after the grant of an assembly to assume a role in bridging the cultural divide. It suggests that this was a role structured by, and subordinated to, the larger political context and the exigencies of bi-ethnic cooperation. On the side of the new French Canadian political elite, for example, demands were presented in the conceptual language of British constitutional thought. As such, they were at least comprehensible, if not necessarily acceptable, to their English-speaking counterparts.

As the balanced constitution remained the touchstone of even Whig political thought (the balance consisting of an 'equitable' division of power among the monarchy, the aristocracy, and the common people), and as the governor and council retained considerable power, conflict regulation within the political system as a whole moved only very gradually away from imposed statecraft towards affiliative trusteeship. Later, as political parties assumed some of the power of the governors, they, and the movements they mobilized for a more popular constitution, provided sites for demotic exclusive nationalism. An important argument of this chapter is that the Patriots were led not by exclusive nationalists, but rather by a bi-ethnic group of liberals cum anti-imperialists, and that the demotic exclusive nationalism that infused the rebellions of 1837–8 represented the spontaneous grafting of popular chauvinism upon an organizational structure formed to mobilize the population for a much less exclusive cause.

Among the British during this period, the domination of the assembly by French Canadians perceived to lack the requisite social status for political leadership led to challenges against the legitimacy of the system. Calls for anglicization were common. In close parallel to developments among French Canadians, the popular chauvinism of the British was grafted onto campaigns spurred by perceptions that the prevailing form of representation was illegitimate. Demotic exclusive nationalism thus ensued from the British, too, reaching its most violent apogee in brutal Loyalist reprisals following the 1838 rebellion. The chapter concludes by analysing the factors leading to the Act of Union, in which the British regime veered quite deliberately, albeit briefly as it turned out, into official exclusive nationalism.

Chapter 3 traces the implications of increasingly representative government for the regulation of exclusive nationalism and conflict generally. Following the Union of 1840, the last vestiges of imposed statecraft rapidly gave way to responsible government in constitutional terms and to affiliative trusteeship in political terms. Despite official expectations to the contrary, bi-ethnic alliances soon emerged that served to accommodate minorities and restrain exclusive nationalism. The chapter analyses the conditions that favoured the formation of broad political alliances, as well as the role of such alliances in curtailing the political articulation and impact of official exclusive nationalism.

Affiliative trusteeship is demonstrated to have been a precariously contingent pattern of accommodation in several ways. A significant portion of the political elite opposed the accommodation of minorities on both procedural and substantive grounds; left to its own devices, it might well have implemented homogenizing measures supported by the majority. In this period, however, this element was precluded from doing so by the force of the alliances; in turn, by the sheer numerical strength of the French-Canadian minority; and, finally, by patterns and underlying norms of political representation that inclined towards trusteeship and facilitated the overriding of majority public opinion relative to key minority interests.

In this context, affiliative trusteeship also emerges as having been important to both the carrying and the (limited) substance of the elements of minority protection enacted with Confederation in 1867. Subsequent experience confirmed, however, that as a protector of minorities, affiliative trusteeship was a form of conflict regulation closely contingent upon the presence of significant minority representation. Where minority representation declined below a certain threshold, institutional pluralism was no longer assured. Provincially, the Roman Catholic minority in several legislatures lacked the force of numbers, as in New Brunswick and Manitoba, to form a strategically vital alliance partner. Pervasive Anglo-Protestant chauvinism provided a strong political incentive for state attacks on the institutional presence of minorities, particularly on the periphery. Federally, although bi-ethnic governments were sufficiently unsympathetic to exclusive nationalism as to oppose it in federal policy and denounce it provincially, constitutional scruples and concern for provincial autonomy prevented forceful direct interventions in wayward provinces. Protestant mass movements in Ontario by the end of the nineteenth century expressed exclusive nationalist views that were articulated, but carried little weight, in elite federal politics.

Official exclusive nationalism arrived within French-Canadian political life much later, in the late 1960s, after a variant of affiliative trusteeship had dramatically shifted to ethnic delegate representation in Quebec politics. In Chapter 4, developments in the dual transition in Quebec in the pattern of representation and the form of exclusive nationalism are closely examined. It is suggested that this important transition occurred not with the election of the Lesage government in 1960, but rather with the explosion of the language issue in 1968, even if key precursors are identifiable early in the postwar period. While 1960 brought to power a more interventionist and inward-focused government, 1968, a year marked by student protests all over the world, marked the historic fusion of a mass movement dedicated to the hegemony of the French language with a political party led by a well-recognized and effective elite. Furthermore, while the Lesage government had pursued economic modernization and had given only an obligatory, superficial treatment of the divisive issues of language and culture, the formation of the Parti Québécois in 1968 injected a powerful exclusive linguistic agenda into official political discourse and policy. This chapter argues that the power cleavage and conflict regulating system collapsed mainly as a result of the popular political mobilization of that and preceding years. Although such mobilization was certainly fed by ethnic cultural and economic competition, on reexamination one must draw attention to the crucial role played by broader factors, including the rapidly increasing penetration of the state in citizens' lives, the consequent need for a more active form of consent, the international climate of protest, and the growing sophistication of Québécois society.

In the final chapter of the historical essay, we assess the implications of these and subsequent developments for conflict regulation in Canada, in particular, the challenges posed in reaching an enduring constitutional settlement in the face of extensive popular political participation. We also explore the basis and emergence within federal politics of new patterns of representation similar to those that appeared earlier in Quebec.

0.8 Methodology and Intended Audience

Given its intended dialogue between theory and political history, this work straddles at least two disciplines, each with its own favoured methods and priorities. Fortunately, important currents in twentieth-century philosophy of history provide support for the interdisciplinary project and the methods proposed here. I digress briefly here to offer several observations on these developments. These are, in a nutshell: (1) that even in its period of initial ardour, historical empiricism did not presume to preclude syntheses addressing present concerns; (2) that historicist methodological arguments have retreated substantially from their high watermark; and (3) that recent contributions to the field are receptive to theoretically-minded historical works seeking to transcend antiquarian interests. I conclude with a brief summary of other considerations of method pertinent to this work. (The reader with little interest in this admittedly rather arcane topic is encouraged to skip, without loss of continuity, to the next chapter.)

John Bagnell Bury's inaugural lecture in 1902 as Regius Professor of Modern History at Cambridge emphasized that history had become more scientific and less beholden to moral philosophy and teleology. In it he left few doubts as to his faith in the mounting empiricism of his day. 'The gathering of materials bearing upon minute local events, the collation of MSS. and the registry of their small variations, the patient drudgery in archives of states and municipalities ... has to be done in faith – in the faith that a complete assemblage of the smallest facts of human history will tell in the end ... We are heaping up material and arranging it ... to build, firm and solid, some of the countless stairs by which men of distant ages may mount to a height unattainable by us and have a history which we cannot win, standing on our lower slope.'[81] Yet even at this, the high noon of preservationism, Bury readily acknowledges that 'all the microscopic research ... the hewing of wood and drawing of water' does not define the boundaries of his discipline. Incomplete as the current state of historical knowledge is, that 'does not mean that we should confine ourselves to the collection and classification of materials, the technical criticism of them, and the examination of special problems; it does not follow that the constructive works of history which each age produces and will continue to produce according to its lights may not have a permanent value.'[82] The value of such 'constructive works' (and Bury's examples are of large-scale syntheses – early imperial Rome, nineteenth-century Germany) inheres not only in the groundwork they lay for yet better syntheses to come, but also in that they are themselves 'characteristic' of the preoccupations and outlook of their own age.[83]

R.G. Collingwood, a generation later, was influenced by the same spirit of empirical meticulousness, most directly from the field of archaeology, and he is best known for his influential suggestion that history ought to aim at self-knowledge of human nature through an imaginative re-enactment of past thought based upon direct evidence.[84] This idea provided the crux of later arguments by J.G.A. Pocock and Quentin Skinner that the measure of history is the fidelity with which past thought is reconstructed, not its discretion or creativity in selecting resources of the past to engage with pressing theoretical or ethical thematic issues of the present.[85] Yet it was Collingwood himself who recalled in his autobiography the realization reached in his later years that the function of history was to inform people 'about the present, in so far as the past, its ostensible subject matter, was encapsulated in the present and constituted a part of it not at once obvious to the untrained eye'; that 'we study history in order to see more clearly into the situation in which we are called to act,' and that any 'realist' position promised on a 'distinction between history and philosophy, or "facts" and "theories" ... must be regarded as suspect.'[86]

Postwar historiography continued to fight the good fight against mechanistically deterministic and highly abstracted flights of historical speculation. Alluding to the hostile critical reception of such works as Arnold Toynbee's six-volume inquiry into the sources of civilization (*per se*!), Patrick Gardiner noted the 'heavy loss of prestige' associated with 'the more ambitious and dramatic undertaking of providing an all-embracing interpretation of the historical process as a whole.'[87] Other notable works sought to defend individual freedom by denouncing the pernicious 'determinism' supposedly lurking in a number of historical works.[88] Sir Isaiah Berlin and others railed against efforts to isolate the fascination with historical law-discovery by associating it with an anti-empirical 'cosmology,' entailing belief in a complex underlying natural order and impersonal forces that restrict individual freedom.[89] As mentioned, Skinner also confirmed more modest (and fastidious) objectives for history, suggesting that explanations of human social behaviour and intellectual commitments must turn on understanding historical actors' own intentions, which are deeply embedded within, if not entirely determined by, complex cultural 'conventions,' hence temporal contexts.[90]

Yet, much of this prescriptive discourse must now seem to us rather overblown. The strength of the social and political sciences, their well-entrenched interest in theoretical generalization, normally at aggregative levels beyond individual actors, has considerably dampened clamorous discussions of determinism versus free will in the critical reception of theories about past and current societies. Furthermore, the equation of all theoretical interest in human behaviour and societies with epistemologically preposterous, teleological quests can no longer be sustained.

At the same time, pretensions of scientific objectivity and method now impose themselves less imperiously upon history, perhaps because our view of science *itself* has changed irretrievably since Bury could conceive of a scientific model for history unproblematically in terms of a linear, cumulative process (of erecting 'firm and solid' stairs).[91] Many historians, including those of the French *Annales* school, for example, have foresworn positivist claims that 'historical research is conducted from some median spot ... that historical texts write themselves from documents.'[92] Others have concluded that, if we are to learn from the past, and to avoid making it 'gratuitously barren,' historians must be free, as Joseph Femia puts it, 'to criticize, to examine historical trends, to make transhistorical comparisons, to impose system where there is none ... to pose artificial questions – our questions – to draw out implications.'[93] Recent works in the philosophy of history, in so far as the field still holds authority, have begun to jettison 'a priori methodological criteria' altogether, in many cases acknowledging the 'relativism that defines the present moment.'[94] Others, perhaps not coincidentally, have devoted considerable intellectual energy to rehabilitating such old masters of 'philosophic history' as Edward Gibbon (*Decline and Fall of the Roman Empire*, 1776–88) and Oswald Spengler (*Decline of the West*, 1923).[95]

Even Skinner, in the face of devastating criticism, now emphasizes that his methodological injunctions as to the primacy of contextual recovery arise merely from his own scholarly undertakings, and were never intended as a general prescription.[96] Moreover, he has reiterated that works of his own preferred genre of intellectual history can serve as a basis for 'reflecting on what *we* believe' by enabling 'testing' of our own beliefs against 'alternative possibilities' from the past.[97] This assertion, assuming that the 'testing' must logically entail some process of bidirectional, even-handed weighing of claims and evaluation, greatly narrows his admonitions to historians 'taking a stand' on past beliefs; what is left is the unremarkable point that, if they choose to do so, they must avoid teleologically conflating 'social explanation' with evaluations of 'truth.'[98]

In short, the former methodological chill on historical works that would select and engage issues of present normative significance, and transcend the (invaluable, though potentially distinct) business of recovering further, unplumbed context, has mercifully thawed.

Fortunately, in the meantime several historically minded theorists have bravely pressed ahead, rather than nervously awaiting this *dénouement*. Writing in the mid-1970s, Skocpol asserts an important role for general theory in historical discussions of her topic of social revolutions. She argues that, 'unfortunately, disillusioned historians sometimes conclude that their discipline should avoid social-scientific theories altogether. They advocate instead analyzing revolutions case by case, each ... in terms of the language of the actors at that time and place. In practice, no such relativist approaches are really possible, for historians must always draw, at least implicitly, upon theoretical ideas and comparative points of reference. But a hiatus of communication between historians ... and social theorists ... *is* always possible.'[99] The 'causal hypotheses to be explored' derive on Skocpol's view from the 'macro-sociological imagination, informed by the theoretical debates of the day, and sensitive to the patterns of evidence' within historical cases.[100] Historical analysis (in her case, comparative) is thus intended to function as a 'valuable check, or anchor, for theoretical speculation.'[101]

We may conclude our brief digression into the philosophy of history with the wisely pluralist and sober counsels of Allan Megill, who has credibly argued for 'multiplicity' in method and subject matter, boundary-crossing between history and other disciplines, and an inquiring spirit. On the last point, Megill argues,

> in a world that no longer believes in a single History, historians can awaken universal interest only insofar as their work addresses theoretical issues ... Accordingly, one envisages (1) a historiography capable of bringing (localized) aid to theory, contributing in serious ways to the discussion of theoretical issues ... (2) a greater attentiveness of historians to theory ... (3) a more self-ironic historiography than the current style, having a greater humility and reflexiveness concerning its own assumptions and conclusions ... Finally, in view of the vast, utterly unmanageable body of *primary* historiography that has been produced, one envisages (4) a historiography more in the manner of meditation or commentary, which, in a Montaignean spirit and in the essay form, would comment on the significance of that body for us, now ... In its meditative mode, historiography would engage not in the dredging up of new facts – would not, that is, engage in historical research as it is normally understood – but would instead engage in the philosophical task of reflecting on the significance of facts already in some sense 'known.'[102]

Many of these characteristics would (I hope) apply to the current work, which, in tracing the development of a specific phenomenon through more than two centuries, certainly could not presume to rely substantially upon 'the dredging up of new facts.' Admittedly, on points on which my interest has been especially piqued (often due to unresolved controversies in the secondary literature), I have often succumbed to curiosity, and have trawled through both archives and printed primary materials readily at hand. More frequently, I have gone straight to sources to which attention has been drawn by specialist historians in order better to understand the context of their testimony. (In these cases I have tried to include in the notes the primary source, as well as the specialist's work that first alerted me to it.) However, in its massive debt to the work of dozens of intrepid historians, this work perhaps most closely resembles a mosaic comprising fragments of varied materials – works of different dimensions and purposes – recombined here to present a novel, integrative *Gestalt* for the Canadian historical case and exclusive nationalism within it.

As such, this work represents at base a modest enterprise of selection, compression, and hypothesis-generation, my major objective being not to break new empirical ground within any single phase of historical specialization, but rather to make new connections among existing, but far too isolated, bodies of knowledge. These bodies on their own offer great fascination and insight to devoted antiquarians or theorists, but together I think they offer much more than the sum of their parts to those sharing my preoccupation with an issue of great present practical significance.

I have attempted this synthesis by juxtaposing its myriad fragments against the lines of its organizing theory. In a few cases, the pieces conform perfectly to those lines; in many others, only partially; and, in still others, not at all. This being an exploratory study, the deviations as well as the congruencies give rise throughout the historical narrative to theoretical ideas and refinements, and I have attempted to provide sufficient detail to support this evolution.

Any credible work that would develop theory in relation to historical experience must in any case accept a formidable, dual challenge: to argue that the history at hand should be read in such a way; and to argue that such a reading has such-and-such implications for the body of theory being developed. Neither of these is at all trivial, and I have had to tread very carefully. Even still, some historians will no doubt find themselves suspicious of the intrusion of *any* abstract, generalizing theory alongside inherently complex subject matter. Conversely, many social scientists, being unfamiliar with at least some of the many controversial interpretive issues inevitably confronted in a work of this scale, may find themselves exposed to higher levels of empirical detail in the narrative exposition than they are accustomed to. Both groups must also be warned in advance that indispensable context, well known to specialist students of Canadian political history, has also been 'read into the record' of the narrative in order to make room for yet another group of readers – namely, generalist practitioners of constitutional law, conflict regulation, and statecraft. Alas it is difficult to accommodate such varied readers, yet I believe that all are indispensable parties to any credible and useful treatment of the topic addressed in this work.

Examining distinct phases of exclusive nationalism by analysing a large chronological span presumes some degree of comparability. Much clearly changed between the Conquest and the founding of the Parti Québécois in 1968: the extent of economic and social development, the strength of imperial bonds, contentious issues of the day, and the cultural boundary delineating the *ethnie* present, among myriad others. Language has become since the 1960s the predominant 'ethnic badge' separating the collectivities of Quebec, and is now strongly associated with nationalism there.[103] Formerly, religion was, of course, much more significant, particularly given the strong Protestant identity and disdain for Roman Catholicism among British immigrants arriving soon after the Conquest (see 1.2). Notwithstanding such shifts of emphasis, however, nations and nationalism do not in general hinge on a unique element of identity.[104] As Liah Greenfeld puts it, the nature of nationalism is 'determined not by the character of its elements, but by a certain organizing principle which makes these elements into a unity and imparts to them a special significance.'[105] Nationalism bears no consistent relationship with territory, language, statehood, shared tradition, history, or race.[106] Nations, as they are self-differentiated, can be based on any of these features, but the precise basis is far less important than the perception of their presence. In 1810, a governor said of the Canadiens, 'Indeed, it seems to be their desire to be considered as forming a separate Nation; *La Nation Canadienne* is their constant expression.'[107] That desire and the underlying perception have remained relatively constant since at least that period, as has the comparable differentiation of those of British extraction (see 1.1 and 2.3). On the other hand, the evolution (in some cases the sea-change) of other elements certainly contributes to causal explanations of different phases of exclusive nationalism.

Finally, I should make clear that I certainly do not claim that this work sets out the only possible thematic scheme for the recombination of the historical 'pieces' germane to its topic, or even that the issues I address here could not be argued from hypotheses quite different from my own. I *do* claim, however, that the exchange of such different perspectives on exclusive nationalism is a conversation manifestly worth having to further understanding of a phenomenon that globally has had a horrendous impact, and on which Canadian political history may offer profound reflections (and vice versa). Of course, I also pledge that my own best interpretive sense has been deployed throughout this work. I welcome others to join the discussion and to advance both its empirical and its conceptual rigour beyond my rudimentary efforts here.

ONE

Conquest and the Height of Imposed Statecraft, 1760–1791

Conflict was regulated in the early post-Conquest era by fiat of the governors and the British government. Ordinary subjects, apart from the raising of petitions and passive non-compliance with civic duties, wielded little influence in state affairs. The imperial regime sought to ensure its own stability in the face of external threats and uncertain local allegiances by cultivating excellent relations with local notables and the Roman Catholic hierarchy. This entailed an even-handed policy that tolerated, sometimes bolstered, a way of life foreign to Britain. British immigrants did not appreciate this policy and pleaded with the imperial government for more popular government and less accommodation of the (French) Canadiens. Protestantism was a major fount of British nationalism in the eighteenth century, and the pleas of British immigrants in Quebec for an officially entrenched hegemony of Protestants represent a classic case of demotic exclusive nationalism. They also revealed a marked power cleavage, for in Quebec, as in Great Britain, elites typically did not share the popular view that a Protestant way of life must be privileged to the exclusion of others.

French-Canadian historians since François-Xavier Garneau have often found in the old Province of Quebec the beginnings of a struggle of a vanquished nation to survive.[1] Lionel Groulx, for example, suggested that the early Canadien society exhibited a determination, as yet inchoate, to maintain 'its integrity, its autonomy as a group and as a race.'[2] Such an interpretation is, by its nature, difficult to contradict. But what it obscures is that the French appear to have lagged the British in developing demotic exclusive nationalism. Although there were sporadic outbursts of popular chauvinism towards the British by the Canadien habitants, these were not coupled with an articulate program, and they lacked the coordination that would only come later with popular political mobilization. Canadiens occupying roles of influence were not as predisposed by their basic political views against the autocratic rule of the governors. As the prevailing mode of representation was not illegitimate for Canadien leaders, they did not attempt to mobilize the people or provide any other openings for demotic exclusive nationalism.

This chapter begins by reviewing (in 1.1) the increasingly well-understood context of British nationalism in the late eighteenth century. The Conquest and early relations between British immigrants and the Canadiens are also discussed. In the next section (1.2), the first and unsuccessful attempt at forming imperial policy for the colony contained in the Royal Proclamation is considered, followed by accounts of the gradual official inclusion of Catholics (1.3), a trend that culminated in the Quebec Act of 1774, and made manifest a power cleavage in much of the English-speaking world (1.4). We discuss (in 1.5) the apparent lag of the Canadiens behind the British in developing demotic exclusive nationalism. An assessment follows of incipient accommodation in the local politics of the colony (1.6). The final historical episode, discussed (in 1.7), is the Constitutional Act of 1791, which was intended to accommodate both Canadiens and would-be immigrants, as well as to advance the system of political representation. The implications for theory of this era of history are considered in the last section (1.8).

1.1 Historical Context, Conquest, and Early Contact

Confronted by perils within and without tinged with Roman Catholicism, British solidarity during the eighteenth century rested largely upon Protestantism.[3] Although the end of the Seven Years War brought respite in 1763, well-founded fears of revenge by Catholic France anticipated further episodes in the intermittent war that had followed the Revolution of 1688 and would not end until Waterloo. Domestically, the spectre of a return to Stuart rule and religious strife still haunted, well after the final deliverance of the Forty-Five (1745–6).[4] The progressively sovereign nation summoned to check these risks had been defined by Protestantism within the dominant political discourse since Elizabethan times.[5] This identity and the fears characteristic of eighteenth-century Britain conspired to embed anti-Catholicism deeply in the national consciousness.[6]

But anti-Catholicism and xenophobia were much stronger among ordinary subjects than among elites. Elites perceived wars over empire with France and Spain as having a narrowly commercial basis.[7] They also recognized after 1746 that Stuart pretensions were finished.[8] Few aristocrats, moreover, considered domestic aesthetic, cultural, and religious sensibilities as the last word.[9] *Gentleman's Magazine* observed in 1766, 'Those who have conversed with persons of different ranks, that have been in France, will find the account favourable, in proportion as their rank is high.'[10] Some partook of a common European intellectual culture, many of whose leading lights, such as Voltaire and Rousseau, were French.[11] Natural religion or scepticism was found by many to be more compelling than mainline Protestantism.[12] Other members of the elite travelled to the Continent and exhibited esoteric tastes primarily for the snob appeal of all things foreign.[13] Until the 'British elite reconstructed its cultural image in the age of revolutions' at the close of the eighteenth century, systematic differences therefore persisted between the identities of elites and ordinary subjects.[14] A sense of 'internal social division along cultural lines' emerged, and drew a 'cultural protest' against the 'cultural treason' and 'moral pollution' of the aristocracy.[15]

In the late eighteenth century, the governing political elite in Great Britain was caught out several times by popular chauvinism and demotic exclusive nationalism. The Jewish Naturalization Act (1753), which would merely have authorized Parliament 'to naturalize individual Jews,' was supported by respectable opinion, but met with a 'torrent of anti-Semitism' in the press and an 'appalling' popular response.[16] Reaction to the Catholic Relief Act of 1778 was yet worse.[17] The act struck out three moribund entries in the long list of statutory discrimination Catholics suffered.[18] Plebeian mobs, which had often been mobilized in preceding years by radical reformer John Wilkes, wrecked carnage and destruction in London in the notorious Gordon Riots. More than 100 burnt homes and 400 casualties, including 200 deaths, were recorded.[19] The mob turned 'its wrath as much against wealthy sophisticates,' identified with cosmopolitan toleration, 'as against the Catholic labourers of the poorer districts.'[20]

The elite's cultural predispositions, distinctive personal tolerance, and willingness from at least 1753 to relax legislative disabilities against religious minorities indicate that the prosecution of war against France, and in turn the conquest of Quebec, cannot be construed as an assault by the British elite on a religion, language, or culture. The wars were precipitated, rather, by the conflicting strategic objectives of mercantile empires. As an address in the Lords in November 1759 frankly acknowledged, the war had been entered 'solely for the Defence of the valuable Rights, Possessions, and Commercial Interests.'[21] France and Spain controlled many colonies, and hence a large proportion of global markets. Jointly, the two blocked 'British expansion in every possible direction,' and were therefore 'simultaneously put to hazard' time and again during the eighteenth century.[22] The battle on the Plains of Abraham in Quebec in September 1759 was merely a distant repercussion of this struggle.

But the military conflict and early contacts were experienced very differently on the ground.[23] For most Canadiens, the experience was one of profound personal loss. Alfred Burt notes that, in Quebec, a town having about 8,000 inhabitants, every building had suffered some damage, while at least a third of the houses were completely destroyed. Shortly after the Conquest, the population was recorded at 3,500.[24] In the countryside, about 1,400 houses were burnt.[25] For the colony as a whole, which had a population of 60,000 to 75,000, the rate of civil mortality in the fighting was perhaps 5 to 10 per cent.[26] A nun wrote, 'A fog of blood veils our country. Our parents and our friends have been taken away from us by the fire of our enemies.'[27] For the nun's compatriots, the 'enemy' was presumably identified as rather more than a competitor with the mother country for global markets. It was undoubtedly redolent of cruelty, sacrilege, and foreign manners and customs.

The strangeness if not the brutality of the connection with an alien civilization was probably also felt by the earliest English-speaking arrivals. Once the fighting stopped, a policy of tolerance was strictly enforced by the colonial authorities to prevent the British military men mopping up after their victory from venting prejudices against the new subjects. Secretary of State Lord Egremont reminded the British commander-in-chief, Jeffrey Amherst, that he was to ensure that his governors 'employ the most vigilant attention and take the most effectual care that the French inhabitants ... be humanely and kindly treated.'[28] Soldiers, in turn, were to be given orders restraining them from 'insulting or reviling any of the French inhabitants ... by harsh and provoking observations on their language, dress, manners, customs, or country, or by uncharitable reflections on the errors of the mistaken religion which they unhappily profess.' There is evidence that the soldiers obeyed and even that they developed amicable relations with some of the Canadiens.[29]

The spirited, opportunistic merchants from the northern American colonies who followed the troops into Quebec also had to accommodate themselves to a foreign environment. Many, particularly in the years to come, found this difficult. Although General Murray observed that they 'readily and cheerfully assisted' the soldiers in the famine-relief effort during the difficult first two years after the Conquest, he was soon complaining that many of the British subjects from New England were fanatical bigots.[30] In a 1764 letter to the Board of Trade, Murray stated, 'Nothing will satisfy the Licentious Fanaticks Trading here, but the expulsion of the Canadians who are perhaps the bravest and the best race upon the Globe ...'[31] In 1765 he was recalled to England at the behest of the merchants and their powerful contacts in London, who had accused him of conducting an autocratic rule insensitive to British interests. About the time of his recall he defended his record thus: 'The Canadians who have lived under my government six years Shall be the best Judges of the truth of that aspersion. They will to a man Vouch that all the Malice and Clamour which have been exhibited in England against me proceed from the protection that I have given them, and the inflexible aversion I have on all Occasions Shewn to the Canadiens against Oppression & the National English Prejudice.'[32] Apparently, British merchants in the province lacked the 'affinity to French culture, language, and custom' of Murray, a Scottish aristocrat.[33]

Apart from Murray's accounts, the attitudes of British merchants towards the Canadiens were also revealed by their actions, and more specifically by their remonstrances with the colonial authorities. In 1764 fourteen 'old subjects,' together with several Canadien new subjects, convened an ad hoc 'Grand Jury.' The notorious jury impugned Murray's governorship and arrogated to itself the right to be consulted about official decisions concerning the province. The old subjects on the panel then added an additional brief, not translated for the benefit of their Canadien colleagues, in which they railed against the inclusion of Catholics in juries. More precisely, they submitted, 'admitting persons of the Roman Religion, who own the authority, supremacy and jurisdiction [of] the Church of Rome, as Jurors, is an open Violation of our most sacred Laws and Libertys, and tending to the utter subversion of the protestant Religion and his Majesty's power authority, right, and possession of the province to which we belong.'[34] This was a classic case of a transient, antagonistic assertion of a distinct identity and an attempt to privilege one way of life over an other by a group initially formed to protest the prevailing system of representation.

The best evidence that the sentiments underlying this show of demotic exclusive nationalism were widely held among the old subjects present in the province is that a public letter of thanks for the 'very spirited and laudable proceedings'[35] of the Grand Jury was signed by 50 people in a community that amounted to fewer than 200 households.[36] On the other hand, it is also true that several of the members of the Grand Jury, including the foreman, later recanted in the face of the fury of their Canadien co-jurors and General Murray. Judiciously, they narrowed the scope of their plea to merely excluding Catholics from sitting as jurors in cases between Protestants. Those who recanted also professed 'that the subscribers of the presentment meant to remove every Roman Catholick from holding any office or filling any public employment is ... a most vile groundless insinuation & utterly inconsistent: Sentiments and intentions such as these we abhor ...'[37] Those who issued this hasty and qualified retreat might well have been sincere. But the civic roles generally envisioned for Catholics remained limited. The same year, a petition of Quebec traders was raised that pressed for an exclusively Protestant assembly, notwithstanding that the Protestants accounted for a fraction of 1 per cent of the population in the province.[38] Two years later, in 1766, a group of merchants mobbed a group of Canadiens peacefully gathering with the permission of the council to petition for equal rights.[39] The traders also complained that Murray had encouraged the Canadiens in their request for French-speaking judges, and that Murray's 'Enacting Ordinances' were 'injurious to the Protestant Cause,' which they felt ought to be privileged.[40]

The ordinance in question had discreetly established quasi-parallel systems for administering civil justice to the new and old subjects according to their respective customary systems.[41] More precisely, in the (middle) Court of Common Pleas, Canadien law, lawyers, and jurors were admitted.[42] According to historian Hilda Neatby, there is 'every reason to suppose that Canadian civil laws and customs remained practically undisturbed,' even for cases involving real property.[43] For British merchants and traders, for whom the English legal system was familiar and thus predictable, and for whom the law was a practical tool in the enforcement of contracts, such pandering to the Canadiens by the governor conflicted with their interests, the expectations of those in the party of the conqueror, and the identity of their nation.

1.2 The Royal Proclamation: Imperial Miscue

In fairness to the merchants, the expectations they held to be reasonable had been injudiciously stimulated by the imperial government. In October 1763, eight months after the Treaty of Paris, the imperial government had declared an umbrella policy for the multifarious spoils of its victory in the Seven Years War: Quebec, East and West Florida, and Grenada. The policy, embodied in the Royal Proclamation of 1763, was developed during a six-month process that was troubled by a late change of ministers at home and a serious development in North America.

The starting point concerning Quebec was that it, together with Nova Scotia, Georgia, and Florida, would serve as a commodious overflow area for the American colonies. Relatively little was known about the natural resources of Quebec, as compared with Nova Scotia, which was understood to be blessed with a superior fishery and with what was rather grandiloquently described as 'that Species of Timber and Wood commonly called Lumber.'[44] Nevertheless, the sheer size of Quebec on the map attracted notice because population pressure was understood to be mounting in the New England colonies.[45]

The president of the Board of Trade, Lord Shelburne, clearly anticipated that immigration into Canada in the wake of the policy would not challenge the predominance of the Canadiens. He noted, 'It is obvious that the new Government of Canada, thus bounded will ... contain within it a very great number of French Inhabitants and Settlements, and that the Number of Inhabitants must greatly exceed, for a very long period of time, that of Your Majesty's British and Other Subjects who may attempt Settlements ...'[46] But sensitivity to this key constraint upon Quebec policy was blunted by the ministerial shuffle necessitated by Egremont's death, and by the added urgency lent by an Indian rebellion known as Pontiac's Rising, a particularly lethal guerrilla war. Quebec, it was hoped, might help to abate the population pressures that threatened to accelerate expansion into territory west of the Appalachians and to exacerbate tensions with the Indians there.[47] There were more than a million inhabitants in the colonies to the South, and if even a small proportion of them could be induced to shift to Quebec they would soon make the province more attractive to the many who might then follow.[48]

Against these exigencies Quebec policy was rapidly overextended.[49] The Royal Proclamation presented the projection of British constitutional and legal structures into Quebec as a virtual *fait accompli*, despite the fact that only a few hundred British immigrants had so far made their way there, and that the administrative and legal apparatus present was inadequate to achieve rapid reforms.[50] Concerned to eliminate a potential foreign conduit of subversion, British law during this period continued to impose restrictions on the scope of toleration of Roman Catholicism. Thus, in Britain, several oaths were a prerequisite to enjoying a range of privileges, including holding public offices of responsibility. Dating from 1558, 1672, and 1714, the oaths included declarations against popery, including one, the 'oath of assurance,' which required the taker to 'declare, that no foreign prince, person, prelate, state or potentate, hath or ought to have any jurisdiction, power, superiority, pre-eminence or authority, ecclesiastical or spiritual, within this realm'[51]

British policy makers did not initially contemplate revising this structure for its new possessions, under the presumption that it would be carried over, at least in form. Restrictive oaths were cited in Murray's Commission and Instructions, and were intended for members of the council, the envisioned assembly, and the judiciary. Several years would be required for this policy to unwind itself officially. Unofficially, Murray made it clear only a year later that he categorically rejected the theory that the 'Popish Laws must be exerted with Rigour' and had no intention of enforcing such laws while he held his commission.[52]

Above all, the proclamation reflected an imperial policy of presenting Quebec as being as hospitable as possible to immigrants from the south. Murray was instructed to advertise the availability of cheap land and to sing the praises of the 'natural advantages of the soil and climate' and 'its peculiar conveniences for trade and navigation.'[53] The proclamation wisely provided a newly fixed boundary between the colonies and the reserved Indian territories. But its promises of English laws and an elected assembly were unrealistic. Prudently, buried caveats rendered the promises technically nugatory, but the document was certainly open to the interpretation taken by the merchants that they would find in Quebec a familiar legal and constitutional environment.

The futility of the policy was perhaps most archly declared in 1767 by Murray's successor, Governor Guy Carleton.

> Having arrayed the Strength of His Majesty's old and new Subjects, and shewn the great Superiority of the Latter, it may not be amiss to observe, that there is not the least Probability, this present Superiority should ever diminish, on the Contrary 'tis more than probable it will increase and strengthen daily ... this Country must, to the end of Time, be peopled by the Canadian Race, who already have taken such firm Root, and got to so great a Height, that any new Stock transplanted will be totally hid, and imperceptible amongst them, except in the Towns of Quebec and Montreal.[54]

In hindsight the early expectations do seem foolish. The ordinary farming folk of the southern colonies, many of whom adhered to dissentient creeds, could scarcely have been expected to find the prospect of living among 65,000 Catholics in an intemperate climate an attractive proposition. With their rugged individualism and democratic traditions, they might have been expected to wait until a Protestant assembly and schools were established before shifting north. But such institutions would clearly be impossible until they did arrive in significant numbers.

The obvious shortcomings of the policy raise an important question:

how serious were British policy makers in their declared intentions? On balance, it would appear that considerable guile was at play. Aimed at shoring up the province as a haven for the excess population from the south, the policy was clearly calculated to appeal to the political outlook of the anticipated immigrants.[55] But it is evident that those who were responsible for the promise of English law and an elected assembly in the proclamation intended that the strong caveats included would be heavily relied upon in the case of Quebec. The proclamation states that the courts of the newly conquered colonies were to settle cases 'according to Law and Equity, and as near as may be agreeable to the Laws of England.'[56] However, Murray's commission, which was presumably written with the particularities of Quebec more clearly in mind, empowers Murray 'to Erect, Constitute and Establish ... Courts ... for the hearing & determining of all causes as well Criminal as Civil according to Law and Equity ...'[57] The reference to English law was omitted entirely, and the terms 'Law and Equity' were synonymous with Canadien law.[58] This interpretation is corroborated by Hillsborough, who helped frame the 1763 policy and later submitted 'that it never entered into Our Idea to overturn the Laws and Customs of Canada, with regard to Property.'[59] Such 'Laws and Customs' were nothing less than the linchpin of the seigneurial (i.e., French quasi-feudal) system. More broadly, Attorney General Edward Thurlow argued in Parliament in 1774 that the proclamation had been a temporary expedient of vague form, not a 'well studied act of state.' It was totally implausible, he submitted, to construe it as 'creating an English constitution, ... as importing English laws into a country already settled.'[60] Referring to the text itself, he defied anyone to find support for the view that the proclamation repealed the old laws of Canada, or introduced a 'new system of constitution.'[61]

Officials were not much more resolute in promises of an elected assembly for Quebec, at least for the short to medium term. There could be little question of opening such an assembly to Canadien participation, given that the newly conquered people would, by sheer dint of numbers, have dominated it. Nor would it be palatable to have an assembly of Protestants purporting to represent the interests of the Catholic population. Perhaps for these reasons, we once again find an important disparity between documents. The passage in the confidential 'Instructions' prepared for Murray upon his appointment to the governorship of Quebec is equivocal as to the early establishment of an assembly, and clearly leaves the governor with much more discretion than is implied by the corresponding passages in such public documents as the 'Commission' and the Royal

Proclamation.[62] The discrepancy was calculated. Another confidential document from Whitehall notes,

> they [the Lords Commissioners for Trade and Plantations] have omitted in these Commissions any Power that it may be necessary to grant to the Governors and Councils of Your Majestys said new Colonies to make Temporary Regulations until Assemblys can be called, because they were of Opinion that an immediate and publick Declaration of the intended permanent Constitution, and an Insertion in the first Commissions of the Power of calling Assemblys so soon as the Circumstances will admit, is expedient ... and will give Confidence and Encouragement to such of your Majesty's Subjects, as shall incline to settle in your said new Colonies ...[63]

The need to present would-be settlers with concrete plans, however optimistic, took precedence over publicly exposing the thorny dilemmas that would almost certainly confront any progression in representative government in Quebec.

Ambiguity in provisions for English laws and a Protestant assembly in Quebec were joined by a lack of substance in plans to orchestrate a change in the religion of the Canadiens. The very terms of the capitulation of Quebec granted the Canadiens the freedom to practice their religion. True, that freedom did not extend initially to being compelled by law to pay the tithe, to which they were accustomed, or to the freedom to receive the authority of ecclesiastical representatives of the Pope. But presumably their faith, not to mention threats from the parish priest, continued to move the faithful to defray the expenses of their parish churches as they were accustomed.[64] As for the lack of local ecclesiastical authority to ordain new priests, this was remedied as early as 1766 when Jean Olivier Briand, with the permission of British officials, was consecrated in France on the orders of the Holy See as the Bishop of Quebec.[65]

Many British Protestants would undoubtedly have welcomed the conversion of the Canadiens to their own faith. But key imperial authorities had no intention of bringing this about heavy-handedly. Governor Murray, who felt himself to be above the fray of political pressures, was at times the point of greatest resistance to any plan of Protestant conversion.[66] While Murray's instructions referred to the importance of establishing a beachhead for the Church of England, Murray baulked at such evangelism. To be sure, Murray himself sometimes professed that he aimed at 'converting a great part of the Canadians,' but the tactics he subsequently employed went little beyond demonstrating by personal example to Canadiens that

Protestants could be equally good Christians.[67] Certainly, he did not treat the long-term maintenance of the Catholic Church in Quebec as a pressing personal concern. Yet this also seems to have been true with respect to the establishment of the Protestant Church. A petition around 1764 of the British merchants and traders who had come to Quebec despaired of Governor Murray's 'discountenancing the Protestant Religion by almost a Total Neglect of Attendance upon the Service of the Church, leaving the Protestants to this Day destitute of a place of Worship appropriated to themselves.'[68] Carleton, for his part, has been observed to have been 'slack to the point of being remiss in "encouraging" the Church of England.'[69]

The failure of the 1763 proclamation suggests that cultural and religious factors were contemplated differently by many leading British policy makers than by those whose behaviour they sought to influence. As Philip Lawson points out in a thoroughly researched work, although such statesmen as the 'broadminded' Shelburne perceived a need to assert political supervision over the church in order to neutralize a potential 'threat to the state's security,' this view, which contained no 'ideological assault on Catholicism,' contrasted strongly with popular sentiments: 'The people who arrived in the province during 1760 to 1764 did not want a tolerant recognition of Catholicism but rather the sort of deprivation and exclusion of papists from social and political life they were used to seeing in Britain and the American colonies.'[70] The preoccupation of policy makers with strategic concerns arising from the imperative of securing a new possession and avoiding conflict with Native peoples appears to have precluded thorough consideration of the cultural and religious outlook of would-be immigrants to Quebec from the south. In their nods to anti-Catholic sentiment, British politicians reflected their environment of 'deep-rooted prejudices in Britain,' but did not produce a realistic and clear project to make English Protestants of the Canadiens. Murray was perhaps ideally placed to urge that the 'political price to pay for showing leadership in the face of anti-papist sentiment' be paid.[71] In the end, Murray himself 'failed to gauge the depth of feeling amongst the small Protestant community ... against conceding ground to Catholics.'[72] The episode of imperial policy surrounding the proclamation thus provides early evidence of the existence of a power cleavage under imposed statecraft.

1.3 Religious Accommodation

British authorities soon acknowledged the lack of credibility in their policy. Cognizant that Quebec would not be as attractive to immigrants as first hoped, officials addressed the task more soberly of tailoring a policy for Quebec that would secure imperial interests with only a slight British presence. The policy required establishing strong ties with traditional opinion leaders and then reinforcing their authority. That this would have the incidental effect of perpetuating, perhaps even fostering, Canadien and British ethnic and religious differences was not of great concern. What mattered was securing the province against a future chapter in eighteenth-century French–English conflict: in a word, Canadien loyalty. Good local relations were also sought because state elites sympathized with the plight of the Canadiens and prided themselves on standing above mass xenophobia.

(Partial) Catholic Inclusion

In 1765 the Privy Council took the positive step of deciding once and for all that Catholic jurors and advocates were not to be excluded from the rudimentary apparatus of justice in the province.[73] Favouring toleration, it also set aside the Board of Trade's recommendation that Catholicism be strictly regulated in order to bring about the eventual conversion of Catholics.[74] Various reports generated prior to the announcement had also argued that customary Canadien property law should not be excluded from the highest court for cases with pre-Conquest origins. The Law Officers went furthest of all: in order to avoid confusion, in all suits relating to property, even those with post-Conquest origins between British parties, local custom was to prevail.[75]

Despite a flurry of papers, only the issue of Catholic jurors and advocates was conclusively resolved at this time. Although a package of the other elements attracted broad and persistent support on the Privy Council, Lord Chancellor Northington twice vetoed it.[76] His objections were both procedural and substantive. Procedurally, the Lord Chancellor held that it was up to Parliament, not the Privy Council, to resolve such questions.[77] Substantively, the Lord Chancellor seems to have objected to the concession of Canadien legal customs and magistrates.[78] It would be eight years before such a controversial policy could be navigated through Parliament, given that 'a bill advocating Catholic toleration in Quebec would touch the rawest of political nerves in England' even though there was 'a growing sympathy both in the parliamentary classes and in ... "polite circles" with the concept of toleration.'[79]

Much of the political will for legislating an end to official discrimination against Catholics in Quebec, some fifty-five years before British Catholics were emancipated, was generated by Carleton.[80] Clearly strong elite will was necessary at a time when a 'public and press campaign against the idea of concessions to Catholics, no matter where' was under way in Britain, and when few 'yet had the courage' to express tolerant views of Catholicism.[81] Carleton was guided by a mixture of strategic objectives and respect for the 'natural Rights of Man.'[82] The strategic issues for this former military man were 'the foundation of all, without which other schemes can be little better than mere castles in the air.'[83] The threat of chief concern to Carleton was that from France, a threat that might conceivably ally itself with American patriots in the event of a rebellion.[84] As he put it in a letter to Shelburne, 'should a French War surprise the Province in it's [sic] present Situation, the Canadian Officers sent from France with Troops, might assemble such a Body of People, As would render the King's Dominion over the Province very precarious ...'[85] With a force at his disposal of just 2,000 men, the rumours or intelligence Carleton had heard of French interest in sponsoring a Canadien insurgency were alarming.

Carleton recommended the urgent reinstatement of the legal *status quo ante*, which he considered to have 'established subordination from the first to the lowest ... and secured obedience to the supreme seat of government from a very distant province.'[86] As he also noted, in his dispatch of January 1768, 'I have given the Military state of this Province, with a scheme for strengthening it by a Citadel; I shall now add, that, was this already constructed, ... still, I shall think the interests of Great Britain but half advanced unless the Canadians are inspired with a cordial attachment and zeal for the king's government ...'[87] This required catering to their self-interest, which was, in part, bound up with 'the quiet Possession of their Property, according to their own Customs, which [for] Time immemorial, has been regarded by them and their Ancestors, as Law and Equity ...'[88] A wholly Protestant assembly, or indeed an assembly of any composition, was to be avoided, despite the ongoing representations of the English merchants. An assembly, 'in a Country where all Men appear nearly upon a level, must give a strong Bias to Republican principles.'[89] Such principles, Carleton presaged, could pose as great a threat to British interests in the colony as a French invasion.

Little during the six intervening years between those statements and the passage of the Quebec Act need concern us here. Though further reports were commissioned by Parliament and submitted by legal authorities during this time, they failed to reach a consensus on several important questions, and, in the end, an inner circle of ministers and officials, including Carleton, who was present in England for the development of the act, exercised preponderant influence.

A summary discussion can scarcely do justice to the complex nuances of rhetoric, tactics, and conviction at play in the parliamentary debate on the Quebec bill. Relatively few opposition speakers suggested that Catholics in Quebec should be left unemancipated.[90] But the exigencies of partisan debate nonetheless generated interesting volleys to assault the government with the awkward semblance, if only occasionally the genuine article, of popular bigotry. One favoured talking point was what could be construed as asymmetrical treatment of the Catholic and fledgling Protestant churches in Quebec. This allowed a member possessing the artful craftiness of the Rockingham Whig Edmund Burke to weave concern for the 'sober Christian professing the Protestant religion' together with a substantive theory strongly favouring religious toleration.[91] Having drawn attention to the discretionary nature of provisions for the support of the Church of England in the bill, so to the delicious irony that a 'Protestant clergyman going into that country does not receive the protection of the laws,' Burke makes clear that his criticism is *not* that this will leave Roman Catholics in the wilderness of despotic papistry. Quite the contrary: he professes that the main drawback is that perverse incentives might wean parishioners from their faith. 'I will suppose this case, when he [a Catholic parishioner] is sued for his tithe, he will declare he does not profess the Roman Catholic religion. He then walks directly in that mass house, or church for whose support he has positively refused to engage himself ... Suppose he abstracts himself from all religion. He pays no tithe. You are encouraging him to be an atheist.'[92] On such unlikely foundations as these, Burke proposes that Protestants pay a tithe also, and, then (in yet another arresting twist), that these funds to be assigned to an Anglican missionary organization, in the absence of any permanent Protestant Church in Quebec. His finale is to conclude with the 'generous example' of the Peace of Westphalia (1648), and the ideal apparently subsequently realized of congregants of different faiths making use of the same parish church for their respective services.

According to the record of debate, the attorney general required fully two hours to extricate himself from the quagmire in which Burke had thus placed him, despite that virtually the entire political elite shared common assumptions about the substantive issues in question.[93] As Burke had acknowledged at the outset, 'there is but one healing, Catholic toleration in this House ... the thirsty earth of our own country is gaping, and crying [for] that healing shower from heaven.'[94]

Another example of tactical opposition might easily be cited. Charles

Fox devised a formula for opposition to the legal declaration of the Catholic tithe in the bill, and rhetorically blended this with fears (prescient, as it turned out) that the measure might convey to the Americans a 'love of despotism.'[95] Clearly the pupil of Burke's, Fox found an object for opposition, not in state-sanctioned tithing for the Roman Catholic religion *per se* ('I profess I do not object myself so much to that part of it'), but rather in a thin technical argument that the tithe was akin to a tax, and that the House of Lords, which had originated the bill, was not to levy taxes. As for the substantive issue of Catholic toleration, Fox allowed himself a brief, but extraordinarily strong parenthesis: 'I think that the persecution of the Roman Catholics, the penal laws of this country, are so repugnant to every principle of toleration, [that] I think there might be some part of his Majesty's dominions an asylum, where the Roman Catholics might go, if persecuted.'[96] Fox and Burke thus conveyed furtive, though powerful support for the most publicly contentious element of the measures without being publicly identified as supporting the government's unpopular measure.[97] Indeed, in radical newspapers such as the *Middlesex Journal*, Burke and Fox shined as the 'most ardent Protestant bigots.'[98] Both of their names were absent from the blacklist published in the *London Evening Post* in October 1774, skewering 'Members who were in the House on the Quebec Bill and who divided for establishing Popery and a French system of Laws in Canada.'[99]

Philip Lawson provides an excellent and uncontested account of the general hostility of the popular radical press in London to the Quebec legislation, and it is unnecessary to rehearse it in any detail here.[100] Suffice to note as an example the heavily reported preparation and delivery of the petition of the London council, which was presented to the King by the mayor and 150 city officials and common councillors. Interestingly, the text of the petition construed the Quebec bill as an assault on the 'great fundamental principles of the constitution of the British monarchy.'[101] Closely juxtaposed in the petition were severely anti-Catholic rhetoric ('the Roman Catholick religion, which is known to be idolatrous and bloody, is established by this bill'), constitutional assertions ('your majesty's illustrious family was called to the throne ... under the express stipulation that they should profess the protestant religion, ... your majesty at your coronation solemnly swore that you would, to the utmost of your power, maintain the laws of God, the true profession of the gospel, and the protestant reformed religion ...'), and bitter protest at the status of representation in the proposed Quebec government ('repugnant to the leading principles of this free constitution').[102] As mentioned earlier, such a formula represents a classic combination that in many eras has generated mobilization conducive to demotic exclusive nationalism.

Although the disposition of historical public opinion is always problematic, not being susceptible to any scientific method of polling, impressionistic evidence suggests that much of the British public opposed the Quebec legislation, and particularly its toleration of Roman Catholicism. A correspondent of the St James Chronicle asserted, 'The Judgement of the Publick upon the Measures of Government has never been, within my Memory, more general, more uniform, nor, perhaps, more in the Right' than on the Quebec bill.[103] Another in a different paper said the bill was 'universally objected to.'[104] The king was reportedly greeted in public with 'No popery, no French Government.'[105] Based on his reading of contemporary newspapers, Fred Hinkhouse concludes, 'The Quebec Act had certainly granted favors to Catholics, and though those Catholics were beyond the seas, Englishmen were keenly aware of Catholics in England, of whose power and position they were constantly suspicious. Many bitter struggles had England had over religion, and many slumbering animosities survived. The Quebec Bill gave occasion for the enemies of Catholicism in England to fan these animosities to a fiery heat.'[106] According to Hinkhouse, in the newspapers, 'the overwhelming bulk of the arguments' were against the Quebec Act.[107]

In Parliament, the Quebec Act easily passed the Lords, where it was introduced. As for the Commons, we have suggested that the vigorous debate there must be understood in the context of passionate public opposition and damning press.[108] It is perhaps telling that, when debate began in the House of Commons concerning the religious clauses that would emancipate the Catholics of Quebec, the government moved to eject the public from the Commons' Gallery.[109] Ultimately the bill passed even the Commons because there was a 'consensus among the social and political elites, including the bulk of the parliamentary classes, that favoured a special tolerant case being made for Quebec.'[110] As the solicitor general, Alexander Wedderburn, asserted, adding credence to Burke's claims of surprisingly uniform tolerance among parliamentarians, 'I believe I should do an injustice if I attributed to any gentleman a desire to convert the Canadians, by an act of force, to the Protestant faith. However desirable it may be, that there should be a conformity of opinion, I do not believe there are any gentlemen in this House who wish to effect the conversion of the Canadians, in any way but by the force of persuasion and conviction.'[111] But Catholic emancipation, even for Quebec, appears to have been achieved despite, rather than on the strength of, public opinion in Britain.

The Quebec Act

As Carleton had recommended, the Quebec Act declared the British government's intention to reconcile itself with the traditional sources of authority within Canadien society. The Catholic Church was to be legally sanctioned in extracting the tithe from all Catholics. The status of its members was to be enhanced by their new capacity to hold the full array of public offices under a modified oath, compatible with their faith. The semi-feudal seigneurial system was confirmed by entrenching the old property law, in addition to the civil laws of the Canadiens. The only export from the British legal system was to be English criminal law. An assembly would not be granted; in light of the unpalatable alternatives, government would continue for the foreseeable future to be by governor and council.

If the Quebec Act was an attempt to reinforce the traditional threads of Canadien society, perhaps its underlying intention was thereby to gain a surer grasp. This suggestion is to be found in the conclusion to Vincent Harlow's magisterial *The Founding of the Second British Empire*:

> The assertion of authority was urgent; in newly conquered or ceded colonies it could temporarily be exercised, but in the interests of tranquility and economy it would be impermanent. Authoritarianism was limited by the facts of empire: distance and diversity. To secure the dependencies, to control democratic instincts, to build up the prosperity of the empire as a whole, it was imperative to create confidence among the local men of influence. So alien law and institutions, indigenous custom and practices, and religions of all kinds were tolerated: the gentry, the princes, zemindari or seigneurs must be won over to accept the imperial rule of which they now became privileged instruments.[112]

Throughout the empire, local notables became indispensable in the campaign of colonial regimes to wrest what could not be won by brute force alone: social and political dominance.

In the list of those who became 'privileged instruments' of the empire, this account might easily have included the Catholic priesthood in Quebec. In an age before mass media and literacy, the church provided the sole channel for articulating not only God's will to Canadiens, but that, also, of secular authority. Many peasants first heard edicts from the governor and council following mass on Sundays.[113] *Some* religion was considered essential for a civil regime. The least desirable scenario for conservatives was not a thoroughly Roman Catholic society, but an irreligious one.[114]

In order to secure the influential backing of the church, the governors often took a hand in its internal affairs. During the process of selecting and gaining official acceptance for a bishop, for example, Murray intervened in favour of Mgr Briand. Briand, not coincidentally, had previously been the only one of the vicars general prepared to offer prayers during mass for George III, even before the fate of Quebec was sealed by the Treaty of Paris. Carleton, for his part, once recommended that French priests hoping to come to Canada be met in London with the impossible obstacle of obtaining a visa.

Yet, even Murray enjoyed relations with Briand that were 'more than honourable; they were cordial. Each frequently used his influence to support the other in managing the clergy and the flocks.'[115] This was still more the case with Carleton. After a decade of dealings with him and his superiors in London, Briand stated in a private letter, 'The faith is perfectly free. I exercise my ministry without constraint. The Governor likes and respects me; the English honor me. I rejected an oath that was proposed, and the Parliament of Great Britain changed it and established one which every Catholic can take.[116]

Briand was blissfully unaware of the rather harsh instructions given to the governor along with the Quebec Act. According to the instructions, all Catholic benefices, including those of the bishop and the priests, were to be filled under the authority of the king.[117] Foreigners were specifically to be barred from such positions. Briand's own episcopal authority was supposed to be limited strictly to functions 'indispensably necessary' to the church. Held under the thumb of the governor, he was not supposed to be allowed to appeal to, or even to correspond with, Rome. These instructions might well have appeared to Briand to breathe life into the proviso of royal supremacy inscribed in the act. The proviso, which Carleton lightly brushed aside in a conversation with Briand, referred to a doctrine remaining on the statute books from the early reign of Elizabeth I, intended to extinguish 'foreign Power and Authority Spiritual and Temporal' – meaning that of the Pope – within the realm.

Yet, it is unwarranted to interpret the overall policy of 1774, as one historian has, as a conspiracy of the British government to undermine the faith and bring a Protestant Reformation to Quebec.[118] Even under steadfastly Catholic regimes, the power of Rome had often been eclipsed. The King of France had always chosen the Bishop of Quebec, and the *intendants* had equally wielded considerable influence in religious affairs. Moreover, the British governor was also to be given a comparable role for the Church of England in the province. The right of the governor to make appointments for both churches arose not only to ensure that the church never became a bastion for subversion, but also because the governor was responsible to decide whether a parish was to have a Protestant or a Catholic 'Incumbent.' According to the instructions, his decision was to depend upon the express preferences of the majority of a parish, with the onus placed upon a Protestant majority to actually 'solicit' a Protestant minister if they so wished.[119] During the British parliamentary debate on the bill, Burke's amendments were defeated that would have either placed the tithes garnered from the dispersed Protestants in Quebec in the hands of a Protestant missionary organization, or made it obligatory for the king to commit such revenues to establishing the Protestant church.[120] In the end, the disposal of Protestant tithes was left wholly at the king's discretion.

Several historians have also suggested that the true policy of the Quebec Act was obstructed by Carleton's inclination to hold a looser rein on the church in Quebec than his superiors in London desired.[121] Carleton did not, as they note, limit to any significant extent the ecclesiastical jurisdiction of the local Catholic establishment. The best evidence to the contrary is to be found in Carleton's discussion of the issue with Briand. According to Carleton, the King himself did not incline to a hard-line position. Soon after having returned from London, where he had been in close contact with government ministers, Carleton construed the King's view to Briand thus: 'The King will not use this power [royal supremacy], and he completely consents and even intends that the Pope will be your superior in the faith, but the bill would not have passed without this word. We have no intentions of directing your religion and our King will not interfere as much as that of France; we do not ask, as you see in the oath, that you recognize this supremacy.'[122] Carleton's words were not an arbitrary dismissal of an official policy he found embarrassing. The evidence Carleton musters here before a sceptical Briand is, in fact, significant. As Carleton notes, an important oath had indeed been changed by the Quebec Act in a way that undermined, rather than reinforced, the doctrine of royal supremacy.

The doctrine of royal supremacy was originally embodied in a 1558 act from the first year of the reign of Elizabeth I.[123] By 1774, it still remained more or less intact in England, and the Quebec Act professes to declare royal supremacy, in the sense of renewing it, as a limitation upon the free worship accorded to the Catholic faith in Quebec. The backbone of that act was an oath required of all clergy and ecclesiastical authority in England. As we have already seen, a similar oath had been mentioned in Murray's 1763 Commission and Instructions. In the Quebec Act, however, the oaths were repealed and replaced with a much looser one. The proposer of the new oath noted in the Commons that a Catholic priest could not take the old oath in conscience.[124] The notion of royal supremacy that thus emerged in the Quebec Act of 1774 was shorn of an element previously at its core: the insistence that the King supplant the Pope as the supreme spiritual authority of the Church. What remained of the doctrine, as embodied in the instructions, was limited to provisions aimed at ensuring that the constitutional sovereignty of the King was not compromised by any openings to the 'great political system of the court of Rome with all of its pretensions.'[125]

1.4 The Power Cleavage

Elites were conscious during this period, both in Quebec and in England, that instituting religious tolerance was not a popular agenda. In 1764 Murray had expressed strong feelings in a letter to Eglinton, a confidant of the King, pledging to resign should the exigencies of public opinion interfere with relaxing the statutory disabilities of Catholics in Quebec. 'I am sure You will do all in your power to assist ... a miserable People, who after having undergone the worst Calamities War can inflict ... must now either abandon their all or submit to the Persecution of the most cruel, Ignorant, rapacious Fanaticks who ever existed ... If the popular Clamour of England will not allow the humane Heart of the King to follow its own dictates & the [anti-] Popish Laws must be exerted with Rigour in Canada, for God's sake procure my Retreat ... as I cannot be the Witness to the Misery of a people I love & admire.'[126] The succinctness of Murray's contrast here between the 'popular Clamour of England' and the 'humane Heart of the King' signals that this was a relatively unproblematic observation within the contemporary context. The power cleavage in both Quebec and England thus appears to have been evident to elites, and it was an aristocratic point of honour not to capitulate to popular chauvinism.[127]

There was an interesting political dimension to the assertion of royal supremacy in the Quebec Act. A letter written by Lord Dartmouth notes that the style in which the free exercise of the Catholic religion was to be made subject to royal supremacy in the act was altered between drafts to appear stronger because of the needs 'to obviate any doubts that might have been created' by a slightly looser formulation and to 'prevent any ill consequences it might be thought likely to have in other parts of his Majesty's Dominions.'[128] This thinly veiled reference to the need to take into account public opinion in America, and perhaps Ireland, echoes

Carleton's own reference to the political context ('the bill would not have passed without this word').[129] Such prevarications over the form but not the substance of Catholic emancipation in Quebec must therefore be understood within the context of the Protestant enthusiasm throughout the empire that buffeted Parliament during the later decades of the eighteenth century (see 1.1). What is most impressive is not that the policy contained obscurantist elements, but rather that the government went as far as it did, in as public an instrument as an act of Parliament.

The reception of the act in North America provides further evidence of a substantial power cleavage during the period.[130] Reaction among the Americans was swift and violent, the act being assimilated to several other 'intolerable acts.' Repeal was immediately demanded. This being unsuccessful, the acts together provided a link in the chain of developments that culminated in the American Revolution.[131] In October 1774, the first American Congress of the colonies thundered that the act fostered 'a religion that has deluged our island in blood, and dispersed impiety, bigotry, persecution, murder, and rebellion throughout every part of the world.'[132] The reaction of the merchants of Quebec, if less hysterical, was no more favourable.[133] In John Manning Ward's words, the act was condemned as a 'statutory embodiment of the Francophile prejudices of the governors.'[134] The British citizens of Quebec and Montreal petitioned for repeal to the House of Commons, tarring the act with the brush of a priestly conspiracy.[135] Meanwhile, their trading partners in London tendered their support for an exclusively Protestant assembly, or at least a council from which Catholics would be barred.[136] As for the retention of Canadien laws by the act, the London traders looked to Ireland for a superior model, as there the assimilation of Irish to English law was rather optimistically understood to be a 'strong ground of union and mutual affection between the inhabitants of the two countries.'[137] Nothing less than a return to the ostensible policy of the 1763 proclamation was endorsed.[138]

1.5 Attitudes among the Canadiens

Surprisingly, the hostile reaction of English-speaking British subjects in North America and their spokesmen in London to the Quebec Act was not mirrored by jubilance among the Canadiens.[139] The clergy and seigneurs praised it, but the Canadien habitants, the bulk of the population, 'were not won.'[140] This was demonstrated most plainly against the background of the American invasion and occupation. The invasion of Quebec in 1775 by a rag-tag force of American revolutionaries prompted Carleton to attempt to mobilize the Canadiens in defence. Bishop Briand and the seigneurs quickly aligned themselves, but the call-up was not very successful. John Hare has calculated that within the fifty-four parishes in the eastern part of the province, more than 750 men, or 17 per cent of those enrolled in the militia, shirked military service for the British.[141] About 80 actively served the American rebels. In ten of fifty-four parishes, the proportion of those refusing to enlist exceeded 30 per cent.

The unimpressive rate of enlistment was in some sense 'quasi-natural' for the ruggedly independent habitants, and had been witnessed even under the French regime.[142] The patron–client feudal ties that kept European peasants in a state of subordination were far weaker in Quebec. Most seigneurs were in fact townspeople with very little inclination to maintain the local involvement, patronage, and social ties essential to commanding influence on their rural estates.[143] Nevertheless, the anti-British sentiments of the rebels seem to have resonated with the sentiments of some of the Canadien habitants. What limited evidence there is suggests that strong antagonism towards the English was common at the time of the 1775 American invasion. Hare notes that, in one parish, the habitants responded with derision to the exhortations of their curé. 'You are an Englishman,' they told him, 'and in obliging us to submit ourselves you want to make us English.'[144] Bishop Briand responded to the curé who had reported the conversation to him that he was receiving the same response: 'My authority is no more respected that yours: it is said of me, as of you, that I am English.'[145]

Whatever animosity may have existed towards the British, however, such sentiments never conduced to an organized and articulate campaign of demotic exclusive nationalism before, during, or immediately following the American revolution and invasion. There is no record of any political statements in favour of privileging the Canadien way of life, and it is implausible that Canadien sympathies for the invaders were generated by nationalist principles. Indeed, passivity in the face of American invasion was an invitation to a force that deeply despised the Canadiens' defining national characteristics, including their religion. The anti-Catholic bombast of the American Congress at the time of the Quebec Act was well known in Quebec.[146] Although raw animosity towards the British may have conditioned the Canadien indifference to the invasion, this stance cannot be called exclusive nationalism.

Canadien society was not yet participant. Its elite had little interest in political mobilization and found nothing illegitimate about rule by governor and an appointive council. The Canadien body politic reflected in the events of the American invasion was divided according to estate in attitudes to the British regime. The first and second estates – the senior Roman Catholic clergy and seigneurial would-be nobility – set aside, or simply did not feel, the national antagonisms of the third estate, the habitants. Divisions among these groups arose not from relations of production, but rather from varying degrees of proximity to state power. Those closer, in the sense that their personal interaction with colonial officials influenced their prospects, had different outlooks from those more peripheral. But collaboration with the imperial power should not be reduced to weakness, complacency, or corruption. For the abstemious Bishop Briand, for example, actions that would have perpetuated national antagonisms would have been not only contrary to the interests of the church, but also, from his perspective, a morally inferior choice. Briand considered that regrets concerning the conquered fate of his people were 'sterile,' and he therefore brought himself to make a genuine reconciliation with the previously despised enemy.[147] His fair treatment by the British elites reinforced his conciliatory attitude.

1.6 Local Politics and Interests

Such demotic exclusive nationalism as existed during the period was exhibited by the English-speaking population (see 1.1 and 1.4).[148] This pattern persisted through the 1780s. In 1787 the Quebec merchants responded to the council's request for suggestions on how to improve commerce in the province with a plan designed to 'give this province the form and figure of a British colony.'[149] The plan proposed to encourage immigration from the south, to cast aside the whole body of French law, except for property law, and to establish schools to teach English.[150]

At the elite level in the council, a body appointed by the governors, the balance of opinion was considerably more accommodating of the Canadiens. Although a minority group of reformers on the council favoured applying English law, their specific proposal did not aim to alter the status quo enjoyed by Canadiens. On their plan, as set forth by Chief Justice Smith, English laws would not have been applied to any suits involving a party avowing Canadien ancestry.[151] The French Party – encompassing a few conservative seigneurs and dominated, despite its name, by a trio of influential English members – demurred in this proposal. As the party was ascendant on the council between 1775 and the early 1790s, Smith's plan was rejected. The 'political faith' of the French Party was that the Quebec

Act was 'the result of the generous and tolerating spirit which distinguishes an enlightened age and nation.'[152] Thus, the act was viewed as the keystone of a legal regime that might be subjected to minor improvements, but not to radical alteration.[153] Governor Haldimand (1778–84) shared this view, considering the act, in his words, a 'sacred charter granted by the king in parliament to the Canadians as a security for their religion, laws and property.'[154]

The French Party countered with its own plan, not only opposing all legal reform, but also proposing to roll back the previous grants of trial by jury for commercial cases and English rules of evidence.[155] Burt characterizes this proposal as nothing less than the 'insistence that all who chose to reside in Canada, having placed themselves under the laws of the country, should conform to its life.'[156] This seems an overstatement. In contrast to the proposals of the Quebec merchants, for example, the proposal of the French Party did not aim to inculcate a particular identity in Quebec. Not unreasonably, it argued for a uniform system of laws, to which 97 per cent of the population was accustomed. Its positions concerning whether juries should decide mercantile causes and whether English rules of evidence should prevail in courtrooms, can also hardly be construed as evidence that the French Party was bent on forcing conformity to the Canadien way of life as such.

Greenwood rightly emphasizes the bi-ethnic nature of both parties, and suggests that political divisions around this time were 'based primarily on class, not ethnicity.'[157] This is an important observation, particularly if restricted to the official commitments of the parties *after* procedures of accommodation driven by common objectives had had their moderating influence. In the council, for example, a compromise bill was finally passed following much debate in 1787; it embodied several elements of Smith's favoured reforms, but did not sanction the introduction of English law.[158]

Even outside the council, committees representing English and Canadien mercantile interests were ultimately able to present a relatively common front after much acrimonious discussion. Together they demanded an assembly that would dilute the power of the arch-conservative council. Significantly, the coalition seems to have evolved considerably between 1787 and 1788. In 1787, the British merchants insisted on making their earlier report (demanding 'the form and figure of a British colony') the basis of their own submission via their agent. The Canadien merchants, in preparing a submission the next year, initially countered with their own demand that the church be released from the (unenforced) royal supremacy entrenched in the Quebec Act. They also wanted more official positions given to Canadiens, and control over appointments vested in the future assembly.[159]

These demands clashed so strongly with the English merchants' position that the two groups initially reached an impasse. After several days of discussions the groups' submissions converged significantly.[160] The committees were mutually dependent: their determination to settle upon compatible submissions was conditioned by their need to convey to decision makers in London that the majority and minority groups of Quebec were not at such great odds that the grant of an assembly would bring irretrievable deadlock or the harassment of the English minority. Such interdependence among groups having common objectives is more often perceived by political elites than by private citizens. Obviously, only a small minority of citizens participate personally at the peak level of organizations, where accommodation and compromise take place. This helps to explain the power cleavage underlying conflict regulation and exclusive nationalism while also underlining the potential for ordinary subjects to reach compromises through common deliberation in the presence of shared interests.

1.7 The Constitutional Act of 1791: Imposed Accommodation

The American Revolution presented two imperatives for colonial policy in what remained of British North America: accommodating the 20,000 Loyalist refugees who had streamed north by 1789, and avoiding a repeat catastrophe through sound colonial government. Accommodating the refugees – many of whom had fought the revolution while favouring the *existence* of local assemblies – required somehow supplanting the *ancien régime* perpetuated by the Quebec Act without breaking that concord with the Canadiens. As many Loyalists had settled in the West, partition seemed appropriate. Assemblies were also needed to levy taxes more locally, and, it was hoped, more legitimately, than in the old Thirteen Colonies. There could be no question of the imperial Parliament subsidizing the colony in perpetuity at the current rate.[161]

The principal architect of the Constitutional Act, Secretary of State William Grenville, believed the trouble in America had stemmed not from excessive autonomy, but from the failure to strike an effective balance among the 'democratical,' aristocratic, and monarchical elements of society, as was the hallmark of the British constitution.[162] This was a fairly conventional, though not uncontroversial analysis of revolution at this time. Arthur Young wrote in 1794 to differentiate Britain from revolutionary France, 'The principle of our constitution is the representation of property ...'[163] Accordingly, the Constitutional Act of 1791 circumscribed the power of the new assemblies by means of executive prerogatives reserved to the governor and the unelected Legislative and Executive Councils in each of the two envisaged provinces, Upper and Lower Canada.[164] The property qualification for electing assembly members was set sufficiently low to provide a broad suffrage for the period.[165] Land in the Lower province would be granted in either freehold or *en fief et seigneurie* at the option of the grantee. The act also provided that a certain proportion of all land grants be reserved to generate revenues for the Protestant ministry, and that the governor be given authority to provide facilities for the Established Church. Both of these provisions were intended to enable the church to minister to the swelling Loyalist population, known to be rife with the religious dissent implicated in the revolution.[166]

The act contravened the views of the British minority in what became Lower Canada by upholding the seigneurial system, opening the popular portion of the government to Canadien domination, and omitting major legal reforms.[167] This was forthrightly accepted by the imperial elite. King George III, himself, stated candidly in a letter to Grenville, 'I am sorry any change is necessary, for I am aware to please all concerned is impossible, and that if things could have gone on in its present state for some years, it would have been very desirable ... [The plan] has been drawn up with ... attention to the interest of the old inhabitants who, by the capitulation, have every degree of right to be first attended to.'[168] At an earlier stage, Grenville had considered enacting some of the merchants' most strongly desired legal reforms as a palliative. Many of his colleagues, however, were unsympathetic, believing that those who had made their way to Quebec ought to be prepared to adapt themselves to the laws and institutions prevailing there.[169]

In the House of Commons, the impact of partition upon the British minority attracted little debate, in part because it could be cogently presented as the least of all evils.[170] As Pitt summed up the question,

> It appeared to ministers ... that there was no probability of reconciling the jarring interests and opposite views of the inhabitants, but by giving them two legislatures ... If one of the parties had a great ascendancy over the other, the party having the superiority was very unlikely to give satisfaction to the other party. It seemed to his majesty's servants the most desirable thing, if they could not give satisfaction to all descriptions of men, to divide the

province, and to contrive that one division should consist, as much as possible, of those who were well inclined towards the English laws, and the other, of those who were attached to the French laws. It was perfectly true, that in Lower Canada there still remained a number of English subjects; but these would hold a much smaller proportion than if there was one form of government for every part of the province. It was in Upper Canada particularly that they were to expect a great addition of English inhabitants.[171]

It would be anachronistic and misleading to label William Pitt the first Quebec separatist, but his argument might nevertheless be held up to those who claim in a much later era that it is impossible to construct a case for separation without resort to exclusive nationalism (more on that in chapter 4). It is in any case striking how little cultural bias imposed itself in the debate. Some speakers, including Pitt himself on an early occasion, espoused a quiet confidence in the superiority of British institutions, and a rather blithe expectation that French Canadians in Lower Canada might, by the power of example, embrace British ways 'from conviction.'[172] But most, such as Burke, were content with the blunt acceptance of live and let live: 'Let the Canadians have a constitution formed upon the principles of Canadians, and Englishmen upon the principles of Englishmen.'[173] Still another, William Grant, most openly espoused what might now be deemed cosmopolitan optimism, emphasizing the strong commonalities in contract law 'in every civilized country,' noting that the advantages of the French 'Code Marchand' were held 'in great repute in that and other kingdoms,' and exonerating French-Canadian laws from claims that they discouraged trade.[174]

Several explanations have been offered to explain the willingness of the British government to compromise the interests of their English brethren in Lower Canada 'on the altar of French Canada,' as Burt put it.[175] Gilles Bourque, for example, suggests that the colony, and hence the two groups of English-speakers, were divided in order to stymie any latent revolutionary potential among them.[176] Tousignant attributes it to an *ancien régime* arrogance on the part of the British colonial administration: the King's servants 'decided the affairs of the empire with the mentality of great feudal lords.'[177]

While these explanations are arguably not strictly necessary, given Pitt's view that his government *was* optimally accommodating both ethnic groups, Tousignant's recognition of the larger pattern of representation – it has here been termed 'imposed statecraft' – is certainly significant in terms of the smooth advance of the measure through parliament. Unlike the Quebec Act, the Constitutional Act of 1791 had few domestic overtones to seize the popular British imagination. No doubt there was also a sense of moral obligation among much of the political elite, to conform to the terms of the previous constitutional settlements, while accommodating the Loyalists as best as possible. As Grenville put it in a letter to Dorchester in 1789, 'a considerable degree of attention is due to the prejudices and habits of the French Inhabitants who compose so large a proportion of the community, and every degree of caution should be used to continue to them the enjoyment of those civil and religious Rights which were secured to them by the Capitulation of the Province, or have since been granted by the liberal and enlightened spirit of the British Government.'[178] Finally, one might detect a certain relativistic respect of British parliamentarians for local attachments. Indeed, by 1791 Grenville was correcting his own earlier use of the term 'prejudices.' 'It had been stated, that the French inhabitants of Canada were so much attached to the prejudices of the Canadians, to their customs, laws, and manners ... He thought such an attachment deserved a better name than that of prejudice. He conceived it was an attachment founded in reason, or in something better than reason; in the best feelings of the human heart.'[179] Simply put, moral obligations dovetailed with impressive broad-mindedness to compel the British political elite in 1791 to comply with its undertakings of 1760 and 1774. The pattern of imposed statecraft provided the British elite with sufficient latitude to do so.

1.8   Early Quebec Settlements: Analysis and Relevance to Theory

The politics of the first two constitutional settlements in Quebec were characterized by a significant power cleavage. Those holding state power or influence were apparently more prepared than others to accommodate the enduring presence of a different way of life within the province, and to repudiate exclusive nationalism. At the same time, the exigencies associated with diverse strategic concerns and the intermittent need to accommodate the parochial views of British subjects both sometimes imposed limitations. The Royal Proclamation of 1763, which aimed ultimately at attracting British settlers from the south so as to avert war with the natives west of the Appalachians, reflected such limitations. In other circumstances, such as when it became apparent that tailoring policy solely to the concerns of British individuals in North America was not strategically vital, the result was more commonly policy that, as the Quebec Act did, tolerated the traditional way of life of a distinct culture, despite the fact that elements of it were despised by the majority of common English-speaking British subjects on both sides of the Atlantic.

In the shadow of the perennial threat of war with France, it was essential to maintain liberal relations with the population that might be called upon to man the ramparts. After the collapse of the policy of the proclamation because of the failure to attract British immigrants, it became clear that that population would be a predominantly Canadien one. The clergy and those presuming to be feudal lords were inevitably the principal partners of the British regime in reconciliation. Alliances in Quebec initially had to be established by the British political elite across the barriers of religion and culture, in short, because the power to thwart invasion or foreign-sponsored insurgency was not confined to, or even concentrated in, their co-religionists. Conciliatory, tolerant attitudes made such alliances fathomable and perpetuated them.

The ordinary English-speaking subjects of the province bore different attitudes and separate concerns. For the time being, the distant security threats could not seem as real and as pressing, because they did not have comparable access to the intelligence information that made Murray, Carleton, and Haldimand and their superiors in London so nervous. Furthermore, from the perspective of a Quebec merchant, success did not depend so much upon building bridges of mutual esteem with individuals outside his ethnic group as in forming trusting personal and commercial alliances within his group, with whom he shared a language and a culturally determined set of expectations including a legal tradition. Maintaining and enlarging the cultural infrastructure of these relationships was understandably a high priority.

A slightly different account can be offered for the division between the quasi-political elites among the Canadiens and their less politically engaged flocks. While all those who suffered through the war with the British were probably predisposed to hostility, this attitude was ill-suited to those whose position depended upon good relations with the prevailing authority. The senior Catholic clergy and the seigneurs both benefited from supportive deployments of constituted authority: the church to enforce its covenants with the faithful, and landholders for the legal sanction to extract their dues. As authority was now vested with an alien elite, it was incumbent upon the clergy to reconcile themselves to this new relationship and build upon it. This fostered genuinely conciliatory attitudes. For the habitants, beyond the reach of British largesse, such incentives were weak or absent. Many might have also harboured natural hostility towards a power responsible for so many casualties in their midst. Whether or not these sentiments were expressed immediately, they appear to have surfaced at the time of the American invasion, when the opportunity arose for a form of passive aggression through refusal to enlist.

Apart from facing very different strategic predicaments, British political elites and subjects clearly had differing grasps of jurisprudence (see 1.1). Although the British law officers were not entirely consistent in advocating the most progressive options, their opposition to discrimination against Catholics in the province was generally stronger than that of any other element of the British regime. The respect accorded their opinions by the British political elite clearly differentiated them from ordinary British merchants in the province who had little appreciation for such niceties, and, indeed, showed a lack of awareness of such contemporary precepts of justice as the right of a conquered people to live according to their own customs and laws until these were specifically altered by the conqueror.

The outlook of English-speaking subjects was probably also constituted by a more determinate set of cultural values than elites'. It appears, for instance, that subjects were far more concerned with the prospects of the Protestant faith in the province than were their political superiors in both Quebec and England. Elites held themselves aloof from the schisms of religious doctrine and took a far more instrumental view of faith (see 1.1 and 1.3) It was speculated earlier that the abject failure of the 1763 policy may have stemmed in part from a failure of British policy makers to anticipate the reluctance of American dissenters to go and live in a Roman Catholic milieu in Quebec. It is possible, similarly, that the Quebec Act was passed without full cognizance of how it would be received by the Americans.

A final question to address is why a comparable form of nationalism to that repeatedly articulated by the British merchants before 1788 did not develop among Canadien subjects during the period. The comparison is not, of course, entirely one of apples to apples. The British merchants of the province were a marginal group numerically. This increased their motivation to lobby for a Protestant assembly that would dramatically shift the balance of power and privilege their way of life. For the Canadiens, militant calls for a return to a French regime or a monopoly of power for French-speaking Catholics would have carried risks of punishment, apart from being useless. Still, the behaviour of the Canadiens in the face of the American invasion exhibited unbridled disdain for the British regime. Minor nationalist currents among the Canadiens were also clearly not entirely eliminated, they simply failed to galvanize much support.[180]

Perhaps the pivotal factor to consider is that the Canadien and British populations in the province varied substantially in their implicit notions of legitimate political representation and in their capacity for popular political organization and mobilization. In this epoch there was as yet no strong feeling among the Canadiens that ordinary subjects ought to be politically enfranchised and engaged. Politics, apart from very sporadic disobedience, was beyond the ken of the habitant, and the lack of representation within the political system probably did not matter much to most. Literacy was an important prerequisite for mobilizing a movement, as the active focus of popular movements such as the Grand Jury was the preparation and refinement of lengthy and sophisticated petitions. Although one did not have to be literate to sign such a petition (many in later periods signified their approbation with an 'X'), a petition clearly required at least a modest organizational backbone, invariably formed by literate and politically activist sections of the population.[181] Within Canadien society the literate segment of the population was small in relative terms, and many of those within it, including the seigneurs and the priests, were inherently conservative and employed their influence to maintain the subordination of their clients.[182] In the absence of a dynamic, literate group of any consequence, no sponsor existed for a political movement onto which popular chauvinism could have been grafted.

Our examination of politics in Quebec between 1760 and 1791 has illustrated the existence of a pronounced power cleavage, one that seems to have stemmed from the greater force of conciliatory attitudes and awareness of external strategic threat among imperial elites, as against the greater religious enthusiasm and commercial concerns of English-speaking subjects. Conflict was effectively regulated on the model of imposed statecraft, even if the legitimate expectations of the British settlers favoured a more representative government. This disjunction provided the impetus for campaigns of the English settlers for an assembly; the campaigns, in turn, provided vehicles for the articulation of popular anti-Catholic chauvinism, thus conducing to what we have termed demotic exclusive nationalism. The Canadiens, who were more accustomed to autocratic rule in the colony, were by contrast relatively quiescent during these early years, and so did not give political expression to cultural antagonism.

Political organization, participatory expectations and mobilization did, of course, eventually arise within Canadien society, with the consequence that the autonomous authority of the political elite was weakened. As discussed in the next chapter, it was a result of this development and the failure of the system of political representation to adapt smoothly to evolving legitimate expectations that would ultimately entrain violent episodes of demotic exclusive nationalism among the Canadiens, and a reaction at least as vociferous among British Loyalists.

TWO

The Decline of Imposed Statecraft, 1792–1839

The imposed statecraft of the British regime achieved major accommodations of the French population in the first three decades of colonial rule in Quebec. Paradoxically, the culmination of this period, the Constitutional Act, also marked the beginning of a long decline of this form of conflict regulation. The impetus for this decline was much broader than the act itself. In an age of revolution, government by cosmopolitan aristocrats alone could not endure, and its constitutional successor was bound to be controversial. Even in Britain, the parliamentary debate over the Constitutional Act impinged upon many severely loaded questions. In the Commons debate, Charles James Fox had the temerity to propose an elected council (albeit one elected 'by persons of property from among persons of the highest property') as a counter-weight to the power of the governor.[1] In so doing, Fox collided with Edmund Burke, his erstwhile mentor, who adverted in his own speech to the destructiveness of the French Revolution, to the role of the crown in maintaining social order, and to the chaos entailed for racially divided societies by democracy premised on the 'rights of man.'[2] In the end, the councils were made appointive, but this could hardly settle the matter once and for all.

In Canada, questions as to the role of various classes in government would be compounded with issues of ethnicity. Otherwise universal questions of political representation – in this period, the balance to be struck among monarchy, aristocracy and democracy (or, at any rate, governor, councils, and assembly) – provided a site for the organization in Canada of mass opinion largely along ethnic lines, and, eventually, for a parasitic exhibition of exclusive nationalism.

After the Constitutional Act of 1791, the governors and imposed statecraft gradually declined as forces regulating conflict in Canada. The legitimate authority of the governors gradually dwindled. Furthermore, in this period the social elite of Britain, as elsewhere in Europe (see 0.5), began to retrench culturally to a more parochial and partial outlook. As Linda Colley observes, 'by the time of Waterloo, a generation of patrician Britons had grown up for whom Continental Europe was more a cockpit for battle, and a landscape of revolutionary subversion, than a fashionable playground and cultural shrine. Out of necessity, therefore, as well as for reasons of prudence and patriotic choice, members of the ruling order were encouraged to seek out new forms of cultural expression that were unquestionably British.'[3] Whereas Murray and Carleton had been inclined to accommodate the Canadiens partly by an ostentatiously aristocratic tolerance, accommodation later grew more narrowly contingent upon whether strategic factors of the moment weighed in favour of conciliation or repression.

Strategic considerations, as a basis for tolerance or opposition to exclusive nationalism, were in turn inherently contingent not only upon empirical facts (e.g., the relative size of an ethnic population, its rate of enlistment in the militia, etc.) but also upon points of geostrategic intelligence (e.g., the probability of Napoleon's electing to invade British North America) and subjective judgment (e.g., the Canadien population's likely loyalties in the event of a French or American invasion). As such, different views as to the appropriate level of accommodation sometimes arose at different vantage points within the political elite. At one extreme were those whose political job descriptions, so to speak, did not require them seriously to assess strategic-factors at all, or who were so far down the strategic-intelligence food chain that loose and malicious rumours informed their judgement. Hence, Murray Greenwood, in his work *Legacies of Fear*, has written of a 'garrison mentality' among many British residents and their local leaders in Canada following the French Revolution.[4] At the other extreme were those holding primary responsibility for the disposition of British troops and imperial resources, whose continued tenure demanded the informed and dispassionate management of risk. Where one stood potentially determined one's view of strategic considerations, and, hence, one's willingness to accommodate. The upshot was occasional divisions of opinion *within* the political elite, and, often, a movement upwards, within the political hierarchy, of the power cleavage. Another factor that began to dispose the political elite against conciliation later in this period was the introduction of mechanisms of constituent control. After the publication of the anti-colonial 92 Resolutions in 1834, moderates were flushed out into the open and largely eliminated from the Patriots, who then became less disposed to compromise.

While imposed statecraft was gradually eclipsed during the period at hand, its later successor, affiliative trusteeship, was only sporadically operative under constitutional arrangements after 1791. As the two major ethnic groups of the colony came to ensconce themselves within separate government institutions, the assembly and the councils, they increasingly talked past each other, having little occasion to engage in order to strike alliances to govern in concert. Each, moreover, served to frustrate the other's agenda, each grew progressively entrenched, and each was composed in a manner illegitimate to the other. For Canadien leaders, the prevailing form of representation lagged expectations; for much of the British elite, it seemed far too advanced. The resulting inflammatory discourse over issues of political representation spilled out well beyond political elites, and became even more polarized by ethnicity at the mass level, providing opportunities for acts of demotic exclusive nationalism on both sides.

Overall, then, during the half-century following the Constitutional Act of 1791, we can trace the gradual decline of the effectiveness of imposed statecraft as a conflict-regulating system, the rise of competing political discourses over forms of political representation in the colony, broad popular mobilization by the political elite on these questions, and the straying of the larger, resulting discourses into exclusive nationalism. The ultimate result of this sequence was the closest approximation to civil war ever experienced in Canada and, following that, a recourse to official exclusive nationalism by the British government.

The chapter is organized chronologically with discussion focused on five major episodes. The first section (2.1) discusses local politics in the shadow of the American and French Revolutions following on the Constitutional Act of 1791. Bi-ethnic alliance formation in the assembly is contrasted with early manifestations of popular protest. The next section (2.2) assesses the increasing pressure placed upon official neutrality from both within and without the political elite, and discusses the factors responsible for the appearance of official exclusive nationalism at the margins of the imperial regime, as well as the response elicited from the Canadien political elite. The third section of the chapter (2.3) contains a discussion of the divisive issues of the 1820s, focusing again on the divergent agendas championed at different levels of the British elite and the Canadien response. The fourth section (2.4) attempts to link the essential ambiguity of the political outlook of the Canadien elite with its strategic and tactical predicament. The fifth section (2.5) discusses the political history of the Rebellions of 1837–8, examining the implications for exclusive nationalism within the Patriots as the mass base gained greater influence within the movement. The sixth section (2.6) discusses the strategic considerations that engendered the Union Act, an act of official exclusive nationalism unprecedented in official state policy to that point. Finally, we conclude the chapter (in section 2.7) with several speculations based on the historical experience considered for a causal theory of exclusive nationalism.

2.1 Popular Politics after the Revolutions: Riots and Early Alliances

In section 0.7, two early stages of exclusive nationalism ('popular chauvinism' and 'demotic exclusive nationalism') were distinguished on the basis of the greater reach of the latter, and, by extension, on the reliance of the latter upon a 'host' political organization. This distinction takes it for granted that, however marked ethnic identity and competition are, a dissatisfied ethnic population bereft of responsive political organization may not be in a position to articulate exclusive nationalism on any large or systematic scale. Within systems in which political representation is at an early stage of development, political elites may, as gatekeepers, control the extent of the dissemination of, and mobilization for, exclusive nationalism. This pattern appears to be borne out by the riots in Lower Canada in 1794 and 1796, which occurred at a point at which the Canadien political elite, divided in itself by class, had begun forming tentative political alliances with its English-speaking counterparts, and had little interest in mass mobilization.

Reaction to the French Revolution was volatile in Lower Canada. Although the English-speaking middle class was initially gratified by news of the curtailment of Roman Catholic privilege and approved the declaration of the rights of man, reaction between 1791 and 1793 swung with word, first, of the growing republicanism and popular disturbances, and, later, of the September massacres and regicide.[5] Most Canadiens, with their identification with the Catholic Church and the *ancien régime*, were probably less supportive than English speakers of even the first phase of the revolution.[6] Although a small cadre of literati among the Canadiens known as the Société des Patriotes supported the aims of the revolution, the French and American agents operating in the province around this time had little success in raising discontent over the tithe and seigneurial dues, which were not in this period particularly onerous or an impediment to access to land.[7]

The riots of the decade were thus the product of other causes.[8] The first riots occurred in 1794, when, on at least two occasions, hundreds of habitants mounted an armed resistance to prevent authorities from arresting a few of the 6,100 men (of 7,000 deemed fit for service) who had failed to comply with a militia call-up. Two years later, riots were again triggered, this time by resistance to the mandatory service in the construction and maintenance of roads known as the *corvée*. Popular chauvinism suffused the turbulence. Greenwood notes that, among the people of the countryside at the time of the Road Act riots, 'the massacre of the English became a topic of tavern oratory.'[9] Anglophobia can also be inferred from the people's receptiveness to rumours during the period that the English were perpetrating unimaginable cruelties and spreading false reports of revolutionary atrocities.[10] Besides the British, the popular fury was also directed against the assembly, which had not only legislated unpaid road *corvées*, but had also passed 'drastic' security legislation in response to an earlier uprising and in the midst of the swirling revolutionary fears then touching the colony. The election of 1796 reflected 'a general alienation from the politics of the government, including those of the Assembly' and it 'dealt a devastating blow' to the incumbents.[11]

The potential for such a 'general alienation' was perhaps fostered somewhat by the gradual political mobilization of the people during this period. While the tradition had been established almost a century earlier, of 'rebellion à justice,' the American invasion and occupation of 1775–6 had brought direct contact with a more participatory society.[12] The practice initiated at this time endured of electing militia captains, who tended to articulate local sentiments. Circulating petitions had also become more common. A conservative seigneur, François-Joseph Cugnet, took umbrage at the fact that 'everyone here, even in the class of the third estate, considers himself entitled to make suggestions to the Councils.'[13]

But, the new popular demands placed on the colonial regime were not yet of sufficient strength or duration to challenge seriously the pattern of conflict regulation. As Jean-Pierre Wallot notes, 'no prestigious leadership channelled and combined with the popular energies' and this 'deficiency of leaders ... aborted the popular furors.'[14] The leading classes were united in sharing a strong identification with the imperial state, and this remained true even after the 1796 election had favoured the very few incumbents and new candidates prepared to articulate popular grievances.[15] Despite the presence after the election of new members, a few of whom had previously been 'imprisoned for seditious offences or on suspicion of high treason,' the assembly opted to renew many of the provisions of the old security legislation.[16] Together with the church leaders, the political elite also sponsored loyalty associations, which lent moral support to the British crown in the war with France. Indeed, the assembly was sufficiently repelled by the French Revolution and convinced of the superiority of the British constitution to commit £20,000 in aid of the war effort in 1799.

Wallot points out that many factors motivated the elite and distanced it from ordinary subjects:

> an undisguised horror of the excesses of the French Revolution, even its principles, and the lightning quick rise of Napoleon, the comparison between the bad memories of the shipwreck of French America ... and the relative material well-being as well as the peace that generally persisted since the Conquest; the linguistic, legal, religious and political concessions since that time, and, above all, the new hopes they had fostered on the new national, political, social and even economic plans; finally, the slowness of the British and Protestant settlement which entertained a climate of false security among the Canadiens of Lower Canada ... All the same, these highly abstract arguments did not always convince the masses.[17]

The social order as it was reflected in state institutions existed in a rough 'equilibrium' with the aspirations of the dominant classes.[18] Given the power of those classes to define the institutions as legitimate, it was possible for the Canadien political elite to maintain a strong state identification.

The equilibrium supported accommodations between the two ethnic groups through the 1790s. While propaganda alluding to 'English domination' swirled around the colony, divisive issues in the assembly were seldom decided by the majoritarian mechanism of formal recorded votes. In the twenty years between 1792 and 1812, there was an average of just six recorded votes per year.[19] Apparently, informal and perhaps somewhat more conciliatory decision-making processes were the norm. Party lines, such as they were, did tend to divide the British merchants from the Parti Canadien. Many divisions, however, turned on competing class interests and not, in the first instance, on ethnicity.

At election time it is true that recourse was occasionally had to chauvinism, as when one prominent candidate resorted to commending a losing colleague in another riding as one who would 'trample the English' if elected.[20] Within newly convened assemblies, there were also sometimes brief shows of strength by the Parti Canadien, after which the assembly would settle into a more accommodative pattern. For example, in the opening session of the assembly in 1793, there initially arose a marked division along ethnic lines concerning whether a French- or an English-speaking candidate for Speaker would be chosen, and whether French would enjoy equal status with English in assembly records.[21] This matter dealt with, however, the split did not endure. As the Lieutenant-Governor Alured Clark put it in late 1793, noting in passing the salience of the popular political context, 'the Canadian members having judged that they had shown their importance, by proving to the people that they were acting in concert and could have their way on any matter debated, and having observed that the English members in general conducted themselves with composure, moderation and reason befitting public service, before prorogation there vanished almost completely the unfortunate distinctions which had at first arisen.'[22] Even at the end of the decade, when ethnic lines of division again became more stark, a group of Canadien members termed *ministérielistes* by Greenwood began to join with English as well as non-partisan Canadien members in opposing constitutional change. This was to represent perhaps the first significant case of bi-ethnic alliance formation within the Assembly of Lower Canada.[23] As popularly elected representatives began to bear some of the load in buffering popular chauvinism, affiliative trusteeship began to be sporadically operative in a pattern of conflict regulation previously characterized solely by imposed statecraft.

2.2 Sectarian Schemes, Constitutional Defences, 1799–1818

Official Neutrality under Pressure

As mentioned earlier, the Constitutional Act of 1791 distributed the political authority that in earlier decades had been vested solely in the governors. The resulting pattern of conflict regulation was more complex and precarious than before, with sources of exclusive nationalism springing up in some cases from within the rather permeable political elite of the period. These sources initially had little influence on state policy, because more powerful actors successfully intervened, but they did contribute to the alienation of the Canadien political elite.

Although the ethnic chasm was effectively spanned by political elites during most of the 1790s, British colonial zealots were already beginning to attack major trusses of the constitutional bridge laid down in 1774 and 1791. The most visible agent of disunity was Jacob Mountain, appointed Anglican Bishop in 1793. Mountain aggressively pursued sectarian political objectives, and he used the seats granted him as Bishop on the Executive and Legislative Councils to boost schemes hostile to Roman Catholicism. At first he incurred several disappointments: Governor-General Dorchester was hostile to his designs, as was his successor, General Prescott. And although Mountain, with the support of Chief Justice Osgoode, managed to secure the recall of Prescott and the appointment of the more sympathetic Sir Robert Milnes in 1799, nothing ever really became of the ensuing initiative to assert the governor's authority to nominate priests.[24] Despite the support of the colonial secretary and the Executive Council for more direct interventions, Milnes was prepared only to issue inducements, not ultimatums, apparently because he believed loyalty to be 'a lively principle in the Breasts of the Canadians' and because he was a 'gentle, timid man who greatly valued his popularity with the Canadians.'[25] Mountain's plea in 1803 that the generous state allowance to the Roman Catholic bishop be diminished was met by the Colonial Secretary, Lord Hobart, with a courteous request that Milnes 'point out ... the propriety of abstaining from any acts that might have the effect of producing mutual uneasiness, or of creating any irritation in the minds of the clergy' or of their flocks.[26] In case his point was not entirely clear, and with an eye to the distribution of the Protestant population, he also enquired whether the Anglican Bishop should not be packed off to Upper Canada![27]

Mountain's ploys in education were also initially unsuccessful. His 1795 proposal to Dorchester to establish throughout Lower Canada parish schools with English Protestant schoolmasters had been set aside. According to Wade, Dorchester had probably rejected Mountain's objective of bringing the Canadiens 'to embrace by degrees the Protestant Religion.'[28] In 1799, under Milnes, however, Mountain successfully backed a second plan, and the Royal Institution for the Advancement of Learning, under whose auspices primary schools were to be created, was formally constituted in 1801. Its board was to include the Anglican Bishop but not his Catholic counterpart; pro-British Canadien schoolteachers were to be appointed in Canadien areas.[29] Ultimately, however, crippling limitations dictated by the assembly and apparently acceded to by the governor and councils made the formal establishment of the Royal Institution a dead letter for many years.[30]

While Mountain was certainly most visible in his religious empire-building, his motivations were not necessarily comparable to those of more powerful decision makers.[31] Milnes's motivation for obtaining greater influence over the Catholic bishop and the priests was very similar to that of the framers of the Quebec Act (see 1.3). The difficulty, as Milnes put it, was that 'all connexion between the Government and the People through that Channel is cut off, as the Priests do not consider themselves at all amenable to any other Power than the Catholic Bishop.'[32] Ideally, influence might be wielded through the priests to gain the election of an assembly more inclined by superior 'education and knowledge of business' to support the 'Executive Government.'[33] Attorney-General Jonathan Sewell believed 'the offices of the [Roman Catholic] Bishop & His Coadjutor ... necessary in Canada,' but desired to 'render the Bishop & all his subordinate clergy equally dependant upon the Crown' to serve the 'purpose of Government' and eliminate any future potential for the church to subvert the government.[34] The view of the Royal Institute was similar.[35] As Greenwood explains, in contrast with Mountain's concerns, 'Sewell's pre-occupation with public education arose largely from a conviction, which he claimed was widely shared, that the "security of the Government of Canada under the New Constitution ... depends much upon the discernment of its Excellency." It was, of course, commonplace at the time that once a man was able to understand even a little about the superb British system of government, he could be nothing but actively loyal.'[36] Increasing the authority of the colonial state, not privileging a way of life, explain the policy of Milnes and Sewell with respect to the Roman Catholic Church.[37]

For Governor Milnes, it appears that the main benefit perceived from improvements to education was in averting the need for future generations to be educated in the republican United States.[38] Given that children of French-speaking families of means were generally educated in the seminaries of Quebec, Milnes may well have been referring to the children of English-speaking residents.[39] Elsewhere in his dispatches there is, moreover, no indication that he favoured the cultural or religious assimilation of the Canadiens.

Still, whatever Milnes's views on assimilation, there is no doubt that privileging an English, Protestant way of life had become, by the late 1890s a nostrum of policy for some English members of the judiciary and councils.[40] The reasons for this partial collapse of official neutrality will be discussed later in the chapter (section 2.7).

Canadien Constitutional Defences

The founding of *Le Canadien* in 1806 launched an indignant rebuttal to the bid of English-speakers for control of the political agenda and to the 'malicious attacks' of the Quebec *Mercury*, their newspaper.[41] The pretensions of merchants, an anonymous writer suggested in the first issue, were a potential menace to the public good.[42] In the edition of two weeks later, another writer demanded to know whether those affecting to be good British subjects intended to make a crime of the French Canadians' affection for 'leur Langue, leurs Usages, leur Religion.'[43] Antagonism thus mounted on the levels of both class and culture.

British constitutional customs furnished an orthodox canon that the Canadien leaders painstakingly absorbed, invoked in asserting assembly prerogatives, and disseminated to the literate classes through Le Canadien. Pierre Bédard declared and never lost his belief in the 'ultimate justice of the working of British institutions ...'[44] His colleague D.B. Viger made his own commitment equally clear, echoing Blackstone in Le Canadien in 1809: 'The British constitution is perhaps the only one in which the rights and interests of the various component branches of society are so carefully nurtured, so wisely counterbalanced and interrelated as a whole, that they provide clarity to and support for one another through the very opposition resulting from the simultaneous exercise of the powers bestowed.'[45] The problem, according to the Parti Canadien, did not rest with a wrong-headed constitution under the British empire, but in the administration of an unimpeachable ministry.[46]

Despite the vigorous arguments in defence of the Canadien-dominated popular assembly, it cannot be maintained that the Parti Canadien was an anti-colonial movement during this period, or that disloyalty to the British empire was common at the elite level.[47] The legitimacy of imposed state-craft, especially of the powerful, unelected executive, was certainly begin-ning to decline. But the determined preference for British over American institutions still moved the political and religious elite to mobilize the people to fight the War of 1812 against the Americans. Sewell himself observed that the people demonstrated 'universally a sincere and loyal desire to assist in every way for the defence of the country exceeding any expectation ...'[48]

Shades of Exclusive Nationalism among the British

As suggested earlier, the regulation of conflict and exclusive nationalism was dependent during this era less upon the autonomous goodwill and cosmopolitanism of aristocratic governors, and more upon strategic con-siderations. This pattern characterized the regime of Sir James Craig (1807–11). Craig was an autocrat who repressed Canadien opinion and political leaders, and retained several viciously francophobic senior advisers and civil servants. Only strategic considerations precluded his endorsing ex-clusive-nationalist schemes to overwhelm and assimilate the Canadiens by means of a union with Upper Canada. Better information within the colonial office displaced the power cleavage upwards during his regime, as it fell to cooler heads there to insist upon more conciliatory and less arbitrary treatment of the Canadiens. There remained, between the centre of state power and ordinary subjects, marked differences in attitudes over exclusive nationalism.

The great clarifying event of the War of 1812 remained in the future during Craig's regime. It therefore remained possible for a governor in ill-health, bedridden, and dependent for information upon British colonial informants to judge Canadien politicians to be disloyal and repress them. In February 1810, Craig dissolved the assembly; March saw the editors of Le Canadien summarily imprisoned. The governor's lengthy May dispatch to the colonial secretary set out a draconian doctrine for the future treatment of the Canadiens. Craig ventured that the Canadiens hated the British and longed for a return to French rule; that royal supremacy should be enforced; and that the assembly should be abolished or a stiff property qualification implemented for representatives.[49] Class prejudices now found an imperious spokesman: 'it really, My Lord, appears to me an absurdity that the Interests of certainly not an unimportant Colony ... should be in the hands of six petty shopkeepers, a Blacksmith, a Miller, and fifteen ignorant peasants who form part of our present House; a Doctor or Apothecary, twelve Canadian avocats and Notaries, and four so far respectable people that at least they do not keep shops, together with ten English members, compleat the list; there is not one person coming under the description of a Canadian Gentleman among them.'[50] Thus, Craig aligned himself closely with the long-held views of the English Party in the assembly.

During the preceding two decades a perceived massive contradiction had arisen for the British of the colony between their increasing economic strength, their stagnant and marginal political influence in the assembly, and the expectation in a British possession some thirty years before the passage of the first Reform bill that political power, even in a Lower House, should follow closely from economic and social status.[51] John Black, an assembly member, complained in 1800 (despite the marked overrepresentation of the English in the assembly) that the English had 'to contend with the passions and prejudices of 38 French, the majority of whom are by no means the most respectable of the King's subjects ...'[52] The populist political leaders of the French Canadians were perceived as subversive 'demagogues'; the threat they posed was feared all the more for their supposed loyalty to France.[53]

English leaders in the assembly were routinely forced to defer to their French-speaking social subordinates and this deprived the constitution of legitimacy for the British. By 1808, the English Party leaders began to move to the Legislative Council from the assembly, and the Executive Council thereafter became something of a reactionary 'star chamber' stacked with British merchants.[54] Still, for a class that had demanded an assembly in the first place, this was something of a last resort. Desperate schemes were therefore formed to assimilate the Canadiens, to fold the double class structure into one, and to end the spectacle of a socially inferior political elite usurping political power by virtue of its ethnic affinity with the electorate.

It is striking that, despite Craig's apparent hostility to the Canadiens, he shrank from the major official exclusive nationalist scheme advanced by prominent English members of the administration and judiciary. It is also significant that his reluctance did not rest upon a personal inclination towards cross-cultural accommodation and toleration, but, rather, solely upon strategic considerations. While an older and more belligerent Chief Justice Sewell now argued in a written submission to the Colonial Office that the Canadiens must be 'overwhelmed and sunk' by English Protestant immigration from the south and by the combined English population of a reunited Upper and Lower Canada, Craig neither subscribed to these particular measures, nor acknowledged this underlying imperative in his own accompanying dispatch.[55] He alluded to Canadien resistance to American immigration as evidence of the sway of national aspirations among them; but he also admitted it was 'another question' to what extent it was 'good policy to admit American settlers.' As for Union, Craig rejected the idea, implying that he expected Lower Canada would maintain a distinct cultural identity: 'Of the success of this measure I confess I have doubts. It would produce a heterogeneous mixture of opposite principles and different interests, from which no good could be expected ... I am more inclined to keep the Province of Upper Canada as a foreign, and distinct population, which may be produced as a resource against that of this Country in case of necessity ...'[56] Craig lived in fear. His rejection of union, the major scheme of anglification advanced during his own and later generations, was probably despite, rather than because of, his personal attitude towards the French Canadiens.

Craig tolerated the opinions of his subordinates and did not dismiss individuals such as Sewell and Herman Ryland for their exclusive nationalist and francophobic views. On the contrary, Ryland, the long-time civil secretary who had broached in 1808 'a general plan for assimilating the Colony in its religion, laws and manners,' enjoyed Craig's 'entire confidence' and was sent to London to remonstrate with the imperial Parliament in 1810.[57] Given Craig's encouragement of Ryland, it fell to London officials to discourage him. The officials suggested either co-optation or intimidation of the assembly leaders, but not a cultural offensive. Ryland reported to Craig from London thus: 'His Lordship [Colonial Secretary Lord Liverpool in Council] then repeated the same question he had before put to me in private, whether the members opposed to Government might not be brought over by the hope of being employed? This question, I must confess, caused me rather a warm sensation ...' He also grumbled that another member of the council was inclined to support a 'namby pamby system of *conciliation* ...'[58]

Governor Craig was himself also subject to criticism from the ranking authorities of the Colonial Office. Two successive colonial secretaries refused to countenance the harsh treatment of the assembly leaders that Craig had meted out. The Colonial Office apparently had a clearer grasp of the strategic context, and this had shifted a power cleavage over accommodation upwards. Lord Liverpool, who served as the joint Secretary of State for War and the Colonies, was sufficiently well informed as to the progress of the war with France as to be able to dismiss outright one of Craig's main concerns. He stated, 'With respect to any military attempt of Buonaparte upon Canada, I can assure you that at present his hands are too full for any such operation. It is evident that he has not the military means of making as large an effort in Spain and Portugal as his interest and reputation require.'[59] Noting that 'the cause of the Canadians would be warmly supported by all the democrats and friends of reform in this country,' Liverpool held that, 'unless a connexion could be proved between the popular party in Canada and the Government of France,' no appeal to Parliament could be made to alter the 1791 constitution.

Craig's successor, Sir George Prevost (1811–15), faced a much altered strategic predicament. The United States had displaced France as the most pressing threat, and in a defence against this enemy, the French Canadiens could be expected to play a much stronger role. This implied a much-altered policy, and the urgency of dispensing with the confrontational policy of Craig's tenure.[60] In rapid succession, thus, Ryland was dismissed, conciliation was extended to the assembly leaders (Bédard, himself, being named to the bench), additional Canadiens were admitted to the Legislative Council, and a large increase in salary (to £1,000 per year) was secured without conditions for the Catholic bishop, who now became the titular Catholic Bishop of Quebec. The Bishop of the Church of England was seriously displeased. With his coterie on the Executive Council, Mountain demanded Prevost's recall to London. Clearly frustrated, Prevost responded thus: 'the great mass of the population was to be soothed to my purposes, not offended on the very subject of their dearest interests. I have found the full reward of my first decision. The Catholic Clergy are my firmest supports & the salary I have obtained for the Bishop has strengthened my claim on their loyalty, zeal, and influence over the people which has given great offence to the Head of our own Church & added to my former disgrace with his Lordship for not yielding the civil administration to his superior Judgment.'[61] Prevost was in the end brought back to England, ostensibly to face separate allegations concerning the conduct of his military command during the war. But the Colonial Office does not appear to have sided with Bishop Mountain. Indeed, Mountain was reproached for his part in the conspiracy against Prevost in 1815 by the colonial secretary, Lord Bathurst, who held, as Manning notes, 'that his complaints against the Roman Catholic bishop and his flock were ill-timed in view of the loyalty and courage they had just displayed in the defence of the province.'[62]

More generally, the Colonial Office confirmed the long-standing policy of accommodating Canadien religious institutions. Upon the advice of Prevost's successor, Governor Sherbrooke (1816–18), Plessis was given a seat on the Legislative Council as the Roman Catholic Bishop of Quebec, a gesture that even Lord Bathurst recognized was technically illegal. Bathurst also later accepted a plan for parish schools that would obviate the existing problem of Roman Catholic children being taught by Protestant schoolmasters. Finally, the same cosmopolitan colonial secretary went so far as to extend personal hospitality to Bishop Plessis, entertaining him on one occasion with pomp and ceremony at his country estate.[63]

This is not to say that Bathurst was sympathetic to the Parti Canadien within the assembly. He was not. But, as Manning explains, his position was based not upon 'questions of race and religion, but of social fitness, and Bathurst, as much as any member of the cabinet, shared the views of Lords Castlereagh and Sidmouth of the positive evil wrought by radicals and "demagogues" – a designation which was freely applied to any politicians who appealed to lower classes. The problem ... was not that of the evils of nationalism but of the evils of democracy.'[64] On the whole, this seems typical of the attitudes of British elites, especially those in the highest echelons of imperial power. Statesmanlike forbearance of Canadien linguistic, religious, and cultural distinctiveness was combined with open disdain at the impertinence and humble social origins of Canadien political representation.

Within the English-speaking population of the colony, exclusive nationalism was a much stronger force. This tendency was best exemplified by the implacable spokesmen of the English merchants at the Quebec *Mercury*. Thomas Carey, the editor of that paper, wrote in 1806 upon learning of the planned publication of *Le Canadien*, 'This province is already too much a French province for an English colony. To *unfrenchify* it as much as possible ... should be a primary object, particularly in these times when our arch-enemy is straining every nerve to Frenchify the universe ... To counteract France we must be Englishmen. After forty-seven years possession of Quebec it is time the province should be English.'[65] As has been observed, even senior officials under Governors Milnes and Craig were apparently partisans of such chauvinism.

2.3 Divisive Issues

The Union Bill of 1822: Divergent Imperial and Local Purposes

During the 1820s, the imperial government was the fount of several ill-advised measures, but it had only a modest impact on the increasingly pitched struggle on the ground. The abortive Union Bill of 1822, set aside by the principled opposition of several British parliamentarians, reflected in its being introduced at all, the increased responsiveness of the imperial government to local elites. On the other hand, its defeat reflects again the upward displacement of the power cleavage, hinting at the different concerns animating the local as opposed to the imperial political elite. Reaction to the rejection of the measure in Lower Canada within the English population tends to confirm the persistence of the (displaced) power cleavage.

Powerful merchants of Lower Canada had considerable influence in London, and, as James Sturgis observes, 'every scheme of anglicisation, direct or indirect, had connected with it promptings of the English community.'[66] One of the most effective representatives of local British interests was Edward Ellice, at once a member of the House of Commons, a Lower Canadian seigneur and merchant, and a close relative of one of the last prominent English leaders in the assembly, John Richardson. Ellice and his ilk were counter-weighted by other influential parliamentarians, notably the liberal and tolerant Sir James Mackintosh. Mackintosh supported the constitutional positions of the Canadien-dominated assembly, and backed its cause at critical junctures in the Commons.[67]

The Union Bill of 1822, pressed by Ellice on the Colonial Office at a time when the latter was seeking an appropriate intervention in a customs dispute between Upper and Lower Canada, was an 'embodiment of the policies of the English party.'[68] The bill, had it passed, would have united Upper and Lower Canada and brought an additional, large and disproportionately well-represented English contingent into the fray with the French-Canadian element. It would have also granted in a stroke the mainstays of the English Party agenda – establishing English as the sole language of record in the written proceedings of the council and, eventually, of the assembly; enacting a property qualification for members of the new assembly; and empowering the governor to influence appointments of Roman Catholic clergy and establish new constituencies so as to stack the assembly with members from the predominantly English-speaking Eastern Townships.[69] This was a list of measures that spoke both to the perceived legitimacy crisis of the assembly and to the local English Protestant chauvinism that had melded with the resultant reaction. In Westminster the policy was intended to turn the assembly over to the English and the mercantile agenda.

The bill failed, however, when Mackintosh objected that such sweeping changes required consultation with the affected parties. Were members, he demanded, 'to shut out all evidence relating to ... [colonials'] feelings, inclinations, opinions, and prejudices?'[70] This was to strike at the essence of ministerial strategy in rushing a measure through late in the session without consultation. Another, sensing the outrage of Canadiens that the legislation would provoke, derided it more directly, as Hansard recounts: 'Would not that very measure [union] ... excite the greatest discontent, if there existed, as he believed there did exist, a sense of spirit amongst the Canadians? It was purely an Upper Canada Bill, having for its object to destroy the influence of the Catholic population over Lower Canada.'[71] In the end, the bill was withdrawn – ostensibly due to the lateness of the session – after fourteen votes were cast against it at second reading.[72]

In fact, the political will propelling the measure, and the interest it aroused within the lightly attended debates, were likely so slight that even moderate opposition made it more trouble than it was worth. By contrast, the bill was accorded the highest importance in Lower Canada by the English Party, which considered it a crucial step to assimilating the Canadiens. In October 1822, a meeting of the Friends of the Re-union of Upper and Lower Canada was opened by the leader of the English Party, John Richardson, who construed union as 'a question of great moment ...; for upon its decision might depend whether inducements would not be held out to them, to become Foreigners in a British Colony; or, for the Inhabitants of foreign origin to become British.'[73] The *Montreal Herald* also shamelessly spouted exclusive nationalism, asserting in an editorial, 'When we hear the Leaders of that party, on every occasion on which the term can be consistently used, still styling themselves "A PEOPLE" when sixty-three years of judicious legislation would have rendered every individual born on Canadian Soil a member of the same political family; which would have spoken the same language; possessed the same institutions, Usages and Customs; ... when we hear this, and witness its effects, we assert that so great an anomaly should not for the prospective happiness of the Provinces be allowed longer to exist.'[74] A petition was raised in Montreal in December 1822 and taken to England, thus ending an unsuccessful campaign to renew the cause of Union.[75] A movement with its origins in a critique of the system of representation on grounds of the social fitness of assembly members had taken popular chauvinism on board and provided a vehicle for exclusive nationalism.

No known analysis has been made of the names of petitioners in Montreal to corroborate the assertion of a letter writer to the *Montreal Herald* that 'all persons of British birth or descent so naturally combine in this District' in favour of Union.[76] It does appear, however, that of the eighteen individuals composing the Montreal General Committee for Petitioning against Union, only one had a name that could be read as being English. In the capital, (the City of) Quebec, by contrast, a similar committee had ten names (of twenty-four) that were probably English.[77] This was the beginning of a long pattern of greater moderation in Quebec than in Montreal, a pattern perhaps resting on the proximity of Quebec to predominantly non-nationalist state elites, including Canadien assembly members, and (by this stage) the majority of the council.[78] This moderating effect was strengthened by the influence of the English-language newspaper, the *Gazette*, a newspaper whose proprietor, John Neilson, was also a leading member of the Committee against Union, and later, of the Patriots.

Canadien Diplomatic Restraint

The upward displacement of the power cleavage on the British side in the decade and a half following the War of 1812 is confirmed by leaders of the Parti Canadien, who distinguished between the attitudes of state elites in Britain and those of the local English population. Canadien leaders, having rejected the official exclusive nationalism generated by English anglicizers, did not meet fire with fire.

An essay written by D.B. Viger in 1826 clearly differentiated between the attitudes of the imperial and local political elite: 'Canadiens know well that they cannot consider in the same light the government of England and [British] adventurers [in the colony] for whom we are only objects of derision, who only see in us papists to persecute and to rob ...'[79] Viger observed that the imperial government, in establishing the constitution of 1791, had lent 'the support of its authority ... to conserve the institutions that our adventurers, the fanatics attempted to shake, worked to destroy.'[80] Great Britain, as Bédard had noted in an earlier essay, also offered protection from the despised Americans.[81] Clearly, for the Parti Canadien at this stage British colonialism was to be preferred to American absorption.[82] The fundamental value of the Canadien political leaders was to conserve the cultural structure of their society in the face of a broad assault by the English Party. Tactically, the conservation of political power was crucial because, as Sturgis notes, 'the loss of political influence would have been the most serious danger because no defences against anglicisation would have remained.'[83] A shared and distinctive culture, the Canadien leaders believed, was what bound their society together.[84] The protection of this culture conferred legitimacy upon the imperial government.

Did this imply, then, that the Canadian leaders believed that their way of life should be privileged in Lower Canada? Viger never states clearly whether the task of conservation should extend beyond defending against the onslaught of English assimilationist policies to include active intervention to consolidate Lower Canada to the Canadien way of life. One comment, however, envisioning the peaceable coexistence of religions, perhaps provides a clue to his larger vision: 'What, then, is the worst problem that the maintenance of our establishments could precipitate? Would it be that one would speak French in Lower Canada, and that a Catholic could, as well as an Anglican, an adherent of Lutheran or Calvinist doctrine, live in security and in peace under its [Lower Canada's] umbrella? Could there be there something to alarm England, inspiring in it the fears for its existence or for its prosperity? If the continuation of this state of affairs is worthy of note, it is because it is enlightened, that it is just.'[85] This envisages a society based on tolerance, 'umbrella' appearing to connote a state that intervenes only negatively in warding off elements hostile to liberal coexistence.

The response to the proposed union of 1822 provides further evidence of the public political values of the elite of the Parti Canadien. Committees against Union sent Louis-Joseph Papineau and John Neilson to London to make known the acute concerns of the assembly and the French-Canadian public over the measure. Papineau and Neilson carefully avoided any suggestion of cultural parochialism in their submission to the imperial government, emphasizing innocuous logistical barriers entailed by Union, given 'the distance, the difficulties, dangers, and expenses of travelling to the scite [*sic*] of the joint Legislature ...'[86] They also pointed out the challenges of amalgamating two quite distinct legal codes.[87] The tone of the discussion concerning the provisions for language was similarly restrained.[88] French Canadians would in the course of time integrate linguistically with the rest of North America, but to be forced to do so was humiliating. Moreover, argued the petition Neilson and Papineau bore with them, to forbid the use of French in the assembly was, under present conditions, tantamount to denying unilingual Canadiens the right to hold seats in the assembly.[89]

Papineau was gratified while in London by the attention he received from officials such as Lord Bathurst at the Colonial Office. Writing to a committee member at home, he observed:

> The anxiety we felt in Canada about the difficulty we might have in seeing the minister could only have rested on a lack of knowledge of this country. They receive all British subjects who wish to see them on public business and answer their communications with exactitude and politeness ... It is only too easy for Richardson or anyone else ... to deceive the ministers and the public and Parliament by false representations. But if there is anyone on the spot to cry 'Wait – don't decide until you hear both sides' they will see the justice of the request.[90]

From the perspective of the Colonial Office, which had originally acceded to the introduction of the legislation, the elements of the bill interpreted in Lower Canada as aiming at anglicization were expendable. Indeed, the colonial under-secretary, Robert Wilmot, strongly denied any intention of touching the Canadians' 'laws, usages, institutions, and religion.'[91] Papineau acknowledged that it was not the imperial government, but rather British colonials, he suspected of harbouring such designs.[92] The under-secretary's disavowal was later echoed by Lord Bathurst, himself, who 'assured Papineau that the clauses on language and the ecclesiastical establishment would be dropped, implied that he thoroughly disapproved of weighting the representation against the French Canadians, and promised that nothing further would be done about the union itself without giving the Canadians plenty of time to be heard.'[93] Canadien diplomacy thus revealed many key imperial backers of union to be animated not by exclusive nationalism, but by the core concern that deadlock and the customs dispute between Upper and Lower Canada be resolved. Perhaps partly because of the restraint of the Canadien elite, entrusting English-speaking interests with preponderant influence was, for the time being, judged unnecessary.

2.4 The Janus Faces of the Canadien Political Elite

Ethnic conflict between the French-speaking Canadiens and English speakers developed and intensified in Lower Canada as a result of a variety of issues. Many of these did not hinge on peculiarly 'ethnic' matters (religion, culture, language) at all. All the same, some quintessentially 'ethnic' issues, particularly hostility to British immigration, appear to have been strongly felt at the mass level. Among the Canadien political elite, an acute tension arose between the need to maintain bridges across the ethnic divide – with both British parliamentary allies and local, English-speaking radicals – and the need to appeal effectively to mass constituencies. At certain points, particularly elections, these tensions made for obvious contradictions in positions adopted. There was thus an irreducible complexity to popular politics, and neither the universal political claims nor the ethnic chauvinism of this era should be explained away. Both figured in the ensuing mass mobilization.

From the turn of the century, divergent policy interests, largely along ethnic lines, had created tensions over the Canadien domination of the assembly and British domination of the councils.[94] Disproportionate participation in various economic sectors caused splits on such economic issues as the well-known controversy of 1805 concerning the appropriation of funds for the jails. As Wade explains, 'The French majority, who represented agricultural interests, favoured customs duties, while the English merchants wanted real estate taxes.'[95] The English merchants also favoured an overhaul in the infrastructure of trade and commerce – banks, roads, and communications – as well as strong American immigration and the jettisoning of the seigneurial regime and the *Coutume de Paris*.[96] None of these proposals was supported by the Canadien bloc, which was more concerned with regional development and the requirements of an agricultural economy.[97]

Increasingly during subsequent decades, the direct source of political conflict became the composition of, and division of powers between, the assembly and the executive. The origins of this conflict were by no means indissolubly nationalist – a parallel conflict also took place in the far more homogeneous Upper Canada under the same constitutional arrangements. In Lower Canada the conflict had deepened during Craig's heavy-handed regime as governor; during the remainder of this period, the English 'plutocracy' had consolidated control of the Councils and administration and used them as a base from which to restrict the power of the Canadien political elite.[98] In the appointive councils the only French-Canadian representation consisted of the crotchety – and normally absent – ministerial seigneurs, who had long since become socially and politically irrelevant within French-Canadian society. A clash between the unelected and the elected institutions of the colony had ensued, giving concrete form to the conflict between the overlapping ethnic and class groups ensconced within them.

Excluding only the period during the War of 1812 and the governorship of Sir John Sherbrooke (1816–18), mutual distrust and unwillingness to concede the jurisdictional claims of the rival legislative chamber created deeply troubled relations.[99] Twenty-one assembly bills were disallowed by the executive, mainly for unstated reasons.[100] A number of the bills related to public finance. The civil list was particularly contentious because many of the positions on it were the sinecures of non-residents, and too few were held by Canadiens, a situation blamed on discrimination. A similar grievance was expressed concerning the composition of the Legislative Council.[101]

Until 1830, leaders of the Parti Canadien, such as Bédard and Neilson, were content to advocate the mere reform of the councils by means of the appointment of larger numbers of prominent Canadiens. After that time, however, the more radical notion of an elective Legislative Council was proposed, an idea that clearly expressed the growing commitment of the Canadien political elite to ideas of popular sovereignty and democracy. For the English minority in the colony and, indeed, the imperial government aside from the parliamentary radicals, such American ideas were anathema.[102]

The Canadien people themselves became more militant and politically engaged after 1827. Their wrath was raised that year when Governor George Ramsay, 9th Earl of Dalhousie (1820–8), summoned the militia, using executive powers. Having abruptly dissolved the assembly before it could renew more contemporary militia laws, Dalhousie was forced to invoke moribund ordinances of the old Legislative Council dating from 1787 and 1789.[103] Protest meetings were organized and attended, among many others, by several Canadien officers of the militia. This led to their dismissal and to the further deterioration of relations between the executive and the assembly. The meetings burgeoned and soon supported a 'groundwork of organization,' in Samuel Clark's terms. Resolutions adopted by the meetings reflected an advanced state of dissent.

Aside from unpaid militia service, the Canadien people felt 'oppressed' by a wide variety of irritants and menaces.[104] As Ouellet notes, these included a hugely expensive St Lawrence canal system foisted on the colony by the mercantile elite; relatively remote, expensive, and discriminatory land registry offices; the banks; attempts at uniting the Canadas; and hordes of land-hungry immigrants. These issues provided impetus for the mobilization of a rural, and predominantly Canadien, population. Within the ensuing, locally rooted discourse, the issues came to be perceived as a 'mortal peril' posed by the British for their nation.[105]

When *Le Canadien* resumed publishing in May 1831, following a five-year hiatus, it adopted the provocative motto 'nos institutions, notre langue et nos lois!' This reflected increasing tensions and ethnic cultural competition. A contemporary remarked, 'even where they reside together, as in towns, they do not associate, but form, as it were, distinct castes.'[106] Voting also appears to have become more ethnically polarized from 1827. Although data are sparse, Ouellet notes that in the Upper Town of Quebec in 1824 only 53 per cent of French-speaking voters had supported a French-speaking candidate.[107] English speakers had given 49 per cent of their votes to Canadien Party supporters. By the 1827 election, however, 80 per cent of French-speaking voters supported French-speaking candidates.[108] In that year only 26 per cent of the English-speaking vote went to the Patriots in the Quebec Upper Town.[109]

The issue of immigration, really code for the complex problem of ethnic coexistence, competition, and survival in Lower Canada, provided a battlefield in which universal arguments concerning democracy or equality of opportunity melded with ethnic chauvinism. Massive immigration had long been openly and enthusiastically promoted by British colonials as a means of swamping the Canadians with a pro-British population, and was an obvious source of conflict between the Parti Canadien and the English Party. Such proposals were naturally vehemently opposed by the Canadiens, who 'had hope,' Bédard acknowledged even in 1814, 'that their population will always be the largest of the country.'[110] By the 1830s, as opinion became increasingly polarized by ethnicity, the Patriot movement itself more often stooped to addressing the issue of immigration in 'outrageously xenophobic terms.'[111] The editors of the official organ of the Patriot party, *La Minerve*, inveighed before the crucial election of 1834 that 'emigrants [both] slothful and employment-seeking, can only be regarded by the native-born as intruders, rejects from their own country.'[112]

This was not an isolated misstatement of more generous views. Nor can such views be disassociated from the revolutionary thrust of the Patriot movement, as one scholar has recently suggested.[113] Prior to the election of November 1834, *La Minerve* gave its front page to a sustained, four-part commentary on the link between revolution and nationalism, entitled, 'Of the Manner in which Nations Are Formed.'[114] The basic thesis of the essay is that nationalities have survived and grown out of foreign domination only through vigorous political resistance and revolution.[115] Nationality, the fount of prosperity and social justice, must be emancipated.

> A nationality is the greatest advantage of a community; by it the prosperity of peoples begins, grows, and is secured. By it, the society frees itself from a foreign domination, often troublesome, almost always exploitive ... Nationality is the regenerative baptism of peoples, the purifying water that washes away the stains of servitude; it is God who endows it with a sublime vocation, ... it is the pact that delivers the members, that breaks their chains, that ... allows them to participate in sovereignty, that makes them the equal of their ancestors, of their neighbours, that places them in charge of exploiting their own resources, and their own affairs ... But ... who profits from a nationality? Everyone! Its benefits reach equally to the rich and to the poor ... To the rich, it procures the increase of its fortune, by the new and solid enterprises in which it can take part ... To the poor, by the increase of the resources of its country and those of its own industry; by the assurance of taking part in the affairs of the country; ... by the certainty of no longer being hurt by a foreigner who fleeces him, in undermining their survival by the sweat of their brows.[116]

Thus far, it *might* be possible to put an inclusive construction on this nationalist outpouring (assuming that the 'foreigner' is maligned for his exploitive dealings, rather than for his cultural differences). However, the argument finally sheds this ambiguity in pressing to the implication that the very presence of 'foreigners' is a menace to the nationality, which, by analogy, is conceived in culturally specific terms.

> In general, Foreign Immigrants who are able to enrich themselves are the worst fear, because they augment themselves in an alarming and absorbent manner. Those who are favoured by the power acquire a character even more dangerous, because it is a powerful means for decimating populations that present to authorities aspects of nationality and of resistance. The administration strives in this way to introduce a foreign population, to amalgamate with the native-born, to destroy the traditional spirit ...; to obtain a majority in the popular assembly; ... to establish legally the reversal and overturning of the

old institutions. It is in this way that the Gauls lost their laws, their customs, their religion, and even their language, by Roman immigration; it is in this way that all the seeds of nations disappear under a foreign domination ...[117]

The cultural preoccupations of this nationalism is confirmed as the essay sets out the duties implied by nationality for subjects. Ordinary subjects, the article concludes, 'must conserve with profound respect the religion, the laws, the mores, the customs and the language that their fathers professed and transmit all with the same attention to their children.' Of more immediate pertinence, they are 'to choose their representatives only from amongst the native-born.'

In view of such writings, some clarification is required of Allan Greer's suggestion that the 'Patriots of the 1830s no longer stood for the simple defence of ethnic distinctiveness, that they now espoused a nationalism linked to universally applicable democratic and egalitarian principles.'[118] Even the Patriots of 1834 should not be reduced to a mere 'Lower Canadian radical movement.' Particularly at election-time, they appended a decidedly chauvinist code to their democratic vision. In short, the Patriot revolutionary political and constitutional agenda was thus at times closely juxtaposed with, and justified by, nationalist imperatives of a chauvinist cast.

To be sure, this was a most delicate business for the Patriots. Even the essay just reviewed did not move beyond a defensive chauvinism into what we would term 'exclusive nationalism' (indeed, it could purport merely to oppose a British immigration policy, itself rooted in exclusive nationalism). Moreover, it was cast in generic form, lacking any specific reference to Lower Canadian demographics; this would extend its appeal beyond French-Canadian habitants to their disaffected Irish allies on the hustings and at the *Vindicator*, who were apt to apply the same analysis to their own homeland. Similarly, the Saint-Jean-Baptiste Society, conceived in 1834 by the editor of *La Minerve*, Ludger Duvernay, aimed 'to promote the interests of the French language and nationality,' but its nods to Irish and American reform traditions also astutely made room for Americans and Irishmen.[119]

In an election speech given in early November of that year, Papineau hedged his position on immigration carefully, first confirming the undisputed legality of immigration within the British empire, but then concluding (to 'cheers') that a tax on immigrants was necessary to defray the expenses they generated.[120] Once the 1834 election was over, Papineau in the same pages furiously repelled Tory accusations that advocacy of the elective principle was in any way predicated upon 'antipathies françaises.' This was not at all, he maintained, 'a war of origin.' In fighting this battle, all 'languages and all origins,' all those sharing the 'opinion of the masses, that is, sharing patriotic sentiments,' were welcome.[121]

Nonetheless, internal tensions are evident in the Patriot elite's position on immigration, comparing the policy on immigration conveyed in *La Minerve* ('Immigration, we oppose, in the manner in which it is practiced now ...') with the more externally driven position stated in the 92 Resolutions of March of the same year.[122] In the third resolution, the Patriotes adopt a markedly different stance: 'Resolved, That the people of this province have always shown themselves ready to welcome and to receive as brethren, those of their fellow-subjects who, having quitted the United Kingdom or its dependencies, have chosen this province as their home, and have earnestly endeavoured ... to afford every facility to their participating in the political advantages, and in the means of rendering their industry available, which the people of this province enjoy ...'[123] More generally, the resolutions were a picture of radical and engaged, but never chauvinist, disputation. Certainly, they assaulted the vestiges of imposed statecraft and the doctrine of the balanced constitution entrenched in the 1791 constitutional settlement. Thirty-eight of the 92 Resolutions plead for more popular and democratic government, including 22 making the case for an elective Legislative Council independent of the executive.[124] Assembly rights, including the control of revenues, were championed in an additional 14 resolutions; tenures and other land issues in 7. Although one of the resolutions declares the refusal of the Canadiens to assimilate, and another two convey thinly veiled threats of revolution in the absence of progress, there is also a clear commitment to the equal treatment of subjects 'without any distinction of origin or creed.'[125]

But to return to my main point, it is important not to obscure either of the Janus faces of the Patriot elite. For to recognize both its culturally neutral, inclusive nationalist face, and its more furtive, ethnic chauvinist face is to cast light on the predicament in which that elite found itself. Whatever their personal predilections, senior Patriots had to address themselves to two very different constituencies. Emphasizing their commitment to equality and popular sovereignty free of 'national distinctions' was crucial to allying themselves with radicals in their shared struggle against tories on both sides of the Atlantic. On the other hand, their very commitment to popular sovereignty entailed, both philosophically and tactically, the mobilization of the predominantly French-speaking mass. This required arguments that would play in the village 'reading rooms,' in which, as Greer notes, 'large audiences could assemble to listen to the news from *La Minerve*.'[126] It remains unclear to what extent American constitutional doctrine could have motivated these audiences, were it not to have been brought home by more substantive cultural and economic concerns. As one politician, Louis-Hippolyte Lafontaine, suggested in February 1837, 'To arouse the people we cannot simply wave the banner of purely abstract questions.'[127]

2.5 The Rebellions of 1837–1838

Preliminary Issues of Evidence

For anyone attempting a synthesis of Canadian political history, there is perhaps no greater occupational hazard than that presented by the Lower Canada rebellions of 1837–8. Although Allan Greer's exceptionally careful and fascinating study of the 1837 rebellion has greatly refined our understanding of this topic, it would be premature to say that a settled consensus has emerged, if only because other specialists have yet to respond with full-scale replies of their own. Crucial issues, moreover, remain unresolved. Perhaps the most significant of these is the extent to which ethnic chauvinism motivated mass, French-Canadian insurgents in the rebellions, and whether their actions offer a case of demotic exclusive nationalism. (Evidence of the demotic exclusive nationalism of the British 'Loyalists' of the colony, which was openly expressed in newspapers, and which almost certainly suffused the extraordinarily brutal reprisals, seems, by contrast, less problematic.) While I have attempted for the sake of brevity elsewhere in this work to avoid explicit historiographical discussions, treating the French-Canadian side of the rebellion requires a preliminary, direct engagement with secondary works and evidence, for which I apologize in advance to theoretically minded readers.

We may begin by contrasting Durham's observations with Greer's 'fundamental reinterpretation.' In a tone of astonishment, Durham, on 9 August 1838 recorded his impressions in a secret dispatch to Lord Glenelg at the Colonial Office.

> The first point to which I would draw your attention, being one with which all others are more or less connected, is the existence of a most bitter animosity between the Canadians and the British ... The hatred of races is not publicly avowed on either side; ... but the fact is, I think, proved by an accumulation of circumstantial evidence more conclusive than any direct

testimony would be ... If the difference between the two classes were one of party or principles only, we should find on each side a mixture of persons of both races, whereas the truth is that, with exceptions which tend to prove the rule, all the British are on one side, and all the Canadians are on the other ... In the next place, the mutual dislike of the two classes extends beyond politics into social life, where, with some trifling exceptions, again, all intercourse is confined to persons of the same origin ... There has been no solemn or formal declaration of national hostility, but not a day nor scarcely an hour passes without some petty insult, ... or even some serious mutual affront, occurring between persons of British and French descent ...[128]

Durham attributes the roots of this antipathy to ethnic competition, incidentally drawing an interesting distinction between mass and elite Canadien views. At some point well after the Constitutional Act, the

Canadians perceived that their nationality was in the course of being overridden by a British nationality ... They have found the British pressing upon them at every turn ... [and] they have naturally resisted an invasion which was so offensive to their national pride ... There seems to me only one modification of this view of the subject. The employment by the Canadians of constitutional and popular means for their national purpose has taught some of them, consisting chiefly of the most active and able, higher political views than such as belong to the question of nationality ... They have also learned to estimate the practical abuses of Government which affect all classes, and to wish for many reforms without reference to Canadian nationality. They even had, to some extent, succeeded in disseminating their opinion to the mass of their countrymen ... but unfortunately, their number is so small as scarcely to affect my opinion of the temper of the Canadian people ...[129]

The rebellion, precipitated when the struggle between the two races became 'too violent to be kept within constitutional bounds,' had served greatly to aggravate the 'sentiment of national hostility.'[130]

By contrast, Greer, inverting Durham's interpretation, argues that the 'lines of conflict then were fundamentally political and incidentally ethnic.'[131] He suggests,

As the struggle between the Patriot movement and the government developed into outright war, the ethnic polarization in Two Mountains and elsewhere in the province became more pronounced and more bitter. The two sides girded for battle, leaving less and less room for polite inquiries. In the confusion and uncertainties of civil strife actors on both the government and the rebel sides had to be able to distinguish enemies ... from friends ... It was only natural, therefore, that in emergency situations people acted as though language was a clear boundary between friend and foe. The inevitable injustices that ensued served of course to embitter the atmosphere and deepen the national cleavage.

Thus, whereas Durham believed that the political struggle of French and English speakers was an epiphenomenon resting upon ethnic distrust and competition, Greer suggests that it was ethnic conflict that was a mere byproduct of a political-cum-revolutionary struggle.

At the same time, Greer does at the outset acknowledge a connection between the ethnic composition of the District of Montreal, which had 'proportionately many more [British] immigrants,' and the fact that it, of the four sections of the province, was the one in which the rebellion occurred.[132] This leads him to note 'parallels between the nationalist movement of Lower Canada and those ... in the small nations of eastern and central Europe.'[133] Nonetheless, Greer attributes Durham's observations of ethnic hostility, made in 1838, after the first rebellion, solely to the deterioration of relations stemming from the rebellion itself. Citing evidence that face-to-face relations between some anglophone and francophone neighbours were peaceable before the rebellion, Greer concludes that prior ethnic conflict was minimal in general, even if this is difficult to square with his account of the 1834 election violence (which 'had all the appearances of a "national" conflict'), and even if he is then left searching for an explanation for why the presence of a 'substantial anglophone majority' should have engendered ethnically targeted violence in the rebellions.[134]

But Greer passes all too lightly over the issue of immigration, and the indication it offers of smouldering ethnic resentment. As quoted earlier, he notes in passing that the arrival of British settlers was often viewed in 'outrageously xenophobic terms.'[135] But he omits the strongly worded observations recorded by the highly astute, and presumably neutral, Alexis de Tocqueville, after speaking to farmers during a visit in 1831: 'They already feel strongly that the English race is expanding about them in an alarming fashion; that it is wrong that they should confine themselves within a compass instead of spreading freely throughout the country. Their jealousy is sharply whetted by daily arrivals of newcomers from Europe. They feel that in the end they will be absorbed. It is apparent that anything said on the subject stirs their passions ...'[136] This account obviously accords closely with Durham's observations just quoted, and it suggests that ethnic antagonism, however repressed in daily dealings, may have been a stronger and more continuous factor than Greer allows.

Alongside the role of acute demographic pressures, one of the important interpretive themes dealt with by Ouellet in discussing the rebellions is the prevalence of different motivations at different strata of the Patriot movement. As he notes, 'to working-class minds, land and immigration were still uppermost in the economic context ... Independence, for most of the peasants, tradesmen, and labourers, was the symbol of the struggle to safeguard their traditions against the English and the Protestants ... The left-wing *patriote* leaders, however, were bent on real social revolution ... Beyond question, the middle-class rabble-rousers and the lower classes they were attempting to arouse were not identically motivated.'[137] Greer, for his part, records the 'ostracism of the 100 or so English-speaking families at St Eustache, St Benoit, and Ste Scholastique' shortly after the major meeting held in the region on 1 June 1837. He notes that the meeting, itself, 'far from fanning the flames of national hostility,' had featured the Patriot elite attempting to reach beyond 'creed, origin and language' to achieve 'understanding and reconciliation.'[138] Greer struggles to explain the subsequent, 'wholly plebeian campaign' of attacks on the property and animals of English-speaking families entirely in terms of a brutal (and 'paranoid' and evidently self-defeating) 'logic' to pre-empt hostile opposition and to convert the families to the Patriot cause. But he cites no evidence capable of excluding ethnic antagonism altogether from the context of either the foreground or the background of these attacks, which occurred months before the first paramilitary clashes between the Sons of Liberty and the Doric Club signalled subsequent violence. Nor does he deal with the depositions cited by Ouellet indicating subsequent hostility explicitly directed at Protestants as such.[139]

Fortunately, the exclusion of prior ethnic antagonism seems superfluous to Greer's major argument. *That*, as I understand it, is to set aside Durham's 'catchy' rhetorical dichotomization (in the *Report*) of a political conflict stemming from democratic principles, on the one hand, and racial/ ethnic conflict, on the other.[140] In this Greer succeeds, clearly demonstrating that the rebellions exhibited both. However, in insisting that the conflict was 'fundamentally political and incidentally ethnic,' Greer himself falls into a similar conceptual trap, and thereby raises thorny and unnecessarily essentialist questions as to the priority of ethnic and political conflict in the preceding decades (which he does not address). My earlier discussion of the issue of immigration has hopefully made clear that ethnic conflict was susceptible to being politicized during this period, even if it was only one dimension of a conflict that in many other aspects did not stem from concerns necessarily ethnically aligned.

Conceptually, it would be an overly narrow concept of ethnic conflict that would equate it with 'primitive xenophobia.'[141] Many types of ethnic competition (for political influence and many other resources) can presumably establish the basic conditions for ethnic antagonism and exclusive nationalism, just as readily as knee-jerk bigotry can. Indeed, it is in general fruitless to attempt to maintain any rigid distinction between local instances of ideological ('political') conflict and those of subterranean 'ethnic' conflict where such cases occur simultaneously in the same locale, address a heavily overlapping set of concerns, and divide essentially along the same ethnic cleavages. Empirically, the actors' own public testimony, where given under duress of various forms, is particularly ill equipped to support such distinctions.

Overall, Greer's evidence seems insufficient to negate the independent and mutually consistent accounts provided by Tocqueville and Durham as to the presence and sources of pre-existing ethnic conflict in the colony. Therefore, it seems most reasonable not to deny the likelihood of popular chauvinism having played *some* independent role in the rebellions. Evidence that members were systematically ostracized in their communities on the basis of their ethnic or religious affiliation is suggestive of crude efforts to alter the cultural 'balance' of the life of these communities (i.e., exclusive nationalism), notwithstanding whether any immediate effort was made to effect the members' religious assimilation or actual physical banishment from the community. But, for that matter, the watertight evidence in both the Archives nationales de Québec and a contemporary memoir as to the organized expulsion of Protestants in Grand Ligne (discussed below) bears unusually strong witness to the presence of demotic exclusive nationalism.[142]

What remains uncertain is the *relative* importance of raw 'ethnic' sentiment as against culturally neutral, economic, and political concerns for rank-and-file French-Canadian insurgents. For the conceptual and empirical reasons discussed, this issue will probably never be satisfactorily resolved. It should also be acknowledged that the breadth of public support for the Patriot's activities in 1837–8 is uncertain. One estimate places the total number of 'disaffected' at 7,000–8,000 of a population of 650,000, and contemporary accounts emphasize that, in areas with little French–English contact, sentiment and participation were greatly muted.[143] Pending uncontemplated discoveries of further evidence, therefore, parts of the following analysis must be considered uncertain in both scope and degree of application.

Elite Alliances, Popular Mobilization, and Demotic Exclusive Nationalism

Until the 1838 rebellion, senior elites succeeded in rendering their dual appeal – to universal political values and nativist loyalties – with such calculated discretion as to avoid rupturing important alliances with English-speaking Patriot elites and British parliamentary radicals. As long as the Patriot movement enjoyed strong leadership, its official political discourse could be shoe-horned into the mould of a culturally neutral, revolutionary struggle, with gestures to ethnic chauvinism conveyed primarily by means of carefully coded ambiguity through party channels such as *La Minerve*. But while this tact simultaneously achieved alliance preservation and mass mobilization, it also left unresolved tensions between the ideological norms ostensibly guiding the elite of the movement, and pre-existing concerns animating the mass base. In a mass-mobilizing movement in which the influence of the rank and file was mounting, such tensions implied the probability of an eventual fragmentation of purpose, and, indeed, the risk of at least a partial descent into demotic exclusive nationalism.

The success of the Patriots in achieving intra-party, bi-ethnic alliances can be gauged from both contemporary commentary and election records. An editorial in the *Quebec Gazette* in the spring of 1831 described the preceding session of the legislature: 'It is not one of the least agreeable features of the Session that there has been a perfect absence of national and religious distinctions, and a complete agreement between the [predominantly English-speaking] Township members and the Representatives from other parts of the Province.'[144] Cooperation between assembly members of the two language groups was evinced especially in the acceptance of prominent English-speakers among the Patriots. As Tocqueville put it, 'there exists in Quebec a class of men who form the transition between French and English; they are the English allies of the Canadians, Englishmen discontented with the administration, [and] French placemen. This class is represented in the periodic press by the *Quebec Gazette*, in political meetings by Mr Neilson and probably several others ... they are more Canadian than English in interest because they oppose the government. Basically, however, they are English in customs, thinking, and language.'[145] In the 1824 election, nine English candidates were elected, of whom four supported the Parti Canadien.[146] In 1827, about five candidates with English names were elected, of whom two supported the Patriots and one was among their most influential leaders.[147] In 1832, there were twenty-one English-speakers elected, of whom five supported the nascent radical wing of the Patriots and several others supported the moderate, constitutional wing.[148] The 1834 election saw nineteen English-speakers elected, ten of whom supported the radical Patriots.[149] As these figures have been gleaned from different sources, and may use different definitions of 'English' members, they may not be comparable. Together, however, they certainly corroborate Tocqueville's observation.

The Patriot elite's cross-cultural alliances also extended beyond Lower Canada to the parliamentary Radicals, such as John A. Roebuck, the Patriot agent in London between 1835 and 1837. Roebuck, as Janet Ajzenstat has pointed out, consistently, and with Papineau's constant approval, represented the party as having no desire 'to maintain in predominance French customs and laws' or to 'prevent any innovation which savours of English habits, manners or feelings.'[150] Appealing to popular chauvinism might gain a movement local popularity, but it had to be done discreetly, so as not to embarrass important allies abroad. Parliament was hardly apt to endorse home rule by a chauvinistic elite incapable of forging alliances with local English-speaking leaders. Such considerations may have informed official policy on issues such as language. As Greer observes, 'in striking contrast with Quebec nationalists of a later age, those of the 1830s did not advocate any use of the power of the state to protect the French language. To the extent that they gave the matter any thought, they seem to have leaned towards what we would call a "policy of bilingualism."'[151] The Patriots never presented themselves as ready to surrender to the insulting schemes of the anglicizers. But as the 1823 submission of Papineau and Neilson on the Union issue suggests, they also purported to accept that over the long term and in the absence of official coercion the French Canadians might acquire the English language (see 2.3).

While these relationships continued to hold strategic value, senior Patriots were clearly in no position to adopt chauvinism or exclusive nationalism overtly. But this is not to say they were above the intentional use of ambiguity, particularly at election time. Interactions between political elites and the masses touching on culture, language, and identity were often ambiguous. For example, in the later years of the period, the term 'les Canadiens' could be understood to mean either those of any origin with a demonstrated attachment to the province and its autonomy, or merely French Canadians.[152] For French-Canadian elites addressing uneducated audiences, it was often possible to create the impression that the sovereignty-bearing subject they envisaged was a French-speaking nation, while at the same time their English-speaking confrères could be reassured that they meant a culturally pluralist, civic society that happened to be composed predominantly of Catholic French-speakers.

Overall, then, popular chauvinism was generally deprived of *official* political support. As late as 1831, Tocqueville observed that 'we have arrived at the moment of crisis ... A man of genius who understood, felt and was capable of exploiting the national passions of the people would here have an admirable role to play. He would quickly become the most powerful man in the colony. But I do not yet see him anywhere.'[153] It was perhaps not that senior Patriots were insensible to 'national passions.' Once Duvernay, the former publisher of *La Minerve*, was in American exile after December 1838, beyond any hope of British favour, his newspaper could let fly with bitter invective almost to rival that of the *Montreal Herald*. The 'Prospectus' for *Le Patriote Canadien*, which he planned to publish from the United States, held, 'from the origins of English domination in Canada, the conduct of the newcomers was marked by insult, arrogance, and outrage against the old colonists.'[154] But such undisguised and broadly directed hostility was rare among senior Patriots in preceding years, having been carefully concealed or camouflaged.

In pressing its cause of popular sovereignty and local government, the Patriot movement itself conformed to a highly participatory ethic, and this shaped internal procedures, as well as the official and (especially) the unofficial ends of the movement. The 92 Resolutions of 1834 met with great popular enthusiasm, and this was channelled through many local organizations established after 1827. Such organizations had earlier aroused protest over the imprisonment of the popular editors of *La Minerve* and the *Vindicator*, the slow pace of the reform of executive institutions, the three deaths caused in 1832 by troops firing on rioters at the polls, and the 1827 call-up of the militia.

All such episodes dovetailed with, and contributed to, the value of popular sovereignty observed by Neilson as early as his 1828 testimony before the Canada Committee:

> Eighteen or nineteen years ago I have heard that the population of Lower Canada considered a popular kind of government a very troublesome one; and they even said that they had all the advantages that they had in the United States without the trouble; they were proud of it; but latterly the people have held very much to popular privileges, because they have been afraid of innovations in their institutions; and the disputes, dissolutions and agitations that have occurred have made them enter more into the prevailing notions of the present time of a representative government.[155]

In March through May 1834, twenty local meetings were held in support of the 92 Resolutions.[156] By the end of 1834, the meetings had matured into an extra-parliamentary movement; the movement altered the nature of political representation. Events between then and 1838 would fulfil the demand cheered at such meetings for the 'Sovereignty of the People.'[157]

Clark astutely explains the implications of the potent combination of local mobilization and the new explicitness of the radicals' doctrine:

> Lack of any sort of party organization within the various electoral districts had made any effective control over the nomination of candidates impossible. Thus there had been no means of passing judgement upon those persons announcing themselves as reform candidates ... Until 1834 the confusion of political issues in the province had not made easy the drawing of sharp party lines, but the 92 Resolutions had provided Papineau and his followers with a distinct party platform; it was now possible to clearly distinguish between the Resolutionists and the Anti-resolutionists ... Thus there emerged through the country organizations a form of constituency control.[158]

Moderates were largely eliminated. In the 1834 election, only four of the twenty-eight assembly members who had opposed the 92 Resolutions were re-elected, most having been deterred from standing by local hostility.[159] Assembly members had become much more closely linked to a disturbed and mobilized citizenry.

The failure of crops and restricted access to capital due to the mounting indebtedness of farmers and an international financial crisis brought heightened tensions in 1836 and 1837.[160] The response of the British government to Patriot demands provided a focal point for public anger. Lord John Russell's 10 Resolutions, based on the report of the Gosford Commission, were passed by Parliament in March 1837. The resolutions flatly refused the continued demand for an elected Legislative Council and responsible Executive Council; they took an equally intransigent position on the old issue of the civil list, and for good measure they appropriated funds controlled by the assembly in order to pay the sizable debts accumulated in the administration of the colony.[161]

The response of the Patriots was two-pronged. Boycotts on imported manufactures were raised to undermine imperial revenues from duties.[162] More important, a credible threat of a sort of American Revolution in Lower Canada was extended, backed by huge public meetings throughout the province.[163] Empowering the people by means of mass mobilization was commensurate with the constitutional objectives, ideology, and ostensible organizational structure of the movement. Newly imported mechanisms of Jacksonian democracy were conspicuously displayed at the public meetings where resolutions were decided with fine flourishes of voting.[164] Substantively, resolutions often included plans for the popular election of military officers and magistrates and, occasionally, broader declarations of citizen's rights.[165] The Permanent Central Committee of Montreal, comprising delegates from local committees, and, later, Patriot magistrates and assembly members, provided direction.

Yet a strong connection with the grass roots limited executive control. Papineau's capacity to restrain mass gatherings in the second half of 1837 seems to have been particularly limited. Despite his pleas for restraint at a crucial meeting of delegates and inhabitants at St Charles in October, the gathering was more receptive to militant speakers and in the end 'unequivocally committed itself to a policy of open rebellion against the state.'[166] The initiative of the movement thus fell to 'more impatient' extremists.[167] A paramilitary organization known as the Fils de la Liberté was organized in Montreal, and it brawled with its British counterpart in early November. Armed hostilities proper broke out mid-month. Between then and 14 December there were three major skirmishes, at St Denis, St Charles, and St Eustache. At St Denis, Dr Wolfred Nelson led the Patriots to their sole victory. In the other engagements, British regulars and volunteers routed Patriot volunteers, inflicting at St Eustache well over 100 casualties, and sacking towns in their path.

Apart from their lack of serviceable weapons and *matériel*, the Patriot forces lacked effective command and discipline. Papineau and O'Callaghan felt it imprudent to risk their lives and quickly fled to the United States. Their example was later followed by most of the other leaders, creating 'a breach between the leaders and their followers.'[168] As John Bumsted observes, 'when agitation turned to insurrection, many moderate members of the élite leadership of the reformers fell away, to be replaced by armed farmers.'[169]

In the absence of effective leadership, it appears that there was among the Patriots a fragmentation not only of tactical military resources, but also of a common sense of purpose. The void was filled on an ad hoc basis responsive to local sentiment. While leaders such as Papineau preached inclusiveness and national reconciliation, mobs pursued their own agendas. Depositions given in December 1837 recount a gathering of 'about 50 people' late one evening at the doorstep of a French-Canadian Protestant, looking for the local minister known to be staying there.[170] The leader of the group, François Molleur, stated, 'We don't want M. Roussy [the local Protestant minister] here, we want only one religion, he must go, if he doesn't go this week we'll come and tear down his house.'[171] According to the depositions, the same threat had been made to at least five other households, and those affected (about fifty people) had been forced to flee, fearing for their security. In another locality, a farmer declared, 'Woe to the English, if the Canadians win.'[172] Others believed that the rebellion was necessary to oppose the English, who 'entertained hostile designs towards them and meant to take away their lands.'[173] Many others clearly hoped to eliminate seigneurial tenure and reduce rents.[174]

A common underpinning of all these elements was the 'growing influence of the "plebian masses"' as Greer explains with specific reference to the anti-seigneurial thrust. The precise balance of motives among Patriot insurgents remains, as discussed, exceedingly difficult to determine. Nevertheless, the pattern, however uneven, of ethnic chauvinism and demotic exclusive nationalism certainly contrasts with the official objectives set out by the political elite of the Patriot movement before 1837.

The renewed strife of 1838 also relied upon, and was strongly influenced in its temper, by 'plebian' participation. As Robert Nelson wrote from a base in Vermont during summer preparations for a second rebellion, 'I continue to receive the most encouraging accont [sic] of the *mass* of the people of L.C., of the unletered [sic] part.'[175] In the middle and lower ranks of the insurgency, Montreal banks, land and the English immigrants occupying it supplied compelling targets, in some cases, for violence.[176] For some rebels, strangling Jews and confiscating their property became an objective.[177]

While elites had been compelled by circumstances to construct their official arguments on civic lines, no similar source of restraint applied to the rank-and-file militia, whose paramilitary activities, free of much command and control, widely distributed the authority to interpret and define the struggle as they saw fit. Beverley Boissery describes this phenomenon in one region: 'In total control of the northern part of the seigneury, the Beauharnois chasseurs made no effort to proclaim a republic, fly patriote flags, or even preach the radically liberal ideology of Nelson and his élite. Some believed a change of government would result in Papineau's elevation to king, changes to the seigneurial system, and the abolition of tithes. The only parts of the patriote gospel they understood or chose to listen to concerned habitant values.'[178] For many insurgents, the British government and finer constitutional theory were clearly too remote to soak up concerns of economic and cultural displacement.

In early 1838, Papineau and his coterie were outflanked on the left by a group that included Drs Robert Nelson and Cyrille Côté, who clearly gained leverage from mass sentiment in extending Patriot radicalism from the constitutional to the social and legal spheres. During brief 'invasions' in March and November 1838, the symbolic declaration by senior Patriots of independence on a republican footing also abolished seigneurial tenure, ties between church and state, and the death penalty; and it enacted trial by jury.[179] The fighting of 1838 occurred in November, but deficiencies of arms and leadership quickly brought a rout: 753 Patriots were imprisoned, and 99 were sentenced to death, of whom 58 were eventually banished to Australia, 27 released, and 12 hanged.[180]

It is important to note that a parallel loss of control and discipline within this highly conflictual environment occurred on the British side. To the dismay of military commanders such as Sir John Colborne and Lieutenant-Colonel Charles Grey, extraordinarily vicious reprisals were dealt by 'irregular' British Loyalist troops to the Canadiens.[181] As Grey put it in a personal letter in November 1838, 'it has been to me a most painful duty. I cannot bear to see the poor wretches of women and children when their husbands, etc., etc. are dragged away by the Volunteers, and in many cases their houses burnt over their heads ... Thank Heaven I have had nothing to do with any burning, nor do I believe have any of the regular troops ... And this was not the worst – I know the Guards shot two men and a woman in cold blood in going into Napierville, and I believe the Dragoons slashed away at the defenceless wretches at the first moment.'[182] From the other side, Le Patriote Canadien described such episodes with understandable outrage: 'Cannibals known under the name of the Queen's volunteers, from the ranks of our most mortal enemies, inflamed by the outrageous language of the newspapers serving a Machiavellian government, competed in cruelty ... without restraint. Theft, pillage, rape, sacrilege, arson, and murder were left in the wake of these bandits without pity – the indelible traces of the most hideous vandalism.'[183] Greer refers to a violent tradition of 'plebeian counter-nationalism of English Lower Canada,' evident from at least 1834, and this probably provides useful context for the volunteers' reprisals. At the same time, however, such violent counter-nationalism was no means restricted to 'plebeian' farmers. Indeed, just as Duvernay's paper suggested, the Tory newspapers of Montreal generated violent attacks on the French Canadians that encouraged and legitimized later physical violence. A single example, from the 12 December 1837 issue of The Gazette may suffice: 'The plain matter of fact is, that the Canadians have ever been against us, and never can be for us until their whole nature and character be changed, or until they have been absolutely, physically, and morally conquered into an acquiescence with the principles of British policy and jurisprudence.' British demotic exclusive nationalism, like its Canadien counterpart, may have manifested its greatest violence in the backwoods, but the attitudes underwriting it were held in many quarters.

In summary, the popular mobilization that culminated in the Rebellions of 1837–8 was orchestrated by a political elite ostensibly in pursuit of culturally neutral reforms, specifically a more democratic, and locally rooted system of political representation. The common ground for the party elite – which included English-speakers O'Callaghan and Drs Wolfred and Robert Nelson, as well as French-speaking figures such as Papineau, Dr Jean-Olivier Chénier, and Augustin-Norbert Morin – was the pursuit of majority rule in the place of an unresponsive colonial administration. Its ostensible intellectual foundations were philosophical radicalism and Jacksonian democracy.[184] The ethnic polarization exhibited at the mass level during the rebellions thus did not arise directly from the central, explicit principles espoused by the group's political elite.

Ethnic strife in the rebellions was instead a byproduct of extensive mass mobilization in the presence of subterranean ethnic antagonism. The emerging ethos of participation, and several confrontations between 'the people and the forces of order' generated a potential for mobilization that was harnessed and propelled forward by the political elite. In the process, however, the universality of its message was compromised by a subtle chauvinism, disseminated through unofficial party channels. Later, elite control of the movement was diluted. The constraints that had bound the Patriote elite in its official political discourse were not so binding at the more homogeneous mass level. Fragmentation associated with mass mobilization thus exposed toxic concentrations of ethnic antagonism and exclusive nationalism to the social enviroment.

In short, aggressive challenges to the legitimacy of the existing mode of political representation, arising partly from concerns not at all unique to nationalism, placed an organized process at the disposal of pre-existing ethnic conflict. In at least a few instances, patterns of demotic exclusive nationalism emerged.

2.6 Official Exclusive Nationalism in the Union Act (1840): Causes

After the rebellions, the British government had to consider whether an increasingly representative government in Canada would regulate conflict and protect the interests of the minority. Pessimism reigned, as Lord Durham and others took signs of mass-level ethnic animosity as indicating poor prospects for bi-ethnic political cooperation. Since the voice of the people would inescapably be heard more clearly in government in the future, the sharp discord of Lower Canadian society could be rendered harmonious, so it was held, only by inducing a uniform scale of values, culture, and language. The Act of Union, aiming to establish English political and cultural dominance in British North America, represents a particularly clear-cut case of official exclusive nationalism. Lord Durham, who best articulated the logic of the imperial perspective, even if his own influence on policy development remains unclear, extolled establishing 'an English population, with English laws and language' and trusting 'its government to none but a decidedly English Legislature.'[185] The resulting policy, perhaps more than any other episode of the epoch, demonstrates in the extreme the contingent nature of the opposition of the political elite to official exclusive nationalism, contingent, that is, upon the deemed best strategic interests of the state. In retrospect, it also marks the twilight of imposed statecraft, for the Act of Union established arrangements for government that soon gave rise to a more representative and responsible form of conflict regulation.

A legislative union was accepted over a federal arrangement because it promised to marginalize the French Canadians more quickly. For greater assurance, the constitution established by the Melbourne government granted equal representation to Upper and Lower Canada in the united legislature at a time when representation by population would have granted Lower Canada almost three-fifths of the seats.[186] In demonstrating the resolve, albeit fleeting, of the most senior imperial elite to privilege a way of life in Canada, the act marks a departure from the historical pattern so far observed. To begin to understand this departure, we will consider the perceptions of contemporary elites as these were distilled in Lord Durham's report.

Despite Durham's lofty eloquence, his approach to the conflict in Lower Canada was remarkably unsubtle and cocksure: a 'fatal feud of origin' *rather than* ideological differences, was the source of the trouble; the feud could and should be stopped by granting the English political and cultural dominance; and the French Canadians were destined to economic and cultural inferiority in any case by their unsustainable petty agrarian existence.[187] Although one modern scholar, Janet Ajzenstat, has upheld the liberalism of Durham's position, she does so only by uncritically absorbing Durham's contention that the Patriots, for all their ostensible radicalism, conspired to pursue a hidden, deeply conservative, agenda inimical to a liberal 'way of life.'[188] Considering the actual issues cited by Durham and picked up by Ajzenstat, however, this reading is empirically untenable.[189] A fairer appraisal must concede that, however constrained by circumstance, and however indirect are the means proposed in the report, Durham resorts to privileging a concrete way of life ('national character'). Thus, he proposes that the state conspire against individual (and collective) cultural choices, breaching at least the concept of liberalism operative here. The outstanding question is, 'Why?'

Durham gleaned his interpretation of the 'racial' roots of the quarrel in Lower Canada both from views prevailing in the Whig and Tory press of London and from local sources.[190] One local consultant, Stewart Derbishire, recorded observations in a surviving report for Durham that are strikingly similar to Durham's own account.

> When to these feelings of aversion towards the intruders is added the alarm sounded of an intention on the part of the 'foreigners' to abolish the laws & language of the 'conquered nation,' to 'anglicise' the Province and destroy every vestige of a distinctive race in the original settlers, – notions diligently inculcated by the revolutionary leaders & ably seconded by the newspaper organs of the English party in the current of contemptuous abuse they have never ceased to pour out upon the *habitans*, & in their frequent demands for measures of vigour to keep them down, – and when the Papineau & his Confederates' appeals to the nationality of this vain people, to their gallantry, to their numbers, to the local and general advantages of emancipating themselves from foreign thraldom & becoming masters of the soil are taken into consideration ... the conduct of the people last Autumn will no longer appear extraordinary.[191]

Such views as to the deeply entrenched nature of the conflict, as well as the position subscribed to by many parliamentarians – that a 'few factious scoundrels' were to blame – combined to influence the decision to dilute the political influence of the French Canadians by uniting them with a larger body of English in British North America.[192]

A legislative rather than a federal union promised to deliver a more powerful anglicizing blow, for the French Canadians of Lower Canada would then be left with no institutional bastion from which to protect their distinctive cultural institutions. But it would also forgo several important advantages of a federal over a legislative union.[193] Indeed, despite Durham's professed desire to raise the French Canadians out of their 'hopeless inferiority' by anglicizing them, he had actually intended until his return to England to concede them a larger measure of autonomy under a *federal* union.[194] Durham reversed himself, turning to a more rapid plan for absorption, only after he had learned of the extent of the renewed fighting in late 1838.[195] Still, even in the report, completed in late January 1839, the cultural incompatibility thesis was not joined with anglicizing measures to equal those ultimately contained in the act, such as, for example, barring French from the legislature. Durham argued, 'A considerable time must, of course, elapse before the change of a language can spread over a whole people; and justice and policy alike require that, while the people continue to use the French language, their Government should take no such means to force the English language upon them as would, in fact, deprive the great mass of the community of the protection of the laws.'[196] As William Ormsby points out, Durham believed his mild method of assimilation to be compatible with conciliation, even if in retrospect he was clearly wrong, both about the efficacy of mild means, and as to whether even mild means, joined with overt intent, would aid reconciliation.[197]

At any rate, such signs of reluctance to assault the French-Canadian way of life as aggressively as the subsequent act suggest that Durham's cultural incompatibility and inferiority perceptions were not wholly responsible for that legislation. Ged Martin argues convincingly that the second rebellion shifted policy, not by confirming or disconfirming the cultural incompatibility thesis, but by demonstrating the belligerency of the French Canadians – whatever its cause – to be a more pressing strategic threat than the foreign policy of the United States.[198] Quickly neutralizing the threat within entailed extinguishing the French Canadians' distinctive influence.

Of course, too, by the late 1830s representative institutions could neither be suspended for long, nor distorted by devices to give grossly disproportionate legislative power to distinct units of population. State and society were becoming more closely intertwined as the state acquired a stronger interventionist economic role, and civic obligations therefore increased. Phillip Buckner observes that many trends of modernization, including 'rapid population growth, steady urbanization, increases in literacy and education, the beginnings of industrialization, [and] the expansion of political participation,' would inexorably 'undermine traditional political authority and create demands upon the government' that required stronger, and thus more accountable, executives.[199]

The Special Council, convened in Lower Canada under martial law after the 1838 rebellion, did not possess the necessary legitimate authority to improve the transportation infrastructure and undertake other major public works blocked by the impasse.[200] While some suggested at the time that indefinite arbitrary rule be substituted for representative institutions or that the French Canadians be 'disfranchised until their political education had been completed,' Durham recommended an immediate grant of responsible government to the united legislature on the basis of representation by population.[201] Although the British ministers were not prepared to go that far, Melbourne himself conceded, 'Swamping them, or any devices by which real power is given to a minority, will not do in these days.'[202] The looming ideological bankruptcy of imposed statecraft was recognized even at the imperial centre.

In a constitution based on the rule of the governor-in-council, the governor was bound to be a declining term in the equation, even as far as the selection of councillors.[203] The elective assembly, once restored, could hardly be expected to acquiesce meekly in a government hostile to popular demands. Civil majorities would increase their influence over government through the assembly, and the remains of imposed statecraft would give way to an uncertain new mode of representation and conflict regulation. But French-Canadian 'demagogues' were perceived to be playing to the worst popular inclinations. If they were entrusted with power, few concessions to the interests of Great Britain and the English residents of Lower Canada could be expected. Thus the character and boundaries of civil society were becoming a vital concern for constitutional policy. There needed to be a moderate, pliable civil majority, because on it would depend the government, the future prosperity of the colony, and the integrity of the imperial connection.

Incidentally, French-Canadian popular chauvinism was by no means the sole constraint identified for constitutional arrangements within an increasingly participant society. Durham observed the bigotry of the British in Quebec in frank and uncomplimentary terms: 'It is not any where a virtue of the English race to look with complacency on any manners, customs or laws which appear strange to them; accustomed to form a high estimate of their own superiority, they take no pains to conceal from others their contempt and intolerance of their usages.'[204] Durham associated such attitudes with subordinate positions in the political hierarchy. Whatever his own radical convictions, he identified a pattern similar to the power cleavage in attitudes of English-speakers towards French Canadians, and he associated ethnic antagonism with the popular democratic thrust.

I have found the main body of the English population, consisting of hardy farmers and humble mechanics, ... [to be] a very independent, not very manageable, and, sometimes a rather turbulent, democracy. Though constantly professing a somewhat extravagant loyalty and high prerogative doctrines, I found them very determined on maintaining in their own persons a great respect for popular rights, and singularly ready to enforce their wishes by the strongest means of constitutional pressure on the Government. Between them and the [French] Canadians I found the strongest hostility; and that hostility was, as might be expected, most strongly developed among the humblest and rudest of the body. Between them and the small knot of officials ... I found no sympathy whatsoever; and it must be said, in justice ... that however little I can excuse the injurious influence of that system of administration, which they were called upon to carry into execution, the members of the oldest and most powerful official families were, of all the English in the country, those in whom I generally found most sympathy with, and kindly feeling towards, the French population.[205]

The English portion of the body politic was unwilling ever again to 'tolerate the authority of a House of Assembly, in which the French shaᵢ possess or even approximate to a majority.'[206] Thus expectations of important elements of civil society were even at this stage a constraint upon conflict regulation in the Canadas. In London, also, political considerations constrained the potential for statesmanship, as Martin and Ormsby have both noted.[207]

The rationale among elites for the Act of Union was not visceral chauvinism, but rather an unusual strategic matrix in which an internal threat was perceived to exceed external security risks. More broadly, the policy was advanced because of the perceived incompatibility between the stable, civil, and responsible government demanded by a progressively participant culture and a mercantile economy, on one hand, and what was perceived as an insoluble and violent mass-level conflict challenging the imperial regime, on the other. As discussed in the next chapter, during subsequent years the Union was unsuccessful in achieving its express purpose of marginalizing the French Canadians. Its rationale, and therefore the force of the policy, rapidly decayed when it became clear that the French Canadians posed no real strategic threat to the colony.

2.7 Imposed Statecraft and Exclusive Nationalism: Analysis and Relevance to Theory

This chapter has argued that the capacity of the colonial state after 1791 to regulate conflict and avert exclusive nationalism became more narrowly contingent upon the perception and assessment of strategic considerations. Such perceptions were susceptible to being warped by fear and poor information. The role of the 'garrison mentality' has already been alluded to. Concern that the French Revolution might 'exercise a dangerous attraction among the Canadiens,' greater fear of France than of the United States as the strategic context shifted, and the outbursts of peasant animus in 1794 and 1796–7 – all engendered fears among the British subjects and their leaders alike and supported a powerful urge to gain a more secure domination.[208] With no reliable support for the British regime apparent within the cultural fortress enclosing the Canadiens, some held that it made little sense to continue to preserve those walls in the manner of the Quebec and Constitutional Acts.[209] Another feature of the garrison mentality was the deterioration of the trust and candid communication essential for conflict regulation. Within the home fort, as it were, a vicious circle ensued, whipping up fears to more and more absurd levels behind rising walls of social insularity.[210]

In some cases, a more detached and informed perspective was available at the centre of state power. Thus, the differences through much of the period between Lower Canadian officials and the Colonial Office over accommodation and exclusive nationalism were due in part to the superior grasp of the geopolitical environment available at Westminster. The detachment of officials in London also inhered in their being less implicated in the contradictions attendant upon the petty power struggles of the colony. The wide social spectrum represented in the Lower Canadian Assembly, a product of an extremely broad franchise for the period, was shocking to aspiring mercantile grandees in the colony. Yet it had been they, broadly speaking, that had militated for an assembly in the first place. From the distance of London, the embarrassment of the ambitious British colonials could not be so keenly felt and did not in itself enclose a confrontational policy. Only the rebellions themselves, risks of continued strife, and the inevitability of strong, elective institutions combined to force the British Parliament to underwrite a form of official exclusive nationalism in the Union Act. While strategic circumstances generally weighed against such measures, extreme circumstances, assessed with the best information available, could generate extreme policy.

The experience of Lower Canada between 1791 and 1840 thus prompts the reflection that the elite–mass division is best conceived in terms of different *propensities* to adopt exclusive nationalism, rather than an absolute distinction. The closer to the centre of political power and the higher within the political hierarchy, the lower the propensity to adopt exclusive nationalism. Under imposed statecraft during particularly tense times, exclusive nationalism tends to be restrained by accommodation and compromise at higher levels than under normal conditions. In such cases, the power cleavage may be said to be displaced upwards. In circumstances of bona fide security or legitimacy crises attributed to a distinct ethnic group, imposed statecraft may not avert official exclusive nationalism at all.

These nuances should not, however, obscure the larger pattern. For even in its declining phase, imposed statecraft was capable of bearing up under heavy loads of popular chauvinism and exclusive nationalism. The power cleavage by and large endured at some level. Manning suggests that it is truly 'remarkable' that 'of all the English and Scottish governors-general who presided over British North America before the Rebellion of 1837 only one may properly be described as pro-English or anti-French.'[211] While this may somewhat overstate the case, it is crucial to distinguish between the positions of political elites and subordinates. In the attempts to assert royal supremacy and establish the Royal Institute of Learning, Governor Milnes and his most senior adviser, Sewell, pursued different purposes from Bishop Mountain and his allies on the councils. As for Craig, clearly he surrounded himself with francophobes. But even he, in view of strategic constraints (not any obvious humanitarian impulses), could not endorse their proposals for either American immigration or union with Upper Canada. In the hands of Prevost, his successor, who suddenly faced an American instead of a Continental French threat, policy changed almost overnight, and the distinctive preferences of French, Catholic Canadiens were accommodated. Anglicizers were certainly heard, even with sympathy, but prior to 1840 they were seldom permitted to achieve their purposes. Certainly there was a close call in the attempted union in 1822, but in that case, too, one must compare the motivations of the provincial English Party with senior London colonial authorities. In such cases, action was taken by local public figures and subjects in order to secure the hegemony of their own way of life in a heterogeneous society. By contrast, senior state elites evaluated and reacted to such causes not so much on the intrinsic criteria of ethnic parochialism as on those of security, stability, or the constitutional evolution of political representation.

In this light, the developments of the 1830s through 1840 reflect not so much the limitations of imposed statecraft in regulating exclusive nationalism as those of the transition to more advanced forms of political representation. As late as 1831, Tocqueville could observe that, strong as the 'national passions' of the people were, the political elite had not come round to 'exploiting' such passions politically. Subterranean ethnic antagonism was a live grenade lacking a political launcher. What was missing, more precisely, was an articulate, political apparatus for popular mobilization within local, like-minded networks. As it happened, the elite of the Patriots soon pledged itself to popular sovereignty, and raised a mass movement that, in the spirit of things, emphasized local participation. On the other side of the equation, participation grew not just out of longstanding ethnic tensions, but also, and probably even more significantly on balance, out of a broad spectrum of other grievances. Needless to say, the elites' subtle nods through party channels to chauvinism in 1834 specifically fanned the ethnic dimension of popular angst, while virtually all official public discourse dealt with more universal themes. Overall, the ultimate dilution of elite authority, the abortive recourse to revolution, and, especially, the ethnic bitterness attending the conflict were all lent by mobilization and concomitant shifts in the popular political process. Papineau's pleas for restraint were easily overwhelmed at clamorous mass meetings, such as the decisive one held at St Charles in October 1837.

As for the Act of Union, while it was perhaps the last major stroke of imposed statecraft, it was imposed, in a sense, precisely *because* imposed statecraft would foreseeably give way to majority government. As Melbourne summed it up well, 'any devices by which real power is given to a minority will not do in these days.' Bare military rule no longer being viable, the legislators of the Act of Union anticipated that state power would settle more squarely upon popular, representative government. It was therefore no longer enough merely to co-opt the seigneurs and Catholic hierarchy of a subject population, as had been possible in the early days of imposed statecraft. A burden of legitimacy to be borne only by a strong civil government had arisen from the need for the colonial state to maintain stability and effect major public works conducive to commerce. This mandated government founded upon popular consent, and hence a reliable majority. The imperative of winning over popular majorities, if necessary by altering the composition of the population, arose then from the anticipated future mode of political representation, not from the past.

It is striking, on this interpretation, how closely intertwined are the proximate causes of exclusive nationalism and the historical evolution of political representation. I've argued in this chapter that exclusive nationalism in this period often flowed out of struggles over the form of political representation. But why in principle should this be so? One plausible logic of explanation might run as follows: (1) through modern times, the advancement of popular sovereignty has been a widely available cause with numerous precedents; it has thus offered a highly articulate, legitimate strategy for political elites on the margin, and, in consequence, a common posture of political opposition; (2) to a much greater extent than other perennial opposition strategies (e.g., fiscal reform, altered foreign policy), the cause of popular sovereignty inherently lends itself to demonstrative mass mobilization, consistent with its substantive thrust that the 'people be heard'; (3) where the policy preferences of a population are strongly correlated with (though not necessarily logically dependent upon) membership within an ethnic group, the mass majority mobilized may in fact turn out to be a relatively homogeneous ethnic group; (4) such mass constituencies may, if different in outlook from their neighbours, influence the evolution of the discourse and political activity according to highly conflictual preferences previously denied (e.g., towards public manifestations of exclusive nationalism); and (5) the threat of this sequence may resolve more powerful groups to forestall the advance of popular sovereignty, and (if feasible) to alter the composition of the population via a counter-official exclusive nationalism. On this hypothetical sequence, then, democratic radicalism and reaction to it may both be conducive to the impact of exclusive nationalism on a society. Conversely, moments of equilibrium in the nature of political representation may undermine, particularly at early stages of development, the motives for mass mobilization, hence opportunities, for the systematic articulation of exclusive nationalism.

To link these abstract speculations with the events of the period, it may first be noted that, by all accounts, habitant anglophobia was at a high ebb during the 1790s, and yet the isolated outbreaks of mob violence in that decade of relative equilibrium were clearly insignificant in comparison with the later insurrections. Later, strong dissonance articulated by segments of the political elite between the actual and the expected pace of evolution of political representation contributed to mobilization and thereby set the stage for exclusive nationalism. Articulate critiques were produced in two diametrically opposed cases: by the British political elite of the colony, which became seriously alienated at the domination of the assembly by men of humble social origins; and, by the Patriot elite, as its procedural expectations shifted progressively towards Jacksonian democratic idealism and radicalism. As this was in both North America and Europe a period of great flux in basic norms of representation, it is not surprising that critiques arising out of both the past and the future of representation should have been set in dialectical opposition in this manner. Dual, simultaneous legitimacy crises thus emerged from directly opposed perspectives, out of a process of democratization perceived at once to be too advanced and too far behind. Dissatisfaction on both accounts gave political opponents legitimate cause for extraordinary escalations of the tone of their attacks or for erecting the organizational structures to bring mass unrest to bear on the issues of principle at stake. This created the potential for waves of popular mobilization, and thus for elite demands for equality and representative government to be joined by some measure of mass ethnic antagonism on both sides.

Whatever the validity of these speculations, study of this period certainly bears out the need to look well beyond fluctuations in national consciousness and ethnic rivalry *per se* in order to explain the variable severity of outbreaks of exclusive nationalism. For it is in any case obvious that there was a very broad range of sources of the great popular anxiety that contributed to the mass political mobilization of the period. Sources of acute dissatisfaction were manifold: divergent, and mutually frustrated policy preferences stemming from the long-standing conflict between agricultural and mercantile interests (as in the jail-funding controversy of 1805); internal-security crises (as in the perceived situation of the English before the War of 1812); conflicts indeed between the 'forces of order and the people' (as in the militia call-up and the shooting at the polls); acute economic pressures (the failure of crops, tightening credit); and multifarious other grievances (immigration, onerous taxation for the canals, difficulties in getting land). Within this list, factors having no necessary connection with national conflict (or the rise of national identity and consciousness) served equally well as those having a major national dimension to direct ordinary subjects to politics, and then to fling aside the ultimately flimsy barriers to violent, exclusive nationalism.

Although conflict regulation would in a later epoch be more chronically disabled by sustained and focused popular political mobilization, the people of Lower Canada, as those of many contemporary European societies, had already gained by 1840 a capacity for extraordinary, if blunt and peripatetic, challenges to elite control of politics and the state. Senior state elites, moreover, had already demonstrated their willingness, albeit under duress of extreme security considerations, to resort to official exclusive nationalism. What remained for the future was the development of more consistently effective mechanisms for popular control over the official agendas of elites, and the sustained collapse of political elites' capacity to champion inclusive political programs and to avert exclusive nationalism.

THREE

Triumphs and Failures of Affiliative Trusteeship, 1840–1896

The pre-emptive campaign of official exclusive nationalism embodied in the Act of Union proved ineffectual and short-lived. French-Canadian leaders, having been collectively labelled as demagogues, instead assumed considerable political risks after Union to join in bi-ethnic political alliances with their counterparts in Upper Canada, now sometimes designated Canada West. Together they would secure responsible government. This marked the final demise of imposed statecraft. Its successor, what I've termed 'affiliative trusteeship' for the discretionary and cross-ethnic coalition-building busily engaged in by Canadian politicians during this period, restrained exclusive nationalism, enabling the system to accommodate minorities, to reduce the impact of popular chauvinism on the state, and to achieve a significant project of political integration, itself inaugurating a new constitutional regime of conflict regulation. However, neither the constitutional arrangements of Confederation nor affiliative trusteeship as a mode of representation provided absolute protection against exclusive nationalism. Indeed, post-Confederation experience in several provinces very clearly exposed the inherent limitations of conflict regulation based on cross-ethnic elite alliances. In particular, such experience tends to suggest that, unless a minority group held a significant share of the population, its value as an alliance partner was insufficient to protect the group from the cultural chauvinism and exclusive nationalism of the majority.

Much of this chapter, being taken up with a period in which official exclusive nationalism was *not* a significant factor, might at first glance seem out of place in a work concerned with the causes of exclusive nationalism. My premise in including it is the speculation that the pattern of elite accommodation during the period was itself largely responsible for containing exclusive nationalism (see 0.6). I want to suggest here that the forces that dampened conflict and favoured integration represent an anti-dote, as it were, to the dynamics that might otherwise entrench exclusive nationalism within the state. Bearing in mind that official exclusive nationalism typically entails an assault by the state upon minority ways of life, aspects of a political system that underwrite the protection of minorities and the even-handed treatment of cultural and religious groups also limit threats of official exclusive nationalism. Accordingly, much attention will be given in this chapter to the political resolution of issues that were particularly divisive along religious and cultural lines, and might easily have conduced to official exclusive nationalism had they not been effectively managed. Besides holding interest in itself, the pattern of representation and conflict regulation and the provisions of minority protection achieved in Confederation will also provide indispensable context for what follows.

The chapter begins (in section 3.1) by considering the nature of representation after the rebellions. Despite significant popular political participation and the radically democratic structure of movements during and immediately preceding the rebellions, much less radical patterns of representation dominated the Union period. Such patterns entailed that representatives, acting as arm's-length trustees of the public interest, affiliated themselves freely with the various incipient parties and coalitions and so served to bridge ethnic barriers and accommodate minority interests. Although such accommodation triggered vituperative reaction among opposition leaders, who could be distinctly less cosmopolitan than, say, the early governors, the mechanism of coalition government proved capable of bringing even the most narrow-minded to compromise. Section 3.2 considers the negotiation of Confederation, the foremost integrative coup of nineteenth-century affiliative trusteeship. Discussion focuses here on how the isolationist tendencies of popular government were overcome, owing, in part, to the attractions of extended political alliances and, in part, to prevailing patterns of representation, which allowed politicians sufficient latitude to conclude such alliances, and to run the gauntlet of agglomerative nation-building, so favoured by nineteenth-century liberals. Consideration is also given to the institutional options weighed and adopted during the period, with particular emphasis placed upon implications for minority protection.

The provisions for regulating conflict within the new Confederation were achieved by a broad coalition, but their ambiguity amidst divergent interpretations of the various parties reflected another limitation of affiliative trusteeship as a bulwark for minorities. Section 3.3 deals with these and other limitations, soon evident in the provinces on the periphery. There, the hard-won minority rights of the old Upper and Lower Canada could not be sustained, as they reflected neither the absolute political dominance of Anglo-Protestants in the outlying provinces nor the more direct, majoritarian politics such dominance there entrained. Indeed, the subsequent assault on the educational institutions of Roman Catholics in New Brunswick and Manitoba demonstrated the dependence of minority protection in this era upon strength of numbers, and the potential for official exclusive nationalism in cases where little more than desperate intercessions of politically impotent minorities and their federal allies stood in the way of the aggressive pursuit of uniformity. Once again, the chapter concludes with an analysis of this historical experience to theories of conflict regulation and exclusive nationalism.

3.1   Union Politics: Affiliative Trusteeship and Sectional Conflict

Official Repression and Reconciliation

In the immediate aftermath of the rebellions, any observer would have been hard-pressed to anticipate strong, collaborative political relationships emerging between the two major ethnic groups of the Canadas. The rebellions were devastating for the French Canadians. Memories were ingrained with stark images of 'houses reduced to cinders, habitants massacred, [and] children and elders left to the violent fury of an unrestrained army rabble,' as one journal editor recalled.[1] Adding insult to injury, derogatory references to the French Canadians were made during the Union debate in the Upper Canadian assembly. A consensus there held that the use of French should be suppressed in a united legislature. As one member put it, 'The necessity of speaking English will force them to learn it, and nothing is better for dissipating their prejudices.'[2] The debate, more than even the Durham report, turned the remnants of the French-Canadian press against Union.[3]

The regime of Charles Poulett Thomson, later Lord Sydenham (1839–41), was characterized by the assertion of outmoded high prerogatives.[4] As his successor, Sir Charles Bagot, put it in a letter to Lord Stanley at the Colonial Office, the government of the colony had been carried only by 'the unscrupulous personal interference of Lord Sydenham, combined with practices that I would not use, and your Lordship would not recommend.'[5] Sydenham had engaged in 'something very like a private quarrel ... with the whole mass of the French inhabitants of Lower Canada.'[6] Sydenham employed the Special Council, established as a provision of martial law by Parliament in February 1838, to pass a series of measures, including local accedence for Union, that would have been unacceptable to an elected assembly.[7] The measures, including provisions for selling off the property of exiled Patriots, charging the Union with the considerable debt of Upper Canada, and reforming the courts on the principles of English common law, were roundly perceived as anti-French. Measures even more specifically antagonistic to the French Canadians appeared with the first election, when Sydenham employed arbitrary authority to marginalize French influence. Constituencies were gerrymandered, polls were located as far as possible from concentrated areas of French-Canadian settlement, and election violence and intimidation directed at French Canadians were tolerated while troops were deployed to protect the other side. The result was that leading French-Canadian politicians, including Louis-Hippolyte LaFontaine, were defeated, even in preponderantly French ridings. Furthermore, only half of Sydenham's appointees to the legislative council for Canada East and none of the executive appointees were French-speakers.[8] Not surprising, most of the energies of the French-Canadian political elite were directed towards repeal of the Act of Union.[9]

This was, in short, hardly an auspicious time for forming alliances across the ethnic chasm. Remarkably, an alliance was nonetheless struck, at first in secrecy.[10] Although French Canadians had not been granted a share of the representation proportionate to their numbers, they retained the upper hand in the legislature. In contrast with the English of Upper Canada, who were riven by a conflict pitting Compact Tories against moderate and radical liberals, French Canadians generally possessed the solidarity of a distressed minority to operate as a bloc. Politicians in Upper Canada who recognized their dependence on French cooperation sought to make common cause; moderate reformers, by dint of their principles and temperament, were best placed to make the advance. Responsible government by party (implying cabinet government arising from, and enjoying a majority within, the assembly) supplied an ideal rallying point for the coalition as it would transfer authority over the composition of cabinet from the governor – who could be variously viewed as embodying both despotic prerogatives and imperial repression – to the local leading party.

Sydenham's despotism was thus met with the concerted opposition of both moderate Upper Canadian Reformers and the French of Lower Canada. In a striking gesture, Reformer Robert Baldwin arranged in 1841 for LaFontaine to take a seat in the legislature in a by-election in Upper Canada.[11] Then, Baldwin himself resigned when Sydenham refused to construct a cabinet reflecting the dominance of Reformers in the assembly.

No French-Canadian politician of any consequence would accept a solitary appointment to the Executive Council, and by September 1842 it was evident that the French bloc as such, as well as their Canada West allies, could no longer be kept out of government. As Reformer and Provincial Secretary West, Samuel Harrison, acknowledged to the governor, 'There is no disguising the fact that the French members possess the power of the Country; and he who directs that power, backed by the most efficient means of controlling it, is in a situation to govern the Province best.'[12] Just eight months after arriving, Bagot (1842–3), Sydenham's replacement, invited LaFontaine to enter the ministry. LaFontaine accepted and secured places for three associates, including Baldwin. Together they would strongly influence the cabinet, which nonetheless continued to include a majority of independent members.[13] While the assembly as a whole voted overwhelmingly (fifty-five to five) in favour of the newly composed ministry, the Tory press railed. The *Montreal Gazette* exclaimed, 'The British party has been deliberately handed over to the vindictive disposition of a French mob.'[14]

As William Morrell notes, although the new government did not command all the powers of a cabinet, its composition now reflected important aspects of responsible government.[15] To win over French Canadians to his administration, Bagot extended considerable control over patronage to his new ministers, and many French Canadians were appointed to various administrative and juridical positions.[16] Bagot also evaded his appointed task of anglicizing the French-Canadian legal system, and he established French-Canadian control over education in Lower Canada by naming a deputy superintendent having close ties to the Roman Catholic clergy.[17]

If Bagot merely ignored the aggressive anglicizing policy inherent in union, Sir Charles Metcalfe, who arrived to take his place in March 1843, dismissed it explicitly: 'If the French Canadians are to be ruled to their satisfaction, and who could desire to rule them otherwise? every attempt to metamorphose them systematically into English must be abandoned, and the attainment of that object, whether to be accomplished or not, must be left to time and the natural effect of the expected increase and predominance ... of the English over the French Population.'[18] Three months later he requested repeal of Article 41, which prohibited the use of French in the legislature. He further concluded that the very project of Union had been 'unwise.'[19] But Lord Stanley at the Colonial Office would not countenance extending conciliation to the extent of negating anglicization. He censured both Bagot's and Metcalfe's policies.[20] Only after Bagot had already admitted LaFontaine and his associates to the council – a step

Stanley had vainly tried to prevent – did the colonial secretary accept that Bagot's French-dominated Executive Council had the prerogative of rolling back the aggressive legislation of Sydenham's Special Council. More generally, as when Bagot indefinitely deferred proclaiming the ordinance anglicizing the courts of Lower Canada, Stanley was a stalwart exponent of assimilation.[21] Metcalfe's request that Article 41 be repealed was refused, and it was not until Metcalfe's ministry in the Executive Council requested repeal that the British government conceded the issue. Even then, Metcalfe's complaisance was criticized by the prime minister, Sir Robert Peel, and a three-year delay ensued.[22]

In the split between Stanley, on one hand, and Bagot and Metcalfe, on the other, the men on the spot were more prepared to abandon official exclusive nationalism in favour of conciliation. At first glance this pattern contrasts with the examples noted in the previous chapter, including the split in 1810 between Craig's local regime and Lord Liverpool in London, where those at the centre of state power were more stalwart opponents of official exclusive nationalism. The common element in these apparently contrasting patterns is that greater empirical familiarity with the security risks in question was associated in both cases with conciliatory strategies. The fear in Lower Canada in 1810 that Napoleon was plotting an invasion was a fear that could be dispelled in England; by contrast, in the 1840s the governors had a finer understanding of security threats *within* North America, and had regained their confidence in the loyalty of the French Canadians. (The ex-governor Lord Gosford had notably been one of the Lords who had opposed Union, contending that in his experience the vast majority of French Canadians were loyal and that the measure was disproportionately 'arbitrary and unfair.')[23] More generally, if reliable information dispenses with more spurious fears than it raises new well-founded ones, if trust and confidence contribute to conciliatory dealings, and if strategic intelligence is *normally* more available at the upper levels of the body politic, these factors may help to explain the often marked power cleavage and its upward displacement during periods of fear and mistrust.

Elite Accommodation and Popular Reaction

The final act of imposed statecraft was to declare its own demise, so to speak, and the supersession of a new mode of political representation. Consistent with the pattern of imposed statecraft observed previously, an explicit connection was made by the governor of the time between the perverse strategic consequences of overt efforts to assimilate the French

Canadians, and the strategic benefits of accommodation. As it had in the past, the advance of a more popular form of representation generated considerable reaction from those who opposed both the procedural and the substantive consequences of more popular government.

Governor Metcalfe, despite his concessions to Reform, clashed with LaFontaine and Baldwin over responsible government and control over patronage. The conflict climaxed when the governor appointed a minor official on his own authority, causing all but one member of the council to resign, and leading, after an eleven-month delay, to the formation of a new ministry.[24] The same issue arose again, early in the tenure of Governor James Bruce, 8th Earl of Elgin (1847–54), when he also attempted to form an executive council not dominated by any one party. A leading French-Canadian politician, Augustin-Norbert Morin, refused Elgin's offer of a seat on the council in 1847. Morin held to dominant public opinion over objective criteria of competency as the basis of government legitimacy, stating: 'The idea of an Executive Council in which perfect confidence and complete unity of sentiments and actions does not prevail would be contrary to that of a government based upon public opinion ...'[25] The 1847–8 election produced a decisive victory for Reformers in both East and West, and the pressures for party government became too strong to resist. A clear preponderance was at last yielded to Reform leaders in the councils.[26]

Immediately preceding his invitation to LaFontaine to form a government, Elgin declared to the colonial secretary his opposition to the assimilatory rationale underlying union. In repeating Bagot's basic argument, Elgin emphasized the loyalty of the French Canadians and highlighted strategic considerations.

> I must confess ... that I for one am deeply convinced of the impolicy of all such attempts to denationalize the French. Generally speaking they produce the opposite effect from that intended, causing the flame of national prejudice and animosity to burn more fiercely ... Let them feel on the other hand that their religion, their habits, their prepossessions, their prejudices if you will, are more considered and respected here than in other portions of this vast continent ... and who will venture to say that the last hand which waves the British flag on American ground may not be that of a French Canadian?[27]

Once again, the British Tories of Montreal threw themselves into virulent opposition to a governor's concessions to the mistrusted French Canadians. Unrest erupted in Montreal after the legislature passed the Rebellions Losses Bill, which indemnified all, including ex-rebels, who had suffered losses inflicted by government troops in 1837–8. An English mob burnt the parliament buildings to the ground, assaulted the governor's carriage, and attacked the houses of several leaders of the assembly. In Canada West, Elgin's immediate acceptance of the full implications of the election result was greeted by cries of 'French Domination.'[28] Meanwhile, British parliamentarians in both the House of Commons and the Lords 'fully sustained' Lord Elgin's decision not to invoke the royal prerogative to disallow the bill, and accepted the precedent he had thus set for extending responsible government to Canada.[29]

Sectional Conflict, Fragile Alliances, and the Implications of Responsible Government

In theory, responsible government promised to bring policy closer to the people. As party rule became an accepted principle, governors exercised less overt influence.[30] Cabinets were formed by, and generally of, representatives of the people. For opposition radicals and conservatives, the constitutional reduction of the aristocratic elements of government raised hopes or fears of unfettered democracy, depending on the perspective. Tories were demoralized in Canada East; in Canada West by the early 1850s, they were searching for direction. Some looked as far as the constitutional designs of the American federalists for a means of checking the power of a supreme cabinet commanding the potent, even intoxicating, legitimacy of popular government.[31]

Yet, in practice, government in Canada hardly provided a vehicle for the popular will. This was not merely a matter of the rapidly diminishing 'paraphernalia' of aristocratic government – the legislative council that remained appointive, privileges for the established churches, property qualifications for members of the legislature – all of which were opposed by advanced reformers termed 'Clear Grits.'[32] More significantly, popular sovereignty was limited because the pattern of political representation, which we have labelled 'affiliative trusteeship,' strongly mediated the connection between electoral intentions and the conduct of public policy.

In several concrete ways, party government did not fully assume its modern form in the Union period. Candidates of the same party sometimes waged elections from opposing sides of major issues.[33] Options confronting the electorate – that is, where ridings were contested at all – did not always bear clear doctrinal stamps. Once members reached the assembly, alignments sometimes shifted, particularly between 1850 and 1858.[34] 'Immense shoals of loose fish' were observed after the 1854 election as being prepared to follow the dominant political current.[35] Thus, changes in the composition of government could bear little relation to the dynamics of electoral strength and depend heavily on the tactics and personal rapport of potential coalition partners. The same 1854 election returned an increased number of opposition Reformers and Liberals in both sections of the province and about the same number of Conservatives. Yet it marked the beginning of a Conservative watershed in Union politics with that party's new dominance of the Western portion of the coalition.[36] Thoroughgoing 'reconstructions' of coalition governments were also undertaken without recourse to the electorate, often on the basis of 'protracted negotiations' among diverse elements.[37] The legislature of this period functioned, in short, as an 'electoral college' for government.[38] Responsible government implied responsibility to the legislature and not, directly, to the people.

Concepts of parliamentary government and representation extolled by respected leaders reflected, in any case, the wide latitude enjoyed by members. For example, given the sensitivities to the church–state issue within the governing coalition, in May 1850 a resolution requesting the British government to transfer control over the clergy reserves to the province was introduced as an 'open question' – a free vote, in modern terms.[39] For many years the clergy reserves in Upper Canada had mainly funded the Churches of England and Scotland, a blatant privilege that greatly irritated the adherents of other Protestant denominations. The resolution of 1850 was an important step to eliminating this arrangement. It also, somewhat furtively, respected the vested interests of existing incumbents, a concession highly unpopular in Canada West.[40] In urging members to vote their consciences, Baldwin presented an uncharacteristically emphatic defence of Burkean precepts of government and their implications for minority accommodation, as contemporary reports of his speech record.

> He held with Burke, that it was not the duty of a member of the Legislature to be a slavish representative of the opinions of his constituents ... He was sent as a representative to protect the interests of the whole community ... He said then that ... [members] were to dispose of this question irrespective of all regard to their political position. What was the object of establishing a government: it was not merely to build a machine as a curiosity, it was to protect the rights of all men, the minority as well as the majority ... If the majority had a right, of their own mere wish, despotically to control the minority, then it became a question whether the despotism of one man was not less dangerous than the despotism of many.[41]

Quoting Edmund Burke's speech to the people of Bristol, which famously construed political authority as a 'trust from Providence,' Baldwin asked his colleagues to ignore the 'considerable excitement' outside the House and to 'deliberate with that calmness which would give weight to their decision.'[42]

Despite their influence among Western ministers, norms of representation premised on trusteeship were candidly expressed by only a few prominent politicians, and were explicitly opposed by Clear Grittism, which, in the early 1850s, was 'in close accord with a restless rural democracy' and which embodied in its opposition members an expressed commitment to (what we have termed) 'ethnic delegate representation.'[43]

Nevertheless, coalitions spanning both sections and major religious groups helped to limit local majoritarian government; they exemplified the latitude vis-à-vis constituent opinion described by norms of trusteeship, entailing fluid lines of party and ministry. While the Reformers of Canada East and West had combined almost seamlessly in the 1840s in pursuit of responsible government, the practical necessity of entering into politically vulnerable compromise was often manifest in the 1850s. Under the leadership, first, of Baldwin and Lafontaine and, then (from late 1851), of Augustin-Norbert Morin and Francis Hincks, the Liberal–Reform cabinets of 1849–54 amalgamated such diverse elements as 'conservative-minded liberals' from the East and Clear Grits from the Western section.[44] The successor Liberal–Conservative coalition, formed by Sir Allan MacNab of the West with the same ministry from the East, was sufficiently pragmatic to encompass fully two-thirds of the assembly.[45]

The discretionary alignments of individual members and the propensity of political groupings to affiliate across sectional and sectarian barriers underpinned an impressive record of minority accommodation. In 1853 the Ecclesiastical Act granted churches the right to establish ecclesiastical corporations, organizations devoted to an array of charitable, educational, and religious purposes.[46] Roman Catholic separate schools for Upper Canada were also enabled on a basis of individual choice by the Common School Act (1850), the Supplementary School Act (1853), the School Act (1855), and the Scott Act (1863).[47] These measures built on the vaguer provisions of the Schools Act (1843) and together they established a pattern of Catholic schools that would endure well beyond Confederation.[48]

These measures were widely unpopular in Canada West. 'Undoubtedly, the vast majority of Protestants in Upper Canada would have preferred to see separate schools abolished,' as Franklin Walker concludes in his study of the issue.[49] Among Western members in the legislature, the measures generated heated opposition – and a measure of rather sheepish and resigned support as well. The ultra reform participants in the ministerial coalition were obliged in 1853, whatever their earlier zealous opposition, to abstain from openly resisting the government's initiatives in separate schools and ecclesiastical corporations. The ministerial Ultras 'chafed painfully,' one being known to 'plunge for the lobby' before particularly awkward votes.[50] The rising tensions ultimately led to the demise of the government, though not to any marked change in schools policy.

For opposition Reformers, the compromises raised the spectre of infidelity and the corruption of responsible government. George Brown, editor of the Toronto *Globe* and opposition member of the assembly from 1851, embodied fear and loathing of popery, Western sectionalism, and a purist view of church–state separation.[51] In Waite's apt assessment, Brown was 'a great journalist and a great Reformer,' but not 'a sober and prudent statesman.'[52] In his maiden address in the legislature, Brown sharply criticized the compromises entailed by elite accommodation.

> Then he came to the present coalition, recounting in sharply documented detail how the Grits had negotiated to enter office with the eastern and western factions they had so utterly condemned ... Indisputably, he declared, *someone* must have swallowed their beliefs ... What had happened to Grit anti-French, anti-state–church professions? ... It all led back to his main charge, that the leaders of the party had betrayed the heart of everything that Liberalism had striven for so ardently. For the essence of the British responsible system was that men took office or resigned it according to the political success or failure of the principles they upheld. If a public man can hold one set of principles out of office and another in office, responsible government is a farce![53]

A far more sympathetic interpretation was presented by Governor Sir Edmund Walker Head, who upheld rather than denigrated the personal integrity of more accommodating leaders: 'it is probably to the action of these very cross interests and their conflicting opinions that the whole United Province will, under Providence, in the end owe its liberal policy and its final success, ... whatever may be the personal convictions, and whatever may be the religious beliefs of a Canadian politician, if he means to lead his countrymen as a whole, he must school his mind to principles of tolerance and he must learn to respect the feelings and even the prejudices of others who differ widely from himself.'[54] The truth probably rested somewhere between the 'schooling of minds' and the 'swallowing' of beliefs. Certainly, John A. Macdonald, Attorney-General West, and future

Prime Minister of Canada, rang true in articulating the liberal case for separate-school provisions in the midst of the 1855 separate-school debate pressed by his Lower Canadian coalition partners. 'The severance of opinion, the right of private judgment tended to the elevation of man, and he should be sorry if a legislature, the majority of whose members were Protestants professing to recognize the great Protestant principle of the right of private judgment, should yet seek to deprive Roman Catholics of the power to educate their children according to their own principles ...'[55] But for many others, coalitions and their demands were mainly expedient. Even Macdonald would occasionally resort to the logic of numbers in making the case for accommodation. As he put it to a Lower Canadian Tory, 'No man in his senses can suppose that this country can for a century to come be governed by a totally unfrenchified government ... So long as the French have twenty votes they will be a power, and must be conciliated.'[56] On balance, it seems that minority rights were protected during the 1850s under the pattern of affiliative trusteeship less because of cosmopolitanism and personal tolerance, still less because majority constituent opinion in the affected areas supported minority rights, and more because the machinery of representational practice, and the balance of power, enjoined cross-ethnic coalitions, hence compromise.

Constitutional Proposals Short of Federation

The sectional 'dualism' of the union was recognized by several quasi-federal devices: dual legal systems, dual ministries, dual seats of government until 1859, and the principle of double-majority.[57] The double majority principle stipulated that legislative measures for a section should enjoy the support of a majority of assembly members of that section. Advocated from 1845, the principle gained little acceptance as a constitutional rule, but was seldom denied as a basis for 'sound politics.'[58] In both 1854 and 1856, for example, the ministry for Canada West was partially reconstructed to regain sectional confidence. Where breached, as with the passage of the 1855 School bill over the objections of a Western majority, the principle was registered in potent opposition assaults, notwithstanding the sometimes marginal significance of the actual measures.[59] John Sandfield Macdonald, a Baldwinite Reformer, advocated 'institutional tolerance' and 'respect for French Canadian culture'; he was the foremost champion of double majority.[60] But the official recognition he sought for it during his leadership of the Western section from May 1862 to March 1864 was 'virtually destroyed' on its first real test in February 1863, when his Scott bill was passed despite receiving only a minority of Upper Canadian votes.[61] After the ministry was reconstructed in May 1863 under strong influence from Brown, the rule lost official sanction.[62]

The double-majority principle acquired little constitutional force because it did not reflect the actual distribution of power under union. Sectional lines of division were, in fact, more deeply cross-cut in the West than in the East by varying views on constitutional and other policy. This tended to give leadership on many issues, particularly those touching on religion or culture, to the moderate, bi-ethnic party consistently enjoying large majorities in Lower Canada.[63] Although various Western brokers of Eastern power rose to prominence during the period, their views were necessarily consonant on such issues with those of the Eastern majority.

Another unrealistic aspect of the double-majority principle was that it would have sometimes entailed combining cultural antagonists in government without a minimum consensus that existing cultural divisions must be accepted as permanent.[64] Brown and his followers, for example, were not content through the early and mid-1850s with mere coexistence; they sought to undermine popery and perhaps even to assimilate French-Canadian Catholics by means of national schools and the consolidation of the two legal systems.[65] Such views were of course anathema to the dominant Conservatives of Canada East. Among moderate Western members, by contrast, opposition to the accommodation of French-Canadian and Catholic interests was not so strong as to preclude otherwise felicitous alignments with ministries, whatever the embarrassments created with constituents. Conservatives governing with John A. Macdonald held with the Ottawa *Citizen* that, under union, 'the evils experienced by Upper Canada have not been practically ... so great as is commonly supposed.'[66]

On a more abstract level, the double-majority principle was not entrenched because there was little conviction among legislators that applying one's conscience in framing measures directed at the other section was illegitimate, and that responsible government ought to be popular, majoritarian government at the sectional level. The union, after all, had been intended to rescue the English Protestants of Lower Canada from their predicament. Many issues in Lower Canada *were* subsequently decided by Upper Canadian majorities in the early 1840s, and even the *Globe* once went so far as to urge that Upper Canadian influence be wielded so that Lower Canadian schools might be 'freed from the priests.'[67] As Careless notes, both sections 'tended to adopt the view that the province was one, or two, just as the occasion suited them.'[68] Prudence may have dictated 'tempering majoritarianism with the spirit of concurrent majorities,' in the parlance of consociational theory (see 0.4), but it was unclear that precedence in the process of accommodation should necessarily be given to compact territorial sections rather than to cross-cutting religious segments. Granting the separate schools desired by a majority of Catholics antagonized a majority in Canada West; respecting majority preferences of the sections would have meant ignoring them within major sects.

Such concerns of minority accommodation hardly troubled Brown, of course, who sought representation by population to establish majoritarian rule in order to overwhelm rather than recognize and accommodate sectional and sectarian differences. From the early 1850s, when a census revealed that the population of Upper Canada had surpassed that of Lower Canada, the equal representation of the Union seemed to Grits an undue constraint upon their own sectional and sectarian agendas.[69] 'Rep by pop,' as the cry was heard, became associated with the Grits' attacks on Catholic institutions, because it threatened 'what, indeed, George Brown made no pretence whatever to conceal – the "assimilation of the laws" of the two sections of the province.'[70]

After his failure to form a governing Protestant, English-speaking coalition after the 1854 and 1857 elections, despite resorting to the theme of 'French domination' in the latter campaign, Brown was compelled to contemplate terms that would be less hostile to Lower Canadian liberals.[71] In February 1858 he accepted a Rouges position construing the national schools of the Grit platform as a more distant eventuality; and during the spring he cultivated a political affiliation that 'many Catholics as well as voluntaryists deplored' with Thomas D'Arcy McGee, a rising assembly member from Lower Canada and an Irish Catholic.[72] Brown also demonstrated greater willingness to 'hear reason' as to the coordinate constitutional changes – perhaps federalism – that would be required to achieve rep by pop.[73] Careless construes such gestures as 'steps towards enlarging his political horizons' and suggests that 'this journalist-partisan of the West ... was moving on from purely sectional campaigning to the wider problem of reaching terms with the East.'[74]

Brown's embrace during early 1858 of a more conciliatory position might be subjected to critical examination. But it seems clear that the accord Brown reached with the Lower Canadian liberal Antoine-Aimé Dorion between 29 and 31 July 1858 represented a substantial weakening of the Grits' position in the face of an opportunity to prove their joint capacity to govern. According to a speech Brown gave at the Royal Exchange on 6 August 1858 to explain the compromise reached, he accepted the necessity of providing constitutional protections for sectional institutions in the form of a written constitution, a 'Canadian Bill of Rights guaranteed by Imperial Statute,' or a 'Federal Union.'[75] As for Catholic education, although Brown was not prepared to accept separate schools on a permanent basis, the principle of voluntaryism could be diluted: 'it is of the utmost importance that, in making the system uniform, it should be rendered as acceptable as possible to all denominations; and if you can show any way in which, without deviating from principle, *facilities can be given* to the clergy of all denominations for the religious instruction of the children, I am prepared to agree to it.'[76] Brown specifically raised the possibility that the clergy might be invited to 'give religious instruction to the children of their several flocks a certain number of hours on so many days of the week.' The apparent acceptance of 'facilities' suggests that government support – probably at a minimum the provision of classrooms and class time – could be offered.[77] Brown also professed a willingness to learn from the Irish common-school model.[78] Many Catholics were apparently impressed. According to the Toronto *Leader*, a majority, 'perhaps a large majority,' of Catholics voted for Brown in the election held in late August.[79] Brown's account of the compromise seems largely consistent with those of Dorion and Joseph Elie Thibaudeau, the latter having been named president of the council.[80]

The Brown–Dorion administration did not command a majority in the assembly and held office for a mere two days before being defeated on a want-of-confidence motion. Still, as Careless emphasizes, 'it was striking that a government had been achieved at all, considering the bitter background of sectional and sectarian conflicts ... The fact was, that the differing interests – Catholic and Protestant, Upper Canadian and Lower Canadian – had been willing to seek a basis of agreement.'[81] The commitment to compromise evinced in the coalition of 1858 represented an abrupt shift for Reform. As recently as the party convention of January 1857, a resolution had been passed calling for the 'gradual assimilation of the local institutions of Canada East and West' over objections that this would tend to alienate Lower Canada from a coalition.[82]

Having brought the most intransigent leader of an intransigent party to compromise, the Brown–Dorion compact demonstrates the contemporary strength of factors favouring cross-cultural coalitions and compromise. The deterioration and collapse of the opposition coalition by April 1859, when the hopelessness of forming a government had become apparent, led to the resumption of tirades against popery at the *Globe* by 1860.[83] This tends to confirm that basic attitudinal change contributed little of the basis of accommodation.

The political failure of Brown's coalition-building efforts and the compromises entailed led many within Reform ranks to despair of achieving their agenda within the existing union. Outright dissolution appeared a simpler solution than either rep by pop or double majority, and, after having gained support in the 'agrarian democracy of the west' following the School bill of 1855, dissolution now found new favour.[84] Brown consistently rejected the idea, as he was concerned to preserve, perhaps through federation, 'the natural unity of the Canadas provided by the great St. Lawrence system' for the sake of trade and defence.[85] The division between the Reform ranks and party leader was clearly manifested at the November 1859 party convention.[86] The convention pitted opponents of dissolution amenable to federation against radicals; for the latter, dissolution was a necessary first step to obtaining a written constitution, total church–state separation, and a polity more directly responsive to popular preferences.[87] Through deft procedural moves, party leaders in Toronto succeeded in derailing the dissolutionist agenda of the 'western agrarian rank and file.'[88] George Sheppard, a radical and now disheartened editor of the *Globe*, pronounced such manoeuvres a 'swindle' and resolved to resign.[89]

Brown, righteous exponent of fidelity though he had once been, was clearly capable of uncompromising leadership within his party and occasionally, of compromise without. His leadership was achieved by subverting the principles of direct representation championed by the old Clear Grit party Brown had inherited and then subdued. More broadly, the strong motivations engendered in Brown for accommodation running against his better judgment, as it were, display with particular force the civilizing influence of affiliative trusteeship.

3.2 Confederation: Constitutional Implications of Affiliative Trusteeship in Its Carrying and Substance

The federation of three provinces of British North America – Canada, Nova Scotia, and New Brunswick – in 1867 would further demonstrate the propensity of political elites during this period to maintain and strike wider connections than those sanctioned by many of their constituents. Intellectually, Confederation confronted the challenge of protecting minorities under representative, majority rule, and dividing sovereignty and the machinery of accommodation between provincial and federal levels. Politically, it required overcoming the opposition of the public and its advocates in the Maritimes, as well as building support in Upper and

Lower Canada, in the last instance largely by means of plural, not very congruent, interpretations of contentious elements.

The topic of Confederation broaches fundamental questions concerning the factors predisposing states to integrative dynamics, factors closely related to the efficacy of conflict regulation, and, (inversely) to the prospects of official exclusive nationalism. The key question, of course, concerns why political elites may, *on balance*, be inclined to build and serve broader political alliances than countenanced by popular opinion. Several recent 'revisionist' works have challenged whether the logic of Confederation was as overwhelming and inexorable as the Fathers and later patriotic historians maintained.[90] Whatever the merits of this argument, it has certainly highlighted political motivations, particularly the interest of key political actors in an enlarged field of political affiliations. The interesting issues of integrative dynamics raised by Canadian Confederation can only be touched upon here. Nevertheless, in the discussion that follows, I wish to highlight three major sources of motivation: (a) thwarted agendas and ambitions within the existing structure; (b) opportunities to shore up weakness by combining with new external allies; and (c) perceived advantages of scale for a political community/state. Additionally, the very pursuit of these objectives arguably depended upon (d) considerable autonomy of the political elite within the pattern of political representation.

Elite Motives for Confederation

By mid-1864 the Canadian political system reached a critical point. Two ministries, those of Sandfield Macdonald–Dorion and Macdonald–Cartier, had been defeated that spring, making four during a two-year period.[91] Neither party could gain a decisive advantage within both sections of the province simultaneously, and governments clung precariously to 'tiny majorities.'[92] Although the resulting discontinuities may not have absolutely halted the administration of the province, they certainly made politics more nakedly a game of 'getting in power and staying in power.'[93] Equal sectional representation seemed to blame; it was also an increasingly indefensible anachronism now that Upper Canada's population already exceeded that of Lower Canada by a quarter and was continuing to grow more rapidly.[94]

Two constitutional remedies, 'rep by pop' and federation, were closely associated and often jointly pursued. Although French Canadians in 1865 held only 49 of 130 seats in the assembly, even Brown had not for many years sought rep by pop without coordinate constitutional changes that, intentionally or unintentionally, would have protected French-Canadian interests.[95] With Dorion he had accepted federation as an option for this purpose in 1858. For John A. Macdonald, rep by pop threatened to diminish the political value of his alliance with the moderate bloc from Lower Canada.[96] Worse, the rising appeal in the early 1860s of 'political platforms asserting the particular viewpoint of one section or the other' worked directly against Macdonald's strength in Upper Canada, and increased the political force behind rep by pop.[97] A British North American federation was a salvation for Macdonald; it might rally a stronger coalition, and, longer term, it opened possibilities of new political alliances.[98]

For George-Étienne Cartier, Macdonald's major political partner, the Maritimes seemed a region with which he could do political business. Cartier viewed the Maritimes as 'mixed,' as against Upper Canada being 'British and Protestant,' and Lower Canada, 'in great part French and Catholic.'[99] This view, together with the greater concern for religious over linguistic minorities, may have influenced Cartier's overall strategic assessment.[100]

> In 1858 he first saw that representation by population, though unsuited for application as a governing principle as between the two provinces, would not involve the same objection if other partners were drawn in by a federation. In a struggle between two – one a weak, and the other a strong party – the weaker could not but be overcome; but if three parties were concerned, the stronger would not have the same advantage; as when it was seen by the third that there was too much strength on one side, the third would club with the weaker combatant to resist the same fighter.[101]

Beyond such considerations of the 'balance of power,' Cartier also held to the nineteenth-century view that increased scale through political integration would foster national development. As he put it during the Confederation debates in Canada,[102]

> the question for us to ask ourselves was this: Shall we be content to remain separate – shall we be content to maintain a mere provincial existence, when, by combining together, we could become a great nation? It had never yet been the good fortune of any group of communities to secure national greatness with such facility ... In ancient times, the first weak settlement increased into a village, which, by turns, became a town and a city, and the nucleus of a nation. It was not so in modern times. Nations were now formed by the agglomeration of communities having kindred interests and sympa-

thies. Such was our case at the present moment ... Now, when we were united together ... we would form a political nationality with which neither the national origin, nor the religion of any individual, would interfere.[103]

Cartier's subsequent career was consistent with this outlook, for he proved 'the moving spirit behind the advance westwards,' in personally negotiating in 1868 with the British government for the acquisition of Rupert's Land and the North-West Territory.[104] In 1871, Cartier spearheaded the entry into Confederation of British Columbia.[105]

It is revealing that even elite opponents to Confederation placed their arguments in this 'agglomerative' cast. Joseph Howe, the most prominent Nova Scotian opponent, for example, rebuffed the nation-building aspirations of the Canadians by asserting that the empire itself formed a greater nation.[106] Howe expressed concern, in the words of a contemporary who knew him, that 'Union would draw away the minds of the people of the British Isles & of Br north America from what he deemed the most vital question of the times – the organization of the empire.'[107] Howe argued that the empire could be brought into a tighter conglomeration by admitting colonial politicians into British Parliament, and by requiring colonies to impose taxes and compulsory service for the military defence of the empire.[108] Among Howe's anti-Confederate peers, several criticized Confederation not because they preferred to 'sulk on [their] own rocks' (in Mill's fetchingly pejorative terms), but rather because they desired an even closer legislative union, probably considering federalism in the harsh light of the American civil war.[109]

The liberal agglomerative impulse may have had its strongest influence upon Confederation indirectly, by helping to shape British public opinion, which in turn, as Martin has forcefully argued, strengthened support and weakened opposition to Confederation.[110] The social elite of Britain believed instinctively, if perhaps ignorantly, that significant synergies in defence would arise from the political merger of British North American provinces.[111] There was also in Britain a belief, perhaps better founded, that political integration would raise the 'standard of public capacity' in the colony, as The Times put it, by introducing 'higher objects of ambition and greater chance of obtaining renown and consideration in the eyes of the world.'[112] As Durham had suggested two decades earlier, British North American union would likely give 'greater scope and satisfaction to the legitimate ambitions of the most active and prominent persons' in the Canadas.[113]

The prospect of 'greater scope' was certainly not lost on British North

American statesmen. Their political ambitions undoubtedly were stimulated by more expansive visions of nationality.[114] In the Maritimes, the Canadians' allies 'saw in Confederation broader fields of enterprise, more spacious meadows of reward, an end to the littleness of provincial pastures,' as Waite evocatively puts it.[115] More immediately, the 'exhaustive festivities' of the Charlottetown and Quebec Conferences served to build and cement new personal and political relationships across the old provincial boundaries.[116] One delegate averred that had Howe been present at the Quebec Conference, even he would have 'played a very different part from what he has done.'[117] Whether this is true or not, overflowing hospitality and stately occasions certainly vested delegates with membership in a new, exclusive, and splendiferous club – and hence with an interest in maintaining the newly enlarged reach of their political world.[118]

Affiliative Trusteeship in the Carrying of Confederation in Canada

The process employed in carrying Confederation reflected on the concepts of representation operative in the colony at the time. Confederation in its final form was not subject to legislative, much less popular, ratification in any of the British North American provinces. It is interesting to speculate as to the likely reception of the BNA bill, had it returned to Canada for discussion and debate, rather than as a *fait accompli* of the imperial Parliament. Upper Canadian Grits might well have taken direction from George Brown and swallowed the broadened provision negotiated in London for minority rights in education. But a positive Lower Canadian reception in the press and legislature – particularly of what became Section 93(4) – would have been less assured. As for New Brunswick and Nova Scotia, Morton argues that it is 'certain' that even the Quebec Plan 'never could have been' accepted there.[119]

The plan for Confederation hatched at Quebec had enjoyed an extended incubation. Peripatetically contemplated for years, a larger federation had been formally proposed by the Cartier–Macdonald ministry in mid-1858, but had met with discouragement at that time by the Colonial Office.[120] The Derby ministry in London possessed insufficient political capital to undertake the project, so the absence of any ready consensus in the Maritimes provided a sufficient pretence to 'adjourn the question' for the time being.[121] Such grounds for refusal implied a future requirement of prior British North American agreement on a plan of union, a requirement that tended to yield the initiative to the colonists themselves.[122] In October

1863, and then in March and May 1864, Brown harked back to the abortive federation scheme of 1858 and proposed a select committee to seek a constitutional solution to the political stalemate.[123] In June, Brown was drawn, despite his preference for a simpler Canadian federation and his instinctive disdain for expedient alliances, to join a grand coalition cabinet committed to seeking British North American federation if readily feasible, or a purely Canadian federation, if not.[124]

Much of the substance of the plan for Confederation, determined by provincial delegates in September and October in Charlottetown and Quebec, was probably conceived during the intense Canadian cabinet discussions of August 1864.[125] In any case, the resulting Quebec Scheme of seventy-two resolutions was published in early November and placed before the Canadian legislature in January 1865.[126] Although the plan was ratified there by March, opposition in the Maritimes (see below) resulted in a delay of some twenty-one months before the London Conference of December 1866 could place the agreement in final form prior to legislative drafting. The British North America (BNA) Act was passed in March 1867 by British Parliament, which, as Morton notes, 'saw in it the first step of a very gradual disengagement in North America.'[127]

In Upper Canada, earlier in the process, several newspapers opposed to the Great Coalition had recoiled from the imputation that they were pressing for a constitutional convention, but they had insisted that 'Parliament should not make sweeping constitutional changes' without a mandate from the electorate.[128] This seems to have been a minority view among elites.[129] Conservative government newspapers emphatically denied the necessity of an election, the Montreal *Gazette*, for instance, maintaining, 'If there be a settled doctrine of the British Constitution it is that the people's representatives in Parliament are not mere delegates charged with certain specific duties, but are, in fact, the people in their political capacity.'[130] A similar position was adopted by the *Globe*.[131] Proposals for an early election were defeated decisively by votes of 84 to 31 and 79 to 19 on separate occasions.[132] As Hodgins notes, 'both George Brown and John A. Macdonald agreed that it would be unnecessary and unwise to hold an election before the implementation of Confederation.'[133] Macdonald seldom expressed interest in entering into what he had once termed 'fruitless discussion on abstract and theoretical questions of government,' but his constitutional designs (see below) revealed little faith in majoritarian democracy. Brown, as late as 1857, was more candid. Disparaging the American political system, he observed that in it 'the balance of power is held by the ignorant unreasoning mass.'[134] In Canada, the government that passed the Quebec Scheme considered it sufficient that enlightened public opinion, as reflected in the newspapers, generally supported the plan of Confederation.[135]

Maritime Opposition and Its Capitulation

For the small, relatively autonomous provinces of Nova Scotia and New Brunswick, Confederation promised to establish a geographically remote federal government in which they could expect to hold only 11 and 8 per cent, respectively, of elected seats.[136] Whatever the anticipated advantages of scale – perhaps the more sophisticated political leadership and administration expected in London, perhaps an independent destiny more permanently independent of the United States – such advantages seemed far less tangible and certain than the wrenching expansion of the boundaries of their political communities and the threatened vulnerability to an 'administration of strangers.'[137] The secrecy of the proceedings at Charlottetown did nothing to allay suspicions; the generous acceptance by the Canadians of equal Senate representation by region went unreported, as did their lofty speeches.[138] Perhaps unsurprisingly, then, a clear division soon manifested itself in Nova Scotia and New Brunswick between governments, which were inclined to support Confederation, and popular majorities. As one Nova Scotian politician, J.L. Shannon, recalled in 1874, 'I was pointed at ... as a man who had sold his country, and eventually lost my seat at the next election.'[139] Later anti-Confederate regimes revealed in government a more qualified position that indeed often seemed rather hollow compared with their trenchant criticism while in opposition.

In New Brunswick, the government of Samuel Leonard Tilley was defeated in the election of February/March 1865.[140] The anti-Confederate campaign maintained that political and economic integration with Canada offered fewer material benefits, and enclosed different priorities and greater costs than the already 'expanding commercial relations' with the much closer American Atlantic seaboard.[141] Naturally, election rhetoric was rather more florid. As Creighton paraphrases, Smith emphasized 'the faithlessness of the spendthrift and turbulent Canadians' and 'the certain exploitation and impoverishment of New Brunswick in the service of western Canadian expansion.'[142] Despite the strength of the case against Confederation in New Brunswick, however, opinion was not resolutely opposed, particularly among elites.[143] Indeed, about half of the leading figures within even the newly elected anti-Confederate government, including Albert Smith, quietly acknowledged support for union 'in the abstract.'[144] During its one year in office, the government revealed a marked discrepancy between its emphatic election rhetoric and its more ambiguous underlying position.[145] The election of June 1866 was won by Confederates, with 26 of 30 seats, having been aided by considerable Canadian financial assistance and the determined intervention of the Roman Catholic archbishop of Halifax.[146]

In Nova Scotia, Premier Charles Tupper meanwhile choose to wait and watch developments in New Brunswick, and so barely mentioned Confederation in the throne speech of February 1865.[147] Tilley's defeat then absolved Tupper of pressing forward with anything more searching than the old chestnut of *Maritime* union. Nevertheless, his government's known commitment to Confederation brought a serious loss in popularity, as evidenced by his party's defeat in the by-election of December that year.[148] Tupper declined again to mention Confederation in the throne speech of March 1866, and it was not until New Brunswick's legislative council had endorsed Confederation that Tupper at last moved a vague motion apparently committed only to renegotiating the Quebec Resolutions.[149] This decidedly weak embrace of the emergent constitutional order was as close as elected governments could come in the Maritimes to endorsing Confederation.

As in New Brunswick, parliamentary opposition also appeared to ebb in Nova Scotia in early 1866. The anti-Confederate leader, Liberal William Annand, very nearly capitulated at this time, probably because he had recognized several powerful sources of momentum behind Confederation, including the persuasive force of British opinion and the general insecurity in Nova Scotia in the face of the Fenian threat.[150] Five other Liberals, including William Miller, did cross the floor of the Nova Scotia legislature in April 1866 to add their support to the motion to proceed with renegotiating union.[151] Knowledge of the imperial disposition on the issue 'provided a discreet cover' for the opponents' capitulation in Nova Scotia and New Brunswick.[152] Sturgis notes that Miller offered 'a public defence [that was] entirely Burkean in its appeal to the importance of changed circumstances and the validity of the independent judgment of elected representatives. If the safety of the people were sacrificed then to what end were the wishes of the people?'[153] Providing representation to the 'nine-tenths of the people opposed,' once his stated objective, had apparently given way to probity.[154]

The various external cues did not resonate with nearly equal volume outside the political centre of Nova Scotia. Joseph Howe's campaign in the election of September 1867 to 'punish the scamps' won 18 out of 19 seats in the new federal House of Commons, and 36 of 38 seats in the provincial legislature.[155]

In continuing to oppose Confederation in Nova Scotia long after serious parliamentary opposition had faltered, Howe pressed an extra-parliamentary, 'popular-cultural' campaign against the union, raising a wide array of conceivable objections.[156] He played the popular-sovereignty card, asserting that 'I have no invincible objection to become a unionist provided anybody will show me a scheme which does not sacrifice the interests of the Maritime Provinces ... If an honest, practicable scheme of union can be arranged, let it be printed, perfect in all its parts ... and, when it has been aired in all the Provinces, let the people accept or reject it. If they voluntarily abandon their institutions, they will sincerely support the union. If tricked and bullied out of what they highly value, they will never be content.'[157] He played the nativist card, attacking the Confederate Catholic archbishop of Halifax, Thomas Connolly, as one who 'is not a Nova Scotian nor is it to be expected that he can feel or resent, as Nova Scotians do, the attempt to break down the institutions of the country.'[158] The imperial-trade card was also laid down ('Why then should Nova Scotia take blankets, broadcloth, crockery-ware or cutlery from Canada duty free, but tax the manufactures of Lancashire, Staffordshire, and Yorkshire? And yet this is just what these cunning Canadians are at'); so, too, the geographic card ('Anybody who looks at the map of British North America ... will perceive that it naturally divides itself into four great centres of political power'); the strategic card ('if we begin ... to build up new nationalities ... How long will the American people, thus challenged, be indifferent ...?'); and, finally, the anti-Canadian card ('Hemmed in by icy barriers at the north, and by a powerful nation on the south, shut out from deep-sea navigation for nearly half the year, with two nationalities to reconcile, and no coal, who will predict for her a very brilliant future).'[159]

Howe was much more 'master propagandist' than philosopher-king. Indeed, he was sufficiently malleable to have avowed in other circumstances, two years earlier, 'I am not one of those who thank God that I am a Nova Scotian merely, for I am a Canadian as well,' and shortly thereafter that he had 'always been in favour of uniting any two, three, four, or the whole five of the Provinces.'[160] True, this last statement was uttered when Howe was influenced by drink and Canadian company; however, it was not strictly inconsistent with Howe's long-standing and very mild caveat that political union with Canada ought not to come *simultaneously* with the building of a rail link between Canada and the Maritimes (as was now proposed), but rather *after*.[161] Indeed, Howe's public root-and-branch anti-confederate campaign substantially exceeded this much weaker position, and so it would appear that it was no deep-seated isolationism that gave rise to his role, but rather the conviction that sharp public objections deserved an advocate capable of presenting all plausible arguments against Confederation.

Howe's brief anti-Confederate phase is interesting, then, in that it provides an early instance of delegate-style representation – albeit one limited initially to the extra-parliamentary sphere.[162] The role of 'tribune' of the people remained vulnerable in this era to a fierce conservative critique.[163] The former governor of Nova Scotia, Sir Constantine Phipps, Lord Mulgrave, observed the shifting tenor of Howe's arguments and suggested that on that basis alone they 'could not be accounted of much worth.'[164] The Halifax *Evening Reporter* accused him of 'demagogue propensities.'[165] A contemporary biographer, the Presbyterian minister G.M. Grant, looked for spiritual malaise and found an 'egotism, which long feeding on popular applause, had developed into a vanity almost incomprehensible in a man so strong.'[166] Such views were clearly partisan, but the very resort to this critique reveals contemporary assumptions as to the impropriety of representing popular sentiments not closely associated with a politician's known prior views.

By mid-1868 it seemed clear to Howe that Confederation could not be stopped. His second campaign in London that winter had been unsuccessful in arousing any will to repeal the new union.[167] Upon his return he conveyed to Prime Minister Macdonald via Tilley that 'the reasonable men' of his party 'wanted an excuse to enable them to hold back the violent and unreasonable of their own party.'[168] In August 1868, discussions with the federal government brought a 'growing split between the "Dominion men" and the "locals".'[169] By October, Howe was rounding the 'sharp corner' of reaching terms for official Nova Scotian acquiescence.[170] The nominally 'better terms' secured for Nova Scotia included an increase in the federal subsidy to match that received by New Brunswick, an increased debt allowance, a cabinet position for Howe, and a role for him in the distribution of patronage at home.[171] Not surprisingly, provincial antis moved to outflank Howe, construing the accord as a 'sell-out.'[172] Some $30,000 in campaign spending, much of it contributed by Canadians, was required to overwhelm the concerted opposition to Howe's by-election campaign of April 1869.[173]

The defeat of anti-Confederates in the Maritimes represented a 'denial of popular feelings,' an integrative coup of affiliative trusteeship.[174] If, as

Sturgis puts it, 'Confederation was one of those ideals which asked men to put aside their petty concerns and jealousies,' it appears that government members were more apt to do so than opposition figures. Government leaders faced clear incentives to endorse an expanding polity, incentives that often crystallized through external exposure and alliance formation.[175] In both Nova Scotia and New Brunswick, anti-Confederate governments lost heart quickly, while defeated Confederates maintained their focus. The axis of deliberation linking the elected political elite of the Maritimes with counterparts in Canada and Britain was generally stronger than the bonds of local public opinion. This was certainly true of Tupper and Tilley, who carried on a continuous correspondence with the Canadians and took considerable political risks. But even erstwhile anti-Confederates in government were soon brought to face externally imposed constraints. Howe, by July 1868, had spent more time as an elected federal MP in England than he had in the Dominion, enough time, notwithstanding continued public opposition, to make him a hard-headed realist.

As noted, externally generated cues and incentives did not resound with equal volume through the ranks of the body politic; those who responded to them by acquiescing in agreements with outside interests faced an uphill struggle to gain popular acceptance at home. Although the political elite of the Maritimes did not by any means uniformly support Confederation, it does seem that government leaders responsible for these questions were, by virtue of their wider connections, subject to greater pressure and incentives to acquiesce in integration than the general public was. Where individual anti-Confederates were brought through their broader alliances to change causes without a public mandate, the integrative force of affiliative trusteeship in nineteenth-century British North American statecraft is again sustained.

Elements of Minority Protection and Their Reception

Confederation not only provided for the political integration of three provinces of British North America, but also enacted measures to regulate conflict between civil majorities and minorities. Three strains of minority protection in the BNA Act can be distinguished: specific guarantees granted to religious and linguistic minorities, anti-majoritarian provisions for the structure of government, and, at least on paper, centralizing elements that concentrated power at the federal level.[176] Affiliative trusteeship was significant to both the carrying and the substance of these aspects. The mode of representation clearly influenced the process through which popular opposition to elite-negotiated guarantees was circumvented. But the inherent limitations of alliance-based accommodation also restricted the faith French Canadians were prepared to place in federally assured protections. As Robert Vipond has pointed out, the immediate reception of Confederation, particularly in Quebec, lent a cross-current to the constitutional doctrine of the Fathers of Confederation and effectively amended it. Thus the capabilities and limitations of affiliative trusteeship emerge as responsible not only for carrying the ostensible conflict-regulating constitutional regime enacted with Confederation, but also for its dulling.[177]

Confederation provided certain weak guarantees for linguistic and religious minorities. The Quebec Resolutions and Section 133 of the BNA Act provided that French would be an official language in the federal houses of Parliament and courts, as well as, of course, in those of Quebec.[178] Section 93 of the BNA Act followed on Resolution 43(6) of the Quebec Conference, a resolution that had guaranteed, without advancing, minority rights in education.[179] Section 93(3) went further in enacting a ratchet provision for separate-school systems, entrusting the federal government with guarding against their disestablishment, not only if already existing by law, but also if 'thereafter established.'[180] It also, rather ingeniously, purported to extend the powers and privileges enjoyed at the Union by separate schools in Ontario to Quebec.[181] More significantly, Section 93(3–4) established a right of appeal to the federal government to intervene with remedial legislation against provincial infringements of specified minority rights in education; this was a provision that had been absent in the Quebec Resolutions. Still, the act did not establish denominational education systems where these were not already established by law, and therefore proved to have little legal impact outside Ontario and Quebec.[182]

The most immediate precursor to Section 93, the abortive Langevin Bill of July 1866, is significant, for in a different setting – the Assembly of the Province of Canada – it failed to secure comparable protections for separate denominational education.[183] The Langevin bill proposed to establish a separate board of education for Quebec Protestants and to guarantee it a proportionate share of school funding.[184] Upon its introduction, the coalition was met with a 'full-scale rebellion of its French-Canadian backbenchers,' who apparently harboured a 'negative attitude toward minority rights.'[185] An 'unwarranted mistrust' was espied in the demand for such rights (at the same time as it was objected that these would place 'constitutional barriers between the two faiths'); the unique concern of the bill with the Quebec Protestant minority was also found inequitable and insulting.[186] The Bell bill was a roughly hewn attempt by a private member to redeem this discrepancy and extend the same to Catholics in Canada West. But it was anathema to Upper Canadian members, who considered it incompatible with their largely non-denominational school system, and who, as noted earlier, were not generally inclined to advance Catholic schools any further than their alliances dictated.[187] The apparent double standard reflected in the hostile Protestant response to the Bell bill provided opponents to the Langevin measure with the leverage to force its withdrawal.[188]

Resolution 43(6) of the Quebec Conference and Section 93 of the BNA Act succeeded where the Langevin bill failed, in part because, in the former cases, the guarantees sought by Quebec Protestants were not uniquely entrenched for them, and indeed, in the BNA Act, appeared to follow partly from those already granted separate schools in Ontario.[189] But equally significant is that negotiations at the Quebec Conference in 1864, between Alexander Galt and Cartier in the fall of 1866, and among the select group of delegates in London in December that year, were all conducted without the participation of rank-and-file assembly members, and, in London, beyond the range of the artillery of British North American newspapers.[190] There, Cartier was also well insulated from the general hostility to minority rights at home. As for Brown, although he personally found constitutionally guaranteed minority rights 'most inconvenient and inexpedient,' he was kept safely in train in the coalition, and his complicity in carrying such rights, however discomfiting, lent itself only to muted protest.[191]

The second element of minority protection carried in the BNA Act consisted of the anti-majoritarian provision for bicameral government in Ottawa and Quebec. Federally, the Senate was to provide a sectional counterweight to population as the basis of representation. Appointive, and subject to a 'materially restrictive qualification for membership,' the Senate was also to place limits on the popular will, and hence protect, so Macdonald envisaged, the property rights of the wealthy 'minority.'[192] For the provinces, Quebec was treated differently from the others. In Ontario, parsimony and Macdonald's view that one chamber was adequate for 'subordinate legislatures' prevailed in favour of unicameral government.[193] In Quebec, an upper house was embraced by Bleus as lending extra weight to provincial rights there. It would also 'give better representation to the English minority,' a factor, according to Waite, that Cartier himself 'had hinted at.'[194]

Finally, a strongly centralized federation promised to prevent provincial infringements of minority rights. As Macdonald bluntly stated in his speech to the Quebec Conference, 'Thus we shall have a strong and lasting government under which we can work out constitutional liberty as opposed to democracy, and be able to protect the minority by having a powerful central government.'[195] Local governments were not to be sovereign, but rather to be 'subordinate to the General Government and Legislature,' in which sovereignty would be vested on a quasi-imperial model.[196] The federal government was entrusted with a broad range of enumerated powers as well as all powers not specifically granted to the provinces – Macdonald said, 'all the great subjects of legislation.'[197] A supervisory role, enacting a federal power to disallow provincial legislation and appoint provincial lieutenant governors, was also entrenched. Some Fathers of Confederation, such as Thomas D'Arcy McGee, conceived as late as September 1866 that such powers would be potent weapons against provincial oppression. As he declared, 'the minorities east and west have really nothing to fear ... the strong arm and the long arm of the Confederate power will be extended over them all, and woe be to the wretch on whom that Arm shall have to descend in anger.'[198] A government newspaper in Quebec agreed that the power of disallowance, in Morton's words, was 'necessitated by the position of minorities within minorities.'[199]

Yet during these years the Bleu press only rarely supported such a centralist view. In the weeks leading to the Quebec conference, Bleu papers had taken 'a position more extreme than that of the Bleu ministers' so as to provide flanking support for the party line.[200] Cartier's own organ, *La Minerve*, had stated, for instance, 'Lower Canada will never consent to allowing its particular interests to be regulated by the inhabitants of the other provinces ... We want a solid constitution ... but we demand above all perfect freedom and authority for the provinces to run their own internal affairs.'[201] Once the Quebec Resolutions were published, the Bleus 'were obliged to recognize the facts' and moderate their position. Nevertheless, they continued to exercise considerable liberality in advertising the agreement as establishing coordinate sovereignty on a conventional federal model.[202] They were obliged to do so, because although the three French-Canadian participants at the Quebec Conference might have accepted that their national privileges could be defended federally by French-Canadian ministers, this view was not broadly held in Quebec, least of all by the Rouge opposition.[203] The Rouges attacked the Quebec Plan as a 'legislative union disguised as a federation.'[204] Public Bleu declarations, as Arthur Silver notes, therefore tended to emphasize '*separation* (from Upper Canada) and *independence* (of Quebec within its jurisdictions)' in a marked derivation from the substance of an agreement that ostensibly imposed collectively significant, central checks on local majoritarian government in Quebec.[205]

A constitution, as Walter Bagehot famously argued, is as much a set of dynamic, 'efficient' conventions as a static, 'dignified' text.[206] The prevalence of the 'federal' interpretation in Quebec at this early and significant juncture formed a sort of 'hidden inner change,' in Bagehot's terms, in the incipient constitutional order.[207] Through the intense discourse on Confederation during late 1864 and early 1865, the sharply centralist elements were blunted. The quasi-imperial relationship between central and local governments earlier envisaged by Macdonald was discounted.[208] The sovereignty claimed for the general government was roundly acknowledged to inhere instead in the imperial power: it did not, it was agreed, flow upwards via colonial governments from the people.[209] Within Upper Canadian Reform political discourse, sovereignty was distinguished from legislative authority.[210] The provinces might not be sovereign, but absolute legislative jurisdiction would be devolved upon them in any case. The insistent protest of the Rouges that the general government might 'exercise its right of veto on all the legislation of the local parliaments' led Cartier to aver that 'the courts of justice will decide all questions in relation to which there may be differences between the two powers.'[211]

Leaving aside the earliest reception of the new constitution, it can be seen that the Fathers confronted a range of abstract possibilities in determining the shape of minority protection under Confederation. Given the choice of a federation over a legislative union, the roles of the two levels of governments in dealing with minority needs were at issue. Closely connected was the question of which minorities were to be protected and over what geographical extent. Another related issue was the extent to which majoritarian logic could be employed to protect provincially concentrated federal minorities.

The great advantage of relying upon majoritarian logic within the provinces was that the French-Canadian federal minority would be transformed into a provincial majority and could thus reliably be expected to seek and secure its own interests. On the other hand, this option did not really promise minority protection at all; it merely reduced the scale and multiplied the possible settings for the treading upon of minorities. By entrusting provincial governments with substantial autonomy to exert local majority will, this option also diminished the extent to which geographically dispersed minorities – not least francophone Catholics – could protect their interests by allying together federally.

But federal minority alliances would not in any case have been able to outface a determined, homogenizing elite majority at that level. Conservatives of an earlier generation had argued that, whereas smaller units of government 'were closer to the people' and 'preoccupied with local or parochial interests,' higher levels of government provided 'forums where more general or "higher" issues would prevail.'[212] Minorities of the Confederation era might well fear, however, that such 'higher' issues would include the pursuit of a uniform national identity. Moreover, in a growing federation there could be little certainty that French-Canadian participation would remain the *sine qua non* of successful parliamentary alliances, or that flanking manoeuvres by Protestant factions could be prevented that might effectively subvert the elite axis with sectarian popular appeals.

Several more tangible factors in Lower Canada entrained majoritarian government at the provincial level as the future bulwark of the French-Canadian minority. First, given the Rouge emphasis on fears of diminished autonomy, the separation argument was tactically useful for the Bleus. Second, as already noted, Lower Canadian constituents, apart from the English-speaking minority, appear to have cared little about minority rights in the abstract, even if they were clearly sympathetic to the particular plight of Upper Canadian Catholics.[213] Third, there was a natural, probably justified, concern that politicians of the Grit mould might break out of the harness of the bi-ethnic alliance and, as they had against the Bell bill, unite in English Protestant majority combinations. As one publication celebrating Confederation put it, 'we have a system of government which puts under the exclusive control of Lower Canada those questions which we did not want the fanatical partisans of Mr Brown to deal with ...'[214]

In short, political leaders in the era of affiliative trusteeship were certainly capable of statesmanship, particularly those veterans who had learned the tactical necessity of cross-ethnic alliances, hence of deviations from constituent opinion. But the era had long since passed when state affairs could be reliably foreseen to be dominated by instinctively cosmopolitan and tolerant statesmen. In the current epoch, French Canadians would understandably rather not take chances.

3.3 Exclusive Nationalism and Its Regulation following Confederation

The central constitutional dilemma, between federal activism and provincial autonomy, did not abate following Confederation. Many English Canadians, as Hodgins notes, shared 'neither the centralist views of their political leaders nor, in some cases, their generous spirit toward the

French.'[215] Cartier, and later Prime Minister Wilfrid Laurier, would confirm provincial majoritarianism as the guarantor of French-Canadian rights rather than risk pitting their minority federal position against dominant Anglo-Protestant opinion.[216] Despite the gradually increasing identification of French Canadians with French or Catholic causes beyond Quebec, senior elite support generally remained weak for the constitutional means and pluralist ends of McGee's envisioned 'long arm of the Confederate power.'[217]

The reluctance to intervene provincially did not stem mainly from antagonism to minorities among the federal elite or from acquiescence in the exclusive nationalism of growing mass movements. Yet the mixed record within the provinces tends to underscore the vulnerability of minority interests under the contemporary system of conflict regulation. The strength of affiliative trusteeship as a bulwark of minority rights was very much contingent upon the numerical weight of the constituency represented by a prospective alliance partner. Even the founders of Confederation, as Ramsay Cook notes, had been 'tolerant realists rather than theorists; where the minority existed in large enough numbers to make its presence felt, it was given recognition.'[218] As we will see shortly, in political communities in which minorities had declining or dispersed numbers and marginal economic influence, they, were vulnerable to an official exclusive nationalism of the majority.

New Brunswick Schools

The bill to establish free, centrally regulated schools supported by direct local taxation, introduced to the legislature of New Brunswick by the coalition government of George Hatheway and George King in April 1871, did not contain, nor had it contained during its three-year incubation, any reference to denominational education.[219] Strong Roman Catholic opposition had nonetheless been raised to the projected powerful school boards, which would supplant parish control without delivering the long-sought separate-school system.[220] Politically, the challenge for the government was to rally to the Common Schools bill the remaining two-thirds of the population, a portion of which, judging from petitions, was incensed by the feature of direct taxation.[221] Only after it had become clear that decisive support for the reforms in the government was not mirrored in popular opinion was the addition made of Section 60, which eliminated public financial support altogether for denominational schools. King, the architect of the Common Schools Act, but the leader of only a minority in the assembly, 'had to be pushed into supporting the non-sectarian clause in order to get the schools act through the legislature.'[222] The addition, approved 25 to 10 in May by the assembly, rallied Protestant opinion, which, apart from an element of the Anglican Church, had declared in favour of non-sectarian schools.[223]

Petitions from New Brunswick Catholics and pleas by federal MPs John Costigan and Timothy Anglin for redress were met by John A. Macdonald with a closely reasoned legal argument justifying non-intervention.[224] Schools in general were a provincial matter under the BNA Act; Catholic schools in New Brunswick were not protected by Section 93(3), which was expressly limited to separate school systems existing 'by Law.' While Costigan and Anglin might argue under pressing exigencies that Catholics enjoyed legally vested rights in denominational schools under the Parish Schools Act of 1858, Section 8 of that act had only accommodated Catholic variants of prayer, and that within a framework premised on individual conscience and undifferentiated 'Parish Schools.'[225] Anglin, who himself had earlier exhibited acute concern over the shortcomings of Section 93 in relation to Catholic schools in New Brunswick, noted that even the lawyers preparing legal challenges on the question found it difficult to accept his innovative interpretation.[226] As Cartier explained to his co-religionists in Quebec, 'the law is hard but it is the law.'[227]

Yet the political debate over disallowance was a broader and more serious matter than legal arguments over Section 93 in relation to the Parish Schools Act.[228] Technically, federal disallowance was not restricted to provincial infringements of minority rights in education, nor even to matters of jurisdiction.[229] Morally, many federal MPs could not absolve themselves so quickly of responsibility for redressing a flagrant injustice that few parliamentarians could deny. Costigan's annual motions for federal intervention gained supporters among Quebec MPs, both Bleu and Rouge. Cartier and the Bleu premier of Quebec, P.-J.-O. Chauveau, were not among them. Cartier responded to Costigan's first motion in May 1872 that it 'tended to place the rights of the Catholics of the Dominion in the hands of a Protestant majority.'[230] But Cartier's strategic constitutionalism did not necessarily appeal to the sentiments of the Quebec electorate and was criticized by such Ultramontanes as Bishop Ignace Bourget of Montreal, whose delayed support probably contributed to Cartier's defeat in the August 1872 election.[231] After the campaign, which featured much discussion in Quebec of the situation in New Brunswick, French-Canadian members from Quebec voted 36 to 4 in support of Costigan's second motion for disallowance, which passed 98 to 63 on 14 May 1873 but was set aside by Macdonald's government for constitutional doctrine and shrewd politics.[232]

Although polite parliamentary disapprobation was expressed to New Brunswick in 1872 and 1875, it is probable that the compromise reached in the province in August 1875 was precipitated mainly by the Caraquet riots during the preceding winter.[233] At the election held in June 1874, 36 of 41 members of the provincial legislature had been elected on pledges of good common-school faith. So the negotiations and ultimate compromise reached by the cabinet with Catholic members of the assembly acting on behalf of John Sweeney, the bishop of St John, were necessarily kept discrete.[234] As it eventually came to light some eighteen years later, it was officially agreed that Catholic students could combine in schools not necessarily in their own vicinity, that they could be taught by teachers educated within Roman Catholic orders, that they could read materials sensitive to a Catholic view of history, and that they could receive denominational religious education at school, albeit outside regular school hours.[235] Substantively, this fell well short of the institutionalized separate-school system that many Catholics would have preferred. A critical historian could certainly also emphasize, 'the furtive nature of the negotiations, the pushing aside of the Board of Education, and the departure from a proper democratic process in virtually amending a law without consulting the legislative body.'[236] Yet as a feat of minority accommodation, the deal that, 'in a sense, legalized within the non-sectarian system ... schools of a sectarian bias' succeeded: new schools were welcomed in Catholic areas and calm was restored for at least a decade and a half until a rearguard local campaign again brought sectarian grief.[237]

The issue of Catholic education in New Brunswick demonstrated the potential for sectarian majority combinations where a somewhat unstable executive lacked preponderant influence within the legislature and a religious minority could command only 10–15 per cent of the seats there. Majoritarian exclusivism in this case was not a function so much of the senior political elite taking an homogenizing doctrine to heart, but rather, of the strong influence within the legislature of popular political opinion on an issue that would obviously and deeply penetrate daily life. Successful management of conflict in such a case depended upon executive control of administration, as well as a high degree of secrecy in negotiations.

Reaction to the Jesuits' Estates Act in Ontario

The pervasive chauvinism of the self-described 'Anglo-Saxon' majority of

Canada collided in the 1880s and early 1890s with the political expression of national and religious ardour in Quebec.[238] The Jesuits' Estates Act (1888), passed by the Parti National government of Premier Honoré Mercier, was emblematic of Ultramontane leanings in Quebec. It drew a range of exclusive nationalist responses within the federal, provincial, and mass political spheres of Ontario. Reaction was most tightly constrained within the bi-ethnic web of federal party alliances; by contrast, it ran rampant within the burgeoning mass movement centred in Ontario that grew specifically to check French-Canadian cultural and religious self-assertion. Ontario provincial politics was caught in the middle: it featured a provincial Conservative party that embarrassed its federal counterpart by resorting to anti–French-Canadian appeals in campaigns against the dominant, and more inclusive provincial Liberal party.[239]

The measure that elicited such great offence among Protestants paid the Roman Catholic Church $400,000 as moral compensation for the usurpation by the colonial government in 1800 of the estate of the defunct Society of Jesus, which had been abolished in 1773 by Pope Clement XIV.[240] Control over the estate had since passed to the Lower Canadian legislature, and then to the Province of Quebec, expressly for the support of higher education.[241] For equity, a Protestant committee for higher education was granted funds under the act proportionate to the Protestant share of the Quebec population.[242] As Pope Leo XIII was himself a party to the settlement, having conferred with Premier Mercier at the Vatican, the measure exemplified for opponents the direct influence of the Catholic hierarchy in Quebec politics.[243]

The Jesuits' Estates Act rankled in Ontario because it defied the culturally engrained expectation there that the Anglo-Protestant tradition, with its close limits upon religion in organized political and community life, would prevail in Canada. Writing of the late 1880s, Margaret Evans observes 'an upsurge of narrow English-speaking nationalism' that 'insisted that the Canadian identity was essentially Protestant and English.'[244] James Miller notes that behind 'Protestant political exclusiveness' lay the beliefs that Catholicism was 'inimical to the social well-being and material progress' of Canada, that Ultramontane Catholicism would have a deleterious 'impact on political life in a plural society,' and that the Catholic clergy had 'an inveterate enmity against the liberal education of the people.'[245] The anti-Jesuit crusade that ensued was not limited to a 'lunatic fringe,' but engaged the 'presumption of Anglo-Saxon superiority' of the majority.[246]

Reaction was not wholly confined to the people. Federal Conservative MP Colonel William O'Brien rejected with colleague D'Alton McCarthy the counsel of fellow caucus members in submitting a resolution to the House of Commons in March 1889 for disallowance. Macdonald's government, which had already declined to intervene, was placed in a delicate political position. O'Brien's resolution was clearly in sympathy with the 'terrible feeling all through every part of Ontario' observed by a Tory newspaper editor.[247] One speaker in the ensuing debate argued that the Canadian provinces 'should be Anglo-Saxon commonwealths' and that the act would 'retard ... the assimilation of these races.'[248] A Quebec Protestant referred to a 'disposition' within the Quebec government to give 'clerical authority' undue influence.[249] The motion itself referred to Jesuits' 'intolerant and mischievous intermeddling with the functions of civil government.'[250]

Yet very few MPs were inclined to accept these views, and despite Macdonald's assurance that dissidents would not have to quit the party, only 8 Conservatives and 5 opposition Liberals supported the motion, as against 188 opposed.[251] McCarthy, who had mused since at least 1886 of a Conservative realignment along a Protestant axis, wrote afterwards to Macdonald, 'The duty of the Conservative party is to hold by and lean on the English Provinces, whilst so far as I can understand yours is rather to depend on Quebec.'[252] In levelling this familiar critique, McCarthy attacked the prevailing pattern of alliances in connection with the latitude, deemed excessive, granted to French Canadians to hold by their own delineation of matters of moral conscience and the role of public institutions.

Ontario provincial politics also established language and religion as the key tactical fronts in the battle against the supposedly expanding reach of French-Canadian culture. Catholic schools were protected of course under the BNA Act, but this did not prevent the Conservative opposition of William Meredith from grasping at the demon of clerical influence in educational policy, as it did in the 1886 and 1890 elections.[253] The use of French as the language of education in the growing numbers of Franco-Ontarian public schools was also criticized, both in its own right, and because such schools often employed Catholic text books.[254] Premier Oliver Mowat's Liberal government had already attempted to ensure that English be taught as at least a second language in Ontario schools. George Ross, Minister of Education, appealed to both imperial magnanimity and the interests of Confederation in reply to an opposition argument that 'the will of the people of Ontario was that it should remain an English-speaking Province,' and that therefore 'extensive teaching of French in the Public schools' must be condemned.[255] Exhibiting awareness of the federal ramifications of provincial policy, Ross responded,

Shall, we, sir, who have taken from that powerful and mighty people the land which they had subdued by their courage, shall we say they are an alien race simply because by the accident of the power of British arms on the Heights of Abraham in 1759 the country has become ours? Is that British magnanimity? ... French Canadians have [since] given a large amount of aid towards the literature and science of the country. We cannot build up this Confederation without the sympathy and active aid of the Province of Quebec, and any one who seeks to put race against race must have his mind made up that Confederation should be broken up to its original fragments.[256]

Continuing with his appropriation of the imperialist rhetoric then in vogue, Ross construed the acceptance of linguistic diversity and the 'greatness of mind' of leading statesmen as the very foundations of the empire.[257] At the conclusion of Ross's 'Great Speech,' 'occupants of the Government benches on both sides of the House burst into ringing cheers, which lasted for several minutes.'[258]

Extra-parliamentary opposition crystallized a few months later in the so-called Equal Rights Association (ERA) founded in June 1889 in Toronto at the Anti-Jesuit Convention. A mass meeting of hundreds of Protestant clergymen, Orangemen, and elected delegates from many Ontario centres, the convention built upon the organizational structure and middle-class demographics of a temperance movement.[259] After various speakers railed at the political 'encroachments of the French Catholic Church' and at the Estates' Act for slowing assimilation, the convention defined its core objectives: 'supremacy of English' in education, an end to Ultramontane meddling in temporal matters, and aggressive policies to curtail separate-school funding.[260] McCarthy, who did not attend but provided intellectual leadership after the convention, was most exercised by the failure of the French Canadians to assimilate, for 'this is a British country' and the modern 'science of language' showed the impossibility of national union without a common language.[261] In 'thought and feeling,' French Canadians must be anglicized. By its apogee, the ERA had established at least thirteen branches in Toronto alone, and mustered 156,000 signatures in Ontario and Quebec for a petition for disallowance.[262]

Although McCarthy felt no compunctions about distilling an exclusive nationalism predicated on language, even he was wary of the religious exclusivism avowed by the Protestant Protective Association (PPA).[263] A secret society whose members swore not to employ, or (later) not to 'keep company' with Roman Catholics, the PPA sought to exclude Catholics from public office and abolish separate schools. The organization claimed as of January 1894 some 49,800 members, organized in 439 councils through-out Canada.[264] According to James Watt, the PPA gained 'national promi-nence' when Sir John Thompson became prime minister, for the 'very fact that a Roman Catholic convert from Methodism should have the highest office in the land aroused the bitter wrath and fears of narrowminded Protestants.'[265]

While the ERA and PPA enjoyed considerable success as fast-burning mass protest movements, in electoral politics the two lacked consistent strategy, organization, and the power to define the main agenda of debate. In some cases, the movements nominated independent candidates. Else-where, candidates of the existing, major parties were 'catechized,' pledging their support for a movement's agenda.[266] Largely on this basis, members of the PPA were elected in 1894 to the Ontario legislature for fourteen, mainly Conservative, ridings, including all four seats in Toronto.[267] But that represented the high-water mark of the movements' political influ-ence in Ontario.[268] Mowat was careful in the early 1890s not to invite sectarian controversy within the realm of provincial politics.[269] Federally, during the election of 1891 the leaders of both major bi-ethnic parties conceived no advantage in politicizing burning linguistic and religious controversies. Attention was focused instead on policy concerning trade with the United States.[270]

The impotence of official exclusive nationalism in Ontario politics, even in the shape of the provincial Conservative party of William Meredith, demonstrates that the demotic exclusive nationalism of the ERA and PPA, despite their deep roots and popularity, were not political wild cards. Meredith's failure to build a winning Protestant front may have resulted in part because he had 'taken up Equal Rights too late and too obviously with an eye on the [1890] election.'[271] Yet on the whole, Equal Rights and the PPA proved substantial liabilities. Not only did they alienate large num-bers of Roman Catholic voters from the provincial Conservative party, but they also brought spirited interventions from both federal political parties that undermined Meredith's credibility and support among moderate Prot-estants.[272] That such federal–provincial incongruities should exist and be brought to bear on provincial politics can be readily explained: while the political infertility of an English-speaking, Protestant official exclusive nationalism may have disappointed some participants in Ontario provin-cial politics, few could conceivably have placed much stock in McCarthy's iconoclastic exclusivism within a federal political sphere of alliances and supporting traditions spanning French and English Canada.[273] In federal political influence in Ontario, a kind of 'long arm' of Confederation demonstrably reached at least as far as Toronto from Ottawa, even if it proved too short to intervene decisively in New Brunswick, or, in the coming years, in Manitoba.

Fin de Siècle in Manitoba: The Defeat of Dualism

It is somewhat misleading to describe the coordinated assault on the cultural presence of French-speaking Catholics in Manitoba in 1889–90 as the 'Manitoba School Question.' Crippling Catholic schools financially, after the manner of New Brunswick, was but one element of the policy. Eliminating the official use of French in government and the courts was another.[274] So, too, was the manipulation of immigration policy: in 1889 only $450 of the $20,000 spent on immigration was spent in Quebec.[275] This conjoint program reflected the belief that Manitoba could not thrive as a bicultural or polyglot society and that homogenization should proceed along British cultural lines; it also hinted at the 'heritage of local hatred.'[276] There have been few clearer instances in Canada of official exclusive nationalism. Consideration must be given to the causes, to the implications of this episode for a theory of exclusive nationalism, and to the ponderous efforts to regulate the conflict federally. The main events will first be reviewed briefly.

On 1 August 1889, the Winnipeg *Sun*, the government newspaper, announced that the government had 'resolved' to legislate in the next session to abolish the use of French as an official language and that it would also attempt to find some way to 'knock out' separate schools, whatever protection the Manitoba Act (1870) had ostensibly provided.[277] The policy was elaborated during the following week by two cabinet ministers. One of these, Attorney-General Joseph Martin, shared the podium with a touring D'Alton McCarthy, who expressed ERA dogma and encouraged Manitobans in curtailing 'the rights of the French language and Catholic education.'[278] Legislation was introduced to these ends in January 1890 and passed in March as the Manitoba School Act and the Official Language Act.

As in New Brunswick, the causes of the assault on dualism did not include a popular movement militating for exclusivist policy. Yet if popular demands were not voiced, the capital to be made by the move within both popular and legislative politics was nevertheless enormous. The craven malfeasance, however marked, of the ministry of Premier Thomas Greenway therefore remains less interesting than broader social and political developments. Foremost among such developments was the minoritization of Franco-Manitobans. As the Brandon *Sun* trumpeted on 17 October 1889, 'To-day the French from the point of numbers, need not be consulted.'[279] Having constituted about half of the population in 1870, the share of French-speaking Catholics had been reduced by 1891 to a tenth; Catholics as a whole, to an eighth.[280]

Among the seven-eighths of the population not Catholic, homogenization enjoyed considerable latent appeal. William Morton observes that the 'great majority of English-speaking Protestants were quietly and resolutely opposed' to the dual educational system and would have eventually sought 'major modifications.'[281] Behind such views Robert Clague discerns the 'inflated prejudices of the frontier' together with the 'racial and religious bigotry' of Anglo-Protestant society across Canada.[282] A vicious circle reflecting the interrelation and effects of such sentiments can be schematically traced from the fear of assimilation and coordinate isolationism of the French Métis, through the imperial subordination of Manitoba to Canada at the hands of Anglo-Protestant migrants, through the rebellion of the Métis (and others) in 1869–70 and 1885; through the execution of leader Louis Riel in November of the latter year; through the reactive assertiveness of the Ultramontanes under Mercier embodied in the Jesuits' Estates Act; through the Anglo-Protestant counter-reaction, already discussed, in Ontario, a reaction that was disseminated in Manitoba by the constant flow of Ontario migrants, the print media, and even by McCarthy's personal appearance.[283] The terminus as well the beginning of this (particular) cycle was the mutual fear and antagonism, now renewed, of Anglo-Protestant migrants and French Catholics in Manitoba.

Yet even relatively cool heads could conclude that the new pioneer society in the West would do well to extricate itself from the irredeemable conflict of the old dual Dominion. The 'melting pot' and, practically speaking, the 'system of "national" schools on the American model' beckoned.[284] Constraints of imagination and perhaps resources made multiculturalism an imponderable successor to biculturalism. As the Rev. Dr George Bryce pleaded,

The problem facing Manitoba was unique. The province was made up of people of many nations. Its speech is polyglot, with the majority English-speaking; it has eight or ten thousand Icelanders; it has fifteen thousand German-speaking Mennonites; it has some ten or twelve thousand French-speaking half-breeds and Quebecers, it has considerable numbers of Polish Jews ... The Icelanders petitioned the educational board ... for liberty to have the Lutherans prepare their candidates for confirmation in the schools: the

Mennonites with singular tenacity have demanded separate religious schools ...
What could patriotic Manitobans do?[285]

Franco-Manitobans were prepared to limit their demands for separate
schools to communities where the population was entirely Roman Catholic or was sufficiently dense to support several schools.[286] But multiple,
peacefully coexisting communities of varying permeability had no place
within the new western Utopia.

Within the Legislative Assembly until the election of 1878, Franco-
Manitobans had held the balance of power, even where they had not held
an outright majority.[287] Subsequently, they had been placed 'in a decided
minority,' and therefore 'sought to safeguard their position through a
policy of political alliances.'[288] The price of their participation had been the
preservation of their schools and of the official use of French.[289] This they
had been granted first by the Conservatives, and then, in January 1888, by
Greenway and Martin on behalf of the Liberals.[290] The precipitous transfer
of allegiance to the Liberals at a time when the Conservatives of John
Norquay had been sharply listing in the assembly unfortunately made the
Franco-Manitoban bloc appear as loose cargo, and this had diminished their
alliance value below even their paltry share of legislative representation.[291]

By 1889, the concessions skilfully wrung from the Liberals the previous
year seemed to be politically superfluous, given that the French Canadians
had become 'politically impotent.'[292] Meanwhile, the Greenway regime no
doubt enjoyed a less comfortable political position than it would have
liked. Despite having raised expectations through a celebrated confrontation with the federally backed Canadian Pacific Railway, the government
had not delivered the cheaper commodity transportation sought by every
grain farmer in the province.[293] The temptation to legislate against an
unpopular minority, thus defying an unpopular Dominion government,
was no doubt immense. Clague is certainly not incorrect in explaining the
Greenway government's assault on the distinctive French-Canadian presence as 'catering to popular prejudice in order to retain the party in
office.'[294]

Yet, most governments must 'cater' to some dimensions of popular
opinion. Many do so, of course, without usurping the position of minorities. The Greenway Liberals, moreover, hardly held on the face of things an
uncommonly weak position: in the election of July 1988, only the previous
summer, they had won 33 of 38 seats.[295] Therefore, the main explanatory
factor is not so much that the collapse of the administration was 'imminent,' but rather that the ties that had earlier and elsewhere bound mid-

and late-nineteenth-century politics had slackened. The principal cross-ethnic alliance in the province had lost its restraining force as the share of power of Franco-Manitobans had been substantially eroded. Thus the endeavour of accommodation within the sphere of legislative politics was supplanted by the limitless political commerce of maintaining electoral viability. Thus the web of power connecting independent brokers in creating and re-creating suitable combinations within the assembly gave way in strategic significance to the axis linking a maturing party with an increasingly dependent and exigent popular majority.[296] As the era of affiliative trusteeship slammed shut in Manitoba, official exclusive nationalism immediately ensued.

The federal government, while not unanimous, could on the whole have little sympathy for the attacks on biculturalism in the West. This much is clear from the federal response to the similar offensive launched by the Legislative Assembly of the North-West Territories in October 1889. That body, which had been elected for the first time in June 1888 without yet being empowered as a responsible government, resolved to petition for the repeal of Sections 14 and 110 of the federal North-West Territories Act (1875).[297] This would have eliminated the legal basis of separate schools and of French as an official language of the assembly proceedings, journals, and ordinances, as well as of the courts.[298] The federal response came in the debate in January 1890 upon the introduction of McCarthy's private member's bill, which specifically advanced the thrust for unilingualism in the Territories.[299] Its preamble, expressing the bill's real point, began: 'It is in the interests of national unity in the Dominion that there should be community of language among the people of Canada ...'[300] The motion put was defeated 149 to 50 on amendment, but not before a Liberal opposition MP, David Mills, plainly exposed the fundamental incongruence of McCarthy's broader, exclusive nationalist agenda with liberalism.[301]

> Does the hon. gentleman understand the character and bearings of the demands that he is making on behalf of the State? Does he know that he is demanding of the French Canadians sacrifices that are dearer than life itself? Does he not know that he is asking for the destruction of one of the most important rights for the existence of which governments are maintained? The state is not an end, the state is a means to an end ... It has not the right to undertake to destroy the mental vision of one section of a population with the design of creating it anew.[302]

Macdonald's famous quip was equally emphatic: 'I believe it would be impossible if it were tried, and it would be foolish and wicked if it were possible.'[303] Undeterred, McCarthy introduced a bill each year from 1891 through 1896 to eliminate the French language as well as the school clauses of the North-West Territories Act.[304] None received the assent of Parliament, most disappearing after first reading.

The acrimonious debate on French-Canadian rights in the Territories confirmed Macdonald's fears of such issues, making him, as well as Thompson and Liberal leader Wilfrid Laurier, for that matter, anxious to avoid a sequel.[305] The legally complex Manitoba Schools Act was instead referred to the courts, to determine in the first instance (in the Barrett case, 1890–2) whether the Schools Act contravened the minority rights in education enjoyed 'by law or practice' guaranteed by Section 22(1) of the Manitoba Act ('no,' said ultimately the Imperial Privy Council in July 1892); and, then, in the second instance (the Brophy case, 1893–5), whether a right of appeal to the federal government lay for the aggrieved minority under Sections 93(3) of the BNA Act and 22(2) of the Manitoba Act, and whether the federal government had the power to take remedial action ('yes' on both counts said ultimately the imperial Privy Council in January 1895).[306] This returned the issue inescapably to the political realm.

In March 1895 the Conservative cabinet of Prime Minister Mackenzie Bowell issued a remedial order demanding that Manitoba restore separate schools supported from public-school funds.[307] But the weak Bowell government at the end of its term failed to reach a negotiated settlement with the Liberal Manitoba government or to pass stronger, remedial legislation. Laurier, pragmatic consensus-seeker that he was, was held tightly in the cleft of the Liberal party, which was seriously divided on the issue, largely English against French.[308] In this predicament, Laurier first prevaricated and then walked the borderline between ambiguity and duplicity.[309] Campaigning in his riding in Quebec East in May 1896, Laurier promised, 'if conciliation fails, I will have to exercise the constitutional recourse provided by law, recourse that I will exercise completely and fully.'[310] By contrast, in Toronto a month later Laurier maintained that he would 'never consent to the coercion of another province.'[311] Provincial rights, before *this* audience, were the 'very basis of Confederation.'[312]

Laurier's extreme contortions to avoid falling into the sort of chasm opening within the Conservative party reflected the increasing strains upon the federal ethnic alliances that at the height of affiliative trusteeship at mid-century had underwritten accommodation and conflict regulation.[313] The unwinding of that form may have owed something to the emergence of less tractable centres of informed opinion, including contemporary mass movements and the increasingly independent print media, both of which tended to shift the role of politicians from trustee to that of malleable opinion broker. Laurier's stance was also pressed upon him in some measure by the urgency of maintaining the bi-ethnic alliance within the Liberal party, by the need to avoid inroads by PPA men in Ontario, and by a full expectation of settling the matter through the 'sunny ways' of negotiating with provincial Liberals in Manitoba.[314] A flippant appeal to both sides of an emotional issue bisecting party lines was, of course, also the path of least electoral resistance: Laurier's Liberals defeated the Conservatives 118 to 88 in the June election; only one member of the PPA and two McCarthyites were elected in Ontario.[315]

The Laurier–Greenway agreement, concluded after the election, restored to Manitobans the right to receive denominational religious education at their schools, and, to Franco-Manitobans and others, the privilege of bilingual education, not limited to French.[316] The settlement clearly offered, as the ensuing Papal Encyclical alluded, only 'partial satisfaction' to Catholics.[317] Notably, it did not permit for the segregation of students within separate schools, nor for infusing the core curriculum with Catholic moral precepts. Still, as long as the deal held – the provision for bilingual education endured only until 1916 – the agreement offered a modest corrective to the policy of 1890.[318] Compromise, not justice in any broader sense, defined the upper limit of federally induced compliance with the 'spirit of Confederation' by the close of the nineteenth century.[319]

3.4 Analysis and Relevance to Theory

British North America witnessed significant progressions during the nineteenth century in the dual pattern of political representation and conflict regulation. Gradual constitutional evolution in representation limited elite interest in mass mobilization, reducing the risks of demotic exclusive nationalism discussed in relation to earlier periods. During the Union period, vestiges of imposed statecraft gave way to government increasingly responsible to the legislature. Politicians exercised their function through the alliances they formed and maintained there, alliances that generally favoured integration and constrained the disintegrative dynamic of exclusive nationalism.

Strangely in retrospect, exclusive nationalist policy had earlier seemed from the distance of London a necessary response to the perceived risk of French-Canadian disloyalty. But in the event, the majority was not denominated, as had been expected, by a monolithic, Anglo-Protestant bloc.

Instead, a French–English alliance under Union jointly pursued a government more responsive to local leadership and less to aristocratic discretion and imperial direction. The relaxation of official exclusive nationalist policy occurred largely because, in the judgment of governors such as Elgin, the new political bridge could withstand the rapid currents of ethnic conflict.

Still, the achievement of responsible government did not entail popular sovereignty in the full sense. Successful alliances governed at arm's length from popular opinion. Although the Clear Grits sought to pander to the various shades of stridently anti-Catholic opinion in Upper Canada, they were obviously an unsuitable alliance partner for Lower Canadian political interests and therefore carried less influence than more moderate and discrete Conservatives. As Head put it, forming a government required a Canadian politician to 'school his mind to principles of tolerance' and to 'learn to respect the feelings and even the prejudices of others who differ widely from himself.'[320] Minority accommodation thus depended upon imperatives stemming from cross-ethnic alliances and, in turn, upon politicians taking liberties with constituent opinion, yielding a pattern closer to trustee than to delegate representation. Such accommodation did not generally depend upon the ready cultural tolerance and cosmopolitanism of aristocratic statesmen.

The forces favouring alliance formation were sufficiently strong to move even the religiously bigoted George Brown, for example, to prepare to welcome Roman Catholic priests into Upper Canadian schools, notwithstanding that Brown had manifestly not undergone a personal conversion to embrace institutional pluralism. Although federal elements were imposed upon the union, and some would have ignored practical difficulties and imposed them still further to limit the legislative domain of bisectional alliances, others believed that representation was legitimately given not only to geographical sections, but also to cross-cutting minorities – in this period, to linguistic-religious constituencies.

Confederation was carried by a broad alliance prepared in several instances to challenge local public opinion. Motivation was lent by the desire to bring new allies to bear on the Canadian political predicament, as well as by the intrinsic attraction of an enlarged political sphere. Externally generated cues registered unevenly within the bodies politic of the Maritimes, but were clearly influential in curtailing opposition. Strong popular opposition in Nova Scotia and New Brunswick found willing elite advocates. Such advocates were nevertheless generally only half-hearted isolationists, readily capable of embracing the inevitable, even unilaterally. Elite discretion was also employed to carry contentious elements of minority protection, which, although limited in reach and effectiveness, were not obviously supported by most segments of majority constituent opinion. The contingent and precarious nature of conflict regulation under affiliative trusteeship limited the attempt to attain a highly centralized union, which, despite a greater capacity, was envisioned as having an uncertain propensity to protect federal minorities.

While the marked tension between minority rights and majoritarian democracy had been managed, if not without strain during the Union period, the precariousness of affiliative trusteeship as a bulwark of religious and linguistic minorities became most evident in provincial politics following Confederation. Provincial political alliances, particularly in New Brunswick and Manitoba, came to depend little upon the participation of religious minorities. In the absence in those provinces of the unilateral accommodation characteristic of the early colonial regime or of federal intervention beyond a temporizing, moral suasion, minorities were therefore vulnerable. Anglo-Protestant chauvinism and anti-Catholicism, characteristic of much of Canadian society, were unbridled and found expression in initiatives of varying breadth in these outlying provinces to impose a uniform civic identity. Accommodation, to the limited extent it was practicable, was slow, dependent upon executive discretion, and, in New Brunswick, clandestine.

In summary, the period at hand illuminates several critical factors limiting the sway of exclusive nationalism and fostering accommodation: the relatively smooth unrolling of self-government ostensibly founded on popular consent; the presence of parliamentary cross-ethnic alliances commensurate with a pattern of trusteeship; and the enjoyment by minorities of sufficient numbers and significant levels of parliamentary representation. In the absence of these factors, particularly in the face of strengthening, mutually dependent relations between state and society, and the rising tendency for parliamentary politics to collapse entirely into the popular political axis, the potential for official exclusive nationalism remained considerable. In the next chapter we discuss a twentieth-century instance in which such risks were realized at a point of rapid acceleration in popular political mobilization.

FOUR

Ethnic Delegate Representation and the Rise of Official Exclusive Nationalism in Quebec

Several twentieth-century cases of exclusive nationalism in Canada well deserve the close analysis they have received in recent years. Anglo-Canadian nativism has been examined in the broad-based hostility in Western Canada towards immigrants and pointed expectations of 'Anglo-conformity' prevalent through the end of the Second World War.[1] Pervasive anti-semitism throughout Canada has been shown as responsible for the failure to accommodate more Jewish refugees before and during that war.[2] In keeping with the narrative of the preceding chapters, however, the emphasis of this chapter rests with the twentieth-century development and rise of official exclusive nationalism in Quebec. It is within that society (and jurisdiction) that the same cultural confrontation received its most sustained development and articulation in the form of exclusive nationalism. Federal responses to developments in Quebec, apart from a brief consideration of the effects of the conscription crises, are deferred until the final chapter.

The centrepiece of this chapter, the episode that much of the remainder seeks to explain, is the acquisition of 'official' status of exclusive nationalism in Quebec politics during and following 1968, when a significant political party, the Parti Québécois, committed itself to imposing French-language unilingualism. While similar policies had already been witnessed elsewhere in Canada (see the previous chapter, on the various schools crises), the extent of this official commitment to exclusive nationalism was unprecedented in Quebec politics. I want to argue that popular political mobilization was the major driver of the official political acceptance of exclusive nationalism, and that, when viewed in historical perspective, commonly emphasized factors – francophone ambitions to reverse urban ethnic inequality, and fresh concerns surrounding cultural survival – can only partially account for such mobilization.

As for the 'historical perspective' I propose to offer, I argue first that ethnic economic competition, and fears of cultural survival in twentieth-century Quebec, long predate the Quiet Revolution, suggesting that these were less dynamic causal variables for the later official exclusive nationalism than commonly recognized. I will also submit that exclusive nationalism was an articulate ideology well before the Quiet Revolution, and had discernible popular appeal. Its earlier lack of impact on the state should be attributed to its rejection by established political elites; to the cooptation and absorption of nationalists through an electoral alliance; and to the lack of dependence of political legitimacy upon participative democracy, even among exclusive nationalists, such that popular opinion in earlier years had little direct, even indirect, impact on state policy. On this basis I conclude that the onset of official exclusive nationalism in Quebec in the late 1960s owes more than commonly understood to the growth and modernization of the state, to the associated rise of a more active form of popular political participation (stimulated, too, by a demonstration effect of anti-colonial militancy), and the evolution of the pattern of political representation.

While the nub of discussion concerns the causal sequence giving rise to exclusive nationalism during the 1960s, roughly half of the chapter deals with antecedent developments in Quebec politics. Part of this preliminary discussion is preoccupied with why something did *not* arise (why official exclusive nationalism was *not* a factor earlier, despite the evident popular appeal of the doctrine), and is therefore more speculative than what follows. In the last part of the chapter I have also included what is properly a (rather lengthy) footnote to the rest of the discussion, to argue that the twentieth-century politics of constitutional autonomy and independence have represented substantively distinct issues from that of exclusive nationalism.

4.1 Nationalism and Conflict Regulation in Quebec prior to 1960

Standard explanations of the increasing political salience of nationalism in Quebec during the 1960s have rightly noted two major factors: first, the role of ethnic economic conflict between (new) middle-class French-speaking Québécois and English-speaking industrialists and managers in Montreal, a conflict that pitted the rising ambitions of francophones against the discriminatory preferences and linguistic obstinacy of anglophones;[3] and, second, the acute anxieties felt during the same decade over the viability of the French-Canadian way of life in Quebec.[4] The historical context typically missing from these accounts, however, is that both factors – ethnically delineated economic conflict and fears about cultural viability – had been sharply felt and articulated much earlier without conducing to official exclusive nationalism. Indeed, in the first four decades of the century, the periodical press was replete with journals calling attention to economic exploitation and injustice.[5] Economic nationalism gathered impressive electoral support. As for the viability of the French-Canadian way of life, demographic perils from both outside (e.g., from immigration) and inside (e.g., from urbanization, materialism, and secularization) French-Canadian society were common topics of public discourse.[6] To be sure, the active defensive front shifted during subsequent decades as language supplanted Roman Catholicism as the first bastion of the French-Canadian identity. But overall, explanations of the rise of nationalism in the 1960s are prone to overemphasizing an increase in the level of conflict and cultural threat during the intervening decades (or the associated jeopardy of francophone middle-class interests) and to underemphasizing the sea-change in the nature of political representation. We will argue here that such change left the political elite by the 1960s with dramatically decreased scope for the sorts of tactics earlier employed to insulate the state from exclusive nationalism.

Our discussion of the precursors before 1960 of the subsequent rise of official exclusive nationalism is divided into four parts. The first reviews the earlier manifestations of ethnic competition and cultural threat in Quebec society; the second discusses exclusive nationalism as an articulate ideology among French Canadians, particularly during the 1930s; the third describes the management of economic nationalism within the political process during the same decade; and the fourth traces the origins of statism and mobilization under Duplessis. (A brief history of separatism during this period is deferred until section 4.4)

Ethnic Competition and Cultural Threat: Earlier Manifestations

It is well known that urbanization prior to the 1960s removed an increasing number of French Canadians from the relative isolation of the countryside and brought them face to face with the spectre of an ethnically stratified class structure in the urban industrial socio-economy. What is not always appreciated is that this process, a key element of many explanations of the Quiet Revolution, was in fact already well advanced by the time of the Second World War. As Lionel Groulx observed in 1939, 'we are no longer predominantly an agricultural country, a country of farmers. We are now hurtling towards the proletariat and no one knows how to apply the brakes.'[7] Indeed, as early as the 1930s, agriculture accounted for just 27 per cent of the labour force in Quebec and 12 per cent of the economy.[8] Although Quebec lagged Ontario in urbanization by three or four percentage points (about ten years), by the 1931 census some 60 per cent of the population was already classified as urban (53 per cent in 1921), a figure that reached 74 per cent by 1961.[9] The professional, commercial, and business classes, various segments of which have been identified as the vanguard of nationalism during the 1960s, had reached almost one-fifth of the labour force by 1931, well on their way to the one-quarter level reached by 1961.[10]

Profound distress over the economic subservience of these social classes of French Canadians did not arise with the 1960s. During the Great Depression of the 1930s, reduced demand for commodities and high unemployment brought heightened awareness of the relative economic vulnerability and weakness of French Canadians. As is discussed later in greater detail, such sentiments were manifest in electoral politics in the weakening and then defeat in 1935–6 of the provincial Liberal regime of Louis-Alexandre Taschereau (1920–36) by the Action Libérale Nationale – a splinter party of Liberal nationalists – allied with dissident Conservatives known from 1936 as the Union Nationale.[11] As Patricia Dirks notes, this development came at a time when 'many organizations and journals [were] focussing attention on the economic inferiority of French Canadians within the province.'[12] In this time of scarcity, French Canadians felt heavily burdened as consumers and as entrepreneurs by high utilities rates in Quebec. A focal point for their general frustration became the utility monopolies ('trusts') owned by foreigners and Anglo-Canadian interests.[13] As Quinn noted at the time, the Union Nationale 'gained many adherents by capitalizing on the prevalent anti-trust sentiment, which was to a very large extent anti-English sentiment ...'[14]

Besides Taschereau and *trustards*, Jews were the other major scapegoat for distresses of both economic and cultural origin affecting French Canadians during the 1930s in Quebec. As Pierre Trépanier notes, during this period 'people in French Canada believed ... that the increasing presence of Jews in Montreal could threaten French Canadian small retailing and small business.'[15] One scholar has observed that the most extreme forms of antisemitism in Quebec were confined to a marginal (albeit vociferous) 'ideological current.'[16] At the same time, the work of other scholars has offered strong evidence that, as Bernard Vigod puts it, 'overt antisemitism became positively respectable [in the 1930s] in student and young nationalist circles, especially in Montreal.'[17] Michael Oliver agrees, arguing, 'anti-

Semitism was a prominent feature of the dominant nationalism of the 1920s and 1930s' and by no means restricted to 'extremist fringe groups.'[18]

Of the several examples of 'respectable,' middle-class anti-semitism during this period, one of the most shocking to postwar sensibilities is the case of Samuel Rabinovitch, a Jewish intern at the Hôtel Dieu Hospital in Montreal forced to give up his position after French-Canadian interns at four hospitals walked out to demand his resignation.[19] Racial hatred and the influence of the Jeune Canada movement were the major motive factors according to Olivar Asselin; this did not prevent support for the strike by 'the Association catholique des voyageurs de commerce, several sections of the St. Jean Baptiste Society, the Chevaliers de Carillon, the Epiciers-Bouchers, and several other organizations,' including professional medical associations in Montreal.[20] The interns' own 'declaration,' reprinted on the front page of Le Devoir by a sympathetic editor, implies that the crux of the issue was that one of fifteen senior-intern positions at a hospital had been given to a Jew (a 'graduate of great distinction'), rather than to a French Canadian.[21] Perhaps most telling of all was the weak response of hospital officials: it focused not on the inherent impropriety of discrimination or anti-semitism, but rather on their inability to find a further qualified French-Canadian candidate.[22]

The campaigns to boycott (primarily) Jewish merchants in favour of their French-Canadian competitors (Achat chez nous) and to reduce the influx of Jewish visitors to the Laurentian resort town of Ste-Agathe similarly reflected easy assumptions about the propriety of discriminating against Jews. Oliver describes the pillars of the Achat Chez Nous movement: 'Tied frequently to parish organizations or to the local St. Jean Baptiste Society, they were fostered by the press, especially the nationalist press ... Achat chez nous swept the province, and nationalists of all hues were in the forefront ...'[23] As for the controversy in Ste-Agathe, which had been preceded by similar conflicts in Val-David and Val-Morin, local vicar Abbé Charland publicly suggested during the summer of 1939 that residents protect tradition by refusing to sell land and houses to 'non-Aryans.' As he put it, 'in every country Jews collide with the national population ... Christians are right to protect themselves from Jews. We all know what control they exercise over commerce. If we rise up against them, it is because we have very reason to protect ourselves. The Jewish problem must also be understood from the spiritual and national point of view.'[24] Another curé justified the ensuing campaign as necessary for the 'defence of the nation.'[25] French and English residents subsequently formed a committee to 'supervise the buying and selling of property in Ste. Agathe to prevent its being acquired by Jews.'[26] Vandals burned a bridge to an island frequented by Jewish visitors.[27] Local backbenchers of the legislature and federal Parliament also weighed in with comments construing the Jews as undesirables, though one, Louis Finch, to his credit, commented that 'merchants, hoteliers, and farmers' all benefited through the tourist season from the increased trade, and that Premier Duplessis had taken an '"energetic attitude" in the face of the situation in stating that he would not tolerate for a single moment acts that tended to trouble the harmony and good understanding between the races.'[28] On the whole, as Oliver explains, anti-semitism during this period was 'not extremely violent; it was wordy and vehement.'[29]

Earlier Exclusive Nationalism as Ideology

As the prominence of priests near the forefront of the Ste-Agathe campaign would suggest, exclusive nationalism in this era generally had strong clerical links.[30] This connection lent it a more intellectual and less political complexion. Individual and corporate morality and only occasionally public policy were therefore the main concerns of the ideological campaigns most nationalists waged. A few nationalist intellectuals attached to the journal *La Nation* – whose influences included the continental *Action Française* and its Maurrasian agnosticism and statism – espoused a doctrine of 'politics above all else.'[31] But the more influential Groulx school and church hierarchy generally upheld the 'primacy of the spiritual,' and viewed democracy, political parties, and the state with at least marked suspicion and often 'antipathy.'[32] Thus, although many nationalist intellectuals were intrigued by the *Action Libérale Nationale* in 1935, for example, close links to an officially neutral church and ideological purism limited their involvement in building the machinery of a permanent mass political party.[33]

The Chinese wall separating many ideological nationalists from electoral, party politics relieved Groulx and others of the task of formulating parsimonious and realistic agendas around which public opinion could be organized politically. Their declinist visions decried, but only rarely sought to resolve, the twin perils of cultural pollution and economic subjugation.[34] Montreal, a rapidly industrializing centre in which international finance and nightlife flowed freely and multicultural life abounded, became in these writings a dystopia of moral decay, a malignant tumour consuming the traditional religious, cultural, and linguistic life of French Canadians. The 'moral decadence of the materialistic American way of life' was held responsible for eroding traditional rural virtuousness and 'the spiritual superiority of an idealistic, Catholic, and French society.'[35] City life, with its cinema, press, and radio, shattered the Arcadian isolation of the past. As an anguished editorial in Le Devoir bemoaned, 'Protestant or materialistic English-language newspapers and magazines have infiltrated and bogged down our country. It is the same with the theatre and, to an even greater extent, with radio. We are surrounded on all sides.'[36]

Such a mentality was hostile to immigrants. Intellectuals articulated the popular hostility towards Jews in particular, and to diversity in general.[37] Jews were the immoral force behind the cinema in all of its debauchery, as well as of the espied 'Judeo-American Finance with Bolshevik sympathies.' In attacking Jews, said Le Devoir, Hitler 'attacks the most formidable power of deceit in the world.'[38] During his stint as president of Jeune Canada, André Laurendeau expressed a dismal view of multiculturalism in the United States, associating it with all manner of spiritual failings. Americans are 'worn down by forces they could never master and by weaknesses which will only worsen with time: different races and nations living within the same State (Blacks and Chinese, Germans, Italians, Jews, Irish, French and the like); and, cancerous growths (atheism, widespread materialism and its repercussions of divorce, family breakdown, and the primacy of money ...)'[39] 'Oriental immigrants,' said a journalist in 1934 in Le Devoir, should pay a police tax of $100 to cover the additional costs associated with their criminality, though, 'of course, exclusion would be even more practical and less costly.'[40]

There was a regenerative impulse also present in the writings of Quebec nationalist intellectuals, and it was often deeply conservative.[41] Groulx sometimes called for the 'reconstitution and maintenance of our peasantry.'[42] Only by assiduously keeping the nation's agricultural vocation could the language and faith be maintained. Groulx believed his nation was 'unhappy and disoriented because it has broken with its past,' that a 'national orientation' was required of schools, and that French Canadians should be imprinted with a 'faithfulness to their origin, history, culture and inborn strength.'[43] 'We have to be French through and through, intransigently, energetically, audaciously – otherwise we shall cease to be.'[44] Groulx also believed that the province of Quebec must become more and more 'an autonomous, Catholic and French state.'[45]

Other intellectual tendencies gave more specific emphasis to preserving the French language. The Jesuit Joseph-Papin Archambault and the Ligue des Droits du Français, for example, had maintained in the second decade of the twentieth century that French was, in the words of Susan Mann

Trofimenkoff, 'both the creator and the guardian of a certain French and Catholic personality.'[46] Archambault and the *ligue* also sought to combat 'the belief that the English language was the magic wand for commercial success' by ensuring that 'the French language had a rightful place in the fields of commerce and industry.'[47] Service on trains, package labelling on biscuits, the names of banks, and the language capabilities of telephone operators were a few of the many targets. In these campaigns orchestrated by the *ligue*, together with *L'Action française* (originally its organ), demands were made directly to businesses to increase both the extent and the quality of their use of French. In a rare foray into the public-policy domain, *L'Action Française* objected at the virtual absence of French services from the federal government and demanded, successfully, that French be included on postage stamps. Within Quebec, Action Française also submitted a brief to the Catholic committee of instruction arguing that the language of instruction within elementary schools catering to French Canadians should be French and that the introduction of English should be delayed. More generally, however, the 'linguistic question in Quebec was a perplexing one' for Action Française and its linguistic program for the province was 'ambivalent.'[48]

Fears about cultural pollution and the status of the French language were often closely connected with status anxieties arising from the proletariatization of French-Canadian rural migrants to the cities. Cultural fidelity could be maintained only by convincing French Canadians, as Groulx put it, 'that remaining French will not detract from their future prospects.'[49] As matters stood, this was hardly the case, argued another contributor in 1922 to *L'Action française*, Joseph Bruchard, who observed prophetically,

> The next generation will no longer find it natural ... that the external appearance of our own streets and highways is English; that everyone who is rich speaks English and everyone who is poor speaks French; that four French Canadians speak English to please one Englishman who does not deign to learn their language; that large industries and businesses are English and that the little shops devoted to small business or to ruin are French, or rather bilingual; that the big firms exploiting our forests, our mines, our fisheries, our waterfalls, etc., provide profits and influential positions to foreigners while they leave to our own people the lowliest jobs and pitiful wages ...[50]

It was, in fact, in the next decade that many of these sentiments found their mark in election campaigns, already alluded to, that weakened and then defeated Taschereau, a leader associated with the Quebec industrial oligarchy. More will be said about those elections in the next section, but the point for now is that ideological critiques of ethnic economic inequality were sharply articulated in this era. Against the backdrop of nationalist hopes having been first raised by the elections of 1935 and 1936 and then doused by resurgent forces of economic conservatism led by Maurice Duplessis, Groulx himself bitterly inveighed in 1937, 'I call an economic regime unacceptable ... that ... places the majority, the native population at the mercy of, or trailing behind, the minority, which inflicts upon it the collective humiliation of making them a people of labourers and domestics; a regime that, in consequence, undermines the confidence of a people in the genius of its race ...'[51] French Canadians, wrote Groulx on another occasion, 'must at very least be masters within their own province ... on this land, which has belonged to their forefathers for three hundred years, French Canadians at least retain the rights and privileges of seniority. Consequently, Quebec's territory ... is a French territory which must be productive for French people.'[52]

At their most constructive moment, sentiments such as these conduced to recognition that more French Canadians needed to be better prepared for leadership roles in industry through broader education in business and economics.[53] But even here, many clerics found commerce to be tainted with materialism, and they were deeply ambivalent as to the desirability of industrialization on free-market, capitalist principles. 'Economic efforts' and 'material wealth' were to serve 'only as a foundation for intellectual and moral superiority,' not 'to amass enormous fortunes, or achieve opulence.'[54]

Leaving aside the positive recognition, qualified as it was, that modernization entailed adaptation, which needed to be accelerated, not retarded, the great preponderance of nationalist ideological criticism was negative, entailing assaults on basic aspects of modern, urban, industrial life, including the international mobility of capital, people, and culture. Contemporary critics accused journals such as *L'Action française* of 'adopting positively Olympian attitudes, interpreting the secret designs of Providence itself,' and indulging in 'Utopian fantasy.'[55] But although Quebec nationalist ideology of the 1920s and 1930s might be judged retrograde, its significance cannot be so readily denied. Though nationalist clerics and intellectuals did relatively little to advance popular political mobilization and organization, they both articulated and shaped emergent raw popular sentiments. Even if popular voices, figuratively speaking, had not yet in this era been furnished with microphones wired to crisp and reliable institutional political amplification, many of their darkest, most medieval urgings – as well as deepest aspirations – were nevertheless being artfully put *for* them. For a time, as we will discuss next, opposition politicians actually joined the chorus, echoing slightly less millennial strains of nationalism.

Earlier Elite Management of Nationalism: Analysis

Fernand Dumont has referred to the 1930s as 'the first Quiet Revolution.'[56] This description points to important parallels in the politics of this decade with those of the 1960s. The comparison is worth drawing out, because understanding the similarities and differences in the politics of the two decades can help to identify the factors unique to the 1960s that gave rise the second time around (so to speak) to much stronger ramifications for political institutions and official exclusive nationalism. We begin here with a brief sketch of what are judged to be the most salient aspects of official politics of the 1930s and complete the comparison with later developments through the remainder of the chapter.

The Action Libérale Nationale (ALN), already referred to, achieved considerable first-time success in the 1935 Quebec election, winning more than 40 per cent (or 26) of the seats it contested, and a similar proportion overall of the popular vote in the same electoral districts.[57] As Dirks observes, 'the surge to ALN had been province-wide.'[58] Even by the standards of the rapid penetration, thirty-five years later, of the Parti Québécois (which won 23, 30, and 41 per cent of the popular vote in the 1970, 1973, and 1976 elections, respectively), this was an impressive result indeed.[59] The ALN was a 'potpourri,' including, as Oliver notes, 'men who had deserted the official Taschereau Liberal party because of a desire for social and economic reform more "liberal" than the Liberals would countenance ... as well as quasi fascists.'[60] The strongest single voice in the party was that of leader Paul Gouin, who set out in the party manifesto a platform that explicitly leaned heavily upon the principles elaborated two years earlier under the auspices of the Jesuit-sponsored Ecole Sociale Populaire (ESP), codified in a pamphlet titled *Le Programme de restauration sociale*. Interestingly, this document, as Quinn explains, was the work of a group, convened and directed by the Jesuits, of prominent lay citizens, who in their individual careers played a 'leading role in all phases of French-Canadian life' and had served as directors of the journal *L'Action nationale*.[61]

As such, both the ESP and the ALN program reflected the views, widely popular at the time, demanding 'economic reconquest' vis-à-vis the 'trusts,' read non-francophone-owned, capital intensive, large-scale industries, including electric power utilities, financial institutions, and the pulp and paper industry.[62] In an important speech on 12 August 1934, Gouin, having alluded to the 60,000 French Canadians at the time of the Conquest, said, 'The time has come ... to assure the national and economic conquest of our people. This is the right of our generation.'[63] Apart from 'breaking the stranglehold' of large institutions, the ALN pledged itself to agrarian, labour, social, and electoral reforms. A few weeks before the November 1935 election, an article in *La Province*, the party organ, suggested that foreigners had reduced the common inheritance of French Canadians to ruins.[64] Another baldly stated, 'this is not a question of party; it is a question of race; it is a question of life or death for the French Canadian nation.'[65] As Dirks sums up the movement, the ALN offered 'a vision of the capitalist system restructured in such a way as to perpetuate the power base of French Canada's traditional elites and increase the possibilities for francophone economic advancement.'[66]

As a political movement, the ALN sponsored a form of economic nationalism that aimed to empower French Canadians, rather than to impose a way of life or alter the demographic composition of Quebec.[67] As such, it differed from the forms of 'exclusive nationalism' noted in previous chapters (and later in the present one). The economic nationalism of the ALN was nevertheless liable to many of the same objections as exclusive nationalism from the standpoint of the established political elite. Fundamentally, it threatened to breach their healthy relations with strategically vital external parties, in this case predominantly non-francophone investors. It threatened, in other words, a form of inter-ethnic conflict typical of nationalism that the established political elite had a strong interest in regulating. As we will see shortly, their efficacy in managing (or more precisely, marginalizing) this conflict is startling by later standards. It is worth briefly dwelling on how they did this and why they succeeded. Although the pattern of representation exhibited does not fall cleanly into either of our categories – 'imposed statecraft' or 'affiliative trusteeship' – elements of both are helpful in explaining the trenchancy of the established political elite.

Taschereau had maintained, even while in office as premier, a strong affiliation with capital through his personal participation on the boards of major corporations, and through treating personally with industrialists. He had upheld the principle, as Vigod puts it, that 'there needed to be flexibility and mutual confidence between business and government which could only be derived from the discretionary and overriding authority of the premier.'[68] Taschereau had also, incidentally, vehemently opposed antisemitism 'at every opportunity': his 'abhorrence of racial and religious prejudice was a lifelong characteristic, and he had the political courage to denounce it in spite of prevailing sentiment.'[69] His strong personal associations with, and public defence of, major corporations had, by the general election of November 1935, proved such an electoral liability as to bring him near defeat, even, as it was, at the hands of an opposition whose eleventh-hour agreement to form a coalition could only partially obscure considerable disunity.

The terms of the hasty coalition of Gouin's ALN with the Conservatives led by Maurice Duplessis granted the ALN a senior role with somewhat more than two-thirds of ridings for the 1935 election.[70] Duplessis was also obliged to issue a joint public statement endorsing the ALN's manifesto as the official policy of the coalition.[71] His guileful nods to this platform, as well as his greater political experience, ultimately underpinned his pre-eminence in the party. There followed, as Dirks puts it, a 'transformation of the *Union Nationale* from an alliance into a traditional, leader-dominated Quebec party,' and, ultimately, a return to policies 'associated with Taschereau.'[72] Duplessis had, it seems, merely 'played the nationalist card,' and deployed nationalism for 'electoral purposes' only.'[73] But he also offered ALN members of the legislature 'their best chance of continuing in public life' and presented himself as prepared to bring 'to fruition whichever parts of the ALN program they wanted to see enacted.'[74]

By the time Duplessis formed his first cabinet following the election of August 1936, he had extinguished the influence of all but one of the prominent members of the ALN party, while retaining a large proportion of backbench support from former ALN members of the legislature.[75] The true colours of the Union Nationale now began to show. Like Taschereau, Duplessis had strong ties to capital, and he was committed to 'the fullest possible exploitation of hydroelectric and other natural resources,' if necessary by foreign or English-speaking capital.[76] Following Gouin's departure in June 1936, Groulx commented that Duplessis appeared 'more worried about reassuring the English than about stimulating French Canadians.'[77] In September, Groulx went further: 'this man always seemed to me of the old school, old hat, passé. He remained with the generation of men in their sixties, with all the empty clichés about bonne entente and "cooperation between the two great races" ... What a restoration of profundity to await from men who intend to do no justice to their compatriots except that which is agreeable to the English minority. Yes! It is a great disenchantment.'[78] Following the Duplessis victory, another nationalist referred to the corruption of the Union Nationale by 'old Tories,' referring to the continuity of the Union Nationale with the Conservative party, from which the preponderance of Duplessis's colleagues had come.[79]

By the standards of modern, participatory parties – especially those founded after 1960 – Duplessis wielded an extraordinarily free hand in discarding elements of his election platform of great popular interest and at the core of his alliance with the ALN. The striking power of Duplessis's autonomous authority must be understood against the form Quebec democracy took during these years. One uncomplicated indication of the status of intra-party democracy is that during some twenty-three years as leader of the Union Nationale Duplessis 'never called a provincial convention at which the rank and file of the party would have an opportunity to discuss policy and demand an accounting of his leadership.'[80] Hence, a sharp contrast must be drawn between the dominant ideological support for extensive popular participation in the official politics of the Quebec of the 1960s, and the long preceding evolutionary period.

Caution about democracy, it should be emphasized, was not the sole preserve of Conservatives, but rather ran deep through French-Canadian nationalist ideology of all shades before the Second World War. Groulx and other clerics had openly attacked it, and 'serious doubts' about democracy were a touchstone of Action française, which had held it to be 'morally corrupt' and divisive.[81] As already discussed, French-Canadian nationalism in that mould had been a narrowly based enterprise concerned with 'doctrine,' not political organization.[82] The ALN inherited that tradition, and, despite its reformist aspirations, was a 'leader-oriented party' that presented itself as above partisanship, and united by familiar and broad nationalist indictments of the Taschereau regime.[83] As Dirks notes, during its brief lifespan the party 'did not look to the mass of French Canadians to provide leadership.'[84] Candidates were selected by local notables. And while the ALN certainly made popular appeals, holding rallies and making radio broadcasts, a good part of Gouin's resources were devoted to the publication of his organ La Province, which reached an audience of enthusiasts and functioned above all as a 'forum for élite thought.'[85] Through its rapid conjunction with the Conservative party and then disintegration, the ALN proved itself to be a loose assemblage of politicos that reflected the fluid political alliances of the era of affiliative trusteeship and the absence of a strong popular voice. Lacking popular ballast in its organizational structure, notwithstanding broad and favourable ideological currents, the ALN was ephemeral, its organization and economic nationalism being quickly swept overboard by the more seasoned, established political elite of the old Conservative party.

Wellsprings of Democracy in the Era of the Chief

Maurice Duplessis led the Union Nationale for the twenty-three years following 1936 until his death in 1959, all but five of them (1939–44) as premier. His was a highly personal, autocratic style of rule that at first glance might easily pass for a sort of vulgar reversion to imposed statecraft. In dispensing public works explicitly upon ridings' voting records, in personally instructing major labour boards, in repressing dissidents (most significantly supposed Communists and Catholic-baiting Jehovah's Witnesses) through ostentatious displays of police force, and in exercising his capacity as attorney general (while premier) to pursue frivolous legal crusades against minor, unpopular figures, Duplessis governed Quebec as his personal fief, sometimes with little regard for procedural justice, and often with utter cynicism.[86] Through his years in office, Duplessis's electoral constituency was increasingly rural, but it was his partnership with business of all sizes that allowed his party to spend heavily at elections, feting voters.[87] Ever the partisan, Duplessis extracted massive contributions to his party's war chest, as well as favourable newspaper coverage.[88] In exchange, his party selectively awarded government contracts, and maintained a highly favourable regulatory and fiscal business environment.[89]

Yet, neither Duplessis's vaudevillian patronage nor his populist sacrifice of small-time 'enemies' of social 'order' should obscure the transformative agenda underwritten by his key, quasi-political alliance with (predominantly anglophone) industrialists.[90] Duplessis courted the capital required to develop the mining, pulp and paper, hydro-electricity, and chemical industries. As he recognized that 'almost all' of this capital 'would have to come from Quebec's English-speaking neighbours,' he undertook to create an image of fiscal sobriety, stability, and labour peace.[91] To the extent that the later Duplessis governments resembled the pattern of affiliative trusteeship, their cross-cultural (albeit extra-parliamentary) alliance-partners were major English and foreign industrialists.[92]

During Duplessis's extended regime of limited public policy innovation, the anachronisms of the Union Nationale multiplied. Mason Wade observes the 'forceful stubbornness' of the party in resisting the 'ever-mounting tide of change.'[93] In terms of both process and substance, major contradictions developed between the structure of Quebec economy and society, on the one hand, and its government, on the other. In these contradictions can be found the impetus for the cascading origins of the rapid mobilization of Quebec society in the 1950s and 1960s. The argument posed here is that nationalist aspirations lent a flavour to this process of mobilization, but that the main impetus of this process, linked to pressures for statism common to modern societies and felt across the spectrum of progressive intellectual opinion in Quebec, were more structural. This argument will then set the stage for the contention in the sections following that the force of exclusive nationalism in the late 1960s arose from the extent of popular mobilization (and not, mainly, the other way around). We will also, in common with the subsequent section, analyse the connection between tendencies towards statism and greater popular involvement in the political process.

In 1958 Quebec political scientist Léon Dion produced a careful assessment of democratization in his province.[94] Dion accepted that many ostensibly democratic institutions in Quebec appeared on close examination to dominated by 'a coalition of great capitalist and clerical interests' and were defined by 'professional politicians beyond any real popular control.'[95] Yet he went on to qualify this familiar critique with evidence of incipient change.

> Rapid social evolution, which has given rise to a modern, urban and industrial society, has provoked the development of new functions and social niches. Democratic attitudes and behaviours manifest themselves among the most diverse groups: among workers within unions; among farmers within cooperatives; among students; among educators and more. This recent development has not been fully recognized. And yet, to me it seems obvious. To demonstrate the full extent of this evolution, let us go back twenty years, and recall the reticence and scepticism surrounding discussions of democracy and the glorification of authoritarian regimes and systems ... What a contrast![96]

Dion's essay presents a useful caveat to the polemical work of this period by future prime minister Pierre Elliott Trudeau. Trudeau was prone to caricaturing the Quebec society he and the journal closely associated with him, Cité libre, sought to change. Trudeau decried the submissiveness of the French Canadians, deploring their 'antidemocratic opinions' and their 'fear of turning to the state,' associating these with their 'narrow societies in the countryside.'[97]

Until recently, indeed, the predominant image of Quebec during the postwar era has remained la grande noirceur (the dark age), generally juxtaposed with the glorious advent of *l'épanouissement* and *la rattrapage* (flowering and catching-up, respectively) of the 1960s.[98] Yet the points raised by Dion's essay make it important not to exaggerate the discontinuities, and in particular to distinguish between the certifiably slow advance of state and party institutions during the Duplessis era, and the much more rapid evolution of civil society during the same period. Structurally, growth rates in overall industrial production *averaged* 10 per cent per year between 1935 and 1955 in Quebec, an impressive figure exactly comparable to that achieved contemporaneously in Ontario.[99] In manufacturing, which accounted for about 63 per cent of the Quebec economy in 1955 (as compared with 68 per cent in Ontario, and 52 per cent in Canada overall), average hourly salaries in Quebec grew from 81 to 85 per cent of comparable levels in Ontario between 1938 and 1955, as labour productivity in manufacturing increased from 77 to 82 per cent of Ontario levels.[100] In the same sector, real hourly salaries more than tripled in Quebec.[101] Overall, postwar Quebec, with its full-employment, high-growth economy, was in many respects in the vanguard of the economic modernization sweeping Canada (and other Western societies) during this era.[102]

As elsewhere, the attendant vagaries and risks of such prosperity raised demands for social intervention on a scale that only the state could manage. These demands were expressed by the opposition press, and by a rapidly growing labour movement that served as the nerve centre for a growing political consciousness in Quebec. The state was called upon to take 'responsibility for the quality of human capital' and to indemnify citizens against the social perils of urban, industrial life.[103] This was an agenda that clearly enclosed major questions of public policy, and posed urgent intellectual and political challenges. To confront these, social groups 'mounted an immense organizational effort,' in the words of Jean-Louis Roy, during the postwar period.[104]

> They renewed their leadership, re-examined their inner workings, re-evaluated their structure, re-defined their objectives, tried to gain a real understanding of other groups and of the state, disseminated their analysis and positions among both specialists and the larger public ... They established locals, permanent [union committees], documentation centres, specialized advisers, and newsletters. Depending on the group, they organized annual or biennial congresses, held symposiums and seminars. They sought to establish contact with groups who were pursuing similar objectives within other societies.[105]

The objectives in question may be summarized under three major rubrics: (a) industrial policy; (b) social policy and education; and (c) electoral reform. Each of these warrants discussion, in order to establish that the associated spheres of controversy were independent of the claims of nationalism, and that together they are representative of the forces pressing for a larger, more interventionist state, and, in turn, for broader participation in collective decision making within Quebec society.

Although extensive discussion of Quebec labour history lies beyond the scope of this work, the central role and profile of organized labour among statist forces deserves brief comment. Quebec unions, whose collective membership rose by 90 per cent between 1945 and 1955 to represent 29 per cent of Quebec's labour force, varied in their level of engagement in policy questions.[106] One of the fastest-growing, and by far the most politically engaged union, was the Confédération des Travailleurs Canadiens et Catholiques (CTCC). Formed in 1921 as an umbrella organization for the Catholic trade union movement, the CTCC displayed in its early years a conservative, and traditional nationalist orientation. Then in 1949, in the crucible of a particularly bitter and celebrated labour dispute over working conditions and pay in asbestos mines (and more broadly, as it escalated, 'industrial democracy'), the CTCC redefined itself as vigorous advocate of the socioeconomic interests of its members, instead of defender of French-Catholic particularism.[107] Although the Asbestos Strike, as the episode is known, was certainly not without 'nationalist overtones' – it pitted French-Canadian workers against English-speaking managers and owners – the union construed its objectives in the universal language of class, not of ethnicity or nationality. In the immediately preceding and succeeding years, other strikes crossed national lines and this fact also adds credibility to Pierre Elliott Trudeau's admittedly tendentious claim that the Catholic labour movement in 1949 was 'striding beyond certain denominational and ethnocentric conceptions of equality.'[108] It also makes it difficult to quarrel with his contention that the Asbestos Strike 'could have occurred solely as a result of forces arising from the industrial world, without any deviations caused by nationalism or denominationalism.'[109]

Precisely the same could be said of the public debate over social policy, which intensified during this period, gradually weakening public anti-statism. Calls from labour on behalf of a growing urban working class for increased state involvement in administering social assistance implied a turn away from the 'solidarity of the family and parish,' the heartland of the traditional French-Canadian identity and way of life.[110] While such class-oriented advocacy could always be translated into the phraseology of national solidarity, there could be no denying that this agenda tended to undermine the rural and clerical pillars of traditional nationalism. It is also worth noting that, in the absence of effective provincial leadership on social policy, the CTCC, for one, specifically advocated during this period an expanded *federal* role in housing policy (in 1946–8), the old age pension system (in 1950), direct transfers to families (in 1952), and health insurance (in 1957).[111]

The structural origins of the severe growing pains experienced in the sphere of education during this period were also manifest. Rapid growth in both the number of students as well as the educational requirements of employers far outstripped the capacity of traditional, church-directed institutions.[112] As Coleman observes, the 'system of education, which had been developed to encourage professional vocations or to return boys to the farm at the age of puberty, had little room for the growing working class.'[113] Despite the rapid growth of postsecondary institutions during Duplessis's administrations, limitations even at the primary level, were a 'major stumbling block preventing modernization of the entire society.'[114] In consequence, education became an enormously contentious issue, emerging as the 'dominant theme' of political criticism levelled by a large array of groups.[115] The Tremblay Commission (discussed below) heard no less than 140 briefs from groups 'dealing in whole or in part with education.'[116] Not even all progressive opposition groups could easily stomach the prospect of further major adventures by their patronage-addicted government in the capital-intensive business of education. Still, initiatives to expand the scope and reach of education ineluctably extended the envisioned role of government and, in the process, established a major arena for public policy disputation.[117] During the following decade, state leadership in education would prove to be the single strongest impetus for popular mobilization.

Democratic reform was the other major impetus for mobilization during the Duplessis years.[118] The patron–client relationships cultivated by Duplessis administrations with major industrialists and local grandees alike were no doubt typical of many traditional societies. But in a rapidly modernizing, and increasingly bureaucratic society, the personal discretion and reciprocity at the heart of such relationships was increasingly dysfunctional for public resource allocation and policy. Managed with cunning and few scruples, they also deeply entrenched the incumbent regime. This, together with a sharply skewed distribution of electoral districts (which allocated two-thirds of seats to rural, predominantly Union Nationale, ridings accounting for just one-third of the population), seriously handicapped the opposition.[119] In the vanguard of the movement to reform patronage and electoral practices were opposition-left intellectuals such as Pierre Elliott Trudeau and André Laurendeau. Advocating that the state be modernized to provide stronger leadership in Quebec they judged that 'if the practice of patronage was curtailed and circumscribed by institutional and legislative changes and the bureaucracy modernized, a majority of Québécois would feel less reluctant to support increased government intervention in, and perhaps control of, crucial sectors of Quebec society.'[120] 'Democracy first' became a rallying philosophy, receiving its most forceful intellectual articulation in *Cité libre*.[121]

Opening the state to stronger popular and technocratic inputs was understood by many politicians to be a crucial precursor to the growth of the state. In December 1959, on the eve of the Quiet Revolution, *Le Devoir* featured a series of commentaries entitled 'Ou va le Canada français?'[122] The thirteen essays, contributed by prominent intellectuals and opposition Liberal politicians representing the gamut of progressive opinion, were each addressed to a common set of themes (e.g., the perceived 'crisis of nationalism'). One of the contributors, Father Richard Arès of l'Université de Montréal, when asked to identify the key issues for a (future) dynamic government in Quebec, underlined in one breath the importance of modernizing the public service and of recruiting ordinary citizens to higher levels of political conscience.

> Do we accept that Quebec is [merely] a large municipality, even a vast administrative bureaucracy, or do we profoundly believe it to be a state, that it must be a great modern state? ... we must recognize that before elaborating a grand political agenda, we must have the means ... This state must depend upon vigilant and enlightened public opinion. Hence the urgency of an ongoing effort of popular education for all echelons of society, of which much has already been accomplished during recent years, but which is still quite insufficient ... it is essential that the man on the street becomes in the full sense of the word, a citizen. Public service of the highest quality, researchers and specialists in great numbers, abundant resources, enlightened public opinion: then, but only then, will the provincial state of Quebec be capable of responding fully to its vocation.[123]

Paul Gérin-Lajoie, a senior figure in the Liberal party of Jean Lesage, agreed, reinforcing the importance of 'intensified popular education' and arguing that only by 'reasserting politics in the spirit of the masses' and 'awakening popular and individual conscience' could any grand political project avoid failure.[124] In abstract terms, we observe here a conscious recognition of the dependence of significant statist initiatives upon greater popular legitimacy and trust, hence a more transparent and open public discourse.

It is crucial for my purposes to emphasize that overall, the powerful thrust towards popular mobilization of labour-based groups, opposition politicians, and statist intellectuals during the 1950s was not dependent upon nationalism of even general form, much less upon exclusive nationalism. While nationalists had certainly become more statist during the course of the 1950s, their statism was an index of the strength of the larger, humanist, social democratic agenda that they shared with vigorous opponents of nationalism; it was derived more from the ramifications (such as an increasingly assertive union movement) of a rearguard provincial government within a rapidly developing society, than it was from recurrent visions of cultural or economic 'reconquest.' To hammer this home, it is useful to clarify the well-recognized division of opposition-left opinion in the late 1950s between *Cité libre* liberals, and neo-nationalists.[125]

Liberal democracy, implying the emancipation of the culturally unencumbered, individual subject, was for Trudeau, and the several small movements he catalysed during the late 1950s, a sufficiently compelling cause to be pursued in its own right.[126] It was certainly not to be confounded with any form of ethnic particularism. By contrast, for Laurendeau and the new breed of 'social nationalists,' democratic reform seemed more politically viable in the broader context of a concrete agenda of advancement for the French-Canadian majority.[127] But an analysis of the content of neo-nationalism reveals a striking pattern: nationalist intellectuals of the late 1950s had become far *less* imperious and exclusivist than the deeply conservative, anti-semitic traditionalists of Groulx's ilk of the 1920s and 1930s. Indeed, nationalist ideology was retrenching to a more universal humanism, less antagonistic to the outside world and the presence of outsiders.[128] By 1959, nationalism in Quebec seemed increasingly preoccupied with how French Canadians could most rapidly blossom economically and culturally in themselves, not how they might stake exclusive claims to turf.

Much less determinate than earlier formulations as to the specific complexion of the French-Canadian identity, the new nationalism sought to apply the fungible resource of national solidarity to the looming process of social transformation.[129] As many others, Gérard Bergeron, a political scientist at Laval, tentatively struggled to define a new, minimalist nationalism shorn of the grandiose messianism of traditionalists.

> Our nationalism ... is far from finding itself ... I dream of a nationalism of 'tragic optimism,' that obeys a sense of history but that still has a sense of

current relevance and political opportunity ... and that produces results. Here, still, a preliminary work of demystification is required ... Nationalism is a way of life centred on the cultural, or better yet, on the collective conscience of participating in an 'ethnie' ... Based on the fact of the 'ethnie,' nationalism indicates concrete general avenues toward concrete ideals and aspirations and not to pure transcendence. It is a means toward human accomplishment, it is not human accomplishment in itself. Nationalism, based on differences defines itself most often 'against.' That's normal. But when it is the most 'against' it is not necessarily the most 'for' the nation.[130]

Traditional nationalism, against the backdrop of Duplessis's burlesque rendering and Trudeau's postwar diatribes, had become palpably un-cool. Even Jean-Marc Léger, best known during this period for his contributions to *Le Devoir* and *Action Nationale* (often on the health of the French language), emphasized the change in priorities from the traditional to the 'new school.' 'While the first body of opinion would seek to struggle against everything that threatens to lessen the French character of Quebec, or which poaches on our government's preserves, the second aims primarily at combatting anything in Quebec which oppresses man, or raises obstacles to his full development ... Why, after all, should one fight for "Quebec's French character" if beneath the surface there lies a threat to human dignity?'[131] This was not to imply that 'survival of the ethnic group as a distinct entity' had ceased for nationalists to be 'the predominant anxiety.'[132] But by 1959, nationalists did not shrink from the brave new world of imminent, thoroughgoing social transformation. For Léger and other neo-nationalists, improving the basis of French-Canadian culture in the 'material well-being' and enlightenment of the masses, had logical priority over 'seeking to impose on our Anglo-Canadian partners an outward respect' for the French-Canadian culture of yore.[133] The vitality of the French language and culture was an 'epiphenomenon' resting upon economic and social circumstances. As things stood, the crude, hybrid language of the unemancipated man on the street could present to English Canada only a 'pathetic image.'[134] The language itself, suggested another, would need to be modernized, a task that required not defensiveness, but rather an end to the slavish mimicry of English by French Canadians. This implied that 'the greatest danger does not come from others, but from ourselves.'[135]

Traditional conservative nationalism had not been totally extinguished by 1959, but its influence was greatly diminished. This can be assessed from the fate met by one of the last, great monuments of traditional nationalism, the report of the Tremblay Commission. While the progress towards an urban industrial society hastened the decline of many traditional values, this elicited a reactionary initiative by the commission to recover what was being lost. The provincial commission, named in 1953, was originally intended as a tactical move in a jurisdictional struggle with the federal government over the division of powers of direct taxation and policy making relative to culture and postsecondary education.[136] The members of the commission included Esdras Minville, who had been a student of Lionel Groulx and a director of La Société Saint-Jean-Baptiste de Montréal.[137] The report issued in 1956 advances an elaborate, traditional interpretation of a French-Canadian culture ordered by a Catholic conception of the good life and 'transcendent' norms.[138] In the Manichean struggle observed in modernizing societies between the materialism and individualism of industrial economies and the spiritualism and collectivism of traditional agrarian cultures, French Canadians had plumped for the moral high ground.[139] It was incumbent upon the Canadian institutional order to respect this defining choice; doing so meant structuring the federal system so as to avoid contaminating the 'ethnic milieu' of Quebec. The 'ethnic environment should be homogeneous; this homogeneity consisting of cultural and lingual unity ... If the data of an outside culture become of current utility or if one of the functions of collective life proceeds from an inspiration foreign to the culture ... the relations of cultural exchange between Man and his social environment are mixed up ... and the nation's renewal organism and ... its survival are threatened.'[140] French-Canadian society depended upon the autonomous, 'organized life' of Quebec – particularly the dominant presence of the Church – to maintain the homogeneous environment and keep the faith through the exigencies of modern times.[141]

Even the quasi-official Tremblay report, it may be noted, vacillated at the border of exclusive nationalist territory. Though it had argued that the state should aid the 'conservation and fruition of cultural values,' the report had also emphatically rejected the idea that a heterogeneous state should actively privilege one particular way of life over others.[142] It had held,

States whose members are of different national cultures should define their policies according to the requirements of the common good ... It does not appertain to them to fashion at their whim the national culture or cultures ...; no more does it appertain to them to raise up a new national culture, for that purpose forcing existing cultures to abandon all or some of their particularism.

> Nor should they adopt the spirit and cultural aspirations of one of the groups, to the detriment of the other group or groups. On the contrary, they have a duty to favour equally the progress of particular cultures ...[143]

Although these arguments are no doubt delivered partly with the federal government in mind (which had released the culturally statist Massey report in 1951) there is a dearth of positive, specifically cultural initiatives envisaged in the Tremblay report for the provincial government. One possible reading is that in the cultural sphere the report presumes a guardian state, mainly responsible for avoiding incursions into the territory of the church and other private organizations, a position that would not logically threaten the comparable institutions of English-speaking Protestants and others in Quebec.[144]

At any rate, the argument had little immediate impact on Quebec policy. While the report might be taken as emblematic of the continuing retreat to Quebec within French-Canadian thought, the report generally 'languished, soon to be labelled retrograde.'[145] Concerned that the report presented altogether too much thorny advice, Duplessis had 3,000 copies of the report locked up at a police station for safe-keeping.[146] Certainly his government took no positive action to bolster the 'cultural and lingual unity' referred to in the report. Subsequent governments paradoxically used the jurisdictional powers reserved to Quebec by the Tremblay Commission to accelerate the very processes of modernization implicated in the report as undermining the traditional culture.[147]

In summary, there are few close intellectual or political parallels to be found on the eve of the Quiet Revolution for the official exclusive nationalism that, as discussed shortly, would clench Quebec politics a decade on. The agenda for the economic and cultural blossoming of French Canada, of which many humanist nationalists and opposition politicians spoke in 1959, pales beside later initiatives to impose French unilingualism in Quebec, and, indeed, was less obviously continuous with such initiatives than, for example, the work of the far more belligerent Groulxian nationalists of the 1920s and 1930s. During the 1950s, the far more significant antecedents of the coming official exclusive nationalism were the forces, structural, social, intellectual, and political, pressing for a larger Quebec state. For not only did such advocacy involve mobilizing from the wilderness the contributions of working-class unionists, intellectual activists, and opposition party cadres, but, equally, with the victory of the Lesage government, it led shortly to new institutional arenas for public policy contestation that legitimized and induced the participation of a huge array of new, assertive actors. Such statism was compelling in the 1950s across the spectrum of the opposition left, across diametrically opposed perspectives on nationalism.

The ultimate result was that political elites would never again govern with the sublime confidence and arrogance of a Maurice Duplessis. Nationalist manoeuvres on the provincial political scene would no longer serve merely as diversions from conservative obstinacy. In a word, the popular will of the majority *ethnie* would no longer be denied by institutions controlled by political elites. Exclusive nationalism would be pressed by the majority onto the official political agenda with much greater vociferousness than ever before.

4.2 State and Society during the Quiet Revolution

The Inclusiveness of Lesage's Nationalism

The Liberals under Jean Lesage defeated the Union Nationale in the 1960 election on promises of stronger state intervention in natural resources, economic development, health care, and education.[148] In office, the Lesage government quickly formed plans to implement a hospital insurance scheme, to nationalize electric utilities, to pour public investment into hydroelectric dams, and to create a ministry of education that would gradually supplant the church in secondary schooling. In initiating such projects during the 'Quiet Revolution' comprising its two terms and six years in office, Lesage's government reorganized and expanded the core infrastructure of an industrial economy.[149] Culturally, it helped to dissolve the fatalism of a traditional society as much as it reflected its rapid secularization. In the decade following 1961, attendance at mass dropped from 61 to 30 per cent in the Montreal diocese.[150] As Nicole Laurin-Frenette summarizes, 'from 1960, it was no longer the Church, but rather the state that watched over the nation and assumed the direction of its destiny ...'[151]

The Quiet Revolution has often been equated with a new phase of Québécois nationalism. Commentators have noted the clear ascendancy on an ideological plane of liberal over traditional nationalism evident by this time.[152] Furthermore, given that many significant policy developments were trumpeted by Lesage's *equipe de tonnère* with suitably sonorous nationalist rhetoric, the lurch towards statism of these years has been interpreted as arising from a fresh and more potent phase of nationalism. It should be pointed out, however, that official *exclusive* nationalism was not a factor during these years. While it is true that new cultural policies were introduced linking state and nation more closely in Quebec, on close examination these were constructed on liberal lines and posed no challenge whatever to pluralism. Official exclusive nationalism did not arise until the *end* of the decade, as will later be demonstrated by considering the record of the Lesage Liberal government, the language policy defended by René Lévesque within the early *sovereigntiste* movement, and the measures taken by Jean-Jacques Bertrand's Union Nationale government. This timing, as well as the shift in positions of the political élite are significant, for they suggest that the most dynamic transformations of this decade relate to the changes in the level of popular mobilization and the nature of political representation.

Although the Liberals under Lésage did what they did in the cultural domain with appropriate fanfare, they did in fact very little. Five days after assuming office in July 1960, Lesage's cabinet boldly proclaimed its intention of preserving the French visage of Quebec.[153] According to Premier Lesage's pronouncement the intent was to celebrate the French language in the course of encouraging Quebec society to 'bloom in its traditions, its spirit and its culture.'[154] Yet, at this point, preserving the French visage was less a matter of repulsing English, and more a matter of providing (mainly) moral support for cultural production, and of encouraging all *Québécois* to speak a form of French less sullied by grammatical defects and foreign lexical impurities. In 1961 a Ministry of Culture was created, ostensibly to foster the arts and letters.[155] An 'Office of the French Language' within the new ministry was given the task of inventing new French words for the features of the modern world that commonly triggered a flood of *anglicismes*. According to William Coleman's careful assessment, the ministry as a whole 'had virtually no impact on the mass of the population.'[156] In large part this was due to Lesage's reluctance to spend heavily in this area, and to his refusal to regulate language.[157]

Lesage's position on the role of the state in culture was flushed into the open several years later by the appearance of the preliminary report of the federal Royal Commission on Bilingualism and Biculturalism (here-in-after, the B & B Commission) in February 1965, and by controversy over a draft white paper on cultural policy submitted to cabinet later that year. The B & B report made it plain that much of the French-Canadian public considered the English influence to be 'harmful' and that francophones were 'rebelling against the obligation of learning English in order to reach positions of authority.'[158] Lesage's canny response was to proclaim that the primacy of French 'must manifest itself ... in all commercial and industrial enterprises in Quebec' – but that it was up to individuals, not the state, to achieve this.[159] As for the white paper, which was never released, Lesage rejected its suggestion that French was losing ground to English, as well as its proposal to make French the 'priority language.' Commenting on the lack of flexibility such a policy seemed to imply, he wrote in an angry marginal note: 'If I want to give instructions to an English-speaking employee, I certainly intend to do so in his language.'[160] In short, while the *dirigisme linguistique* of the Lesage government may well have given offence to those fond of Joual, the heavily anglicized French street dialect of Montreal, it did not propose any serious measures to alter the balance among real language communities in Quebec.

Mobilization during the 1960s

Meanwhile, a participatory culture was rapidly evolving in Quebec, a response to increases in both the supply and the demand of popular mobilization. On the demand side, the Lesage Liberals exemplified the opposition consensus evident in 1959 (see above) in seeking to achieve more 'citizen participation in public life' in order to 'revitalize the state.'[161] The project of nationalizing the patchwork of privately owned electric utility companies in Quebec was championed by René Lévesque, then minister of Natural Resources, who launched a 'personal campaign,' unauthorized by cabinet, to mobilize public opinion on the issue by 'speaking throughout the province.'[162] Subsequently, the 1962 election was called and decisively won on the issue.

Educational reform was advanced in part through the public consultations of the Parent Commission. The commission, in turn, suggested that in future 'some voice had to be given to the diverse range of organized social groups with a stake in education in the province. The normal electoral bodies had to be supplemented by "corps intermédiares" that would provide these groups with an opportunity to participate in the planning of education.'[163] A permanent intermediary body, a Superior Council of Education, was consequently created by Bill 60, explicitly with reference to concepts of 'organic democracy,' providing for the tempering of old-style 'intermediate bodies' representing vested interests, with groups purporting to represent the broader base of stakeholders.[164] At least in abstract form, Gérin-Lajoie recognized the far-reaching consequences of more 'direct democracy.' As he observed with considerable prescience, 'Whatever will be the government elected in twenty years, it will reflect the views of the population, and I accept that.'[165]

On the supply side, a boom in postsecondary education had conferred upon more citizens the sophistication required for more advanced forms of participation. Continued popular demand for improvements in public services in key sectors, not least education, lent the motivation for focused group participation.[166] The perennially powerful urge of French Canadians to better their collective standing in Quebec now found in the young nationalist wing of the Lesage Liberals a receptive and relatively open channel of political expression. Lévesque could claim in 1962 with perhaps some justification that nationalization was a necessary expedient, a symbolic outlet 'which will relieve that dangerous, growing impatience in Quebec and ward off a possible explosion.'[167] From the perspective of the older generation, Lesage included, the supply of popular participation exceeded all expectation. 'Jean Lesage, who in many ways was an eminently traditionalist leader, several times drew back in exasperation at the swift democratization that went so far as to affect his own status or the role he was exercising ... More and more people were demanding participation in management and in decision-making ... This "liberation" went well beyond the bounds of pure politics. The pendulum swung so far that leaders in every field, from bishops to parents, were caught off guard. Quebec was up against the first authority crisis in its history.'[168] The 'liberation' signalled an incipient crisis in the prevailing mode of political representation. By 1966, according to Denis Monière, citizens' groups began to 'proliferate.'[169] Some of these groups, as we shall see, would challenge the capacity of traditional political elites to maintain pluralist linguistic policies.

The Widening Power Cleavage

As we have argued, popular mobilization and newfound influence in Quebec during the 1960s was generated by much more than ethnic inequality. All the same, such rising influence was incommensurate with the perpetuation of such inequality. Broad francophone support was arrayed for state interventions that would remove selected economic functions from the private-sector domain of anglophones and deliver them up to a public domain dominated by francophones. But this was to broach a massive problem that could receive, as Lévesque had put it, only symbolic relief from the proposed measures. While the Liberals could print posters in its 1962 campaign depicting fists clenching bolts of electricity under the slogan 'Maître chez nous,' Hydro-Québec, even with its immense feats of engineering and construction, could hardly offer a global solution on its own.[170] Urban folklore had long had it that 'labour spoke French, and management, English' and the general truth of this had never ceased to rankle. In fact, the average income of those of French origins ranked seventh out of eight ethnocultural groups in Montreal in 1961.[171] In the private sector, salary earners of French ethnic origin in Montreal earned some 29 per cent less than those of English or Scottish origins, most of which (17 per cent) was attributable to factors attached to ethnicity itself, rather than, for example, to education or occupation.[172] One significant disadvantage was that in communicating with anglophone superiors, francophone professionals and administrators spoke in French less than a quarter of the time.[173] Moreover, it remained uncertain how quickly a French presence would assert itself in a Montreal business world populated with many well-entrenched anglophone professionals and owners. Thus, as French-speaking Québécois entered the political marketplace during the early 1960s, they demanded schemes to improve the economic position of francophones.[174]

Many francophones, concerned with *la survivance* of their culture, were also alarmed by numbers reported following the 1961 census revealing that the birth rate among younger francophones was no longer substantially greater than that of younger anglophones.[175] Their worst fears deepened when it was confirmed that immigrants were assimilating predominantly to the wealthier, English-speaking community in Montreal.[176] In the atmosphere of demographic crisis, many French-speaking Québécois came to favour simply eliminating altogether the distinctively anglophone corporate presence and power-base by compelling everyone to speak and write in French at work. What was sought with increasing forcefulness was not only greater economic power for francophones, but also an interlocking hegemony of the majority language and culture.

Yet this went well beyond anything the traditional political elite was prepared to champion. By 1965, Lesage's precarious combination of strong rhetorical support and weak policies in the realm of linguistic nationalism began to totter. In October at a special congress of a Lib̀eral student organization at which several cabinet ministers, including the premier, were present, the Université de Montréal delegation proposed a resolution demanding unilingualism in the province, charging that bilingualism was causing French to degenerate.[177] After a passionate debate, the resolution was withdrawn at the insistence of Lesage himself, causing its backers to leave in protest. Amended so that French would be recognized as the *langue prioritaire*, the motion passed with the support of the English-speaking contingent present, but against the opposition of the smaller number of French-speakers remaining. An advocate of the amended resolution asserted that 'the French Canadians can only count on themselves for maintaining the quality of their language, and that they would not gain its improvement by eliminating English.'

On such political foundations as these, priority for French rather than official unilingualism was inscribed as official policy in the Liberal manifesto of the next election. This, it should be made clear, was a thoroughly symbolic concession, with little or no policy force in terms of 'privileging in the sense of imposing a way of life.' To be sure, it proposed to elevate the prestige of the French language of the majority, but it proposed few if any concrete measures to achieve this. A proposal that would have done just that met a different fate. An initiative was raised in October 1965 of legislating a requirement for French to be used in collective agreements imposed by management, in the internal regulations of firms, and in the work process itself at the level of the shop floor.[178] However, even this mildly interventionist proposal was apparently something of a *coup*, having been publicly sprung by a rogue minister without Lesage's consent. Lesage, evidently mortified and about to embark on a trip abroad, declared he did 'not fully understand' his minister's initiative, and would have to take up the question with him upon his return.[179] Nothing further was heard of the proposal.

Internecine divisions of this sort within a public environment of mounting separatism and continued inequality presaged the departure of a section of the Liberal party in 1967 to form the Mouvement Souveraineté-Association (MSA). A year later, the MSA would go on to merge with the Ralliement national (RN) and draw upon the membership of the soon-to-be-defunct Rassemblement pour l'Indépendance Nationale (RIN) to form the Parti Québécois (PQ).

Although the dam was clearly at the bursting point, the established political elite was still attempting to channel the raging currents of increasingly articulate popular demands through liberal floodgates. The central figure in the innovation within the party system, René Lévesque, repeatedly denounced, both before and after his departure from the Liberal party, the sorts of exclusive nationalist policies in the sphere of language his party would later champion. Indeed, in 1965 at the time of the declaration of priority for French, and later in the nascent MSA, Lévesque made clear his opposition to any sort of official unilingualism.[180] In an informal talk to students at Laval, Lévesque held up as a paragon of just language policy the example of Finland, where bilingualism was the rule in documents of both the central administration and local governments in areas where at least 10 per cent of the population used the other official language.[181] (In

Quebec, as Lévesque noted to the students, approximately 20 per cent of the population was generally deemed to be anglophone.)

Three years later, in April 1968 at a general assembly of MSA delegates, Lévesque was forced to threaten his own resignation in order to block a resolution advanced by François Aquin advocating that government-funded education in English be substantially curtailed in Quebec.[182] Having flatly told Aquin before the assembly that he intended to 'fight as strongly for the rights of anglophones as for sovereignty,' Lévesque now expressed the common concern of political elites to avoid the serious international repercussions of exclusive nationalism.[183] He pleaded with the 1,700 delegates, many of whom were sympathetic to the much more radical linguistic exclusivism of the RIN, that in the interests of 'friendship with our neighbours to the East, West and South' a sovereign Quebec 'must make it a point of honour to demonstrate a great respect for the rights of its important linguistic minority ...'[184]

Inflexible commitment to such a restrained and liberal policy provoked frustration among many of the young delegates. One remarked ingenuously, 'We have [had] enough of moderation and of humanistic democrats ... We will march on with Lévesque if he is really the only one that can bring us power. But after, we will know what to do.'[185] A perspicacious journalist, after witnessing the spectacle of a division between party leader and delegates, observed that a democrat such as Lévesque was bound to embrace the rigours of a popular process, even if it was just such a process that was causing his principled leadership to falter.[186]

4.3 The Rise of Official Exclusive Nationalism

The International Context from Quebec: Thinking Globally

Internationally, 1968 marked the emergence of the new social movements that have profoundly altered politics in the industrialized world. The famous demonstration in Paris in May by nearly a million marchers brought an 'indictment,' as Alain Touraine put it, of 'new forms of power and oppression that are less specifically economic and more social, cultural, and political than in the past.'[187] At Columbia University, students occupied an administration building to protest the lack of regard shown by autocratic officials to the plight of disadvantaged blacks displaced by campus expansion. In Chicago, thousands of students confronted delegates and then police to challenge bourgeois American political values and the war in Vietnam.[188] In all three cases, 'new forms of opposition and contestation' were deployed in the quest to force the bureaucratic creatures of traditional elites to be more responsive to novel agendas and participants.[189] In their tactics and their ideals, protests such as these reinforced a legion of causes the world over and partly subverted the paradigm of politics as industrial relations.[190]

Quebec politics encountered a 'rupture' of its own in 1968 as exclusive nationalism erupted there in step with militancy throughout the West.[191] The synchronism between protest without and within Quebec stemmed in part from common intellectual foundations, established over the previous decade. In Montreal as in Paris, the militancy and the conceptual vocabulary of anti-colonial struggles influenced intellectuals. Drawing upon such inspirations to the American and European New Left as Franz Fanon and Ernesto Che Guevara, Québécois activists moulded a popular political culture in Quebec that was exceptionally receptive to the international wave of protest.[192] A member of the terrorist Front de Libération du Québec, Pierre Vallières concluded his celebrated prison diary, *White Niggers of America*, with Guevara's exhortation to revolution.[193]

An indication of the influence of the international climate upon popular culture in Quebec can be gained by considering the press. By 1968, even a daily such as *Le Devoir* no longer stigmatized militant tactics as subversive, even if it could not always resist gently lampooning them. A sardonic piece in the newspaper in the autumn provided students with a list of back-to-school necessaries that included a gas mask, a recipe for Molotov cocktails, posters of Guevara and Trotsky, works by Marcuse, and a list of snappy terms for use in meetings, including 'situationism,' 'student power,' and 'permanent protest.'[194] In more serious coverage, the daily ran front-page photographs of the 'confusion' in Chicago and a weighty three-part analysis of the global role of student protest.[195] When youth in Quebec did not fail to take such cues, the paper printed sympathetic editorial comment, thus reinforcing the impact of student mobilization for a variety of movements, most notably exclusive nationalism.[196]

The Aquarian age of popular protest and participation that rapidly accelerated in 1968 seriously challenged the legitimacy of affiliative trusteeship, of permitting elite reluctance to undermine the long-standing economic and political alliance with the powerful English-speaking minority to constrain direct majority rule. Mobilization led to symbolically charged confrontations with elite-driven policy concerning culture and language. As the political landscape was altered beyond recognition during the ensuing years with the creation of a new political party committed to internal democracy, conflict regulation was gravely weakened, the power cleavage closed, and the previously excluded nationalist segment gained sympathetic political representation in full proportion to its presence in Quebec society. As ethnic delegate representation came to define the emerging standard of legitimacy, official exclusive nationalism soon formed the new orthodoxy.

Protest in Quebec: Acting Locally

During 1968, the contradiction between the procedural and substantive ideals of democratic liberalism became ever more painfully evident. Although other members of the Quebec political elite would show themselves to be even more intransigent than Lévesque in rejecting popular chauvinism, events demonstrated that popular exclusive nationalism was being articulated with greater force and effectiveness than ever before, and that it could not easily be resisted.

In June 1968, in St Leonard, a suburb of Montreal, a citizens' group known as the Mouvement pour l'Intégration Scolaire (MIS) took control of the local school board with an agenda of forcing state-funded Catholic schools to use French as their sole language of education.[197] The impetus for the movement was that the large Italian community was sending the vast majority of its children to bilingual schools, in which up to 70 per cent of courses were given in English.[198] The new board's initiative was met by Italian parents in September with a boycott that kept some 1,700 children out of classrooms.[199] In the tense atmosphere that ensued, a second conflict was precipitated by an unrelated administrative decision of a regional board to move the francophone students at a secondary school to make way for anglophones. Some 85 francophone students occupied the school amid protestations of support from all manner of nationalist groups, one of which construed the issue as a 'touchstone for the status of the French language as the national language of Quebec.'[200] Six days into the occupation an agreement was reached that allowed the francophone students to keep their school.[201]

The principled response of the Quebec government of Bertrand to the larger issue was to proclaim in law the prerogative of parents to choose the language of education for their children. The initiative, Bill 85, placed Lévesque in an awkward position. Having refused to provide political leadership on the issues underlying the St Léonard affair (pointedly telling the leaders of the MIS that 'the integration of immigrants will not be done by knocking heads or by ordering people to speak French'), Lévesque now found himself struggling to square his new role as tribune of grass-roots nationalists, with his own, apparently sincere, liberal convictions.[202] During the parliamentary debate on Bill 85, Lévesque scribbled notes revealing the extent of his own compunctions: 'Bill 85 – how to reconcile that which we want, respect for others + influence [*rayonnement*] for the national language? Status quo at least preserved – why not? Awaiting an inquiry. It is no longer, sometimes, reason but passions that prevail ...'[203] Under the circumstances of a rapidly deteriorating situation on campuses and the streets (protest that, as Jacques Parizeau had noted, had served to triple the rate of membership enrolment in his party), Lévesque decided, apparently with heavy heart, that immigrants *could* be compelled to assimilate to the ranks of francophones and that the growth of English-language schools could be stopped, save for any natural increase in the Canadian-English population.[204] He then adopted a posture of strenuous opposition to the legislation. In any event, such violent popular opposition greeted the introduction of Bill 85 in November 1968 that a surprised Bertrand, suddenly stricken with a cardiac condition, was forced to send the measure to expire quietly in committee before second reading.[205]

When sufficient nerve was found a year later to reintroduce and pass the measure in a somewhat different guise, tumultuous demonstrations attracted tens of thousands of protestors, many of them young students.[206] Although the new version aimed to ensure that students attending English schools would acquire a knowledge of French, to encourage immigrants to learn French and choose it as the language of instruction for their children, and to subject to public scrutiny violations of the right of workers to use French, these concessions were insufficient to quell the public opposition manifested on the streets by some 200 organized groups as well as in opinion polls.[207] One poll of 5,000 Montrealers revealed that of francophones indicating a preference, 64 per cent opposed Bill 63 (as the 1969 version was known). Among students, opinion was even more decisive: 88 per cent of those indicating a preference were opposed.[208]

Significantly, the balance of opinion was entirely different within the National Assembly, in which Bill 63 enjoyed the support of the entire political elite, except for the dissenting votes of Lévesque and his four colleagues. Nonetheless, the nature of political process was changing forever, and elite liberal policy preferences could not hold out for much longer. With even the Union Nationale having adopted internal democracy (in 1965), Bertrand had been confirmed as leader in June 1969 against the 'ultra-nationalist' Jean-Guy Cardinal, with only 59 per cent of delegates' votes.[209] Permissive language policy would be spectacularly overturned by the language laws of the 1970s, when the 'divorce' an editorialist observed during the furore over Bill 63 'between parliament and a important fraction of public opinion' would be mended by elected officials prepared to execute the exclusivist will of a dominant section of the francophone majority.[210] That development is discussed in greater detail later. But, for now, the crucial point is that, as Gérard Bergeron emphasizes, the 'eruption' in 1968 rose up from the dense core of the body politic, not from the visible layers of the political elite. 'The language question, in particular, was being politicized. Not by the political leaders ... but at the grass roots ... Until the St Leonard affair in 1968, there had certainly been awareness of the significance of language among the governments of the Quiet Revolution. But it required this eruption from below in the protests of francophone citizens of a suburb of Montreal for language immediately to become and remain a political question.'[211] The concern of the political elite for harmonious relations with minorities made it extremely reluctant in the 1960s to adopt the sorts of decisive policies later enacted to assert the cultural and economic hegemony of French-speaking Québécois in Montreal. Liberal values were also apparently influential for some. As Bertrand put it, 'Democracy demands that one extends [the free choice] to others that one demands for oneself.'[212] Indeed, sensing the deluge that was to come, political elites recognized the importance of a dyke to protect individual freedoms from the surging struggle to advance the status of francophones and their language. The unsuccessful campaign platform of the Liberals in 1966 included a call for the formation of a human rights commission and a declaration of the rights of man.[213]

The Fusion of Ethnic Delegate Representation and Official Exclusive Nationalism in the Parti Québécois

The founding of the Parti Québécois in October 1968 was the pivotal event in the historic fusion of popular sovereignty and popular chauvinism, the fusion that ushered in the age of official exclusive nationalism in Quebec. 'Participation was the key word at the convention as delegates debated hundreds of amendments submitted by riding associations to the draft program drawn up in April.'[214] The statutes of the new party entrenched the substantial degree of popular control sought by 'participationists,' a dominant element sceptical of the democratic credentials of the ex–Liberal party elite.[215] In this environment, René Lévesque was unable to obstruct the exclusive nationalist forces arrayed before him. As John Saywell observes, 'A program far more radical than that advocated by the leaders was finally adopted. On the sensitive subject of minority language and educational rights the convention agreed to the continuance of English-language schools on a limited basis, but declared that immigrants would be required to speak French and attend French-language schools, that English would not be an official language, and that businesses would have five years to convert to French.'[216] Although eight years were required for the fledgling party to mature sufficiently to be entrusted with a mandate to legislate these policies, the sometimes grudging acquiescence of its leaders in a participatory process and their willingness to abide the popular consensus, however exclusivist, were already unmistakable by the end of the founding convention. As an affiliative trusteeship (of sorts) was finally hobbled in Quebec provincial politics, ethnic delegate representation emerged. Exclusive nationalism was not merely grafted temporarily onto the new party, but would increasingly define the core of its official ideology.[217]

Official Exclusive Nationalism in Office in Quebec

After being elected to a second term in 1973, the Liberal government of Robert Bourassa demonstrated the extent to which exclusive nationalism had come to dominate the official policy of all major Quebec parties. Bill 22, passed on 31 July 1974, was the first of two major language laws enacted during the decade. The preamble to bill 22 proclaimed the new orthodoxy. It stated, 'it is incumbent upon the government of the province of Quebec to employ every means in its power to ensure the pre-eminence of that language [French] and to promote its vigour and quality.'[218] In substance, the measure eliminated access to bilingual schools for children lacking a 'sufficient knowledge' of English, in practice, for children not from anglophone families. Essentially, the flow of immigrants and francophone defectors to the English language was to be stopped. Bill 22 also encouraged businesses to establish programs of francization, consisting of plans for more francophone managers to be hired and for unilingual anglophone managers to learn French and employ it in written documents.[219] Other provisions of bill 22 included making knowledge of French a requisite for accreditation by professional bodies, and requiring the use of French on public signs (though other languages were also permitted).[220]

Here was a policy of which French-speaking Québécois could approve. Polls showed that 71.6 per cent of a sample (of which sample 76 per cent were francophones) favoured compelling non–English-speaking immigrant children to attend French school. (A minority of almost 20 per cent – or about a quarter of the francophone portion of the sample – believed that even anglophones should not retain the right to send their children to English school.) In another poll, fully 90 per cent of francophones favoured government intervention to make French the language of public administration, labour, and business.[221] Among the political elite, the leaders and Quebec caucuses of all major federal parties were now left isolated in Quebec as the supporters of liberal policy.

The language legislation of the Bourassa Liberals overran the recommendations of the Commission of Inquiry on the Position of the French Language and on Language Rights in Québec, known as the Gendron Commission, after its chairman, Jean-Denis Gendron. Named in 1968, the commission comprised five members, including an anglophone constitutional scholar, Edward McWhinney. The commission's report, tendered in 1972, had recognized that measures were required to ensure 'far greater vertical mobility in commerce and industry on the part of French Canadians' and that the language of work was an key concomitant. But it had proposed, for the time being, mainly symbolic measures to elevate the status of French.[222] Thus it had hoped that 'psychological persuasion and example, in preference, if at all possible, to criminal law-based sanctions' would help to extend the 'French fact.'[223] Within the workplace, the immediate objective proposed had been merely to 'implement a language policy which will allow both French- and English-speaking people to use their own language in work communication.'[224] In education, the commission had notably recommended that all children in Quebec acquire, 'at the earliest possible age' a 'mastery' of both languages, but it could not bring itself to recommend any immediate measures to limit free choice.[225] Overall, the bicultural Gendron panel had presented a brave, if often furtive and qualified embrace of a pluralist cultural policy for Quebec at variance with the support for official exclusive nationalist policy within majority francophone public opinion, and with subsequent government policy.[226]

After the election of the Parti Québécois in 1976, perhaps the most significant development in exclusive-nationalist language policy was not a new direction in policy – Bill 101 only built on the base established by Bill 22 – but rather an explicit official exposition of the logic of the emerging language policy. In March 1977, the government released a white paper titled *Québec's Policy on the French Language*, perhaps the greatest monument to official exclusive nationalism in Canadian history. The author of the paper was Camille Laurin, a minister of the Lévesque government, and a former psychiatrist. Laurin diagnosed the troubles of Quebec society in psychological terms, observing that 'as long as a people feels insecure, threatened and vulnerable to attack from without, it will tend to withdraw.'[227] In Quebec, 'chronic insecurity ... bred legitimate feelings of distrust,' a pathology that threatened to spread to 'incurable xenophobia.'

The treatment Laurin prescribed with great candour was to indulge the longing for francophone hegemony that had lingered at the mass level since the conquest. The society the government of Quebec wished to build was 'essentially French.' The use of French 'will not merely be universalized to hide the predominance of foreign powers from the French-speaking population; this use will accompany, symbolize and support a reconquest by the French-speaking majority in Québec of that control over the economy which it ought to have. There will no longer be any question of a bilingual Québec.'[228] As Laurin took the view that a great deal of culture is embedded in language, the aims of his exclusivist language policy went far beyond giving economic superiority to francophones to include 'protecting and developing ... a mode of being, thinking, writing, creating, meeting, establishing relations between groups and individuals ...'[229] The whole French-speaking Québécois way of life, incarnate in language, was to be privileged.

The bewitching vision of a monolithic Quebec was directly transferred from the white paper to the preamble of the first draft of the new language law, Bill 1. The preamble contained a description of the body politic that was extraordinary, bearing in mind that Montreal, the locus of ethnic conflict, enjoyed a 34 per cent minority having a primary language other than French.[230] 'The National Assembly, being aware that the French language has always been the language of the Québec people, that it is, indeed, the very instrument by which they have articulated their identity ...'[231] The last clause of the draft bill was equally noteworthy: it gave priority to the act over the Quebec Charter of Rights.

Both elements provoked an outcry from the anglophone minority and, indeed, from the Quebec Human Rights Commission. Partly because of these reactions, and partly because of the desire for a rapid passage, Bill 1 was rewritten to remove some particularly noxious elements (including the original preamble) and tabled again as Bill 101.[232] Overall, Bill 101 was essentially a package of amendments to the general policy set out in Bill 22, rather than a startlingly new initiative.[233] Stricter criteria for access to English schools were introduced so as to erect an even more effective bar against immigrant assimilation to the anglophone community. In lieu of English tests for five-year-olds, the principal criterion for admission to English schools became whether a parent had attended English school in Quebec. If a parent had not done so, with few exceptions, admission was denied. Chapter 7 of the legislation required that signs, posters, and firm names be in French only. Even small shops with overwhelmingly non–French-speaking clienteles were prohibited from displaying signs inside or outside their businesses in other languages.

Provisions in chapter 5 barred those lacking a knowledge of French from the professions, a measure gratuitously discriminatory for non–French-speakers seeking to serve predominantly non-French-speaking communities.[234] The negative incentives for firms to acquire francization certificates were also increased; operating licences in addition to official largesse were now to be denied to firms with more than fifty employees lacking one. The francization program, at least as envisaged in the act, aimed at 'the use of French as *the* language of work and as *the* language of internal communication.'[235] No qualifications were offered as to the appropriateness of conducting business in other languages under certain (reasonably foreseeable) circumstances, such as where fluently multilingual francophones find themselves overwhelmingly outnumbered by speakers of another language, or simply desire to practise speaking another language. This, hence, was no mere promotion of linguistic courtesy, non-discrimination, and competence within a multicultural society. It was a crude assertion of exclusive linguistic rights arising not from individuals, not from communities, but rather from 'majority rule' as such.[236]

Many non-francophones in Quebec took umbrage at the measures, which seemed to devalue their presence. Four years after the measure was passed, Lévesque himself referred to a poll showing that six out of ten anglophones believed 'the Quebec government does not want them.'[237] Equally telling was the flow from the province of English-speakers. Between the 1976 and 1981 censuses there was a net decline in Quebec of some 95,000 anglophones, or 12 per cent of the population having English as its mother tongue.[238] Although the hurt and anger concomitant with such large population movements might elsewhere have triggered an insurgency, in Quebec civil violence was avoided, perhaps because anglophones were able to relocate with their property elsewhere in Canada. The most serious costs of Bill 101 were therefore not civil war, but rather a sharp shock to pluralism in the world, considerable loss of international prestige for Quebec, and (presumably) some loss of continuity in the lives of those who left the province because they no longer felt they fit in.

In July 1977, when Bill 101 was passed, there were few vestiges left of the power cleavage. Although 32 of 86 members present in the National Assembly voted against the measure, this division probably roughly paralleled the division within public opinion.[239] Perhaps the only sign of reluctance whole-heartedly to embrace exclusive nationalism among the governing political elite was exhibited by several PQ cabinet members, including Lévesque.[240] In rising to defend his government's measure only 'half-heartedly' in the National Assembly, Lévesque professed to be 'humiliated' to be obligated by circumstances to pass such a measure. He also tried to erase the element of revenge unmistakably expressed in the white paper, and further pledged that in future – as if the time had not yet come – the affirmation and defence of French in Quebec would cease before it prevented the anglophone community from maintaining and expressing itself freely.[241]

4.4 Constitutional Autonomy: Exclusive Nationalism?

Why This Digression Is Necessary

Little attention has been given so far in this chapter to the evolution in twentieth-century Quebec of constitutional autonomy. Independence, when rhetorically predicated on the existence of a nation, is perhaps as obvious a manifestation of generic nationalism as one might encounter. That is not to say, however, that aspirations for autonomy are tantamount to *exclusive* nationalism. Indeed, in Quebec, autonomy has not been consistently motivated by, or coupled with, exclusivist designs. Many important nationalists, and particularly those among the political elite, have advocated greater autonomy for Quebec on grounds that are not in the least exclusivist, envisaging in key instances a new state at least as pluralist as modern Canada. Furthermore, much of the obvious stimulus for autonomy has been distinguishable from the impetus for exclusive nationalism, having often arisen from episodes causing alienation within and from Canadian federalism, rather than (as for the instances of exclusive nationalism discussed in this chapter) from circumstances *within* Quebec society. Independence, finally, on a theoretical plane must be firmly distinguished from exclusive nationalism.

To be sure, there are no syntactical or logical barriers to espousing constitutional autonomy as a means to separate a minority from its friends elsewhere, in order, *then*, to impose the way of life of the majority. Such arguments would obviously elide separatism and exclusive nationalism. But while they have certainly appeared in Quebec, they have by no means been universal, and indeed have very rarely been articulated by the senior political elite. The relevance of the subsequent discussion to the larger theory here is to set aside the argument that might assert that while established political elites have had exclusive nationalism of the linguistic variety thrust upon them, they at least kept pace with, if not led, popular opinion before the late 1960s in asserting a discreet type of exclusive nationalism in the form of Quebec-autonomy/separatism. (That, if it were true, would undermine the sequence of popular political mobilization leading to a change in the pattern of political representation, leading to a breach of the power cleavage – the heart of my argument.) For interest sake, I will also argue that as late as the 1980 referendum on sovereignty-association, the terms of the 'Yes' campaign, as set out by the executive of the PQ, carefully avoided any admixture of exclusive nationalism and sovereignty.

Conscription and the Souring of French-Canadian Nationalists on Confederation

In 1913, the Canadian parliamentarian and French-Canadian nationalist Henri Bourassa began a series of articles about nationalism in Quebec with a sweeping proposition: 'The nationalist movement was born with the official participation of Canada in the South African War.'[242] During the decade and a half following the Boer War crisis, a period that imposed additional strains by the disillusioning crises in French education in Ontario and the Prairies, Bourassa had nevertheless bravely espoused an optimistic vision of entente, his 'nationalism' articulated mainly in the insistence that the French-Canadian minority, in deference to its role as founding partner and to its differences of language and religion, be recognized as a distinct and equal partner to 'English' Canadians, particularly in matters bearing on fundamental constitutional questions.[243] The autonomy Bourassa sought for French Canada (and indeed for Canada as a whole) consisted in a retreat from the imperial military obligations thrust, as he saw it, upon Canada.[244] To his opposition to imperialism, Bourassa added public faith in reciprocal accommodation and in the good intentions of English Canadians.

> We are the neighbours and associates of an English majority. We do not want our fellow citizens to reinforce the ties that attach us to England, nor to upset to their own advantage the equilibrium of the two races in Canada. In return, we must not injure their national feeling and natural touchiness by desiring a strengthening of political ties with France, or a rupture of the Canadian Confederation ... Resist firmly the political absorption of Canada in the

Empire and the extinction of our nationality in Canada. Honour the faith
that we have placed in England and in the Anglo-Canadian majority: that is
the best means of making them keep their word.[245]

Two years later, in 1904, Bourassa blended an assertion of duality with
claims of nation status for Canada as a whole, and a dismissal of the attacks
on Confederation by a Quebec writer, J.-P. Tardivel.[246]

> Our nationalism is Canadian nationalism, founded on the duality of races
> and on the particular traditions that duality brings ... The fatherland for us is
> all of Canada, that is to say, a federation of distinct races and of autonomous
> provinces. The nation that we want to see developed is the Canadian nation,
> composed of French and English Canadians, of two elements separated by
> language and religion, and by legal structures necessary to conserve their
> respective traditions, but united in a fraternal bond, in a common attachment
> to the common fatherland.[247]

Bourassa, a leading spirit of French-Canadian nationalism until the mid-
1920s, thus early situated French-Canadian constitutional discomfiture
within a context much broader than that of ethnic conflict and competition
in Quebec.

One of the great tragedies of Canadian federalism is that Bourassa's
optimistic assertions of Canadian dualism were soon overtaken by the
First World War. The war, which much of the French-Canadian elite
quickly supported in principle, made mounting demands on Canadian
resources and lives that grossly outweighed both the limited local interests
perceived at stake, as well as the attenuated sense of personal injury felt by
many French Canadians (and many Australians and New Zealanders, for
that matter). The failure of senior officers, particularly Colonel Sam Hughes,
Conservative minister of the Militia (1911–16), to accommodate a culturally distinctive and prominent presence for French Canadians within the
Canadian military also did not make enlistment any more attractive.[248]

The announcement of compulsory military service in May 1917 consequently brought nothing less than the 'political isolation of French Canada,'
the humiliation of many political allies of federalism in Quebec, and the
declining influence there of Bourassa's earlier pan-Canadian formulation
of French-Canadian nationalism.[249] Equally damaging as stories of Orangemen zealously directing recruiting efforts in Quebec was the rhetorical excess of English-Canadian politicians.[250] Arthur Meighen, the minister
responsible for conscription, let slip that 'the most backward elements' of

Canadian society were opposed to conscription.'[251] In the federal election campaign of late 1917 Unionists pointed to French-Canadian Liberals as traitors, despite their support for the war.[252]

The pro-conscription Union government that swept to power in the December 1917 election had not a single supporter among French-Canadian MPs.[253] The polarization of Canadian society now cut cleanly through its political elite. In the wake of the Conscription campaign the English-Canadian political elite now proved sufficiently numerous and united to govern as an ethnic bloc (though thankfully not for long), without recourse to the cross-cultural alliances that Confederation had been founded upon. In Quebec, Bourassa's hopeful *bonne ententisme* of the pre-war years became increasingly untenable. Days after the election, he himself thundered furiously in *Le Devoir*,

> The anglo-saxon bloc ... is nothing less than solid. It is not the union for 'winning the war' that aligned the anglophone forces – that, *that* is the pretext, the smoke screen, the fake flag that conceals the smuggled goods – it is the union for crushing Quebec. This fine plan, conceived with hatred and dishonesty, has attained its predictable result: it has brought four million Anglo-Protestants against all that is Catholic and non-British; it has revived and raised the distrust of two million French Canadians ... against all that is English and Protestant; in a word, the supposed 'National Union' has disunited the Canadian nation and planted a new seed of disintegration in the already deeply cracked soil of the British Empire.[254]

Younger nationalist voices in Quebec were disinclined to stop there, to construe the empire as the sole constitutional dock at which this bitterness should be heaped. The Quebec legislature itself witnessed a motion and brief debate in 1918 on the withdrawal of the province from Canadian Confederation.[255] More significantly, Bourassa's federalist and integrative leadership for French-Canadian nationalism gave way during the following two decades to the parochial and often exclusive nationalism of Groulx, accelerating the psychological retreat, not merely from the British empire and monolithic conceptions of the Canadian nation, but now from Canadian confederation itself. During this phase, the elision of exclusive nationalism and constitutional autonomy was more common.

In 1920, *L'Action française*, which had originally been spawned by writings on federal French language rights in *Le Devoir*, passed under the directorship of Groulx.[256] In 1922, the journal published a monthly series of articles, 'Our Political Future.' The premise of the series was that

Confederation had been placed on a path to destruction and that independence for Quebec seemed virtually inevitable.[257] Without sounding any calls to immediate action, the series addressed the issues an independent 'French state' might face. Joseph Bruchard, addressed what Groulx termed an 'internal obstacle' – namely, the presence of foreigners.[258] Bruchard granted anglophones in his hypothetical state bilingual schools, but hoped that after perhaps two centuries of continued co-existence they might 'deign to speak our language among us.'[259] But he was more firmly exclusivist in conceiving of the use of sweeping legislation to 'undertake a French restoration of our territory from one border to the other,' envisioning 'sparkling French signs thrust up from our soil.'[260] By 1924, one of the writers for *L'Action française* bluntly declared its support for the dissolution of Confederation and the 'constitution of a French state in Eastern Canada.'[261] But this proved to be the high-water mark of separatism in *L'Action française*. Thereafter, it took the view that the envisaged Catholic, French state could subsist as an autonomous province of the Canadian federation.[262]

This generated a minor schism, as younger radicals at the most extreme node of nationalist discourse articulated an even more enthusiastic elision of separatism and exclusive nationalism. Dostaler O'Leary, for example, was a prominent young member of both *Jeune Canada* and the *Jeunesses Patriotes*, a frequent contributor to *La Nation*, and a forthright advocate of fascist corporatism.[263] O'Leary explicitly rejected the constitutional conservatism of Groulx, arguing that 'the realization of a French state in Confederation is a utopia.'[264] 'And it is because it is absolutely impossible within Confederation to be entirely French Canadian that we want to leave.'[265] O'Leary's blueprint proposes a separate state modelled loosely after the authoritarian dictatorships of Mussolini and Salazar that 'will protect the collectivity before individuals' and will 'speak of duties before speaking of rights.'[266] This would be a state 'fully Catholic and fully French ... a state in which the personality of our people will affirm itself fully, entirely, totally.'[267] How so? Through quotas, as in Europe, for Jewish 'lawyers, doctors, engineers, architects, etc.' that would limit numbers to the proportion of Jews in the population (and do the same for English-speaking civil servants); through compelling by law all those who work with the public 'to speak French *correctly*'; and (anticipating later language legislation) by requiring the ubiquitous presence of French on public signs, in advertising, and on restaurant menus.[268]

The Bloc Populaire Canadien was founded just five months after the plebiscite of April 1942 once again divided Canada over conscription.

French Canadians voted overwhelmingly 'no' in the plebiscite, the vote in Quebec showing 73 per cent against, in stark contrast to the vote in 'English' Canada of 80 per cent in favour of releasing the federal government from its pledge of March 1939 not to impose conscription.[269] The result of the plebiscite on conscription made French Canada feel 'more isolated and different than ever,' confronted as all of Canada now was by the 'brutal realization' of the country's 'essential dualism.'[270] The Bloc responded to the crisis by demanding, as Bourassa had earlier in similar circumstances, the restoration of the dualist spirit of the 1867 constitution, as well as many of the federalist remedies actually instituted in ensuing decades: federal and provincial bilingualism, a new flag and anthem, more francophones in the federal civil service, a cessation of appeals to the privy council, and a distinctive Canadian diplomatic presence abroad.[271] But now federalist reforms were joined with much stronger demands for provincial autonomy than Bourassa had made earlier. As Maxime Raymond, leader of the Bloc, put it, 'The Bloc considers provincial autonomy as the backbone of the country. Without it, Canada risks sagging under legislation that is too uniform, under a centralism that does not take account of geographic, economic or ethnic particularity, and under the quarrels that tend to the violent rupture of Confederation.'[272] In the end, the Bloc failed at the polls, garnering only 15 per cent of the vote (and four seats) in the 1944 provincial election, 8 per cent (and 2 seats) in the 1945 federal election.[273] But in linking conscription with the threatening growth of centralized federal policies, the movement staked a public claim for the importance of the Quebec state.[274] From our perspective, the Bloc's commitment to bilingualism simultaneously with a more autonomous and stronger Quebec state, together with its origins in federal policy rather than internal ethnic conflict, signify a renewed separation of the thrust for greater Quebec autonomy from that of exclusive nationalism.

Postwar Demands for Autonomy and Sovereignty

Duplessis, whether from conviction or tactical political considerations, distinguished himself from earlier Conservative Quebec premiers by a distinctly antagonistic relationship with the federal government. Seizing upon everything from minor symbolic issues (protocol for appointment of lieutenant-governors; unilateral federal redistribution of seats for Parliament) to more substantial ones (constitutional amending formulas, division of the tax base, university funding, and federal entry into provincial social welfare policy spheres), Duplessis entered into a series of public confrontations with successive prime ministers to escape 'federal tutelage' and assert Quebec autonomy.[275] As Conrad Black puts it, Duplessis 'canalized Quebec nationalism into a battle that was frequently indistinct as to what it was for, but very descriptive in what it was against. Centralization meant a virtual unitary state ... It meant depriving Quebec of the ability to defend its own cultural, religious, and national prerogatives.'[276] To recall our early discussions, Duplessis had little intention of actually exercising such cultural or religious prerogatives in any systematic, positive fashion. Whatever his own disposition, his symbiotic relationship with Anglo-Protestant capital would have strongly deterred anything along the lines of O'Leary's agenda. Defending the old bicultural framework in Quebec of educational, health and welfare institutions, while advancing the cause of Quebec autonomy therefore presented an obvious strategy, one that avoided any elision of autonomy-seeking and exclusive nationalism. Duplessis's dramatically pitched battles with the federal government over taxation and new federal programs permitted him to assert not only Quebec autonomy, but also his opposition to an extensive modern welfare state.

The May 1980 Referendum on Sovereignty in Context

As already discussed, the provincial political elite of virtually all partisan stripes in Quebec, under duress of francophone majority opinion, embraced an exclusive nationalist language policy during the 1970s. It is important to note, however, that the sovereignty and exclusive language agendas were kept in virtually watertight compartments. Although the PQ was patently freighted with both cargoes, it remained within the scope of the party elite's influence to insist that they be kept apart. Under the influence of René Lévesque, sovereignty was consistently presented as an option for all.[277] This discussion will place the 1980 referendum in the context of the evolution of the PQ's sovereigntist agenda.

The PQ arose from the confluence of three separatist movements: the RN, RIN, and MSA. Of the three, the RIN represented the closest elision of separatism and exclusive nationalism. Founded in 1960, the movement patterned itself after anti-colonial movements in the developing world, alluding in its manifesto and other declarations to federal centralization, to the 'economic and political tutelage of foreigners' in Quebec, and, above all, to the consequent need to 'accelerate the establishment of national independence for Quebec.'[278] At least two executives of the movement, Pierre Bourgault and André d'Allemagne, also held that the 'corrupted

French of French Canadians could not be dissociated from their status as a colonized and dominated people' and so alongside its independence and social-democratic agendas the movement held a 'forthright commitment to the full preeminence of French within Quebec.'[279]

It was this exclusivist element of the RIN that precluded a simple merger with the MSA. Several rounds of talks between the two movements foundered when the MSA refused to compromise public funding for anglophone institutions in a future independent Quebec. In the end, d'Allemagne was told in June 1968 by Marc Brière and Jean-Roch Boivin of the MSA that 'the English of Quebec have a right to their schools, their universities, and to their hospitals, financed by the government ... These are not temporary rights; they are inalterable ... They are historic and sacred rights that must be inscribed in the Constitution [of an independent Quebec].'[280] Lévesque terminated the talks the following month when it became evident that no agreement would be forthcoming on, as Lévesque put it, 'a thing as fundamental as the respect of minority rights.'[281]

The principled position taken by the MSA in dealing with the RIN did not represent an abrupt about-face or an anomaly. To be sure, Lévesque's work of the previous year, *Option for Quebec*, which set out the sovereigntist proposal, had rhetorically addressed itself to a monolithic body politic. ('We are *Québécois* ... At the core of this personality is the fact that we speak French.')[282] Moreover, the public declaration announcing the merger between the MSA and RN articulated the intangible, but symbolically portentous objective of the 'creation of a sovereign state of the French language.'[283] Yet, the same declaration also pledged 'recognition of the educational rights of anglophones' and *Option for Quebec* volunteered to address, in concert with the rest of Canada at the time of separation, 'the question of minorities.'[284] And although Lévesque maintained (the entirely reasonable position) that 'in our homeland we must be able to earn our living and pursue our careers in French,' he certainly did not suggest anything along the lines of compelling in all organizations, including ones staffed predominantly by anglophones, to tolerate only French.[285] *Epanouissement*, protection of the French culture from erosion, even symbolic 'priority' were clearly part of the sovereignty package, but not cultural hegemony, or, to repeat the core of our definition of exclusive nationalism, 'altering the balance.'[286] Of course, such exclusivist policy is not for that matter explicitly excluded either. But our point is not that the PQ executive, certainly by 1972, felt it possible to avoid all exclusivist policy, but rather that they did not cite as an advantage of sovereignty that it was a precursor for (what we would deem) official exclusive nationalism.

If not to vouchsafe exclusive-nationalist policy, why then replace Confederation with sovereignty-association? Three major reasons were emphasized during the early years of Lévesque's sovereigntist proposal, reasons that may be summarized as Quebec statism, the obsolescence of Canadian federalism, and the psychological benefits of the very act of national self-assertion. Taking these in turn, the argument for a 'massive transfer of fiscal resources' to the state of Quebec, turns in *Option for Quebec* and *Prochaine étape* (1972) upon three contentions.[287] First, that the role of the state in fields such as education, social welfare (hospital insurance, family allowances, pensions, and medicare), and 'scientific and industrial research' had not yet reached maturity for the purposes of Quebec.[288] Second, that state capitalism and planning on the model of Hydro-Québec, Société Générale de Financement, Soquem, and the Caisse de Dépôts represented an important growth vector for Quebec and would be enhanced with the full backing of a strong separate state.[289] Third, that in order to 'secure the safety of' (not to *impose*) the 'collective "personality"' (read: majority francophone culture), the Quebec government required control of 'citizenship, immigration, and employment,' as well as of 'films, radio, and television.'[290]

Canadian federalism is argued to be irretrievably 'archaic' because its duplication of institutions and services makes it inefficient (an interesting argument, given that sovereignty would eliminate overlap only at the cost of forgoing *all* benefits of scale in building a *fully* dedicated, parallel, bureaucratic apparatus within Quebec), and because the radical decentralization required to resolve such duplication and to accommodate the distinct policy priorities of Quebec would not be in the best interests of the rest of Canada.[291] Finally, it is adduced in favour of sovereignty that the very act of assuming it would be psychologically emancipatory for Quebec society. Having been subjected to the status of an 'internal colony' by the English-Canadian metropole, Quebec stands to gain a heightened sense of efficacy through sovereignty: 'There is now among us the capacity to build our society ourselves and the more we take charge in accepting our responsibilities, the more we will discover ourselves effective and capable of succeeding as well as others, all things considered. There will be no valid excuse because it will be up to us only to find solutions to our problems that suit us, because no other person is capable, nor desirable, to rule in our place.'[292] To pursue sovereignty would be to 'bring us together, united and strong enough to confront all of our possible futures.'

By the time of the May 1980 referendum on sovereignty-association, three years had passed since Bill 101 had been legislated – within Confederation. This initiative achieved, the PQ's case for the 'yes' side did not rest upon official exclusive nationalism. On the contrary, the 'yes' side conscientiously framed its argument to appeal to Québécois of all ethnic or linguistic persuasions, and pledged its tangible support for a pluralist, multicultural society within an independent Quebec.

The terms of the pro-sovereignty PQ campaign were set-out in a white paper tabled 2 November 1979 entitled *Québec-Canada: A New Deal*.[293] Consistent with earlier sovereigntist appeals, the white paper emphasizes the dysfunctionality of Confederation. The Canadian federation is an inescapably centralized system in view of the division of powers and taxation under the BNA Act, the growth of the state in post-war times, and the legitimate interest of the rest of Canada in a centralized system.[294] As structured, the federation precludes the desired integration of the social security system in Quebec, maintains overlapping jurisdictions, is culturally invasive (given the role of Ottawa in 'asserting a Canadian identity distinct from the American identity'), and reduces Quebec to 'a beggar vis-à-vis the federal government.[295]

To be sure, the white paper opens with an emotional and somewhat exclusive appeal, referring to a set of 'our ancestors' that assuredly represents only *pure laine* stock.[296] Yet, the document also offers both symbolic and concrete concessions to minorities, committing to policies tantamount to official multiculturalism (though assuredly not under that brand name).

> Thanks to the contributions of citizens with different languages and religions, Quebec society, long a homogeneous one, has become quite diverse: it includes English-speaking Quebecers and those of all origins who, with their francophone compatriots, are helping to build Quebec. Sovereignty will not change the policy Quebec has always followed regarding the various cultural communities that make up its people and reflect the cultural riches of our planet. It is in the interest of those communities, as well as of Quebec, that they assert and develop that part of themselves which is essential to their heritage. The Quebec government undertakes to put at their disposal the community facilities and cultural instruments with which they will be able to develop their heritage on their own. Those various communities enrich Quebec, and Quebec offers them the ideal surroundings in which to live and grow according to their aspirations.[297]

The cultural policy envisaged for the majority, moveover, proposes to define culture in broader terms than language or religion, such that cultural sponsorship is construed less as intervening within ethnic competition and conflict, and more a matter of scattering fertilizer in every field. The beneficiaries are inherently plural groups ('artists, creators, and researchers'), and the policy tools are neutral ('expansion of cable distribution and community media ... film and book policies, assistance programs, prestigious and varied museums, sports, parks and recreation').[298]

Reaction to the case for sovereignty made by the PQ elite was mixed. Graham Fraser, a journalist for the *Montreal Gazette*, observed succinctly that 'the English in Quebec go virtually unmentioned in *A New Deal* as a scapegoat, but rather get the promise of a bilingual ballot on the referendum' and pledges concerning its rights.[299] On the other hand, perhaps the most telling indication of the pluralist assumptions and comportment of the 'yes' campaign consisted in the furious rantings of a living traditional nationalist, François-Albert Angers, who offered from within *indépendantiste* ranks a four-part post-mortem in *Le Devoir*, presenting an extraordinary diatribe against Lévesque's 'false democratic scruples' and 'almost morbid fear of falling into racism.'[300]

> Today, after the referendum, in which ... by false democracy and against all good sense, we have given the right to pronounce on self-determination to all Canadian *Québécois*, without distinguishing national affiliation, a serious reflection imposes itself on all those who still dream of an independent Quebec as to what sort of Quebec they want to build. And if it is a French Quebec they envisage, major changes of attitude will be necessary. Based on current trends, what is in store is an entirely different Quebec from that which we have worked to liberate: a bilingual and bicultural Quebec, [indeed] multilingual and multicultural. We will lose our Quebec, even in acceding to political independence.[301]

Needless to say, it would not have been tactically wise for Angers or other *indépendantiste* critics to make such views known *during* the campaign, and so the PQ elite was, perhaps unusually, in a strong position to set out from above a distinctly multicultural vision for an independent Quebec. (On the other hand, I am unaware of any opinion research that would quantify the portion of the francophone public that shared Angers's reaction to the PQ's platform. It therefore remains a matter of conjecture to what extent the specific circumstances of the referendum enabled the PQ elite to 'reopen' a power cleavage.) Sovereignty was rejected in the 1980 referendum by 59.6 per cent of voters (including, incidentally, 52 per cent of francophones). McRoberts interprets the result as evidence that, through measures such as Bill 101, 'the Lévesque administration may have eased some of the cultural insecurity that could otherwise have led to support for sovereignty.'[302] Certainly it seems clear that the pluralist assumptions underpinning the 'yes' campaign gave little scope to any unfulfilled exclusive nationalist sentiment among voters.

To summarize, we conclude that no *a priori* elision of separatism and exclusive nationalism can be presumed. Certainly, many on the fringes of electoral politics, such as Groulx, Bruchard, O'Leary, Bourgault, and Angers, have sometimes envisaged constitutional retreat as a means to exclusivist ends. But others, including many nationalists (of varying hues) within the political elite, such as Henri Bourassa, Raymond, Duplessis, and the proponents of the sovereigntist platform of the PQ to 1980, never linked their initiatives for greater constitutional autonomy (in the form of anti-imperialism, dualist conceptions of federalism, provincial autonomy, and sovereignty) with exclusive nationalism. To generalize, constitutional retreat has generally ensued from the shortcomings of Canadian federalism in the view of francophone Québécois; exclusive nationalism by contrast has always responded to circumstances within Quebec society, even where it has been embraced simultaneously with constitutional retreat.

Autonomy, Exclusive Nationalism, and Liberalism: A Philosophical Sidebar

A final, more subtle argument to address is that separatism, when propelled by the national aspirations of a majority *ethnie*, inherently constitutes exclusive nationalism; that in seeking greater autonomy, most particularly on behalf of Quebec francophones, *all* political elites in Quebec (from Duplessis onward), have engaged in a form of official exclusive nationalism. This discussion may be reduced to two questions. Is the ethnically concentrated nature of the primary constituency for national autonomy tantamount to proof of the exclusive nationalist character of the initiative for autonomy? And are political objectives, such as autonomy, which differentially accommodate a national majority, inherently exclusive nationalist? These two issues may be termed the 'national subject' question, and the 'national object' question.

To take the 'national subject' question first, it is useful to recall that our concept of exclusive nationalism (unlike the concept of 'ethnic nationalism,' unfortunately prevalent in the literature) refers not to the ethnic exclusivity or particularity of the prime *constituency for* a form of nationalism, but rather to a specific class of ends sought – namely, 'to privilege one recognizable way of life over others, in the sense of imposing it on others ...' Barring claims for consensus in modern democracies, neither the substantive nor the procedural liberalism of measures can be judged from whether their supporting majorities happen to be largely denominated by ethnic characteristics. To argue the contrary would be to engage in a form of logical fallacy at the communal level known for individuals as *ad hominem*, or attacking the characteristics of the speaker rather than his or her arguments.

Although the 'national object' question could also be quickly dealt with through reference to our definition of exclusive nationalism (not just *any* national objectives, only those that impose a way of life), it is worthwhile pausing here to address briefly the bearing of liberalism on the pursuit of independence, in the case where it is constructed to provide differential relief or benefits for certain ethnic or national groups present. Is the nation-state (or the seeking of it) inherently illiberal? Given that it is difficult or impossible to attach an ethical value to the majority or minority status of *ethnie* within *existing* states (this having been almost always decided arbitrarily, often by force), I think that liberalism can have virtually nothing in its own right to say about initiatives to redraw the borders of states. The exception, of course, would be where this redrawing is proposed *so that*, as a *second* step, the polity can embrace exclusive nationalism as official policy (or otherwise employ the state in illiberal fashion). Now, one might argue that, political resources being scarce, there are higher liberal priorities than constitutional upheaval from the perspective of achieving substantive justice, but this sticky argument about resource deployment has at least been addressed (if not totally convincingly) by separatists in arguing that the act of achieving independence would unshackle the spirit of progress needed to confront even greater structural issues of fairness in society. One seeking to deny liberal credentials to separatism might also argue on empirical grounds that a byproduct, historically, of erecting new nation-states has been the despotic treatment of minorities by majorities. But given recent examples, perhaps most significantly the Czech and Slovakian republics, this argument might be defeated by reasonable grounds for new optimism.

Finally, one might argue that to seek particularist objectives, such as independence, on behalf of ethnically delineated groups is to reinforce the organization of opinion (and identity) within the body politic along ethnic lines, and, further, that such cleavages are not the most efficient from the standpoint of achieving more substantially transformative liberal agendas. But while this certainly represents an interesting avenue for speculation, it seems doubtful that any generalizations will be found possible here. Most would accept that 'national exploitation' is a legitimate category well known to history, and *in such cases* (themselves prone to definitional uncertainty) it would be contentious to suggest that alternative lines for organizing public opinion (class, gender, theories of economics, etc.) would necessarily give rise to the greatest emancipation of the greatest number of individuals. It is difficult or impossible, in short, to construct knock-down arguments against bare separatism from liberal theory. Such arguments must instead depend on serious issues of practical viability, and on global interests in a manageable international order.

4.5 Analysis and Relevance to Theory

We have argued that official exclusive nationalism, the third and terminal phase in the progression traced in this work, arose in Quebec during the late 1960s. As previous forms, its presence was no doubt a political manifestation of ethnic competition for symbolic and concrete forms of influence. But in reconstructing the *causal sequence* (as distinct from the general *context*), it is inadequate to stop there. Attributing causality for any intensifying (or weakening) phenomenon logically depends upon evidence not just of the static presence, but also of the changing intensity, of an independent variable. In Quebec between 1930 and 1960, it is unclear that either ethnic competition or cultural insecurities intensified. To encounter the election rhetoric presented by the ALN in 1935, and the electorate's considerable support for the party, is to recognize that it is far from certain that French Canadians were any more content with their lack of participation in guiding and profiting from capital in that decade than they were thirty years later. To read *L'Action française* of the 1920s (and *L'Action nationale* in the 1930s) and to witness evidence of pronounced ethnic tensions during the 1930s is to encounter a painful awareness of, and distress at, the threat of massive discontinuities in the cultural life and identity of francophone society. Therefore, we have argued in this chapter that the most obviously dynamic variable was not the extent of ethnic competition or the presence of deep cultural insecurity, but rather the transformation of the state and, specifically, its much increased interdependence with broader ranks of civil society.

Earlier political forms in Quebec featured narrower forms of such interdependence. In the days of Taschereau and of the early Duplessis administrations, the legitimate role of the provincial state was to secure economic growth within a highly capital intensive, resource-extraction-based economy for a population rapidly outgrowing its agricultural land base. Social welfare, conceived in terms of Christian charity and the integrity of parish life, was not the responsibility of the state, but of the church. Democracy, even among the regimes' critics, lacked legitimacy. Governments' major affiliation, which under the circumstances crossed ethnic lines, was with capital. During subsequent decades, however, legitimate expectations of the government's role (if only slowly its actual fulfilment) extended to managing the social externalities of a booming capitalist economy and of developing human resources. This extended role was desired by a broad coalition of forces not at all restricted to, or even concentrated in, nationalists of any persuasion, and particularly not traditional or exclusive nationalists. As Roy observes, 'the modernization of *Québécois* society *presupposed* collective choices that only the state was able to assume.'[303]

This extended role for the state demanded a much closer and co-dependent relationship between government and civil society. The concept of 'organic democracy,' championed by educational reformers of the early 1960s, provides one indicative example. On an ideological and tangible level, the late 1950s witnessed agreement, outside the Duplessis regime and its defenders, that the growing authority of the state must be exercised through the deliberation, cooperation, and consensus between government and constituents. As the statist Liberals came to power, this then informed the methods actually employed to achieve change. One tangible product of this collaboration of state and organized interests could be seen in the more than 200 groups that mobilized the public to protest Bill 63.

Simultaneously, changes in the legitimate comportment of the subject, in part imported from anti-colonial and new-left civil protest abroad, dovetailed with the local drive to organize. The organized masses poured onto the streets and into party conventions, demanding that leaders set aside their past alliances and liberal squeamishness to execute the majority's bidding. The legitimacy of the political process within parties such as the nascent PQ now depended upon little-mediated 'participation.' In subsequent years, national emancipation was achieved in a fashion that, while no doubt easing status and cultural insecurities, unfortunately also overran the freedom of individuals to live their lives by their own cultural lights.

It is one of the defects of the lack of differentiation within the contemporary conceptual vocabulary of nationalism that conscientious proposals for constitutional change presented by liberal nationalists should be tarred with the same brush as bona fide exclusive nationalism. Liberalism, it has been suggested cannot speak, at least not on philosophical grounds, to the question of where state borders should be drawn. It speaks only to the prerogatives of individuals, and on that basis to the proper constraints on majorities. Although in Quebec emotional appeals have sometimes been made to an exclusively francophone heritage of the 'nation' within arguments for a sovereign state, we have noted that, as late as 1980, the PQ government of Quebec conscientiously managed to maintain a multicultural and pluralist blueprint for its envisaged sovereign country.

FIVE

Other Legacies of 1968

As official exclusive nationalism took root in Quebec, the need to confront it was felt by many federal Liberals. Two policies gathered support: establishing demonstratively plural federal institutions, and constitutionally entrenching basic liberties. The limited reach and effectiveness of the measures ultimately taken reflected the popular underpinnings and coordinate sovereignty of modern Canadian federalism. Provinces have emerged as formidable champions and instruments of majority popular will, and pluralism has proven difficult to dictate from the centre. Another constraint to federal efforts has been the risk of driving Quebec from the Canadian federation. Thus, as dissatisfaction in Quebec mounted with even the mild rebuke to official exclusive nationalism delivered by the Constitution Act of 1982, initiatives were framed to soften such censure. These initiatives, the Meech Lake and Charlottetown Accords of 1987 and 1992, were met with substantial public opposition on grounds of both process and substance. Meanwhile, the federal party system has changed during the past decade in a way that has also altered the pattern of political representation and the institutional basis of conflict regulation in Canada.

In this chapter we first briefly consider (in 5.1) the objectives and reception of official bilingualism and multiculturalism. The next major section (5.2), which contains several parts, will assess the intentions and outcome of the federal attempt to regulate exclusive nationalism constitutionally. The unsuccessful subsequent initiatives to temper constitutional censure of exclusive nationalism with explicit recognition of the distinctiveness of Quebec society are then discussed (in section 5.3). This discussion brings out the apparent constraints upon conflict regulation in Canada in an era of popular sovereignty. The issue of the changing mode of political representation is explicitly raised in the next section (5.4) Finally, the implications of these developments for regulating future conflict in Canada are contemplated, necessarily somewhat tentatively. The main point throughout the chapter concerns the nature and causes of the key constraints affecting the regulation of official exclusive nationalism and other forms of conflict in Canada.

5.1 Demonstrative Pluralism: Bilingualism and Multiculturalism

Official bilingualism was the most significant federal response to the increasing 'disengagement' of the Québécois from the federation.[1] The Official Languages Act (1969) sought to ensure, as Trudeau put it, that Quebec is 'not a ghetto for French-Canadians, that all of Canada is theirs.'[2] More tangibly, the act addressed the 'precipitous decline of the French-speaking proportion of the total Public Service' noticed by the B & B Commission.[3] Thereafter, the rules and orders of the federal government and courts were to be published, and government services provided, in both official languages where 'significant demand' existed, including Ottawa. This would place a premium on French-language skills in the federal public service and augment the ranks there of French Canadians. On a symbolic level, official bilingualism was intended to bring greater recognition of the French fact in Canada as a whole.[4]

Unfortunately, at the time of its introduction, most of the popular recognition garnered for the French fact was closer to derision than to acceptance. Although the support of official bilingualism for linguistic equality was unopposed by the provincial premiers and by the leaders of all federal parties, 'large sections of the Canadian people were opposed to it in theory and practice. Indeed, there were many signs throughout the year of a bilingual backlash.'[5] At second reading some seventeen conservative backbench opposition MPs, mainly from the West, voted against the bill.[6] Charles Taylor provides an incisive analysis of popular resistance to the implementation of official bilingualism. 'To some extent, Trudeau's remarkable achievement in extending bilingualism was made possible by a growing sympathy towards the French fact among political and social élites in COQ [Canada outside Quebec]. The élites pushed the bilingual process at a pace faster than many of their fellow citizens wanted. For many people lower down in the hierarchy, French was being "stuffed down their throats," but because of the élite-run nature of the political accommodation process in this country, they seemed to have no option but to take it.'[7] Ordinary citizens were gradually acquiring greater influence over the process of minority accommodation. Elites retained the capacity to transcend majoritarian impulses in legislation, but encountered difficulty in actually fostering good will and conferring public recognition.

In fairness, popular hostility to official bilingualism was not wholly a product of narrow cultural horizons. The most intense rejection of the policy came from citizens of neither British nor French ancestry, a group that felt excluded by the recognition inherently conferred by the policy upon the 'two founding peoples.'[8] Their sentiments were sufficiently strong and widespread for the B & B Commission to dedicate a fourth volume of its report to 'other ethnic groups' and, ultimately, to provide impetus to multicultural policy.

Official multiculturalism sought to 'support all of Canada's cultures,' based on the premise that 'cultural pluralism is the very essence of Canadian identity.'[9] The original policy objectives, as tabled in a House of Commons paper, were fourfold: (1) to assist interested cultural groups to develop themselves; (2) to assist such groups to 'overcome barriers to full participation in Canadian society' by confronting discrimination and fostering a broader sense of belonging; (3) to promote 'creative encounters and interchange among all Canadian cultural groups'; and (4) to promote official language education.[10] Running through these objectives is a celebration of cultural pluralism in Canada, tempered by a pledge that cultural groups not be hermetically sealed enclaves nor traps preventing individual mobility within a modern economy in which rapid, complex, and quasi-standardized communication are generally vital.[11] Practically speaking, the policy did not attempt the (perhaps impossible) task of preventing immigrant families from identifying more strongly over successive generations with mass North American culture.

Despite receiving the general approbation of the federal political elite, multiculturalism attracted 'vociferous debate' and 'little support.'[12] The *Toronto Star* unsympathetically demanded, 'can we survive as a nation that relies for strength on fragmentation?'[13] More recent popular antipathy to multiculturalism will be discussed later (in section 5.4). At the time of introduction, opposition to multiculturalism and to Trudeau's assertion of its compatibility with official bilingualism was particularly strong in Quebec. There, the press suggested multiculturalism would undermine the 'image of two nations, politically, sociologically, or culturally.'[14] Premier Robert Bourassa declared that language and culture are 'inseparable' and insisted that Quebec must have 'cultural autonomy.'[15] The opposition of the provincial Liberal political elite to multiculturalism policy may have reflected mainly a tactical move to avoid being flanked by the Parti Québécois, but it clearly underlined the division between the federal and provincial Liberal parties within Quebec and probably reflected the differing compositions of their constituencies.

5.2 Why the Constitution Act of 1982 Did Not Assume Its Projected Form

Sources of Trudeau's Constitutional Agenda

Prime minister of Canada almost continuously from 1968 to 1984, Pierre Elliott Trudeau consistently repudiated popular chauvinism and exclusive nationalism. Trudeau's defence of minorities was rooted, somewhat unusually for an elected Canadian statesman, not principally in the demands of political expedience, but rather in an explicit and cogent set of abstract philosophical and political values. Trudeau's rapid progression from novice member of Parliament to leadership of the federal Liberal party between 1965 and 1968 undoubtedly reflected strong internal demand for avowed French-Canadian federalists within the party.[16] One could therefore abstract from individual agency in explaining his influence, and emphasize the systemic imperative of cross-ethnic alliance formation and brokering (a theme of chapter 3). This view would certainly be consistent with the differences between Quebec federal and provincial Liberals noted. But here it seems most interesting to touch on the personal values and experiences that tended to distinguish Trudeau from exclusive nationalists in Quebec and that engendered there a particularly robust power cleavage in federal politics during a period in which the mode of political representation and conflict regulation was evolving.

Trudeau's political philosophy was marked by an evangelizing liberalism and universal humanism. 'The history of civilization is a chronicle of the subordination of tribal "nationalism" to wider interests,' he wrote in 1967.[17] His liberalism was partly founded on a personalist Catholic esteem for the capacity of individuals to define their own identities.[18] As he once stated in Parliament, 'The individual's freedom would be hampered if he were locked for life [by illiberal policy] within a particular cultural compartment by the accident of birth or language.'[19] The state, he believed, must respect this capacity by not impinging on the individual's choice of cultural affiliation and 'scale of values.'[20] Another foundation for Trudeau's liberalism was his belief that challenge, rational enlightenment, and 'the exchange of ideas' ultimately bring some form of human progress and that the state should not obstruct it.[21] 'In the field of political culture, no less than in other fields, our [Québécois] institutions do not deserve to survive at all unless they can successfully survive external competition.'[22] Faced with the risks of cultural discontinuity, Trudeau generally appeared supremely indifferent.

If he was so, Trudeau's uncommon personal experience was undoubtedly an important factor. Born to a Scottish mother and French-Canadian father, Trudeau held a cosmopolitan outlook that was reinforced by postgraduate study and extensive travel abroad. Randall Collins, an American sociologist, suggests that diversity of cultural exposure is related to the development of relativistic ideas; lower diversity, by contrast, makes individuals more likely to perceive 'an alien and uncontrollable world surrounding familiar local circles.'[23] Guy Laforest has made a similar connection in contrasting Trudeau with the society of his origins.

> It is possible to understand why Trudeau can brush off so rapidly the greater dependence of the individual upon the community that characterizes Quebec, why he can absolutize the capacities of any French Canadian ... to compete successfully without additional state protection ... Trudeau ... benefited from exceptional familial and educational circumstances ... [and] extrapolated the potentialities from his own personal story to all French Canadians ... his uncommon means explain his ability to outdistance the community without losing his identity.[24]

Within mainstream Québécois society, the wider concentric rings of identity could not be as well developed.

In pondering the sources of legitimation for a pluralistic federation such as Canada, Trudeau eschewed populist jingoism. 'Any expenditure of emotional appeal (flags, professions of faith, calls to dignity, expressions of brotherly love) at the national level will only serve to justify similar appeals at the regional level, where they are just as likely to be effective ... in the last resort the mainspring of federalism cannot be emotion but must be reason ... If politicians must bring emotions into the act, let them get emotional about functionalism.'[25] Despite his overarching statism, Trudeau had no interest in forging a pan-Canadian nation-state. The legitimacy of the Canadian federation was to depend, rather, on the material progress it brought and the quality of justice it dispensed.[26] A liberal, but certainly not with any bent for promoting cultural uniformity, Trudeau was concerned that minorities be buffered from the 'homogenization and depersonalization of mass society.'[27] Trudeau's multicultural policy is perhaps best termed 'managed syncretism,' entailing support for a fluid pluralism through judicious state intervention.

Such a policy has probably never enjoyed majority support (see 5.2 and 5.4) in Canada, but Trudeau's leadership on unpopular issues was consistent with his position on political representation. Although a liberal, Trudeau exhibited a streak of Burkean conservatism. He embraced a limited measure of elite tutelage to protect minorities from the wrath of hostile majorities. As he most succinctly summed up his position, 'too much authority, or too little, and that is the end of freedom. For oppression also arises from the lack of order, from the tyranny of the masses: it is then called the Reign of Terror.'[28] Trudeau rejected majoritarian formulations of liberal democracy.[29] Limits to what citizens can require of their legislators he believed should be constitutionally entrenched. In the face of the St Leonard crisis in 1968, for example, Trudeau reiterated his advocacy of a constitutional charter to protect minority linguistic rights.[30] 'In Canada, authority to legislate with respect to some of the rights regarded as fundamental lies with the provinces, [and] authority to legislate with respect to others of these rights lies with Parliament ... Only by a single constitutional enactment will the fundamental rights of all Canadians be guaranteed equal protection. A bill of rights so enacted would identify clearly the various rights to be protected and remove them henceforth from governmental interference.'[31] Trudeau apparently believed that political leaders retained sufficient legitimate authority in the late twentieth century to establish boundaries to popular sovereignty with a strong Charter and that such a Charter could be wielded by jurists to manage the exclusive nationalism of the provinces.

But subsequent experience must qualify this view.

The Advent of Popular Participation in Constitutional Affairs

While Confederation had been enacted without the ratification even of provincial legislatures, constitutional agreements reached in 1964 and 1971 among the federal and provincial executives were scuttled after receiving nothing more than adverse comment from public opinion leaders in Quebec.[32] Standards of public accountability in constitutional affairs would continue to evolve through subsequent decades, with significant substantive consequences for the constitution and, more broadly, for conflict regulation in Canada. The evolution was not, however, entirely continuous. Formal consultative initiatives launched in 1970–1 and 1977 brought increased popular involvement in constitutional affairs.[33] As Peter Russell notes, the Special Joint Committee of the Senate and the House of Commons on the Constitution of Canada had 'held meetings in forty-seven cities and towns across the country, received 8,000 pages of evidence, and heard evidence from 1,486 witnesses at meetings attended by 13,000 Canadians.'[34] However, the report released in 1972 by the committee, chaired by Senator Gildas Molgat and MP Mark MacGuigan, was greeted with a 'deafening silence.' Constitutional issues as yet attracted limited public interest, and what interest did exist focused on the discourse of political elites.[35] Furthermore, while the election of the PQ in 1976 spurred interest in constitutional issues and generated a flurry of public participation during the hearings of the Pepin–Robarts Task Force on Unity (1977–9), the recommendations of the task force were quickly dismissed because they contradicted the intentions of the Trudeau government.[36] Despite early gestures to public participation, 'constitutional politics remained fairly elitist, and it was the aspirations of governments, not people, that really counted' during the 1970s.[37]

Against this background, the process of patriation in 1980–1 was a major advance for the cause of popular involvement in Canadian constitutional affairs. In December and January 1980–1 a parliamentary committee conducted extensive public hearings. More than 250 hours of the sessions were televised, and many proposals developed during the hearings were accepted.[38] The so-called people's package of 2 October 1981 proposed an amending formula that would resolve future deadlocked constitutional negotiations between the federal and provincial governments by means of national referenda.[39] Trudeau declared his intention to 'proceed unilaterally with patriation,' in essence 'appealing over the heads of provincial politicians directly to the people.'[40] Volatile and rights-conscious public opinion was thus recognized as a powerful lever for prying provincial governments from their intransigence. In recognition of the federal nature of the country, concurrent majorities in four regions, Ontario and Quebec among them, were to furnish the standard of consent for such plebiscites.[41]

Trudeau's relatively open process of constitutional development reinforced democratic idealism, and established a significant precedent. As we discuss in the next section, the ill-fated Meech Lake Accord of 1987, which sought the symbolic consent of Quebec to be governed by the constitution, ultimately collapsed three years later when two provincial legislatures failed to ratify the agreement before the deadline passed.[42] Despite the new requirement for provincial legislative ratification, the Meech Lake process was more elite-dominated than even Trudeau's early attempts at patriation. This proved its most vulnerable flank during an era in which deep procedural bows to popular sovereignty have become de rigueur.[43] The Charlottetown Accord (see 5.3), concluded in 1992, was submitted to a national referendum. This established a new standard of public consent, the full implications of which continue to emerge.[44]

The Constitution Act: Ambivalence before Exclusive Nationalism

The Constitution Act (1982) does not so much regulate exclusive nationalism as cast it publicly in the uncomplimentary light of liberal doctrine. Legally, under the Charter of Rights and Freedoms enacted with the new constitution, governments retain considerable scope for inculcating a particular religion, culture, or language in the population, such as by denying immigrants all choice in their process of acculturation.[45] The forced assimilation of the Italians of St Leonard to the French language community is thus, for example, left unabated, and what limited injunctions against exclusive nationalism the Charter does include – the requirement that provincial governments offer some categories of anglophones and francophones education in their mother tongue, for instance – are so circumscribed as to barely exceed the minority language 'guarantees' of Bill 101. Other rights mentioned in the Charter that are in sharper conflict with the original policy of Bill 101, such as freedom of expression, are greatly diminished by the inclusion of an override (also known as the 'notwithstanding clause') that permits governments to ignore major portions of the Charter in enacting right-infringing legislation for up to five years at a time.

The override clause was included in the constitution at the insistence of the provincial premiers, who argued that parliamentary supremacy must be protected and the power of unelected jurists, limited. (As the former Liberal senator and constitutional scholar Eugene Forsey lamented in a public letter after the accord of November 1981, 'The Provinces have shot it full of holes ... [The Charter of Rights] is now being disembowelled.')[46] Clearly, the premiers also anticipated that any government invoking the override clause would, in doing so, wave a 'red flag to opposition parties and the press,' as the president of the Canadian Civil Liberties Association put it.[47] Still, the override provision essentially vitiates the core rights guarantees of the Charter in cases where policies infringing rights are demanded by aggressive provincial majorities or especially vociferous minorities. Certainly this is true of exclusive nationalist policies enjoying militant and organized support. In the context of Canadian federalism, the override clause has also had the incidental and perverse effect of enraging the public *outside* the province invoking it, and, in turn, of deepening the feelings of alienation and insecurity within. This was demonstrated conclusively in late 1988 when the Quebec government chose to invoke the override clause to insulate a modified version of the French-only sign provision of Bill 101 from the Charter. As will later be discussed, the controversy raised across Canada by this decision was perhaps the most potent factor of all in the demise of the Meech Lake and the Charlottetown Accords.

The relative ease with which the override clause was invoked in Quebec is largely a function of the ambivalence of francophones there towards the Charter. Alan Cairns judged in 1990 that the Charter 'has not taken root among the Quebec francophone majority in the way it has elsewhere.'[48] On a substantive level the Charter did not depart materially from the principles recognized in Quebec's own Human Rights Act, except in recognizing the minority language education rights of a limited category of anglophones in the province.[49] (Despite having been itself the author of exclusive nationalist language policy in education, the Quebec Liberal government of Premier Robert Bourassa had passed the Human Rights Act in 1975, protecting basic personal rights and liberties.)[50]

The new constitution was particularly vulnerable in Quebec as a result of the unfortunate circumstances of its negotiation. At the constitutional conference in November 1981 the Quebec delegation was not only the sole party to reject the accord, but also, to the discredit of the other participants, the only government unrepresented at the eleventh-hour bargaining session at which the basis of the final agreement was reached. This exclusion, perhaps unintentional, reinforced the isolation of Quebec and provided grounds for the common view there that the province was not morally bound by the accord. (Jean Chrétien, it should be noted, avows that the separatist PQ government had privately made known its categorical unwillingness to endorse any conclusive agreement to renew the Canadian constitution.)[51]

In the face of the furore among exclusive nationalists in Quebec, the federal government itself chose at the committee stage to weaken the section guaranteeing minority language rights (Section 23) by introducing a partial escape clause in Section 59(2) specifically for Quebec. This was to bring the guarantee much closer to the policy of Bill 101, and indeed, into almost exact correspondence with Lévesque's personal preference (which his cabinet colleagues had forced him to compromise slightly in 1977) for English-language education to be restricted to the children of parents educated in English in Canada.[52]

Nevertheless, Quebec nationalists emphasized their government's lack of involvement in the final process and, of course, denounced the resulting substance. This served to strip the Charter of legitimacy in Quebec and paved the way for a legislative counter-attack. Bill 62, introduced in the National Assembly in May 1982, provided that *all* Quebec legislation would henceforth automatically include an override clause.[53] This would demonstrate just how effortlessly a creative and determinedly exclusive nationalist government could render the 'red flags' imperceptible.

Analysis

The decision of senior Canadian political elites to weaken the Charter by means of the override clause was intimately bound up with their commitment to popular sovereignty. Besides their concern to maintain their own spheres of legislative competency, the provincial premiers were animated by a belief in the functioning of majoritarian democracy at the provincial level and by a desire to avoid 'indirect legislation' in other jurisdictions, particularly Quebec.[54] At the negotiating table, Premier Peter Lougheed of Alberta resisted entrenched language rights on the grounds of opposing 'any coercion, any scheme that indirectly legislates in Quebec.'[55] The premier of Saskatchewan, Alan Blakeney, was also concerned on grounds of principle to abide popular sovereignty within the provinces. 'Canadians ought not to have taken away from them the fundamental right to participate in political choices, in particular they ought not to have eroded under the guise of advancing their freedoms their right to make important social choices, and to participate in those decisions ... I believe the citizen believes that he has a right to a voice in those decisions.'[56] In post-1968 Canada, the potential for popular militancy also explains in part why the views to which Blakeney refers are given so much credence. Asked by Trudeau whether he would accept entrenched minority language rights, Premier Lévesque reportedly replied, 'No, there would be riots in the streets of Montreal.'[57] Besides elite receptiveness to democratic ideals, thus, the risk of rapid popular mobilization deters any pointed confrontation of exclusive nationalism.

As we have seen, the collapse of the power cleavage in Quebec after 1968 was compounded by an incapacity of federal elites to erect a constitutional buffer to exclusive nationalism of their own. As with the collapse of the power cleavage in Quebec, this incapacity to regulate exclusive nationalism ultimately arose from a rejection of the elite tutelage concomitant with affiliative trusteeship and from the acquiescence of elites in the rise of popular sovereignty. Later constitutional debate would focus not on whether there should be escape clauses for official exclusive nationalism, but on whether, within a certain range, it should be tacitly accommodated.

5.3 Failed Initiatives: Constitutional Rigidity in an Age of Popular Sovereignty

The Meech Lake Accord and Why It Failed

The scope of the constitutional revisions of the late 1980s was limited from the outset to making constitutional amends with Quebec. This was an undertaking not obviously sanctioned by public opinion outside the province. Yet, the support of key elite elements created this early opportunity to accommodate Quebec. The Conservative federal government, elected in 1984, contained many provincialist Québécois. In Quebec, Bourassa's federalist Liberals had replaced the PQ in office late the following year. Provincial Liberals in Quebec had publicly advanced an agenda for constitutional change during both their election campaign and public declarations during the spring of 1986. The publicity so garnered 'pre-empted any remaining reluctance among the premiers,' as slowness to proceed at this juncture might well have seemed a rebuff in Quebec, and have ultimately tilted the delicate partisan balance there in favour of sovereigntists.[58] The key constraint to regulating ethnic conflict in Canada, the threat of secession, was thus to have sway in the ostensible loosening of the constitutional bonds binding official exclusive nationalism in Quebec, as well as in the modest recognition yielded claims there for greater influence and autonomy.

Four of the five constitutional amendments agreed to by the provincial premiers and the federal government would have devolved influence to *all* of the provinces, not merely to Quebec. None of these purportedly devolutionary changes were particularly dramatic departures from the existing practice of Canadian federalism, despite the deep forebodings of trenchant federalists.[59] By far the most significant element of the agreement, at least as far as the subsequent debate was concerned, was the proposed addition to the constitution of a new interpretive clause. The ostensible purpose of this new clause was to relieve the contradiction between nationalist policy making in Quebec and the rights and freedoms mentioned in the constitution. Although the constitution was, for reasons already discussed, a blunt instrument for attacking exclusive nationalism in Quebec, it still remained an irritant to exclusive nationalists there. The very mention in the Charter of minority education rights, freedom of speech and so forth undermined the legitimacy of language legislation before the already unsympathetic and increasingly rights-conscious anglophone society inside and outside Quebec. Thus, the 'distinct society clause' (DSC), as it was called, was to recognize that 'Quebec constitutes within Canada a distinct society' and to affirm the 'role' of the Quebec government 'to preserve and promote the distinct identity of Quebec.'[60]

It is extremely dubious whether the DSC agreed upon by the senior Canadian political elite would have had any material effect on the contradiction (mild as it is legally) between existing exclusive nationalist policy in Quebec and the Charter.[61] The DSC included explicit recognition of the linguistic duality of Canada and gave this characteristic 'paramountcy.'[62] It will never be known for certain how the conflict between the Quebec government's roles in promoting the 'distinct society' and in preserving linguistic duality would have been resolved by jurists in adjudicating any exclusive nationalist policies not shielded by the (unchanged) override clause. However, there is no reason to believe that the net effect would have been great, and, indeed, it seems fair to conclude that in agreeing to the DSC the first ministers made a symbolic, not an appreciable legal accommodation of nationalism in Quebec.[63]

But in doing even this, they incurred the indignation of a majority of anglophone Canadians.[64] Meech collapsed when two provincial legislatures outside Quebec, backed by strong national popular opposition, did not ratify the agreement before it expired in June 1990. The reasons for public opposition to the agreement vary tremendously, and indeed, in some cases are diametrically opposed. They remain worthy of a brief discussion, because they established important constraints upon later and future attempts at constitutional evolution.

In December 1988 the Liberal government of Quebec, under tremendous pressure from mobilized exclusive nationalist opposition, invoked the override clause to impose a modified version of the French-only sign law. The earlier sign law, passed as part of Bill 101 and thus predating the Charter, had lacked a reference to the override clause and was therefore quashed in rulings by two courts in Quebec and the Supreme Court of Canada. Bill 178, as the modified sign law was titled, made it plain to many Canadians that the Charter was already too permissive of exclusive nationalism, even without the ostensible further dilution of rights by the proposed DSC.

There are two faces to the reaction of Canadians to Bill 178, a reaction that greatly influenced public attitudes to the DSC, and thus to the Meech

Lake Accord of which it was crucial part. On the one hand, there was a position built on a individual-rights consciousness, fortified by the political and juridical discourse surrounding the Charter during the preceding eight years. That such a consciousness has taken hold within a significant segment of the population there can be no doubt: an opinion poll published in February 1990 showed that 77 per cent were opposed to Quebec language legislation conflicting with the Charter of Rights. Furthermore, although 66 per cent of those registering an opinion were opposed to the Meech Lake Accord (the vast majority of them, presumably, because of the DSC), 59 per cent would have accepted the DSC had it been clear that it would not enable Quebec to 'pass laws that conflict with the Charter.'[65]

On the other hand, there was also a certain tribal quality to the protest that was not clearly linked with any consistent commitment to the protection of minority linguistic rights. A study published in 1989 revealed that, as of 1987, support for official language minority rights was actually much weaker among anglophones than among francophones in Canada. Anglophone citizens, moreover, appeared to be particularly prone to applying what the authors deemed 'double standards.' The study revealed that while fully 80 per cent of anglophones in the nation-wide sample strongly supported the provision of federal government services in English within Quebec, only 31 per cent of anglophones felt the same way about providing such services in French outside Quebec.[66] Attitudes such as these precipitated grass-roots movements in 1989–90 that, although local phenomena, enjoyed considerable mass support across the country.[67] A popular movement known as the Association for the Preservation of English in Canada vented popular chauvinism in small-town Ontario, advancing resolutions in municipal assemblies to establish 'official unilingualism' at the local level.[68] According to a poll in July 1990, these initiatives enjoyed the support of some 46 per cent of Canadians outside Quebec expressing an opinion.[69] Interestingly, the same poll showed that the most trenchant opponent of Meech Lake among political elites – Clyde Wells, premier of Newfoundland, a former constitutional lawyer for the Trudeau government, and a strong advocate of minority rights – drew a majority (52 per cent) of his considerable national public support for his position from those who also favoured the French-only resolutions of the Ontario municipalities.[70] As in a much earlier era, the dissimilar perspectives of strange bedfellows together tilted the political process against conciliation.

As suggested by the segment of public opinion that would have opposed the DSC even had it not yielded Quebec any further latitude with the

Charter (about 41 per cent of those expressing an opinion), there were also other issues at stake with the DSC than a supposed erosion of Charter-guaranteed rights. Many of these related to the Charter not as a legal document, but as a revered and relatively immutable icon that differentially recognizes, and thus allocates status to, various segments of Canadian society.[71] As several scholars have noted, the DSC derogated somewhat from the presumptive equality of the provinces and from the official 'ethnocultural pluralism' of Canada.[72] Furthermore, in emphasizing the mediation of membership in Canadian society by membership in linguistic communities, the DSC also collided with a pan-Canadian 'civic identity,' supported and reinforced outside Quebec by the Charter.[73]

The Meech Lake Accord was trenchantly opposed by a variety of organized groups purporting to represent, among others, women, aboriginals, multicultural groups, visible minorities, and persons with disabilities. Women's groups, for instance, were indignant that the section guaranteeing equality of rights between the sexes was not excluded from the ambit of the DSC. (Although commentators have noted that the outrageous scenarios contrived in their protest betrayed an 'incredible ignorance of Quebec society' and gravely offended women in Quebec, the protest was certainly successful in raising the public profile and influence of the feminist organizations involved.)[74] Cairns discerns that many of the groups newly involved in constitutional politics became enmeshed within a mounting 'counter-discourse' characterized by 'minoritarianism.'[75] The 'counter' aspect derives from the emphasis the groups place upon issues of 'status,' 'identity,' and 'recognition,' instead of the conventional constitutional preoccupations of the defense of negative individual liberties, the workings of federalism, and, one might add, the retention of Quebec within Canada.[76] As Cairns notes, the issues of special interest to the Charter counter-culture had pan-Canadian dimensions, and this brought them into conflict with a strong provincialist element of the 1982 constitution, the amending formula.[77]

The amending formula requires unanimous provincial consent in order to amend certain parts of the constitution. The amendment of other parts requires the agreement of seven of the ten provinces, representing at least 50 per cent of the Canadian population. Both types of amendments have been proposed in the major rounds of constitutional negotiations thus far. Their acceptance in agreements has tended to be intertwined in that amendments governed by one rule have been accepted by some provinces in return for the acceptance of amendments governed by the other. This pattern has necessitated unanimity for complex constitutional accords as a whole and in turn has required protracted negotiations to reach agreements among the provincial premiers and the prime minister.

This personal and rigorous process of elite accommodation now seems an artefact of the bygone era of affiliative trusteeship. It certainly tends to breach both the substantive and the procedural expectations of contemporary Canadian society. Substantively, the intensive process of first ministerial negotiations 'can facilitate agreement by building solidarity among the participants, [but] it runs the risk of isolating them from their larger constituencies.'[78] This was of course true of the very heart of the agreement, the DSC. Procedurally, the complexity of the trade-offs involved, and the tremendous effort required to arrive at agreements, meant that the Meech Lake Accord could not accommodate extra-parliamentary group input. Although public hearings were conducted in a number of provinces in the course of the ratification process for the accord, these appeared a 'sham' to participants in light of indications that the accord was a 'seamless web,' or 'done deal,' and therefore not amenable to alteration.[79]

The illegitimacy of 'executive federalism' as a means of constitutional reconciliation was recognized in the sober post-mortems conducted after the collapse of the Meech Lake Accord. The 1991 report of the Beaudoin–Edwards joint Senate and Commons committee on the amending procedure acknowledged that the public had little tolerance left for constitutional proposals perceived to be the 'product solely of eleven first ministers making deals behind closed doors.'[80] The deference of citizens to elite-driven processes has declined, and their capacity to detect incongruities and mobilize articulate opposition have increased. As Simeon cogently observes, these factors, above all, defeated the Meech Lake agreement. 'The failure to recognize this profound change is, I believe, perhaps the single most important reason for the failure of Meech ... it simply was impossible to contain the debate. Too many groups had come to perceive a direct stake in the Constitution; and too many of them had the knowledge, political sophistication and communications networks for élite politics to prevail.'[81] In a post-Charter Canada, as Cairns observes, 'There is now a public base to the constitutional order, whose implications need to be worked out.'[82]

The Defeat of the Charlottetown Accord

The new 'public base' seemed exceedingly well entrenched during the Canada Round of constitutional deliberations. An unsuccessful national referendum defeated the Charlottetown Accord, concluded in August

1992 after almost two years of public consultation.[83] Fully four separate consultative initiatives had been involved in developing the proposals; each had failed to find a formula acceptable to all. In addition to the Beaudoin–Edwards committee, already mentioned, the Citizens' Forum on Canada's Future was launched in November 1990. Over the course of six months it directly engaged some 400,000 Canadians in talking about core constitutional and political issues.[84] In July 1991 the Royal Commission on Aboriginal Peoples was appointed and charged with providing comment on emerging constitutional ideas. Finally, after the release of the Mulroney government's own constitutional proposals in September 1991, another joint parliamentary committee (later known as the Beaudoin–Dobbie Committee) was struck, and in its most successful phase conducted five constitutional conferences, each of which brought together academics, interest-group leaders, politicians, and interested citizens from across the country.[85]

Public consultation, however intense, could not of course dispense with the necessity of involved negotiations among the plethora of legislative parties to any settlement. Talks were conducted beginning in the spring of 1992 among provincial, territorial, and federal delegations, with special representation given to four aboriginal organizations. Two further major meetings were held during the summer, the last of which included Quebec, which had otherwise held itself aloof from the meetings in order to construct the final agreement as a compact between itself and the rest of Canada. The Charlottetown Accord proposed a new Canada clause, which recognized eight 'fundamental characteristics' of Canada. One such characteristic was the distinct society of Quebec, this time specifically qualified with reference to the 'French-speaking majority,' 'unique culture,' and 'civil law tradition' of the province. These explicit elements, together with the commitment declared in another of the eight characteristics to 'the vitality and development of official language minority communities' throughout Canada, made the Canada clause an even narrower loophole for official exclusive nationalism in Quebec than the DSC of the Meech Lake Accord had been.[86]

The Charlottetown Accord was nevertheless rejected in the national referendum conducted 26 October 1992 by 54.2 per cent of voters. Electorates supported the accord in three Maritime provinces, in one territory, and, by a slim margin, in Ontario. In the other territory and six provinces the accord was rejected. The reasons for public rejection of the agreement had little to do with the provisions for aboriginal self-government, and much to do with the concessions made to Quebec.[87] Diametrically opposed interpretations readily coexisted at the mass level in Quebec and in the rest of Canada concerning whether Quebec or the rest of Canada had gained greater advantage. Many Québécois rejected the accord because they deemed the concessions made to their province insufficient; many other Canadians, because they perceived the same concessions to be excessive. In Western Canada slightly fewer than half of respondents (a proportion representing more than three-quarters of the 'no' constituency there) cited the Quebec concessions in response to an open-ended question asking which part they 'particularly dislike.'[88] Another poll showed that in British Columbia only 39 per cent approved of recognizing Quebec as a distinct-society, and just 11 per cent approved of the guarantee in the Accord of 25 per cent of the seats in the House of Commons for Quebec.[89]

As with the rejection in public opinion of the Meech Lake Accord, there was a certain antagonism present in the reaction of English Canada to Quebec's gains. A particularly scholarly empirical study, *The Challenge of Direct Democracy*, found that raw feeling for Quebec was correlated with the vote, that it 'overwhelmed ideas,' and influenced attitudes to the distinct-society clause.[90] Anecdotal evidence at the time seems consistent with this analysis. June Callwood, an English-speaker from Toronto, stated upon her return from a campaign swing to the West for the 'yes' side that she 'came back disheartened because of the animosity against Quebec ... [Supporters of the 'no' option] see it as a way of voting against French on the cereal boxes.'[91] Certainly, there is little reason to suppose that the public rejection of the Charlottetown Accord was animated by a dispassionate concern over the implications of the Canada clause for Charter principles.[92] Any suggestion to this effect would face the difficult task of explaining public apathy in the face of a gaping escape clause proposed for future aboriginal governments that might wish to breach Charter rights. Cairns suggests this apathy demonstrates that 'Aboriginals were defined as being on the periphery of a fundamental constitutional norm for other Canadians.'[93] Perhaps it also shows that the concern of most Canadians for minority rights stands in direct proportion to their identification with the individuals most likely to be affected by an erosion of the rights in question. More concern is felt for anglophones in Montreal over the recognition of the 'distinct society' than is generated for nonconformist aboriginals who might (hypothetically) be subject to repressive measures by exacting aboriginal governments. If this hypothesis is correct, then strong in-group preferences would appear to be a guiding factor in mass constitutional politics.

Even if the popular rejection of the Charlottetown Accord turned to a greater extent than seems likely upon principles genuinely held and disinterestedly applied, the principles typically invoked in Canadian constitutional discourse rest in varying degrees of tortured opposition, and it remains to be seen whether a formula simultaneously bespeaking the equality of individuals, of provinces, of founding nations, and of aboriginal and non-aboriginal peoples can command sufficient popular sympathy.[94] No realistic constitutional proposal can bear untempered witness to all of these principles, but compromise provides weak flanks for opponents to attack to great popular acclaim. James Tully reflects that citizens evaluated the Charlottetown Accord against their own 'immanent standards,' and that in that light it 'looked a mess.'[95] As Alan Noël puts it, the Charlottetown agreement 'was a document that could appeal to no clear conception of justice,' having been produced by 'hard and rapid bargaining.'[96]

Certainly, there was also at play in the defeat of the accord a more transient reaction against unpopular provincial and federal leaders. Prime Minister Brian Mulroney was seen by some as having 'elevated contempt for the popular will to a governing principle,' having introduced, among other things, an unpopular new sales tax against the will of 80 per cent of public opinion.[97] Some 22 per cent of the respondents of a poll suggested that they opposed the accord because politicians supported it.[98] Mulroney himself had a net conversion score of *minus* 18 per cent, implying that a significantly larger proportion of individuals were influenced by his participation in the 'yes' campaign to vote *against* the Accord than to vote for it.[99] One individual who campaigned for the 'yes' side observed 'very strong anti-government, anti-establishment feeling right across the Western provinces'; another commentator declared a 'crisis of legitimacy' that engulfed social, besides political, elites.[100] The 'crisis,' if such indeed it was, reflected the vulnerability of a thinly veiled exercise in elite-directed statecraft, in this case where the elite proponents enjoyed little public esteem.

5.4 Towards Ethnic Delegate Representation?

The New Constitutional Politics

As Russell observes, 'Canadians have come to aspire to a more democratic form of constitutionalism.'[101] Much of this aspiration is concentrated in the organizations that seek to be accredited more routinely in the constitutional process. In this sense it can be understood partly as a legacy of 1968. As Philip Resnick acutely observes, 'some of our own social movements, from feminists to environmentalists, have learned to spurn an all-too-

Canadian deference to authority ... The Burkean notion of members of parliament (or legislatures) owing their electors nothing but their consciences carries less weight, as does the derived notion of first ministers with parliamentary majorities being free to act pretty well as they wish, even in constitutional matters. Decidedly Rousseuean and Jeffersonian notions of popular sovereignty have suddenly begun to take hold.'[102] The Jeffersonian (or Jacksonian) impulse, initially articulated by the movements with a pointed interest in constitutional affairs, reverberated through much of Canadian society.

It is an impulse that dovetailed with the thrust to participation common to the advanced industrialized world. As an important recent study by Neil Nevitte points out, the marked increase in Canadians' level of political interest and propensity for protest, and their declining deference to authority of all kinds, including government, has occurred in parallel with similar trends in other industrialized societies.[103] Drawing on essentially the same body of theory as Rosenau (see 0.5), Nevitte finds powerful support for his thesis concerning the rise of 'new politics' and a strident 'politics of participation' in comparative longitudinal data collected in 1981 and 1990.[104] Within economies highly dependent upon technology, hence high levels of education, 'Cognitive mobilization implies that ... publics are better equipped to evaluate political information relatively independently.'[105] Such skills, together with 'fundamental shifts in the value systems of mass publics' have undermined 'citizen attachments to political parties' as well as respect in general for 'traditional hierarchically organized representative institutions.'[106]

Under these conditions, the legitimate pattern of political representation is apt to shift. Impressionistic evidence supports the increasing prevalence of norms of delegate representation in the popular political culture. As the Report to the People and Government of Canada of the Citizens' Forum conveyed, 'a group in Ontario reflected the consensus of most Forum discussions in reporting: "The government must be changed. We must have a system whereby our elected representatives truly represent and reflect the wishes of their constituents." ... Another expressed with passion the sentiments shared by many participants in saying, "As for the government itself, recall and direct responsibility to the electorate should be implemented. You do not rule us, you work for us. Stop being so secretive, try honesty and straightforwardness."'[107] In the light of the vehemence and specificity of such comments, Cairns's remark that the implications of the 'public base' of the constitution 'need to be worked out' seems optimistically understated. If statecraft is reduced to articulating without ameliorating the perennial squabbles of a society riven by deep divisions, then the constitution is likely to prove rigidly inflexible until and unless it verges on collapse.[108] 'Constitution-making,' Thomas Courchene concludes, has 'ceased to be an exercise in statecraft and degenerated into a process of brokering among uncompromising and unreconcilable special interests.'[109]

Developments in the Federal Party System

One might argue that the new politics and the new social movements are two sides of the same coin. Both seem to emanate from societies in which providing for the basic physical needs of members no longer dominates the public agenda. Both apparently germinated near the end of the 1960s. Both embody a thrust to transform the vehicles for popular political participation. Yet formulated as a dual category, the new politics/movements contain strong internal contradictions. This becomes evident in considering one of the most significant innovations in the Canadian political system of the 1990s, the emergence of the Reform Party of Canada.[110] Reform sits squarely astride these developments, embodying simultaneously an enthusiasm for a 'democratic populism,' and a sour reaction to the inclusion of special interest representation in the political process.[111] Reform has been supported since its founding in October 1987 not so much by young, highly educated 'post-materialists,' as by a greying, alienated constituency concerned with issues of physical security, moral and fiscal rectitude, and the changing cultural face of Canada.[112] Indeed, the party could easily be defined as reactionary relative to the new politics/movements, if not for its championing, however qualified, of constituent assemblies, recall mechanisms, weaker party discipline in Parliament, and wider use of referenda, all of which are intended departures from the hierarchical structure of politics.[113] In fact, Reform leader Preston Manning has also led a party that has engaged its mass membership in a more vigorous and interactive internal discourse than other federal parties. It is worth asking, therefore, whether Reform does not actually represent one face, albeit a surprising one, of the new politics.

In locating Reform, the historically specific context in which the party arose should not, of course, be overlooked. An advocate of the 'reactionary' interpretation might well argue that the party's appropriation – or so it may be construed – of the agenda of popular democracy was opportunistic and contingent upon the specific misalignment of public opinion and existing political options during the leadership of the Progressive Conservatives by Brian Mulroney.[114] The PCs, the established competition for any new contender on the right, had notably moved from its position of ambivalence on cultural issues in the 1970s to one of actually 'outbidding' the Liberals by the 1984 election on the 'pro-French' dimension.[115] The same party, previously home to small business and fiscal conservatives, had also had the gall to implement in office a highly visible and perplexing tax, the GST.[116] Opportunities abounded, in other words, for an outflanking manoeuvre presenting a blunt appeal to public opinion. Various democratic paraphernalia dug up from the older legacy of Prairie alienation, populism and protest, supplied colourful rhetorical material.[117] As this theory might have it, Reform is not emblematic of significant contemporary structural changes in the pattern of Canadian politics.

Yet analysing on this basis Reform's deployment of at least the style of popular democracy misses the substantial continuity of the party's innovations with prior developments in the major federal parties. As David Smith clearly traces, the internal structure of the Canadian party system has evolved significantly in several distinct steps since the mid-fifties.[118] The 'disintermediation' of the process of regional and cultural conflict in Canada took a major step forward as early as the Conservative government of Prime Minister John Diefenbaker (1957–63). As Manning has invoked the image of 'One Nation,' Diefenbaker's mantra in office was 'One Canada.'[119] Diefenbaker's *modus operandi* was to supplant the existing practices of accommodation within the federal cabinet under provincial notables in favour of a direct connection between himself and the Canadian people *en masse*.[120]

The rhetorical consolidation of sovereignty in an undifferentiated mass base of Canadian society was given increasing substance in the Liberal governments of the 1960s. As Smith explains, 'Unlike their predecessors in office, both Liberal leaders experimented with party reorganization and ... reforms in the 1960s. Participatory democracy, the sophisticated use of polling and public relations agencies, the use of the mass media, and the emphasis on the leader (to the detriment of regional chieftains) all reflected the same motivation as their major government politics, which was to speak to Canadians directly, in a national language, and without intermediaries.'[121] It was, of course, the entering wedge of these initiatives that caused such high tories as George Grant such heartburn.[122] To Grant, it all seemed so American. Following the victory of Liberal leader Lester B. Pearson in 1963, Grant 'lamented' the passing of a mode of politics that, as he thought, had 'stood in firm opposition to the Jeffersonian liberalism so dominant in the United States.'[123] Perhaps anticipating the later theorists of new politics, Grant perceived that the conservative tradition had failed in the teeth of an emergent urban, technology-based industrial complex.

We have already traced, in relation to constitutional affairs, the subsequent growth of popular political involvement. Suffice to say at this point that the democratization of Canadian political parties followed a similar pattern. Formal initiatives to open 'decision making to rank-and-file participation' and to allow the political agenda to be 'defined by the mass and not by the elite' arose well before the acquisition of real popular control.[124] This pattern had the effect of entrenching expectations without wholly satisfying them. At the same time, the major federal parties in Canada presented something of a 'cartel' in colluding to articulate only a limited range of public opinion relative to cultural and regional issues.[125]

Like its nineteenth-century precursor, the Reform Party of George Brown, Manning's Reform Party seized the opportunity to criticize both the process and the substance of accommodation surrounding cultural and regional issues within the major parties. Manning's resort to 'democratic populism' is a twentieth-century advance on Brown's argument that the exigencies of alliances were making responsible government 'a farce,' but both capitalized on the dissonance between elite opinion within the governing party and a major fraction of public opinion on the (existing) western periphery. As it did in the 1850s, the critique resonated strongly with partisans of the modern Reform Party. A survey of delegates at a Reform convention in 1992 revealed that an astounding 80 per cent of respondents agreed that 'the central question in Canadian politics is the struggle between political élites and ordinary people.'[126]

It would be a serious error to overlook this perception's empirical basis relative to cultural policy, to suggest that it is a figment of overwrought, alienated imaginations. Of course, the perception must be set in the context of the particular segment of public opinion constituting the Reform constituency. In the same survey, fully 60.3 per cent of those asked disagreed with even the mild statement that 'a bilingual federal government is necessary,' and just 1.9 per cent agreed that the 'federal government should increase its efforts to further multiculturalism.'[127] Such results are probably not fully representative of overall public opinion in Canada. Still, it is worth noting that in the course of its consultative efforts (with the 400,000 participants), the Citizens' Forum heard between twenty and forty times as many negative comments about official multicultural policy as positive ones.[128]

Even more significantly, an analysis of data collected in 1987, the same year Reform was founded, hints at the structure of opinion underlying the divisions between elites and the population at large. The study, by Paul Sniderman, Joseph Fletcher, Peter Russell, and Philip Tetlock, revealed a gap of 9–17 per cent between Canadian anglophone 'decision makers' and citizens in support for bilingualism in federal government services.[129] Among anglophones the proportion of decision makers expressing 'strong support' for government services in French outside Quebec was 157 per cent of the proportion of citizens holding the same view. Interestingly, the authors of the study found that positions on official bilingualism are quite strongly correlated with levels of egalitarianism and social tolerance. On measures of social tolerance the power cleavage was pronounced. Citizens had a 39 per cent higher index score than decision-makers on an item measuring intolerance to homosexuals; similarly, they were 40 and 58 per cent more negative in their attitudes towards immigrants and Jews, respectively.[130]

Nevitte suggests that one of the preoccupations of the emerging constituency for new politics is the 'need for belonging.'[131] Unless a postmodern, syncretic identity gains greater popular appeal, this might well imply a tendency for individuals to pour more of themselves into exclusive cultural spaces reflecting highly specific ethnic and historical roots. Nevitte also observes that, despite the 'striking jump' between 1981 and 1991 in the level of support among citizens for the principle of tolerance in the abstract, this disguises what is in fact a rising level of social intolerance when evaluated by the more concrete and telling measure of willingness to reside near common outgroups.[132] Given that level of education and urban residence do not dispel, but actually mildly increase levels of social intolerance, there is little reason for confidence that societies at a more advanced stage of development will be societies more instinctively apt to embrace the accommodation of socially unfavoured groups.[133] There is little reason for confidence, therefore, that the new politics in Canada will not in future be led by conflicting factions having little propensity or capacity for accommodation and conflict regulation.

On the other hand, the future is not now – yet. In terms of both process and substance, the Reform Party has in some respects sharpened the pre-existing thrust to make public policy flow more directly from emergent popular opinion. It is arguably the most significant institutional torch-bearer in Canada of the new politics. But even the Reform Party of Preston Manning has, to an impressive extent, been firmly led by its leader.[134] Moveover, the leader of Reform remains subject to external pressures very similar to those faced by George Brown: the electoral imperative of reaching beyond an existing narrow regional and demographic constituency to build a broader coalition. This often requires transcending the views of party activists. The initiative to build a united conservative party open to strong participation, even leadership, from Ontario represents but one, particularly salient example. Similarly, Manning also singlehandedly reversed his party's position on the issue of whether Sikhs could wear turbans in the RCMP, an issue on which the party had previously adopted an exclusivist position in clear conflict with its officially liberal (though often intentionally ambiguous) ideology.[135] Manning is also said to be cognizant of the dangers of giving rein to popular chauvinism, and at early party conventions was careful to construct proceedings in ways that would not thwart strong executive leadership.[136]

Still, a party that is ostensibly committed to executing faithfully the present state of popular preferences, to 'aggregative' rather than 'integrative' democratic processes (in Michael Atkinson's helpful terminology), might well have difficulty in permanently nullifying more directly democratic practices within the party itself.[137] Indeed, Flanagan notes that by the 1994 Ottawa party convention, the point at which his interesting narrative trails off, the well-known incongruence between rank-and-file views and party policy had created irresistible pressures for greater popular influence. As he narrates,

> The process that led to this spate of social and cultural resolutions was notably different from what had prevailed at previous assemblies. Almost all of these motions, as their sometimes awkward wording suggests, came straight from constituency associations ... During the assembly, there were no warnings from the head table to remain moderate ... In practical terms, Manning must have sensed there was little he could do to hold off these resolutions, even though he had always tried to avoid the topics of many of them. In 1989 the Edmonton assembly had ended in confusion over what had been passed and not passed; and in 1991, at the Saskatoon assembly, Manning had manoeuvred to defeat almost all resolutions from constituency associations. He had then decreed that the 1992 Winnipeg assembly would craft an election platform out of existing policy, not make new policy. With much media commentary about the gulf between his moderation and the conservatism of party members, the delegates could not be denied a chance in 1994 to take a stand on contentious social issues.[138]

Substantively, the outcome of the 1994 Ottawa convention was the passage of a series of resolutions taking aim at an astonishingly broad spectrum of vulnerable outgroups in Canadian society: immigrants (reducing numbers, and curtailing in some cases the citizenship rights of children born to immigrants); welfare recipients (mandating workfare); gays and lesbians (precluding homosexual marriage); violent criminals (initiating 'two strikes and you're out' policy for serious assaults); visible minorities (proscribing affirmative action); and official linguistic minorities (advocating repeal of Official Languages Act).[139] Given that the elitist arguments needed to maintain strong executive control over party policy do not come readily to the lips of avowed populists, there can be little doubt that Manning or his successor will have difficulty before the same wrenching choice as René Lévesque faced in 1968, between the procedural dictates of popular democracy, and the substance of the broadly liberal compromises traditionally upheld by the political elite. The future of conflict regulation in Canada, the extent to which ethnic delegate representation will replace affiliative trusteeship in an era of new politics, and the extent to which minorities will be protected from the wrath of the majority may hang in the balance.

Unpopular Institutions

Given their unpopularity, many distinctive aspects of Canadian public policy must be attributed to the distinct political values of Canadian political elites. Rick Ogmundson and Lee Fisher postulate that many Canadian–American differences in policy cannot be explained with reference to 'mass public opinion,' but only with respect to 'differing *élite* political cultures,' which in some measure 'derive from the distant past.'[140] One might here raise the example of nineteenth-century liberal concepts of political nationality, of which George-Etienne Cartier was Canada's most important exponent (see 3.2).[141] This view, that a diversity of cultural elements need not be corrosive of political fraternity nor, even, of a common meta-identity inhering in such diversity itself, is apparently not firmly rooted in popular experience, particularly outside the fashionably cosmopolitan cores of major cities. Alan Cairns and Cynthia Williams also confirm the salience of distinct elite political values. As they observe, governments in Canada should not be understood 'as passive recipients of society's demands, mechanically translating public pressures into policy outputs. State élites have their own agenda, derived from their visions of desirable futures and from their official responsibility for the long-run health of the government and people over whose affairs they preside. Policies relating to language and the Charter, in particular underline this leadership role ...'[142] The capacity of elites to continue to exercise this leadership within the realm of conflict regulation, however, must ultimately turn upon the prevailing mode of legitimate political representation. That policies unsanctioned by public opinion remain in force in Canada should not be mistaken for evidence of a deferential population. Most policies represent the accretions of several generations of politics, and although it is considerably less costly politically to maintain an unpopular policy than to implement one anew, it remains uncertain how long policies that resist majoritarian logic and embrace a permanent multiplicity of overlapping cultural identities as the very essence of Canadian nationhood will persist in the altered political landscape.

5.5 The Future of Statecraft in Canada

Interestingly, although James Tully and Alain Noël have each recognized an immense clash of beliefs inherent in Canadian constitution-making, neither has apparently lost his faith in the capacity of democratic deliberation to reap mass-level consensus.[143] The 'gap between negotiators and deliberators' witnessed after the Charlottetown Accord is attributed by Tully to the lesser enjoyment of citizen-deliberators (relative to elites) of the 'interactive experience' that helps to free individuals 'temporarily from their own background understanding' to reach compromises.[144] What is needed, he suggests, is for Canadians 'to engage in more exchanges and become a little more intercultural.'[145]

This identifies a shortcoming in classical consociational theory, which, in presupposing the maintenance of heavy cultural barriers, undoubtedly neglects the necessity of cultivating fraternity and common perspectives in the long-term management of conflict.[146] Nevertheless, it needs to be understood that intense popular political engagement does not necessarily advance 'interculturalism' any more than the deliberations of Athenian citizens brought them into sympathy with the (remote) Spartans. As Peter Russell observes with respect to the hearings in Manitoba and New Brunswick during the Meech Lake ratification stage, the 'process showed how divisive popular participation in constitution making can be if it is carried on in balkanized enclaves.'[147] Of course, for the vast majority of citizens, such enclaves – their families and places of work, local meetings in school gymnasiums, and the letters and editorial page of their local newspaper – are just the sort of settings in which they typically conduct their political deliberations.

Furthermore, as indispensable as 'interculturalism' is to a permanent solution to conflict in segmented societies, it is no more an adequate, short-term response to potentially serious intra-state conflict than cultural exchanges, intermarriage, and athletic competitions are sufficient short-term solutions to inter-state conflict and war. It remains true that 'political élites understand the complexities of multiracial or multicultural societies, or at least have a heightened appreciation of their explosive possibilities' and that ordinary citizens are more apt to favour majoritarianism than minority rights.[148] More enlightened and less dangerous policies are therefore more likely to be accepted by elites, even if legitimate implementation remains a critical issue. Although the increasing penetration of university education within society at large might be expected to induct proportionately more citizens into the 'culture of tolerance' that guided most university-educated voters in the Charlottetown referendum in favour of accommodation, the dissemination of information alone, as through an intensified popular political discourse, does not invariably improve support for minority accommodation.[149] Indeed, in their study of the sources of the 'no' vote in the referendum on the Charlottetown Accord, Johnston and colleagues concluded, 'Although information, as distinct from education ... increased liking for specific minorities, it reduced support for minority rights in the abstract.'[150] Clearly, the increasing salience of mass electronic communication with remote strangers holds hope, particularly for the cross-cutting segments mediated by the Internet (as opposed, in some instances, to talk radio). But for the time being, gratuitous extensions of popular democracy in the realm of conflict regulation would seem to be markedly incautious, particularly where popular involvement consists of the public aggregation and self-reinforcement of monolithic local opinion.

All this is not, of course, to imply that there is presently a great deal of latitude for elite-dominated processes in constitutional processes. Entrenched expectations appear to require a considerable degree of popular consent for constitutional change.[151] Affiliative trusteeship, certainly in the absence of extraordinarily compelling statesmen, or as-yet-undiscovered mechanisms of legitimation will have an increasingly restricted compass. Yet, these limitations do not dispense with the imperative of thinking about how, within the limited range of motion available, the constitutional political process ought to and can be conducted.[152] Aspects of Canadian political history engaged in this work provide indispensable context for such a reconsideration, which unfortunately cannot be attempted here.

5.6 Conclusion

Conflict regulation in Canada was frustrated in the closing decades of the twentieth century by the incapacity of federal political elites to realize their agendas. Official bilingualism and multiculturalism have been successful in the narrow sense of establishing federal programs that survive today and that (in the former case) have brought far more francophones into the federal public service. But such programs have been largely outfaced by public resistance in their broader role of garnering symbolic recognition for minority cultural and linguistic groups. Initiatives for major constitutional change, with one notable exception, have been thwarted entirely. The exception, the Constitutional Act of 1982, was substantially altered in relation to Trudeau's original design. As such, what was envisaged as a decisive confrontation with exclusive nationalism became instead a blunt, but galvanizing insult to exclusive nationalists. Subsequent high-profile initiatives to assuage such insult have met with harrowing failure, and indeed have tended to salt the wounds.

The reasons for the failure of these strategies are complex. But in some ways they all relate to the common premise that elite consensus can underwrite dramatic, symbolically portentous policy shifts to reform the political and civic relations of majorities and minorities. The perverse consequences of these attempts – the manifestation of grass-roots linguistic chauvinism precipitated by official bilingualism, the choruses of assimilationist views raised by multiculturalism, the constitutionally entrenched subservience of individual rights to popular sovereignty at the provincial level of the 1982 constitution, the public displays of penuriousness in the refusal to accommodate Québécois aspirations through the Meech Lake Accord, and the echoes of anti-Quebec sentiment heard after the Charlottetown Accord – all hint at the difficulty of reforming popular predispositions and civic relationships through a sort of monumentalist politics. In an age of increasingly direct democracy and ready popular mobilization, highly visible moves within the closely contested realm of culture and identity are readily vitiated by popular reaction.

Conflict regulation, it should be noted, has not been equated in this chapter with the untempered suppression of exclusive nationalism. Indeed, in the view of most practitioners in Canada, regulating the French–English conflict in the 1980s and 1990s has required, among other things, beating a symbolic constitutional retreat from the moral position taken by the 1982 Constitution Act. To a degree, as we have seen, this view is motivated by the embrace of popular sovereignty and its full implications for majoritarianism and individual liberties. But it is also a function of the special circumstances engendered by the risk of Quebec secession. Factoring in such risks should not be construed as placing expedience before liberal principle. For the principles ultimately at stake are vividly clear. If one accepts that minorities in present-day Canada would be at greater risk in the aftermath of secession, particularly in view of the potential for economic and social trauma, and that the mutual suasion of Canada and Quebec would be diminished in any subsequent intercessions, then there is much to lose from the standpoint of upholding individual liberties and managing conflict by exacerbating the risk of secession. Quibbling over minor symbolic accommodations of exclusive nationalism may, in this respect, be counter-productive.

The position underlying the analysis of this chapter, therefore, is that the interests of managing conflict in Canada require striking a balance between containing the risk of secession, on one hand, and, on the other, upholding the Charter, which despite its legal weaknesses, certainly defends minorities in some contexts, as well as providing a moral injunction against exclusive nationalism. This balance is inherently difficult to strike, and is subject to tactically oriented shifts. The calculations involved have tended to be inscrutable to all but the most devoted observers and practitioners of constitutional politics. While the near victory for secession in the 1995 referendum may perhaps bring the salient considerations into sharper relief, the rise of participatory constitutional politics certainly hindered achieving a stable compromise to that point.

It is unhelpful, of course, to argue from hindsight that any of the failed constitutional strategies struck a balance preferable to the current predicament. But if one abstracts from the substance of those strategies, one must still record as unfortunate the consistent failure of carefully formed strategies for regulating conflict, and the diminished potential this suggests for cogent leadership in this sphere. Only a true cynic could aver that rudderless drifting is a more promising state of affairs than intelligent, if sometimes fallible, navigation. As for the future capacity and responsiveness of conflict regulation in Canada, that might be seen to depend in the first instance on the nature, causes and reversibility of the increasingly direct-democratic political process in this realm. However, the preliminary indication from the preceding chapters is that political representation has become progressively more direct over the past two centuries in Canada due to mainly structural factors. This is not to deny a place for inspired leadership through what may well prove to be the trailing edge of the potential for statecraft. But it certainly is to call attention to the need to give serious consideration to how, more generally, conflict might be attenuated in an intermittently antagonistic, segmented society in a way that is compatible with increasingly direct democracy. On what scale, on what legitimate basis, and through what processes politics may entrain reconciliation within divided societies remains the central issue of our time.

The Lessons of History

The influence of exclusive nationalism on Canadian politics and policy has varied historically. Its varying force can be understood in part as a function of the changing relationship of political elites to popular constituencies, that is, of the pattern of political representation and conflict regulation. The historical essay presented a narrative of the changing nature of conflict regulation and the related penetration of official politics and policy by exclusive nationalism. In this summary, I draw together the interpretive themes of the work by linking them with my theoretical model. I conclude by reviewing the major implications of this work for a theory of exclusive nationalism and for the practice of conflict regulation in Canada.

Canadian Political History in Light of Exclusive Nationalism

A basic premise of my theory is that the epicentre of exclusive nationalism is located well outside the central political arena in which statecraft has traditionally been conducted by the political elite. I have suggested several reasons why elites have been less apt than ordinary citizens to embrace exclusive nationalism. The first is that elites have been more receptive to strategic constraints in the international environment that weigh heavily against exclusive nationalism. Consciousness of external strategic threats, for example, made such leaders as Carleton, Prevost, and Elgin acutely aware of the imperative of maintaining strong ethnic alliances at home. The greater receptiveness of elites to social and diplomatic pressures from abroad was also a factor in the concluding of the grand integrative project of Confederation, particularly in New Brunswick and Nova Scotia, where the project was unpopular. Lévesque, in his earlier guise as a trenchant opponent of exclusive nationalism, emphasized the value of 'friendship with our neighbours to the East, West and South' in making the case for not impinging on the rights of minorities.

A second, rather less steady, factor was the sometimes broader cultural horizons of the political elite. Consistent with the widening schism in contemporary Britain, Governor Murray sharply rejected the fanatical chauvinism of his Protestant brethren. George Ross, Minister of Education in Ontario under Premier Oliver Mowat, appreciated the contribution of French Canadians to the culture of the country. In the twentieth century, the cosmopolitan and bicultural Trudeau rejected the inward preoccupation within Quebec and seemed supremely indifferent to the risks of cultural discontinuity. Elite cosmopolitanism has sometimes not, however, been sufficient in itself to sustain the power cleavage. One need only think of Governor Craig, Ludger Duvernay, George Brown, D'Alton McCarthy, Camille Laurin, and Preston Manning to recognize that subtle nods to philistine chauvinism have long posed the temptation of a strong local following for ambitious or insecure figures.

Third, even in the absence of broader cultural horizons and ingrained habits of tolerance, the exigencies of maintaining alliances with elites of other cultural persuasions helped dampen the articulation of residual prejudice. This was witnessed, for example, in the participation of the Ultras in the Liberal–Reform coalition of 1851. A fourth and final factor must be the liberal political principles of such men as Grenville, Viger, Mills, and Bertrand, all of whom rejected in principle the state imprinting an official religion or culture on a heterogeneous population.

Together, these factors have historically given rise to the power cleavage, the division repeatedly observed between elite positions and mass sentiments over exclusive nationalism. The power cleavage in earlier times, under normal circumstances, prevented the latent potential for exclusive nationalism in popular chauvinism from being realized. The power cleavage has never, however, been a perfect barrier. Two related categories of failure have been realized: the loss of control of the political elite over a mobilized movement, and their own acquiescence in exclusive nationalism. These failures have occurred especially (though not exclusively) following turning points in the long evolution of forms of legitimate political representation, an evolutionary path I segmented into three modes, imposed statecraft, affiliative trusteeship and ethnic delegate representation. Rapid corrections in the level of popular political involvement occurred as imposed statecraft gave way to affiliative trusteeship, and as the latter gave way to ethnic delegate representation; they were triggered after periods in which the rate of evolution of the prevailing form of political representation had at first slowed, increasingly lagging burgeoning legitimate expectations. Nevertheless, at such turning points the initiative shifted from the elite to the rank and file of movements, pressing popular sentiments to particular effect. The growing expectations of popular influence that were instrumental to such developments were created by several factors, chief among them the evolving international context of democratic norms and the developing popular capacity for articulate political participation. Opposition elites, who have frequently seized upon slow progress in popular government as an effective challenge to existing regimes, have frequently encouraged and catalysed popular political mobilization, at times with obliquely chauvinist rhetoric. Two major forms of exclusive nationalism ensued, as will be reviewed shortly.

Military rule in the immediate aftermath of the Conquest gave way to the autocratic rule of governors, which in turn gave way to the regime established by the Constitutional Act of 1791, a regime aiming at a tripartite balance of power among monarchy, aristocracy, and democracy. In declining extent from that early sequence until the gradual grant of responsible government in the 1840s, conflict regulation was imposed by fiat of the governors, appointive councils, and the imperial government. This system, which we have termed imposed statecraft, was at no juncture wholly legitimate before every segment of the population. For instance, although the seigneurs were generally content not to have a popular assembly during the early decades after the Conquest, the British merchants were severely distressed. Their protests on the issue provided forums for the first recorded articulation of demotic exclusive nationalism in Canada. As for the regime inaugurated with the Constitutional Act, although it was not subjected to any articulate root and branch critiques in the first decade after its introduction, such vestiges of despotic rule as the corvée and militia duty were felt heavily by the habitants; their anger was manifested in sporadic riots exhibiting popular chauvinism.

If imposed statecraft was never entirely legitimate in the early decades, its legitimacy later rapidly declined. This was particularly evident by the 1830s, as expectations of popular sovereignty were racing, on one hand, and the evolution of the system of representation ground to a halt, on the other. The Canadien political elite and their democratic British colleagues articulated opposition with increasing volume in Lower Canada that clearly reflected the growing international influence of Jacksonian ideas and philosophical radicalism. They mobilized the population, which was exercised at any rate with its own variety of grievances, ranging from violence at the polls, to immigration, to oppressive militia ordinances. The movement was at first defined from the top, as witnessed, for example, by the formulation of the 92 Resolutions, a document of strident tone that nonetheless explicitly welcomed immigration from other parts of the British empire and that focused the critique on the prevailing system of representation. While the population had certainly gained the political consciousness to be capable of participation within a structured movement, it did not yet dictate objectives. However, as elite voices were progressively diluted, the elite lost control and the mass base sheared off and took on a life of its own. The bloody struggle, infused to some extent by ethnic animosity, directed against the (even more) violent *anglais*, was grafted onto the movement by its followers, rather than by its bi-ethnic traditional leaders. Such was the complexion of demotic exclusive nationalism.

The struggle of the Canadiens and their English allies in the early nineteenth century against the existing form of political representation rested in dialectical opposition with the struggle of the English social elite of the colony. This group looked to their distinct interests in monopolizing administrative power, as well as to their haughty notions of the status prerequisites for holding major political responsibility. Their leaders, including governors and the colonial office, held that democratization, which also implied a diminishment of the imperial connexion, was moving not too slowly, but too quickly. As their dissatisfaction mounted with the reforms pressed by the Parti Canadien–dominated assembly, the chauvinism and paranoia of petty British leaders in the colony was welded onto the rearguard Whig critique, and it occasionally afflicted even senior officials, including Governor Craig's advisers. Still, advocates of official exclusive nationalism during the period were generally confined to subordinate tiers of the imperial political system. In this respect they did not compare to the more concerted British parliamentary exhibition of early official exclusive nationalism in the Act of Union.

In the Act of Union a determined effort was made to assimilate the French Canadians. This was an effort that certainly dovetailed with popular chauvinism, but that was ultimately driven by the need to assure trust within a civil political arena becoming increasingly pivotal to the underwriting of the infrastructure and stability required for commercial prosperity. Above all, the policy was a product of an internal security risk seeming unusually larger than external risks. That this unenlightened venture was premised primarily upon strategic considerations and the need for trust-based collaboration rather than a cultural vendetta is made clear by the swiftness with which it was abandoned as it became evident to the governors on the spot that the cause for concern had passed.

The form of government that the Canadien elite had sought with eloquence and increasing commitment since Bédard's time was one in which
the executive would serve the people. This vision was achieved as responsible government was granted in several stages and imposed statecraft gave
way entirely through the 1840s to affiliative trusteeship. It was achieved
because the fears of such observers as Lord Durham that local leaders were
mere spokesmen for popular prejudices were not realized. In the event,
governing political elites acted not as servants of popular chauvinism, but
rather as trustees of the broader public interest. The system that therefore
evolved fostered alliances, and these were led particularly by men such as
Baldwin, who clearly articulated his role as trustee and was committed to
joint accommodation and to the pursuit of principled causes across the
ethnic divide. During the Union period the political elite exhibited varying
affinities with popular views, although a politician actually hoping to form
a governing coalition had, as Governor Head put it, to 'school his mind to
tolerance' (see 3.3), or at least to mute residual personal prejudices. Alliance pressures, of course, greatly supplemented, in some cases substituted
for, principled opposition to exclusive nationalism. Trustee conceptions of
political representation, as well as fluidity of partisan affiliation supported
a continuous process of coalition formation and development.

By the mid-1860s strategic partisan interests in forging a wider circle of
political alliances augmented a liberal, agglomerative impulse in giving
impetus to Confederation, perhaps the greatest coup of nineteenth-century affiliative trusteeship. But the reliance of conflict regulation during
this period upon shifting political alliances rooted in varying shades of
expedience also reduced the stock that the francophone majority of Quebec was prepared to place in centralized conflict regulation. The result was
an early constitutional tradition that gave pride of place to provincial
majoritarianism as the protector of the most significant federal minority,
Catholic francophones in Quebec, and that gave only a limited role to
federal intervention.

A necessary, perhaps obvious, condition of accommodation on the
pattern of affiliative trusteeship is that political alliances with minorities
carry sufficient strategic political value to be at least occasionally indispensable to the formation of governments. This condition lapsed in both New
Brunswick and Manitoba after Confederation. A majoritarian resort to
official exclusive nationalism ensued. Such strikes against minorities could
be parried only weakly by the federal government, which although strongly
opposed on balance to exclusive nationalism in its own sphere of control,
was divided as to the merits of legislating in provincial domains.

As already noted, the potential for exclusive nationalism appears to be particularly strong at points of rapid acceleration in the institutionalized levels of political influence enjoyed by ordinary citizens. In the later part of the twentieth century the most dramatic and visible surge of participation and subsequent rise of exclusive nationalism occurred in Quebec during the 1960s. Manifested in extra-parliamentary popular mobilization and in the rapid democratization of the political process within parties, this surge was precipitated partly by the intensifying mutual dependence of state and society through a process of rapid modernization of public institutions. This was also a period that coincided with an increasing potential for popular political organization and participation. As higher education was rapidly expanding in Quebec, the improving analytical sophistication of citizens enforced a shift in the basis of legitimacy away from charismatic authority towards performance criteria. Mobilization was then further elicited by a very dynamic international context of protest.

The birth of the Parti Québécois brought an historic fusion of high levels of mobilization and participatory expectations with popular chauvinism, which had mutated somewhat in Quebec over the preceding decades as the urban status order had displaced traditional forms of competitive differentiation. The fusion brought the collapse of the power cleavage and of the existing system of conflict regulation. Lévesque and other members of the political elite were willing agents of this change, as they deliberately sought to create a party that would be steered by its rank and file membership. The Parti Québécois was constituted on this basis and was composed overwhelmingly of francophones. This crowning of ethnic delegate representation as the new standard of legitimacy brought a marked reduction of the conflict-regulating potential of the political system. The passage of Bill 63 in 1969 (providing for freedom of parental choice in language of education) with overwhelming support from the political élite of the Quebec National Assembly was a heroic last stand amidst massive demonstrations on the streets. Thereafter, official exclusive nationalism of various shades would be enshrined in Quebec as the new orthodoxy.

It was an orthodoxy that could be only partly offset by constitutional initiatives from the federal sphere. Trudeau was in some senses a late embodiment of affiliative trusteeship within federal politics, wielding a relatively free hand in promulgating unpopular, pluralist policies in the realm of language and culture. But his constitutional precepts were not widely shared by provincial elites, who, as Premier Alan Blakeney among them, gave precedence to majoritarianism at the provincial level over regulating exclusive nationalism. The threat of popular mobilization in

Quebec and of precipitating the secession of that province continued subsequently to preclude any more effective confrontation of exclusive nationalism. Indeed, later constitutional initiatives proposed to allay rather than strengthen the moral condemnation of exclusive nationalism implicit in the Charter of Rights.

Fine-tuning the constitution so as to manage the risk of secession has, however, proved difficult because the amending formula entails a process incommensurate with a meaningful role for many mobilized constituencies, and because the mechanism of plebiscitary democracy, introduced to the constitutional realm with the Charlottetown Accord, tightly constrains the potential for generally unpopular, minority accommodation. On other fronts, the nature of party politics, as of new constitutional politics, shows signs of being fundamentally altered in the context of structural changes in popular expectations of involvement in the development of policy.

Exclusive Nationalism in Light of Canadian Political History

I considered in the introduction explanations of nationalism that emphasize the consolidation and differentiation of distinct cultures, and the competition of large groups thus demarcated for various forms of power and status. The theoretical thrust of this work is that among the causal underpinnings specifically of exclusive nationalism must also be included an array of other dynamic factors. In particular, the factors affecting the integrity of the power cleavage, which has traditionally formed a barrier between inveterate popular inclinations and the conduct of state policy, appear to be pivotal. Long-term trends and short-term fluctuations in the mode of political representation and conflict regulation can narrow or close the power cleavage, and these fluctuations, we have argued, are largely independent of processes of cultural differentiation, ethnic competition, or variations in popular chauvinism. This can perhaps best be seen on the level of individual agency, as many of those who were instrumental in bringing home the global context of evolving democratic norms were not animated by ethnic chauvinism, but rather by liberal convictions. Certainly this was true of John Neilson through the *Quebec Gazette* in the 1820s, Wolfred Nelson in his role in the Patriots in the late 1830s, and Pierre Trudeau and other writers at *Cité libre* in the 1950s. Even such a leader as René Lévesque, who was instrumental in effecting the transition from affiliative trusteeship to delegate representation in Quebec, was distinctly uncomfortable with the ethnic exclusivism that the new mode of representation appeared to entrain. In Quebec, efforts to advance the cause of popular sovereignty dovetailed with the increasing capacity of citizens for sustained involvement in political causes – another factor that owes little to fluctuations in the strength of popular chauvinism. Also independent of such chauvinism was the intensifying dialectic of control (or increasing co-dependence of state and society) over the course of modernization, witnessed during the 1960s in Quebec.

If many dynamic factors separable from ethnic consciousness, competition, and antagonism have affected the mode of representation and in turn the prospects for exclusive nationalism, it is also true that the incidence of popular chauvinism has been much broader than that of official exclusive nationalism. In 1765 Governor Murray could speak of Protestant 'Fanaticks' and the 'National English Prejudice'; a few years later, Canadien habitants were talking about 'bashing "*les Anglais*".' Mass xenophobia and popular chauvinism have been visited upon most if not all eras of Canadian history in the interim. Indeed, it is at the very least a useful exercise to treat these as constants in striving for more complete explanations of the impact of exclusive nationalism as a systematic force. What has varied quite independently is the extent to which support for various sorts of religious, cultural, or linguistic crusades has penetrated the central political arena and institutionalized political discourse and activity. While popular chauvinism and the factors that feed it have long provided a latent potential for official exclusive nationalism, all of the factors that determine the nature of the political process and the level of extra-parliamentary mobilization have determined the extent to which that potential has been realized.

I therefore conclude that in analysing the causes of exclusive nationalism it is essential to consider not only the perennial, if mutating, insecurities of large groups, and their inveterate preferences for hegemony over inferiority in the changing realms of being and endeavour in which they stake their identities, but also why such insecurities and ambitions are successful in penetrating the central political arena at specific historical moments. Adequate causal explanations of exclusive nationalism must subsume the major causes of popular mobilization, and in particular, basic incongruencies between the state of society and prevailing forms of political representation. Exclusive nationalism is a greater risk in the wake of discontinuities in the evolution of popular sovereignty within political systems, and, unfortunately, at later phases of majoritarian democracy. What must remain uncertain for now is whether the onset of ethnic delegate representation may at some future time permanently cripple the regulation of domestic ethnic conflict, making erstwhile options of last resort, namely secession and resettlement, necessary evils.

Exclusive nationalism clearly raises serious moral questions. I personally tend to think about these in the rather unfavourable light of liberalism. Others will have their own views. But it is in any event insufficient for any of us to moralize. Regulating conflict requires considerable practical discretion in balancing the protection of individual rights today with the maintenance of a vital institutional context for their future protection. In striking this delicate balance much ultimately depends upon the extent to which effective statecraft, perhaps of a less ostentatious and overt form than in the past, can be resurrected. The maintenance of independent, juridical spheres charged with upholding the sanctity of individual, self-regarding choices might also make a modest contribution. But in an age of increasingly direct democracy, more still will depend upon the ascent to pluralist attitudes and values of citizens themselves, perhaps even upon their finding inspiration and models for emulation among the greatest statesmen of Canadian political history. Perhaps most of all, however, it will depend upon the web of individuals' own professional, business, and cultural alliances continuing to expand beyond their native communities.

Notes

Introduction: Exclusive Nationalism and Conflict Regulation

1 Several of the best-known large-scale historical works on Canada that al-
lude to nationalism are Donald Grant Creighton, *Dominion of the North:
A History of Canada*; Ramsay Cook, *The Maple Leaf Forever: Essays on
Nationalism and Politics in Canada*; Léon Dion, *Nationalismes et politiques
au Québec*; Denis Monière, *Ideologies in Quebec: The Historical Development*, trans. Richard Howard; Susan Mann Trofimenkoff, *The Dream of
Nation: A Social and Intellectual History of Quebec*; Louis Balthazar, *Bilan
du nationalisme au Québec*; Fernand Dumont, *Genèse de la société
québécoise*.

2 However, the implications of *recent* Quebec politics for theories of nationalism have been examined in several works. See Hudson Meadwell, 'Breaking the Mould? Quebec Independence and Secession in the Developed West,'
in *Notions of Nationalism*, ed. Sukumar Periwal, 129–61; Mary Beth Montcalm, 'Quebec Nationalism in Comparative Perspective,' in *Quebec: State
and Society*, ed. Alain Gagnon, 45–58; Katherine O' Sullivan, *First World
Nationalisms: Class and Ethnic Politics in Northern Ireland and Quebec*;
Michael Keating, *Nations against the State: The New Politics of Nationalism
in Quebec, Catalonia, and Scotland*.

3 Peter Alter, *Nationalism*, 2d ed., 1. See also Walker Connor, 'A Nation
is a Nation, is a State, is an Ethnic Group, is a ...,' in *Ethnonationalism:
The Quest for Understanding*, 90–117; Louis Snyder, *The Meaning of
Nationalism*, 4.

4 Carlton Hayes, *The Historical Evolution of Modern Nationalism*, 6; Hans
Kohn, *The Idea of Nationalism: A Study in Its Origins and Background*, 15;
Thomas Spira, 'Nationalism: Recent Research and New Opportunities,' in

Nationalism: Essays in Honor of Louis L. Snyder, Michael Palumbo and William Shanahan, 34; Alter, *Nationalism*, 4; Miroslav Hroch, 'National Self-determination from a Historical Perspective,' in *Notions of Nationalism*, ed. Sukumar Periwal, 65; Montserrat Guibernau, *Nationalisms: The Nation-State and Nationalism in the Twentieth Century*.

5 Both congruence and symbiosis are loosely implied in Lord Acton's famous observation that nationalism aims to make 'the nation the mould and meas-ure of the state' (Lord Acton, 'Nationality' [1862], in *The History of Free-dom and Other Essays* ed. J.N. Figgis and R.V. Lawrence, 299; quoted in Hans Kohn, *Prophets and Peoples: Studies in Nineteenth Century National-ism*, 37, and in Smith, *Nations and Nationalism*, 113). Gellner's definition of nationalism (political principle that 'the political and the national unit should be congruent') has been influential (Ernest Gellner, *Nations and National-ism*, 1). See Eric Hobsbawm, *Nations and Nationalism since 1780: Pro-gramme, Myth, Reality*, 9. But even Gellner's own work suggests that the nationalist program goes well beyond seeking congruence, certainly in any straightforward sense (*Nations and Nationalism*, 57). See also Kohn, *The Idea of Nationalism*, 18–19.

6 Hayes drew attention to the cultural nationalism of Herder in *Historical Evolution of Modern Nationalism* (27–33). See also John Plamenatz, 'Two Types of Nationalism,' in *Nationalism: The Nature and Evolution of an Idea*, ed. Eugene Kamenka, 22–8; John Dunn, *Western Political Theory in the Face of the Future*, 73; Gellner, *Nations and Nationalism*, 57; Hroch, 'National Self-determination,' 73; Smith, *Nations and Nationalism in a Global Era*, 13; John Hutchinson, *Modern Nationalism* (London: Fontana, 1994), 46–7.

7 Thus, a Canadian political scientist, Léon Dion, has defined nationalist movements in terms of collective action 'undertaken under the influence of a perception of the national community's will to exist ... aiming to mobilize the community's members so as to promote a sense of solidarity ... and [pro-mote] projects relating to the organization of the cultural, economic, and political life considered proper for that community': Léon Dion, *Québec: The Unfinished Revolution*, 108–9.

8 Hayes, *Historical Evolution of Modern Nationalism*, 13–231. Cf. Alter, *Nationalism*, 27, and John A. Hall, 'Nationalisms, Classified and Explained,' in *Notions of Nationalism*, ed. Sukumar Periwal, 8–33.

9 Hayes, *Historical Evolution of Modern Nationalism*, 17–22, 64–9, 165, 196, 212.

10 Kohn, *The Idea of Nationalism*, 329, 351. Cf. Plamenatz, 'Two Types of Nationalism,' 25, 33–4.

11 Anthony Smith, *Theories of Nationalism*, 197.

12 Ibid., 208.

13 Ibid., 215–27.

14 Ibid., 216–20.

15 Blurring such distinctions is also responsible for an often obtuse evaluative discourse, which has tended simply to weigh good against bad manifestations of nationalism as a compound, abstract whole, as though the proverbial two Janus faces or sides of the coin of nationalism are necessarily fused together. This seems analogous to weighing the merits and demerits of 'killing,' a category that similarly relates to a vast range of distinguishable forms and contexts, whatever their shared and ethically uninteresting correlations with elements such as 'adrenalin,' 'testosterone,' 'aggressiveness,' and so on. Many manifestations of nationalism (e.g., genocide and peaceable autonomy-seeking) are also not related in any causal or morally pertinent way. The development of international norms connected with nationalism, as well as the study of the phenomena thus delineated, will depend upon substantially improved categories that are more closely connected with the implications of the program.

16 Smith, *Nations and Nationalism*, 113. See also works cited n. 6, above.

17 Smith, *Nations and Nationalism*, 97.

18 Keating, *Nations against the State*, 7–8.

19 Ibid., 3, 6. Smith modified his own typology in a later work to emphasize the nature of the 'concept of the nation' used by nationalist movements, rather than their sociological circumstances: Anthony Smith, *National Identity*, 81–2.

20 For literature implicitly assuming the distinction between inclusive and exclusive nationalism, see Hayes, *Historical Evolution of Modern Nationalism*, 308; Kellas, *The Politics of Nationalism and Ethnicity;* 135; Dunn, *Western Political Theory*, 78; Smith, *Nations and Nationalism*, 151; Alter, *Nationalism*, 26–35; Hall, 'Nationalisms, Classified and Explained,' 18–20; Vesna Peši , 'The Cruel Face of Nationalism,' in *Nationalism, Ethnic Conflict, and Democracy*, ed. Larry Diamond and Marc F. Plattner, 133; Ghia Nodia, 'Nationalism and Democracy,' in *Nationalism, Ethnic Conflict, and Democracy*, ed. Diamond and Plattner, 15; Guibernau, *Nationalisms*, 63–4.

21 Hence, Yael Tamir suggests that a liberal form of nationalism might endorse 'distributing an equal number of cultural vouchers to each citizen, and allowing individuals to consume culture according to their own preferences': Yael Tamir, *Liberal Nationalism*, 54–5.

22 Keating, *Nations against the State*, 7; Smith, *Nations and Nationalism*, 99–100. Note, however, that the same limitation – capturing only fractions of movements – also applies to the ethnic/civic distinction to the extent that

it is employed to describe not only the sociopolitical origins, but also the objectives of nationalism. On balance it seems better to accept the challenge of focusing upon subsidiary levels of analysis (episodes, sections/currents of movements) in order to avoid categories that are simpler but of narrowly academic interest.

23 Alter, *Nationalism*, 26.

24 Thomas Pogge, 'Group Rights and Ethnicity,' in *Ethnicity and Group Rights*, ed. Will Kymlicka and Ian Shapiro, 188.

25 Donald Horowitz, *Ethnic Groups in Conflict*, 196. Horowitz cites several examples, speaking, for example, of the 'growing narrowness of Sinhalese conceptions of nationalism through this century,' which came to imply that Tamils were 'not included in the political community' (197). More generally, he observes that 'ethnic exclusivism is quite common' and that 'homogeneity is an exclusivist goal with a powerful appeal' (197). See also Stephen Van Evera, 'Hypotheses on Nationalism and War,' in *Nationalism and Ethnic Conflict*, ed. Michael Brown, Owen Coté, Jr, Sean Lynn-Jones, and Steven Miller, 29, 34.

26 Michael Hartney, 'Some Confusions Concerning Collective Rights,' in *The Rights of Minority Cultures*, ed. Will Kymlicka, 206.

27 Joseph Raz, *The Morality of Freedom*, 369–72, 426–7; Will Kymlicka, *Multicultural Citizenship: A Liberal Theory of Minority Rights*, 80–2; Sir Isaiah Berlin, *Four Essays on Liberty*, 124–44; John Stuart Mill, *On Liberty* (1859), ed. David Spitz, 64.

28 Chandran Kukathas, 'Cultural Toleration,' in *Ethnicity and Group Rights*, ed. Kimlicka and Shapiro, 79–83; Kymlicka, *Multicultural Citizenship*, 91–2; John Stuart Mill, *Considerations on Representative Government* (1861), ed. Currin V. Shields, 229–37; Mill, *On Liberty*, 60–3.

29 Adeno Addis, 'On Human Diversity and the Limits of Toleration,' in *Ethnicity and Group Rights*, ed. Kimlicka and Shapiro, 138–9; Leo Strauss, *Liberalism Ancient and Modern*, 226; Brian Barry, *Justice as Impartiality*, 170. See also the literature on fascism: Walter Laqueur, *Fascism: Past, Present, Future*; Michael Burleigh and Wolfgang Wippermann, *The Racial State: Germany, 1933–1945*; A.J. Nicholls, 'Germany,' in *European Fascism*, ed. S.J. Woolf, 61–87.

30 Jeremy Waldron, 'Minority Cultures and the Cosmopolitan Alternative,' in *The Rights of Minority Cultures*, 100–2, 108–9; David Miller, 'Group Identities, National Identities and Democratic Politics,' in *Toleration, Identity and Difference*, ed. John Horton and Susan Mendus, 110–17; cf. Kymlicka, *Multicultural Citizenship*, 103–4.

31 Admittedly, some liberals, including Mill, have sometimes acknowledged substantive goods in this range, often on the basis of (entirely plausible) speculation that individual autonomy is ultimately conducive to both diversity and sincerity: Mill, *On Liberty*, 54, 59.

32 I am aware that these claims together import a 'comprehensive view of the good' into politics and as such are unlikely to be acceptable to all. My own view however is: (1) epistemological perfection seems unattainable for any basis for civility (though I can' t be sure!); (2) conjointly, the assumptions proposed, which represent a fairly 'thin' (i.e., not very imposing) view of the good, are likely to attract sufficient overlapping consensus within many Western societies, sufficient, that is, to sustain the centrality (in the abstract) of self-regarding individual preferences; (3) at some point politics rightfully becomes a sphere of partisan deliberation and negotiation; and (4) even scholars must attempt to span scepticism with at least modest substantive commitments and constructive engagement. See Brian Barry's argument against epistemological restraint, supporting (only) moderate scepticism in, *Justice as Impartiality*, 172, 180–1; also Berlin, *Four Essays*, 172. Cf. John Rawls, 'Justice as Fairness: Political Not Metaphysical,' 239–48; Rawls, *Political Liberalism*; and Thomas Nagel, 'Moral Conflict and Political Legitimacy,' 215–40. In response to this stance of 'privatization,' see the collection of essays in *Toleration, Identity and Difference*, ed. Horton and Mendus, and Charles Taylor, 'Shared and Divergent Values,' in *Reconciling the Solitudes: Essays on Canadian Federalism and Nationalism*, 175.

33 Kymlicka, *Multicultural Citizenship*, 94–5, 152–72; Kymlicka, *Liberalism, Community, and Culture*, 198–9; Chandran Kukathas, 'Are There Any Cultural Rights?,' in *The Rights of Minority Culture*, ed. Kymlicka, 252; Kukathas, 'Cultural Toleration,' 71–2, 89; cf. Leslie Green, 'Internal Minorities and Their Rights,' in *The Rights of Minority Cultures*, ed. Kymlicka, 264–6; Mill, *On Liberty*, 95–7.

34 Yael Tamir and Will Kymlicka may be partial exceptions. Kymlicka seems to place stock in 'Terms of Integration' for immigrants, which, he thinks can rightly be wielded by states to supplement (already powerful) market pressures on immigrants, affecting their choice of languages. He appears to have reified his concept of 'societal culture,' so that myriad policy choices are reduced to the rather imposing question of whether immigrants are to 're-create their own societal cultures' (as a complex whole) *or not*. See Kymlicka, *Finding Our Way: Rethinking Ethnocultural Relations in Canada*, 27–8, 50–1; and Kymlicka, *Multicultural Citizenship*, 95–7. For my response to Yael Tamir, see n. 39, below.

35 Kukathas, 'Cultural Toleration,' 79–81; Immanuel Kant, *Critique of Pure Reason* (1781), trans. Norman Kemp Smith, A747/B775, A752/B780–A753/B781.

36 Michael Sandel, *Liberalism and the Limits of Justice*; Charles Taylor, 'Atomism,' *Philosophy and the Human Sciences*, vol. 2, 187–210.

37 For the definition of a public good, see Friedrich Hayek, *Law Legislation and Liberty*, vol. 3, 43–6; on resource transfers, or 'reparations,' see Green, 'Internal Minorities and Their Rights,' 260; Kymlicka, *Liberalism, Community, and Culture*, 189–91.

38 Michael Walzer, 'Pluralism: a Political Perspective,' in *The Rights of Minority Cultures*, ed. Kymlicka, 153.

39 Yael Tamir, *Liberal Nationalism*, 54–5. For similar earlier proposals see Ronald Dworkin, 'Comment on Narveson,' *33–4;* and Milton Friedman, *Capitalism and Freedom*, 86–91. Unfortunately, Tamir goes on to envisage future liberal national entities that would legitimately build their unity 'on a distinct cultural foundation,' making them 'more accessible to certain individuals ... than to others' (145–9, 163). Assuming that such entities would be territorial states (not entirely clear from her argument), this seems at odds with her earlier commitment to a best-efforts cultural pluralism. One weak point in her argument is the claim that advantages of scale necessarily attach to civil majorities, as such, rather than to groups of greater absolute numbers and territorial compactness (56). It is certainly true that minorities are at a disadvantage within many states, but this results from the very patterns of cultural preferment that, in the end, she commends. I think her argument that 'alienation and irrelevance' necessarily attend a culturally neutral state is seriously overstated (149). With Jeremy Waldron, I believe that her claims as to the essential interpenetration of culture and state politics (à la Clifford Geertz), which she uses to attack state cultural neutrality, hinge upon decided ambiguity in the scope and scale of the 'culture' in question. Cf. Waldron, 'Minority Cultures and the Cosmopolitan Alternative,' 93–114. See also the recent collection of essays *Nested Identities: Nationalism, Territory, and Scale*, ed. Guntram Herb and David Kaplan, especially Alexander Murphy, 'Rethinking the Concept of European Identity,' 53–70, and Rex Honey, 'Nested Identities in Nigeria,' 175–96.

40 Will Kymlicka, *Finding Our Way: Rethinking Ethnocultural Relations in Canada*, 51–2.

41 Waldron, 'Minority Cultures and the Cosmopolitan Alternative,' 93–103.

42 Smith, *The Ethnic Origins of Nations*, 221.

43 Theda Skocpol, *States and Social Revolutions: A Comparative Analysis of France, Russia, and China*, 28.

44 Ibid., 30.

45 Gellner, *Nations and Nationalism*, 111.

46 Plamenatz, 'Two Types of Nationalism,' 23.

47 Benedict Anderson, *Imagined Communities: Reflections on the Origins and Spread of Nationalism*, 19, 84; Gellner, *Nations and Nationalism*, 111, 119.

48 Anthony Giddens, *A Contemporary Critique of Historical Materialism*, vol. 2, *The Nation-State and Violence*, 186–92, 201–14.

49 Karl Deutsch, *Nationalism and Social Communication: An Inquiry into the Foundations of Nationality*; Deutsch, 'Nation-Building and National Development: Some Issues for Political Research,' in *Nation-Building*, ed. Deutsch and William Foltz.

50 Walker Connor, 'Nation-Building or Nation-Destroying,' *World Politics* 24 (1972): 329.

51 Ibid., 341.

52 Vaclav Havel, 'Needed: A New Spirit for A New World,' trans. Paul Wilson, *Globe and Mail*, 28 February 1995, A21.

53 Connor was probably the first to compile statistics concerning the 'remarkable lack of coincidence that exists between ethnic and political borders.' He calculated that, as of 1971, only 9.1 per cent of the 132 contemporary states were ethnically homogeneous. Moreover, he observed that in 53 per cent of the other cases ethnic minorities comprised more than a quarter of the population ('Nation-Building or Nation-Destroying?' 320). Gellner, considering the same issue in linguistic terms, estimates that at the extreme outside, only one-tenth of the 8,000 language communities in the world have exhibited nationalism. On the basis of this result he observes: 'Most cultures or potential national groups enter the age of nationalism without even the feeblest effort to benefit from it themselves. The number of groups which ... could try to become nations, which could define themselves by the kind of criterion which in some other place does in fact define some real and effective nation, is legion. Yet most of them go meekly to their doom, to see their culture (though not themselves as individuals) slowly disappear, dissolving into the wider culture of some new national state. Most cultures are led to the dustheap of history by industrial civilization without offering any resistance.' Gellner argues that this puts the lie to the 'social metaphysic' of nationalism of 'nations as a natural, God-given way of classifying men, as an inherent though long-delayed political destiny' (*Nations and Nationalism*, 47).

54 Breuilly, *Nationalism and the State*, 19–20.

55 Hobsbawm, *Nations and Nationalism since 1780*, 101.

56 Anthony Smith, *The Ethnic Origins of Nations*, 130, 132, 156–7; Breuilly,

Nationalism and the State, 359–62; Tom Nairn, *The Break-Up of Britain: Crisis and Neo-Nationalism*, 343; Michael Hechter, *Internal Colonialism: The Celtic Fringe in British National Development, 1536–1966*, esp. chaps. 2, 10; Gellner, *Nations and Nationalism*, 73–5, 97; Plamenatz, 'Two Types of Nationalism,' 27; Hobsbawm, *Nations and Nationalism since 1780*, 160.

57 A major empirical study by Ted Robert Gurr corroborates the argument that economic, cultural, and conventionally considered political power differentials are not strong causes of 'ethnonationalism.' Indeed, Gurr finds that, in terms of all of these dimensions, ethnonationalist groups tend to be somewhat better off on average than other groups (*Minorities at Risk: A Global View of Ethnopolitical Conflicts*, 46, 82).

58 See note 53, above.

59 Arend Lijphart, *The Politics of Accommodation: Pluralism and Democracy in the Netherlands*, 10, 112, 125, 134, 145; Lijphart, *Democracy in Plural Societies*, 116.

60 Adriano Pappalardo, 'The Conditions for Consociational Democracy: A Logical and Empirical Critique,' 365, 375.

61 Eric A. Nordlinger, *Conflict Regulation in Divided Societies*, Occasional Papers in International Affairs, no. 29 (Cambridge, MA: Center for International Affairs, Harvard University, 1972), 75. Donald Horowitz notes that the very process of elite accommodation may not be popularly accepted: 'From the perspective of a group member, multiethnic bargaining may be illegitimate, a form of appeasement or dealing with the Devil' (*Ethnic Groups in Conflict*, 565, 569–77). See also his 'Ethnic Conflict Management for Policymakers' in *Conflict and Peacemaking in Multiethnic Societies*, ed. Joseph V. Montville, 115–30.

62 Nordlinger, *Conflict Regulation in Divided Societies*, 64, 66, 70, 73.

63 Ian Lustick, 'Stability in Deeply Divided Societies: Consociationalism versus Control,' 325–44.

64 Ibid., 330. See also Hechter, *Internal Colonialism*.

65 Sammy Smooha and Theodor Hanf, 'The Diverse Modes of Conflict Regulation in Deeply Divided Societies,' 31.

66 Ibid., 32.

67 Nordlinger notes that majoritarianism stands in opposition to virtually all significant conflict regulation practices (*Conflict Regulation*, 33–4). Lijphart similarly argues that 'majority-control democracy spells majority dictatorship' in an unequally segmented society. Lijphart, *Power-Sharing in South Africa*, 106; quoted in Kenneth D. McRae, 'Canada: Reflections on Two Conflicts,' *Conflict and Peacemaking in Multiethnic Societies*, ed. Joseph V. Montville, 101.

68 Although Lijphart offers a brief account of the historical development of the Dutch political system in *The Politics of Accommodation*, his intent in that case is to isolate a consistent pattern, rather than to consider long-term trends in the underlying conditions for elite accommodation.

69 James Rosenau, *Turbulence in World Politics: A Theory of Change and Continuity*.

70 Ibid., 6–11.

71 Cf. Samuel Huntington, Michel Crozier, and Joji Watanuki, *The Crisis of Democracy: Report on the Governability of Democracies to the Trilateral Commission*, 59–118.

72 Rosenau, *Turbulence in World Politics*, 97, 239, 368.

73 Ibid., 381.

74 Ibid., 397.

75 Ibid., 401.

76 Kedourie, *Nationalism*, 90–1. For useful background concerning the Concert of Europe and its decline, see Gordon Craig, 'The System of Alliances and the Balance of Power' in *The New Cambridge History*, vol. 10, *The Zenith of European Power, 1830–1870*, ed. J.P.T. Bury, 250–64, 271; John Lowe, *The Concert of Europe: International Relations 1814–70*; and Alan Sked, *Europe's Balance of Power, 1815–1848*, 98.

77 Smith, *Ethnic Origins of Nations*, 167–8; see also Anderson, *Imagined Communities*, 20; and William Pfaff, *Civilization and the Furies of Nationalism*, esp. Chapter 3, 'Internationalism.'

78 Hobsbawm, *Nations and Nationalism since 1780*, 89.

79 Ibid., 83.

80 Dunn, *Western Political Theory*, 65.

81 J.B. Bury, 'The Science of History' (1902), in *The Varieties of History: From Voltaire to the Present*, ed. Fritz Stern, 219–20.

82 Ibid.

83 Note that Bury himself had devoted much of the previous four years to completing his first edition of Edward Gibbon's *The History of the Rise and Fall of the Roman Empire* (London: Methuen, 1897–1901). In a balanced appraisal, John Matthews has recently noted that Gibbon 'tended to follow the grain' of contemporary historians (29), and that 'Gibbon made more use than most modern scholars of the great commentaries of seventeenth- and eighteenth-century editors, some of them unsurpassed to this day ...' (26). John Matthews, 'Gibbon and the Later Roman Empire: Causes and Circumstances,' in *Edward Gibbon and Empire*, ed. Rosamond McKit-terick and Roland Quinault, 12–33; see also Patricia Craddock, *Edward Gibbon, Luminous Historian, 1772–1794*, 143.

84 R.G. Collingwood, *The Idea of History* (1946), rev. ed., ed. Jan Van Der Dussen, 231–302; Collingwood, *Essays in the Philosophy of History*, ed. William Debbins.

85 Quentin Skinner, 'A Reply to My Critics,' in *Meaning and Context: Quentin Skinner and His Critics*, ed. James Tully, 234.

86 R.G. Collingwood, *An Autobiography*, 106, 114, 148. See Allan Megill, '"Grand Narrative" and the Discipline of History,' in *A New Philosophy of History*, ed. Frank Ankersmit and Hans Kellner, 163.

87 Patrick Gardiner, 'Introduction,' in *The Philosophy of History*, ed. Gardiner, 1.

88 A representative example is Karl Popper, *The Poverty of Historicism*.

89 Sir Isaiah Berlin, 'Historical Inevitability,' in *Philosophy of History*, 161–86.

90 Quentin Skinner, '"Social Meaning" and the Explanation of Social Action' (1972), in *Method and Context*, 79–96.

91 Arthur Danto, 'The Decline and Fall of the Analytical Philosophy of History,' in *New Philosophy of History*, 70–85; Thomas Kuhn, *The Structure of Scientific Revolutions*.

92 Philippe Carrard, 'Theory of a Practice: Historical Enunciation and the *Annales* School,' in *New Philosophy of History*, 123.

93 Joseph Femia, 'An Historicist Critique of "Revisionist" Methods for Studying the History of Ideas,' in *Meaning and Context*, 168–74

94 Hans Kellner, 'Introduction: Describing Redescriptions,' in *New Philosophy of History*, 16; Danto, 'The Decline and Fall.'

95 Albert Cook, *History Writing*, 55–72, 196–203; McKitterick and Quinault, eds., *Edward Gibbon and Empire*, especially the editors' introduction and Peter Ghosh, 'The Conception of Gibbon's *History*,' 271–316; Craddock, *Edward Gibbon*.

96 Skinner, 'Reply,' 284, 232, 248, 287. In fairness, even in a much earlier writing, Skinner allowed that a historian might be 'more interested – as he may legitimately be – in the retrospective significance of a given historical work or action than in its meaning for the agent himself': Skinner, 'Meaning and Understanding in the History of Ideas' (1969), in *Meaning and Context*, 44. For particularly incisive critical essays on Skinner's methodology see Kenneth Minogue, 'Method in Intellectual History: Quentin Skinner's *Foundations*' (1981), in *Meaning and Context*, 176–93; and Femia, 'An Historicist Critique,' 156–75.

97 Skinner, 'Reply,' 287; see also Skinner, 'Meaning and Understanding,' 35–6, 67.

98 Skinner, 'Reply,' 236–9.

99 Skocpol, *States and Social Revolutions*, 35.

100 Ibid., 39; emphasis added.

101 Ibid.

102 Megill, 'Grand Narrative,' 173. See also Cook, *History Writing*, which concurs on the issue of evidence, arguing that 'any discourse, historical or other, must be judged by the aptness of the statements and assertions it includes and coordinates, and not by the labor of prior substantiation ...' (205). To this modern judgment may be added that of Edward Gibbon, who dispensed with this issue more than two centuries ago in replying to a critic, 'If my readers are satisfied with the form, the colours, the new arrangement which I have given to the labours of my predecessors, they may perhaps consider me not as a contemptible Thief, but as an honest and industrious Manufacturer, who has fairly procured the raw materials, and worked them up with a laudable degree of skill and success': Edward Gibbon, *A Vindication of Some Passages in the Fifteenth and Sixteenth Chapters of the History of the Decline and Fall of the Roman Empire* (1779), reprinted as *Gibbon's Vindication*, ed. H.R. Trevor-Roper, 74, see also esp. 75–81. For an outstanding example of a recent synthesis written almost exclusively from secondary sources see Linda Colley, *Britons: Forging the Nation, 1707–1837*. For a well-received work based on secondary sources relating to Canadian political history see Denis Monière, *Ideologies in Quebec: The Historical Development*, trans. Richard Howard, which won a Governor General's Award in 1977 in its original French version.

103 The term 'ethnic badge' belongs to Hobsbawm, *Nations and Nationalism since 1780*, 68.

104 Gellner, in *Nations and Nationalism*, observes the potential for continuity between pre-industrial and industrial identities based on 'high religions' (72). These sometimes 'become the basis of a new collective identity,' which may then be overlaid with territorially more specific characteristics. Thus, in Algeria, with its particular brand of Islam: 'The shrines had defined tribes and tribal boundaries; the scripturalism could and did define a nation' (73). Within industrial society, nations generally seize upon functionally equivalent 'diacritical markers,' which may consist of race, culture, or language (74).

105 Greenfeld, *Nationalism*, 7.

106 Ibid., 40; Connor, 'A Nation is a Nation,' 95; see also Smith, *Theories of Nationalism*, 150.

107 Craig to Liverpool, 1 May 1810; quoted in Fernand Ouellet, *Lower Canada, 1791–1840: Social Change and Nationalism*, trans. Patricia Claxton, 52. In Canada the pages of the influential *Le Canadien* from 1806 expressed the fear that Canadiens might be mistreated by the British in connection

with 'their language, culture and religion.' From 1831 the motto of that paper was 'nos institutions, notre langue et nos lois.' Clearly, several cultural traits, most prominently religion and language, merged from an early state as the basis of Canadien identity.

Chapter 1: Conquest and the Height of Imposed Statecraft, 1760–1791

1 François-X. Garneau, *History of Canada, from the Time of Its Discovery till the Union Year (1840–1)*, trans. Andrew Bell; Lionel Groulx, *Lendemains de conquête*; Groulx, *Histoire du Canada français depuis la Découverte*, 4th ed., v. 1; Maurice Séguin, 'La Conquête et la vie économique des Canadiens,' 308–26; Guy Frégault, 'La colonisation du Canada au XVIIIe siècle,' 53–81; Frégault, *Canada: The War of the Conquest*, trans. Margaret Cameron; Michel Brunet, 'La Conquête anglaise et la déchéance de la bourgeoisie canadienne (1760–1793),' in *La Présence anglaise et les Canadiens*, 49–109; Brunet, *Les Canadiens après la Conquête, 1759–1775. De la Révolution canadienne à la Révolution américaine*. Cf. Francis Parkman, *The Old Régime in Canada*; William Kingsford, *The History of Canada*, vols. 4 and 5; Alfred L. Burt, *The Old Province of Quebec*, 2 vols; Fernand Ouellet, *Economic and Social History of Quebec, 1760–1850: Structures and Conjonctures*, trans. Institute of Canadian Studies; Hilda Neatby, *Quebec: The Revolutionary Age*; Ramsay Cook, *Canada and the French-Canadian Question*, 129–42; Mason Wade, *The French Canadians*, 1: 47–93; Fernand Dumont, *Genèse de la société Québécoise*, 89.
2 Groulx, *Lendemains de Conquête*, 212. Translations of quotations appearing in this and succeeding chapters are by the author unless otherwise noted.
3 Linda Colley, *Britons: Forging the Nation, 1707–1837*, 18; Paul Langford, *A Polite and Commercial People, England, 1727–1783*, 351.
4 Langford, *Polite and Commercial People*, 202; Colley, *Britons*, 25.
5 Liah Greenfeld, *Nationalism: Five Roads to Modernity*, 45.
6 Nicholas Rogers, *Whigs and Cities: Popular Politics in the Age of Walpole and Pitt*, 380. See also Philip Lawson, *The Imperial Challenge: Quebec and Britain in the Age of the American Revolution*, 27, 43, 103; Colley, *Britons*, 22; Langford, *Polite and Commercial People*, 291–2.
7 Gerald Newman, *The Rise of English Nationalism: A Cultural History, 1740–1830*, 75.
8 Colley, *Britons*, 22–3.
9 Newman, *Rise of English Nationalism*, 1–48.

10 *Gentleman's Magazine* 36 (1766): 592; quoted in Newman, *Rise of English Nationalism*, 37.

11 Newman, *Rise of English Nationalism*, 10.

12 Langford, *Polite and Commercial People*, 242; Newman, *Rise of English Nationalism*, 7.

13 Langford, *Polite and Commercial People*, 322, 328; Colley, *Britons*, 166–7; Newman, *Rise of English Nationalism*, 42–4.

14 Colley, *Britons*, 177.

15 Newman, *Rise of English Nationalism*, 99.

16 Langford, *Polite and Commercial People*, 223–5; Rogers, *Whigs and Cities*, 89–92.

17 Radical reaction was also bound up with the Quebec Act of 1774. Rogers, 'Crowd and People,' 41–2; Newman, *Rise of English Nationalism*, 208; Langford, *Polite and Commercial People*, 549–52.

18 For example, the 1534 Act of Supremacy, the 1661 Corporation Act, the 1662 Act of Uniformity, the revised Coronation Oath of 1689, and the 1673 and 1678 Test Acts.

19 For casualty figures see Nicholas Rogers, 'Crowd and People in the Gordon Riots,' in *The Transformation of Political Culture: England and Germany in the Late Eighteenth Century*, ed. Eckhart Hellmuth, 39.

20 Newman, *Rise of English Nationalism*, 209.

21 Lords Proceedings, 13 November 1759, *Proceedings and Debates of the British Parliaments Respecting North America, 1754–1783* (hereinafter cited to as *Proceedings*), ed. R.C. Simmons and P.D.G. Thomas, 1: 298.

22 Vincent Harlow, *The Founding of the Second British Empire*, vol. 1: *New Continents and Changing Values,* with portions by A.F. Madden, 20.

23 Trofimenkoff, *Dream of Nation*, 20.

24 Burt, *Old Province of Quebec*, 1: 5.

25 *Boston News-Letter*, 6 December 1759; quoted in Frégault, *Canada*, 251.

26 In 1761 General Murray estimated that the population of the province as a whole had declined by 10,000 in the previous two years: see Murray to Pitt, 17 February 1761; cited in Groulx, *Lendemains de Conquête*, 35. Of those, only approximately 4,000 can be attributed to emigration (including 2,000 disembarking French soldiers): see ibid., 43. Assuming the estimates to be accurate, and assuming that Murray's estimate included the departure of French soldiers, much of the remaining number of 6,000 must be attributed to fatalities.

27 [Sister Marguerite-Marie], *Les Ursulines des Trois-Rivières depuis leur établissement jusqu'à nos jours*; quoted in Brunet, *Les Canadiens après la Conquête*, 19.

28 Lord Egremont to Amherst, 12 December 1761; quoted in Burt, *Old Province of Quebec*, 1: 26.

29 General Gage's 'Report of the State of the Government of Montreal,' 20 March 1762, *Documents Relating to the Constitutional History of Canada, 1719–1791* (hereinafter cited as *Constitutional Documents*), ed. Adam Shortt and Arthur G. Doughty, 2d ed., 92. Burt notes that at least one soldier was summarily hanged for looting: Burt, *Old Province of Quebec*, 1: 13. Amicable relations were evidenced by a large number of marriages contracted between British officers and Canadiens: see Wade, *French Canadians*, 1: 50.

30 General Murray's 'Report of the State of the Government of Quebec in Canada,' 5 June 1762, in *Constitutional Documents*, 80.

31 Murray to the Lords of Trade, 29 October 1764, *Constitutional Documents*, 1: 231; quoted in Hilda Neatby, *The Quebec Act: Protest and Policy*, 15.

32 Murray to George Ross, 4 December 1765; quoted in Wade, *French Canadians*, 1: 58. As for Vouching, see the letter of twenty-one seigneurs to the King *ca* 1766, lamenting the *fait accompli* of Murray's departure: 'Our protector, our father is taken from us; like a father he listened to our complaints; like a protector he remedied or at least alleviated them promptly, and he comforted us by his kindness; without him what will become us? The old subjects, at least the greater number of them since the date of civil government have only sought to oppress us, to render us their slaves and perhaps to seize our property': Douglas Brymner, ed. *Report on Canadian Archives*, 19.

33 Lawson, *Imperial Challenge*, 48–51. See Gerald Browne, 'James Murray,' *Dictionary of Canadian Biography*, vol. 4.

34 Presentments of the Grand Jury of Quebec, 16 October 1764; *Constitutional Documents*, 214–15; quoted in Neatby, *Quebec Act*, 12.

35 Burt, *Old Province of Quebec*, 1: 100.

36 According to data cited by Burt, there were 'exactly two hundred "Protestant housekeepers" [presumably 'householders'] in total between the towns of Quebec and Montreal.' Montreal apparently had a somewhat smaller British community than Quebec, with a total of about 100 males, not all of whom were householders. It can be deduced that the 50 signatures collected in the town of Quebec were collected in an English enclave of more than 100, but fewer than 200 heads of households: see Burt, *Old Province of Quebec*, 1: 92. Although Burt claims that the Grand Jury did not represent 'a fair sample of the community' (1: 100), this rate of support seems significant.

37 Statement of English Jurors, [1764]; quoted in Neatby, *Quebec Act*, 13.

38 Petition of the Quebec Traders, [1764], in *Constitutional Documents*, 232.

39 Burt, *Old Province of Quebec*, 1: 105.

40 Petition of the Quebec Traders, [1764], in *Constitutional Documents*, 1: 233; quoted in Harlow, *Founding*, 2: 672.

41 'Ordinance Establishing Civil Courts,' in *Constitutional Documents*, 205–10; cited in Neatby, *Quebec*, 53. A caveat was that the jurisdiction of the common pleas court was limited to cases of amounts greater than £10. Furthermore, suits involving amounts greater than £20 could be appealed to the King's Bench, where English Law prevailed.

42 Ibid.

43 Neatby, *Quebec*, 53.

44 Enclosure in letter from the Lords of Trade to Egremont, 8 June 1763, in *Constitutional Documents*, 138–45.

45 Burt, *Old Province of Quebec*, 1: 75. In the enclosure to the letter to Egremont (see previous note) the need, arising from 'Justice and Humanity as well as sound Policy,' to reserve the lands to the West for the Indians is mentioned. Immediately following that discussion, Canada is cited with Florida and the West Indies as the 'Places where Planting, perpetual Settlement and Cultivation ought to be encouraged,' in contradistinction to the lands to the west: enclosure, in *Constitutional Documents*, 140.

46 Enclosure, in *Constitutional Documents*, 142.

47 Ibid., 137; Burt, *Old Province of Quebec*, 1: 69; Harlow, *Founding*, 1: 173–4; Neatby, *Quebec*, 8–9.

48 Burt, *Old Province of Quebec*, 1: 75.

49 For an solid account of the development of the policy, and the subsequent 'hasty public compromise' entailed in the Royal Proclamation, see Lawson, *Imperial Challenge*, 28–38.

50 Harlow, *Founding*, 1: 174–6. Harlow states, 'The fundamental mistake on the part of Halifax, surely, lay in attempting to condense a highly complicated and evolutionary policy in the summary terms of an edict ... it would have been extremely difficult in a formal and public instrument to have conveyed the provisional character of the intended arrangements ...' (1: 175–6).

51 1 George 1, c.13 [1714]. Other oaths stemmed from 1 Eliz. 1, c.1 (1558), and 25 Charles 2, c.2 (1672).

52 Murray to Eglinton, 27 October 1764; quoted in Wade, *French Canadians*, 1: 56; see also Governor Murray to the Lords of Trade, 29 October 1764, in *Constitutional Documents*, 1: 231.

53 'Instructions to Governor Murray,' in *Constitutional Documents*, 1: 198–9; quoted in Burt, *Old Province of Quebec*, 1: 74. One of Murray's subsequent official statements turned the harsh winters into an asset: frost and snow, it was said, 'not only contribute to fertilize the earth, but they certainly render

land-carriage [by sleigh over packed snow and ice] three-fourths cheaper
here than in other countries' (quoted in Burt, *Old Province of Quebec*, 1: 82).

54 Carleton to Shelburne, 25 November 1767, ibid., in *Constitutional Documents*, 281.

55 Burt, *Old Province of Quebec*, 1: 71.

56 Note the italicized phrases (my emphasis) in these excerpts: 'We have ... given
express Power ... to our Governors ... that *so soon as the state and circumstances ... will admit* ... they shall ... summon and call General assemblies' ;
'We have given Power ... to the Governors ... to erect ... Courts of Judicature
... for hearing ... all causes ... according to Law and Equity, and *as near as
may be agreeable* to the Laws of England' (Royal Proclamation of 7 Oct.
1763, in *Constitutional Documents*, 165).

57 Commission Appointing James Murray, Captain General and Governor in
Chief of the Province of Quebec, 21 November 1763, in ibid., 176.

58 Indeed, the term 'equity' in Murray's ordinance of 17 September 1764, in
conjunction with the establishment of the Court of Common Pleas, determined that Canadien law would prevail there in what was effectively the
court of the Canadiens: see Ordinance Establishing Civil Courts, 17 Sept.
1764, in ibid., 205. Lawson appears to have missed this point in *Imperial
Challenge*, 49.

59 Hillsborough to Carleton, 6 March 1768, in *Constitutional Documents*,
1: 297; quoted in Burt, *Old Province of Quebec*, 1: 148.

60 *Proceedings*, Commons Debates, 26 May 1774, 455.

61 Ibid., 456.

62 Note, first, the passage in the confidential instructions: 'so soon as the
Situation and Circumstances ... will admit thereof, You shall ... summon ... a
General Assembly ... You are therefore, as soon as the more pressing Affairs
of Government will allow to give all possible attention to the carrying this
important Object into Execution: But, as it may be impracticable for the
present to form such an Establishment, You are in the mean time to make
such Rules and Regulations, by the Advice of Our Said Council ...' *Constitutional Documents*, 185. Compare that with the promise contained in the
commission, a public document: 'And we, do hereby give and grant unto you
the ... full power and authority ... so soon as the Situation and circumstances
of our said Province under your Government will admit thereof, and when
& as often as need shall require, to summon and call General Assemblies of
the Freeholders and Planters, with your Government ... And we do hereby
declare that the persons so Elected & Qualified shall be called the Assembly
of that our province of Quebec; and that you ... by & with the advice and
Consent of our said Council and Assembly ... shall have full power and

authority to make ... Laws Statutes & ordinances for the publick peace, Welfare, & good Government of our said province ...': ibid.

63 Report on Commissions for Governors, 6 October 1763, in ibid., 160.

64 Governor Carleton testified as follows before a House of Commons Committee on 2 June 1774:

Q. Have the clergy in Canada since the peace enjoyed and received the tithes and parochial dues?
A. They have received the tithes and parochial dues as formerly; there may be some who have not, but very few ... (*Debates of the House of Commons in the year 1774 on the Bill for Making More Effectual Provision for the Government of the Province of Quebec* [hereinafter cited as *Debates*] 103).

65 Neatby, *Quebec*, 108–11.

66 Lawson, *Imperial Challenge*, 48.

67 'Instructions to Governor Murray,' 7 December 1763, 1: 191; Murray to Halifax, 26 June 1764; 'Governor to the Earl of Halifax,' in *Constitutional Documents*, 1: 210–11; quoted in Wade, *French Canadians*, 1: 53.

68 Petition of the Quebec Traders, [1764], in *Constitutional Documents*, 234.

69 Gerald Browne, 'Guy Carleton,' in *Dictionary of Canadian Biography*, vol. 5.

70 Lawson, *Imperial Challenge*, 47.

71 Ibid., 48.

72 Ibid., 51.

73 Harlow, *Founding*, 2: 673.

74 Lawson, *Imperial Challenge*, 69.

75 Harlow, *Founding*, 2: 674.

76 R.A. Humphreys and S. Scott, 'Lord Northington and the Laws of Canada,' 42.

77 Ibid., 47. See also Lawson, *Imperial Challenge*, 82–3.

78 Humphreys and Scott, 'Lord Northington,' 52.

79 Lawson, *Imperial Challenge*, 98. See also Pierre Tousignant, 'The Integration of the Province of Quebec into the British Empire, 1763–91,' in *Dictionary of Canadian Biography*, 4: xli–xlii.

80 Sir Reginald Coupland, *The Quebec Act: A Study in Statesmanship*, 92–6; Browne, 'Guy Carleton.'

81 Lawson, *Imperial Challenge*, 101.

82 Carleton to Shelburne, 25 November 1767, in *Constitutional Documents*, 1: 282; quoted in Burt, *Old Province of Quebec*, 1: 142.

83 Ibid.

84 Burt, *Old Province of Quebec*, 1: 141. Burt concludes, 'in view of the

chronic hostility between Britain and France in that age, Carleton could not envisage an American war from which France would long hold aloof, though he might conceive of a French war without a rebellion in the old colonies' (140). This interpretation is shared by Coupland, *The Quebec Act*, 60–1; and Neatby, *Quebec*, 88, 100. See also Carleton to Hillsborough, 20 November 1768, in *Constitutional Documents*, 1: 326.

85 Carleton to Shelburne, 25 November 1767, in *Constitutional Documents*, 285; cited Burt, *Old Province of Quebec*, 1: 143.

86 Carleton to Shelburne, 24 December 1767, in *Constitutional Documents*, 1: 289; quoted in Burt, ibid., 1: 144.

87 Carleton to Shelburne, 20 January 1768, in *Constitutional Documents*, 294.

88 Ibid.

89 Ibid., 296.

90 For a discussion of the few opposition figures who did attack the bill as a plan of 'popish despotism' see Lawson, *Imperial Challenge*, 144; see also *Proceedings*, Commons Debates, 26 May 1774, 4: 449; 5: 151; and Lords Debates, 17 June 1774, 230.

91 *Proceedings*, Commons Debates, 7 June 1774, 5: 131–3.

92 Ibid., 5: 132.

93 Ibid., 5: 133.

94 Ibid., 5: 131.

95 Ibid., 4: 471.

96 Ibid.

97 Note that in this period no official transcripts of debates were maintained, and that, of press reports, 'very few corresponded at all closely' to what was said in debates: (*Proceedings*, 5: vii).

98 Lawson, *Imperial Challenge*, 138.

99 *Proceedings*, 5: 144.

100 Lawson, *Imperial Challenge*, 138, 145–51. Lawson's account is corroborated by the earlier work, Fred Hinkhouse, *The Preliminaries of the American Revolution as Seen in the English Press, 1763–1775*, 170–6.

101 Printed in *London Magazine*, June 1774, 301–2; existence of petition cited and discussion of press reception in Lawson, *Imperial Challenge*, 148.

102 *London Magazine*, 301.

103 P.C.D., *St James Chronicle*, 9 July 1774; quoted in Hinkhouse, *Preliminaries*, 172.

104 *London Packet*, 8 June 1774; quoted in Hinkhouse, *Preliminaries*, 171.

105 *St James Chronicle*, 23 June 1774; quoted in Hinkhouse, *Preliminaries*, 171.

106 Hinkhouse, *Preliminaries*, 176.

107 Ibid., 174.

108 Lawson, *Imperial Challenge*, 133–4, 145.

109 Ibid., 128, 138.

110 Ibid., 144.

111 *Proceedings*, Commons Debates, 26 May 1774, 4: 467.

112 Harlow, *Founding*, 2: 799. The quotation cited from the conclusion of the book was in fact written by A.F. Madden following Harlow's death.

113 See F. Murray Greenwood, *Legacies of Fear: Law and Politics in Quebec in the Era of the French Revolution*, 19.

114 Ibid., 217–18, 224.

115 Burt, *Old Province of Quebec*, 1: 85.

116 Briand to Papal Nuncio in Paris, 10 March 1775; quoted in Guy-Marie Oury, *Mgr Briand: Évêque de Québec et les problèmes de son Époque*, 181.

117 Instructions to Governor Carleton, 1775, 3 January 1775, in *Constitutional Documents*, 603.

118 Neatby, *Quebec*, 139.

119 Instructions to Governor Carleton, 3 January 1775, in *Constitutional Documents*, 603. The instructions also provided for minority rights: the Protestant or Catholic minority of a parish was explicitly permitted to use the parish church when not in use for worship.

120 House of Commons, 7 June 1774, in *Debates*, 217–6.

121 Neatby, *Quebec*, 140; Harlow, *Founding*, 2: 716; Burt, *Old Province of Quebec*, 1: 173.

122 Briand to Papal Nuncio in Paris, 10 March 1775; quoted in Harlow, *Founding*, 2: 716, n. 100.

123 An Act to Restore to the Crown the Ancient Jurisdiction Over the State Ecclesiastical and Spiritual, and Abolishing All Foreign Power Repugnant to the Same, 1 Eliz. 1, c.1 (1558).

124 House of Commons, 8 June 1774, *Proceedings*, 165–6; *Debates*, 250.

125 The quotation is from one of three legal reports prepared prior to the drafting of the Quebec Act, Plan of a Code of Laws for the Province of Quebec; Reported by the Advocate-General, James Marriott, London, 1774, 14 June 1771, in *Constitutional Documents*, 1: 483. See also Attorney General Thurlow's speech in the House of Commons, 26 May 1774, *Proceedings*, 457; and, 'Report of Solicitor-General Wedderburn,' in *Constitutional Documents*, 1: 427; cited in Lawson, *Imperial Challenge*, 121–2.

126 Murray to Eglinton, 27 October 1764; quoted in Wade, *French Canadians*, 1: 56, and in Lawson, *Imperial Challenge*, 48.

127 Lawson makes an interesting contrast between the position of Shelburne and Murray and that of the 'bigots' who went out to Quebec: *Imperial Challenge*, 47.

128 Dartmouth to Lord Mansfield, 1 May 1774, in *Constitutional Documents*, 551, n. 1.
129 See n. 122.
130 John Derry, *English Politics and the American Revolution*, 23.
131 Ibid, 112–13.
132 Address to the People of Great Britain, 21 October 1774; quoted in Wade, *French Canadians*, 1: 65. See also Burt, *Old Province of Quebec*, 1: 168.
133 Burt, *Old Province of Quebec*, 1: 184.
134 John Manning Ward, *Colonial Self-Government: The British Experience, 1759–1856*, 12.
135 Petition to the Commons, 12 November 1774, in *Constitutional Documents*, 593.
136 Case of the British Merchants Trading to Quebec, 31 May 1774, in ibid., 512, 519.
137 Ibid., 516.
138 Ibid., 515.
139 Burt, *Old Province of Quebec*, 1: 181.
140 Ibid. W.P.M. Kennedy, *The Constitution of Canada, 1534–1937: An Introduction to Its Development Law and Custom*, 2d ed., 67–8.
141 John Hare, 'Le comportement de la paysannerie rurale et urbaine de la région de Québec pendant l' occupation américaine 1775–1776,' *Mélanges d'histoire du Canada français offerts au professeur Marcel Trudel*, 148–9.
142 Ibid., 147.
143 Ibid., 149.
144 Ibid., 146.
145 Ibid.
146 Wade, *French Canadians*, 1: 66.
147 Oury, *Mgr Briand*, 177.
148 Greenwood, *Legacies of Fear*, 52.
149 Burt, *Old Province of Quebec*, 2: 150.
150 Ibid.
151 Ibid., 2: 149.
152 Neatby, *Quebec*, 161.
153 Burt, *Old Province of Quebec*, 2: 44.
154 Ibid., 2: 47.
155 Ibid., 2: 149.
156 Ibid., 2: 151.
157 Greenwood, *Legacies of Fear*, 37.
158 Burt, *Old Province of Quebec*, 2: 153.
159 Neatby, *Quebec*, 255.

160 Greenwood, *Legacies of Fear*, 40.

161 In 1788, for example, this subsidy had amounted to some £153,000. See Harlow, *Founding*, 2: 754; David Milobar, 'Conservative Ideology, Metropolitan Government, and the Reform of Quebec, 1782–1791,' 60–1.

162 Harlow, *Founding*, 2: 758. See also Greenwood, *Legacies of Fear*, 44–5; Milobar, 'The Reform of Quebec,' 63; Pierre Tousignant, 'Problématique pour un nouvelle approche de la constitution de 1791,' 181–234; Kennedy, *Constitution of Canada*, 78–87. See also Grenville's speech in the Lords, 30 May 1791, *Parliamentary History* 19: 656–7.

163 Arthur Young, *The Example of France ... a Warning to Britain* (1794), 106; quoted in Harold Perkin, *The Origins of Modern English Society, 1780–1880*, 39. Perkin notes that in the House of Commons 'three-quarters of the Members between 1734 and 1832 were landowners or their near-relations, and those of the rest who were not their friends or nominees were rich business and professional men often with one foot on the land': ibid.

164 For a scholarly consideration of the constitutional relationship between the governor and the councils, see Henri Brun, *La formation des Institutions Parlementaires Québécoises, 1791–1838*, 39–46.

165 For a comparison of the suffrage in Britain and Lower Canada during the period, see Jean-Pierre Wallot, *Un Québec qui bougeait. Trame sociopolitique du Québec au tournant du XIXe siècle*, 285.

166 Harlow, *Founding*, 2: 735.

167 The population of what would become Lower Canada in 1789–90 was 161,311, of which about 150,000 were French-speaking Canadiens. Greenwood, *Legacies of Fear*, xiv.

168 King George III to Grenville, 13 October 1789; quoted in Tousignant, 'Problématique,' 225.

169 John Hare, *Aux origines du Parlementarisme Québécois, 1791–1793*, 87; Tousignant, 'Problématique,' 190.

170 In eighty pages of recorded debates on the issue, mentions of the predicament of the English in the future Lower Canada (considering their reinforced minority status) amounted to fewer than seven pages, more than half of those minimizing the significance of such concerns: see *Parliamentary History of England* 29 (1791–2): 104–13, 359–430. (The mentions fall on 109, 113, 401–9.) The bulk of the two recorded debates was taken up with the issue of whether the Legislative Council should be appointed or elected, and behind this of the proper balance between democracy and the rights of man, on the one hand, and monarchical and aristocratic government, on the other hand; the issue was considered in the light of contemporary events in France: see the discussion in chapter 2.

171 House of Commons, 11 May 1791, *Parliamentary History* 29: 402.

172 House of Commons, 8 April 1791, *Parliamentary History* 29: 113; see also Tousignant, 'Problématique,' 230.

173 House of Commons, 11 May 1791, *Parliamentary History* 29: 403.

174 Ibid., 408.

175 Burt, *Old Province of Quebec*, 2: 205.

176 Bourque, *Question nationale*, 337.

177 Tousignant, 'Problématique,' 194.

178 Grenville to Dorchester, 20 October 1789, in *Constitutional Documents*, 2: 988; quoted in ibid., 229.

179 House of Lords, 30 May 1791, *Parliamentary History* 29: 656.

180 See Brunet's discussion of an obscure group who called themselves 'Les Canadiens Vrais Patriotes': *Les Canadiens après la Conquête*, 266–8.

181 Ouellet, *Lower Canada*, 204; Helen Taft Manning, *The Revolt of French Canada, 1800–1835: A Chapter in the History of the British Commonwealth*, 54.

182 Jean Hamelin, *Économie et société en Nouvelle-France*, 127–37.

Chapter 2: The Decline of Imposed Statecraft, 1792–1839

1 *Parliamentary History of England*, vol. 19, 11 May 1791, 411.

2 Ibid., 6 May 1791, 364–7; 11 May 1791, 419–20.

3 Linda Colley, *Britons: Forging the Nation, 1707–1837*, 166.

4 F. Murray Greenwood, *Legacies of Fear: Law and Politics in Quebec in the Era of the French Revolution*, xii.

5 Ibid., 59–67; Fernand Ouellet, *Lower Canada, 1791–1840: Social Change and nationalism*, trans. Patricia Claxton, 44.

6 Ouellet, *Lower Canada*, 44.

7 Greenwood, *Legacies of Fear*, 59–60, 67.

8 Greenwood notes that, 'of the dozens of depositions, voluntary examinations, government reports, and other extant documents bearing directly on the militia and Road Act riots none refers to abolition as a factor motivating rural rioters': ibid., 97.

9 Ibid., 90. Greenwood also notes the significance of anglophobia in the 1794 riots. In May 1794, 'much talk of violence, dangerous assemblies of the disgruntled, and rhetoric which sounded sympathetic to revolutionary France had surfaced. Violence, threatened and actual, flared in many rural parishes, but most dramatically at Charlesbourg, a village just north of Quebec. For several days and nights up to three hundred habitants, armed with muskets, pikes, pitchforks, and hunting knives, formed patrols to

defend themselves against an expected attack of city folk bent on enforcing conscription. Some of the farmers, by their own sworn admission, also thought this might prove a good time to bash "les Anglais'" (82).

10 Ibid., 99.

11 Ibid., 86, 88.

12 Ibid., 101; Mason Wade, *The French Canadians, 1760–1967*, vol. 1: *1760–1911*, 2d ed., 101.

13 Wade, *French Canadians*, 1: 101.

14 Jean-Pierre Wallot, *Un Québec qui bougeait. Trame socio-politique du Québec au tournant du xixe siècle*, 296. See also Jean-Pierre Wallot, *Intrigues françaises et américaines au Canada, 1800–1802*, 18–23.

15 Ouellet, *Lower Canada*, 46–9; Greenwood, *Legacies of Fear*, 88. See also Wade, *French Canadians*, 1: 99; and F.X. Garneau, *History of Canada*, vol. 2., trans. Andrew Bell, 227.

16 Wade, *French Canadians*, 1: 129.

17 Wallot, *Québec qui bougeait*, 275.

18 Ouellet, *Lower Canada*, 51. Note, however, that even during the 1790s Canadien leaders in the Assembly were beginning to press for more representative government. See Greenwood, *Legacies of Fear*, 74.

19 John Hare, 'L'assemblée législative du Bas-Canada, 1792–1814: Députation et polarisation politique,' 361–95. See also Wallot, *Québec qui bougeait*, 303, n. 94.

20 Depositions of farmers Jean-Marie Renaud et al. and of farmer Louis Paquet, 23 December 1794; quoted in Greenwood, *Legacies of Fear*, 98. Greenwood also notes that, in the same 1792 election, but in an urban riding, Panet supported Adam Lymburner, a prominent English merchant.

21 Ouellet, *Lower Canada*, 47. In both instances the French-speakers' cause prevailed. See also Pierre Tousignant, 'La première campagne électorale des Canadiens en 1792,' 138; and Garneau, *History of Canada*, 2: 214–19.

22 Alured Clarke to Henry Dundas, 3 July 1793; quoted in Ouellet, *Lower Canada*, 47–8. The same point is acknowledged in Gilles Paquet and Jean-Pierre Wallot, *Lower Canada at the Turn of the Nineteenth Century: Restructuring and Modernization*, Canadian Historical Association Historical Booklet no. 45, 11.

23 Greenwood, *Legacies of Fear*, 188. The *ministérielistes* also joined with the Parti canadien in blocking several of the measures aimed at anglicization discussed below.

24 Helen Taft, *The Revolt of French Canada, 1800–1835: A Chapter in the History of the British Commonwealth*, 35.

25 Milnes to Portland, 1 November 1800, *Documents of the Canadian Constitu-*

tion, 1759–1915 (hereinafter cited as *Documents*), ed. W.P.M. Kennedy, 242; Milnes to Hobart, 15 August 1803, *Report on Canadian Archives* (hereinafter cited as *Report*), 1892 (Ottawa, 1893), 16. The description of Milnes's character is from Manning, *Revolt*, 36. Cf. Jean-Pierre Wallot, 'Sir Robert Milnes,' in *Dictionary of Canadian Biography*, vol. 7.

26 Mountain to Milnes, 6 June 1803, *Report*, 1892, 16–22; Lord Hobart to Milnes, 9 January 1804, *Report*, 1892, 22.

27 As Hobart dryly put it (with what must surely have been considerable amusement) in his letter of 9 January 1804, 'A consideration arises with respect to the Policy of fixing the seat of the Protestant Church Establishment, and the Residence of the Bishop in that [Upper] Province. Upon this point I request to receive your sentiments and those of the Bishop, with whom you will naturally consult.'

28 Wade, *French Canadians*, 1: 103.

29 Greenwood, *Legacies of Fear*, 179.

30 Wade, *French Canadians*, 1: 104.

31 Greenwood, *Legacies of Fear*, 178–9.

32 Milnes to Portland, 1 November 1800, 239.

33 Ibid., 243.

34 Sewell to Milnes, 29 May 1801; reprinted in Wallot, *Québec qui bougeait*, 171–7. Contrary to Wallot's suggestion, there is no evidence in this document that Sewell aimed to diminish the spiritual influence of the Bishop.

35 Wallot, *Québec qui bougeait*, 172.

36 Greenwood, *Legacies of Fear*, 178–9.

37 Wallot, *Québec qui bougeait*, 179, n. 13.

38 Milnes to Portland, 1 November 1800, 243. Milnes states in his letter, 'there can be no doubt that the liberality with which His Majesty has lately been pleased to provide the Means of Education in the Province will go a great way to secure the affection and loyalty of the rising Generation who would otherwise be in danger of imbibing Principles inimical to His Majesty's mild and paternal Government by the necessity which has hitherto existed of their being sent to the neighbouring States for education': ibid.

39 Ouellet, *Lower Canada*, 71.

40 For Herman Ryland's views, predicated on Canadien disloyalty, see Ryland to the Lord Bishop of Quebec, 3 February 1806, and Ryland to Peel, 27 June 1811, in Robert Christie, *History of Lower Canada*, vol. 6, 84–5 and 226–7; cited Greenwood, *Legacies of Fear*, 177. For the views of Bishop Jacob Mountain see, Louis-Philippe Audet, *Le système scolaire de la Province de Québec*, v. 3, 10–16.

41 Lawrence Smith, '*Le Canadien* and the British Constitution, 1806–1810,' 95.

42 Letter to the editor signed Cauis, *Le Canadien*, 22 November 1806.

43 *Le Canadien*, 11 December 1806.

44 Manning, *Revolt*, 68.

45 Ouellet, *Lower Canada*, 103.

46 Manning, *Revolt*, 68; Henri Brun, *Le Formation des institutions parlementaires Québécoises, 1791–1838*, 58–9.

47 Greenwood, *Legacies of Fear*, 197–8.

48 Sewell to Prevost, 3 July 1812; quoted in Ouellet, *Lower Canada*, 113.

49 Craig to Liverpool, 1 May 1810, *Documents*, 256–66.

50 Ibid.; also quoted in Wade, *French Canadians*, 1: 112.

51 Ouellet, *Lower Canada*, 39, 61. Ouellet notes that, with the transition to shipbuilding and forestry, the economy came to be even more strongly dominated by the British than it had during the pre-eminence of the fur trade. The British were also very strong in other sectors of the economy, and their accumulation of capital was reflected in major property acquisitions. At the turn of the century they owned almost a third of the seigneurial land, and during the decade following 1802 they acquired sixty townships and twenty seigneuries.

52 Quoted in Gilles Bourque, *Question nationale et classes sociales au Québec, 1760–1840*, 166.

53 Mason Wade, 'Quebec and the French Revolution of 1789: The Missions of Henri Mezière,' 364–8; see also Ryland to the Lord Bishop of Quebec, 3 February 1806.

54 Manning, *Revolt*, 213, 113.

55 Jonathan Sewell, 'Observations of Chief Justice Sewell on the Union of the Provinces,' *Documents*, 268; Craig to Liverpool, 1 May 1810, *Documents*, 261.

56 Craig to Liverpool, 1 May 1810, *Documents*, 263.

57 'Observations Relative to the Political State of Lower Canada By Mr. Ryland, [May 1808],' *Documents*, 248; Craig to Liverpool, 1 May 1810, 267.

58 Ryland to Craig, 23 August, 1810, *Documents*, 272, 274.

59 Lord Liverpool to Sir James Craig (confidential), *ca* 12 September 1810, reprinted in Charles Duke Yonge, ed., *The Life and Administration of Lord Liverpool*, v. 1, 312–14; cited in Manning, *Revolt*, 227.

60 James Sturgis, 'Anglicisation as a Theme in Lower Canadian History, 1807–1843,' 216.

61 Prevost to Adam Gordon, 21 July 1814; quoted in Manning, *Revolt*, 103–4.

62 Manning, *Revolt*, 236.

63 Ibid., 238. Nevertheless, Bathurst felt no personal affinity for Catholicism. Sturgis notes that Bathurst once professed to being 'violently anti-Roman Catholic': Sturgis, 'Anglicisation,' 217.

64 Manning, *Revolt*, 234.

65 *Quebec Mercury*, vol. 2, no. 43 [1806]; quoted and attributed to Thomas Carey in Albert Faucher, 'Le Canadien upon the Defensive, 1806–1810,' 254.

66 Sturgis, 'Anglicisation,' 215.

67 Manning, *Revolt*, 165.

68 Ibid., 153. See also K.L.P. Martin, 'The Union Bill of 1822,' 42–4; Sturgis, 'Anglicisation,' 219; Martin, 'Union Bill,' 54.

69 'Proposed Act of Union, 1822,' *Documents*, 307–11.

70 Hansard, 2d ser., vol. 7 (1822): 1704.

71 Ibid., 1713. The member was Henry Bright.

72 Ibid., 1731.

73 *Montreal Herald*, 16 October 1822.

74 Ibid., 2 November 1822.

75 'Petition from Montreal For Union,' December 1822, *Documents*, 319. Cf. corresponding petition from Quebec City, ibid., 324.

76 Letter to editor, signed 'An Old Loyalist,' *Montreal Herald*, 23 October 1822.

77 'Resolutions of Quebec Committee,' *Report*, 1897, 23.

78 See 'Petition from Legislative Council of Lower Canada Against Union,' 1823, *Documents*, 331, but also the 'Minority Resolutions' passed by a dissenting minority of six English-speaking Legislative Council members: ibid., 330.

79 D.B. Viger, *Analyse d'un entretien sur la conservation des établissemens du Bas-Canada des loix, des usages de ses habitans* (1826; reproduced as CIHM 21200), 32.

80 Ibid., 31.

81 Pierre Bédard, 'Mémoire au soutien de la requête des habitans du Bas-Canada à son Altesse Royale le Prince Regént' (1814), *Documents*, 286.

82 Louis-Joseph Papineau evidently shared this view. See the excerpt from his 1820 speech comparing the benefits of British as against French colonial regime, made on the occasion of the death of George III, quoted in *Papineau: textes choisis et présentés par Fernand Ouellet*, 2d ed., 21–2.

83 Sturgis, 'Anglicisation,' 211.

84 Viger, *Analyse*, 32.

85 Ibid., 31.

86 *Letter from J.L. Papineau and J. Neilson, Esqs. Addressed to His Majesty's Under Secretary of State on the Subject of the Proposed Union of the Provinces of Upper and Lower Canada* (1824; reproduced CIHM 38456), 8.

87 Ibid., 9.

88 Ibid., 20–1.

89 'La Pétition des soussignés, ... de la province du Bas-Canada,' *Documents*, 334.

90 Papineau to Guy, 13 March 1823; quoted in Manning, *Revolt*, 168.

91 Manning, *Revolt*, 164.

92 Ibid.

93 Ibid., 168.

94 This explanation is emphasized in Donald Grant Creighton, *The Commercial Empire of the St. Lawrence, 1760–1850*.

95 Wade, *French Canadians*, 1: 105.

96 Ouellet, *Lower Canada*, 62; Wade, *French Canadians*, 1: 117.

97 Paquet and Wallot, *Lower Canada*, 12–13.

98 Manning, *Revolt*, 10.

99 Testimony of Neilson, 1: 122–3.

100 See speech of Sir James Mackintosh in the House of Commons, 2 May 1828, Hansard, 2d ser., vol. 19 (1928), 326; quoted in Peter Burroughs, *The Canadian Crisis and British Colonial Policy, 1828–1841*, 32. See the Testimony of Neilson, 1: 67–8, for a litany.

101 Ouellet, *Lower Canada*, 197–200; Sir C.P. Lucas, introduction to *Lord Durham's Report on the Affairs of British North America*, ed. Lucas, 1: 38–52, 58–64.

102 Manning, *Revolt*, 208.

103 Samuel Clark, *Movements of Political Protest in Canada, 1640–1840*, 260.

104 Ibid., 263; W.H. Parker, 'A New Look at the Unrest in Lower Canada in the 1830's'; repr. in *Constitutionalism and Nationalism in Lower Canada*, ed. Ramsay Cook, Craig Brown, and Carl Berger, 58–66.

105 Ouellet, *Lower Canada*, 176.

106 Testimony of McGillivray, *British Parliamentary Papers*, 1: 100.

107 Ouellet, *Lower Canada*, 206.

108 Ibid., Table 59, 375.

109 Ibid., Table 77, 384.

110 Bédard, 'Mémoire,' 286.

111 Allan Greer, *The Patriots and the People: The Rebellion of 1837 in Rural Lower Canada*, 133.

112 *La Minerve*, 8 September 1834; quoted in Ouellet, *Lower Canada*, 178; see also edition of 6 November 1834.

113 Greer, *Patriots and the People*, 165; cf. Gérard Filteau, *Histoire des Patriotes*, 72–6.

114 D.M., 'De la Manière dont se forment les nations,' *La Minerve*, 8, 11, 15, 18 September 1834.

115 Ibid., *La Minerve*, 11 September 1834.
116 Ibid., 15 September 1834.
117 Ibid., 18 September 1834. *La Minerve* should be distinguished from *Le Canadien*, which sought to minimize rather than inflame chauvinism during this period. In an editorial of 5 November 1834, the latter paper maintained that, although the designations of 'parti canadien' and 'parti anglais' had become 'rallying slogans in hotly contested elections' and had 'remained until the present in the mouth of the people,' they did not at all reflect ('at least among the Canadiens') 'any hostile national spirit,' 'national fanaticism,' or *'exclusivism.'*
118 Greer, *Patriots and the People*, 165.
119 Elinor Kyte Senior, *Redcoats and Patriotes: The Rebellions in Lower Canada, 1837–38*, 12.
120 Louis-Joseph Papineau, 'Discours dans l'election du quartier ouest,' *Le Canadien*, 3 November 1834.
121 Louis-J. Papineau, 'Aux libres et indépendants électeurs du Quartier Ouest de Montréal,' *La Minerve*, 8 December 1834.
122 Editorial, *La Minerve*, 6 November 1834; 'The Ninety-two Resolutions of 1834,' *Documents*, 366–88.
123 'The Ninety-two Resolutions of 1834,' 366.
124 A content analysis of the document reveals this breakdown of emphasis: desire for more popular form of government than the status quo under the 1791 constitution (38; nos. 9–46); assertion of the rights and prerogatives of the Assembly (14; nos. 5, 64–4, 79, 80); criticism of the present colonial administration in Quebec and London (7; nos. 47–9, 51, 84, 85, 92); criticism of the Tenures Act and other land issues (7; nos. 56–62); professions of loyalty and liberal values (4; nos. 1–4); administration of justice, including criticism of English unilingualism (2; nos. 77–8); inequitable distribution of offices (2; nos. 75–6); threats of disloyalty in absence of reform (2; nos. 50, 86); refusal to assimilate and defence of French culture (1; no. 52); miscellaneous interpretations and declarations (15; nos. 6–8, 53–5, 63, 81–3, 87–91). 'Resolutions,' 366–87.
125 'Resolutions,' 366.
126 Greer, *Patriots and the People*, 140.
127 Undated letter, LaFontaine to Girouard; quoted in ibid., 283.
128 Durham to Lord Glenelg, 9 August 1838, in *Correspondence Relative to the Affairs of British North America*, 152–3.
129 Ibid., 153–4.
130 Ibid., 154.

131 Greer, *Patriots and the People*, 183.

132 Ibid., 43, 49.

133 Ibid., 49–50.

134 Ibid., 168.

135 Ibid., 133.

136 Journal entry of 29 August 1831, in Jacques Vallée, ed., *Toqueville au Bas-Canada*, 100; quoted in Ouellet, *Lower Canada*, 177. In a journal entry several days later, Toqueville, like Durham, clarifies that among 'Canadiens belonging to enlightened classes' he had discovered less of an abiding concern than he had expected to 'conserve intact their origins, and to become a people entirely apart.' While the 'instincts of the people are against the English,' he discovered among many of his interlocutors that 'their hatred is directed still more against the government than against the English race in general': Entry of 1 September 1831, in ibid., 104.

137 Ouellet, *Lower Canada*, 296.

138 Greer, *Patriots and the People*, 174.

139 Ouellet, *Lower Canada*, 296, 402, nn. 65–6.

140 Greer, *Patriots and the People*, 155.

141 Ibid., 182.

142 See note 170.

143 Senior, *Patriots and Redcoats*, 196–7; Garneau, *History of Canada*, 2: 445; Charles Grey to Earl Grey, 17 April 1839, in *Crisis in the Canadas: 1838–1839, The Grey Journals and Letters*, ed. William Ormsby, 199. It must also be borne in mind that many of the participants themselves had been placed under severe physical duress to participate.

144 *Quebec Gazette*, 31 March 1831; quoted in Manning, *Revolt*, 321.

145 Vallée, *Toqueville*, 101; quoted in Ouellet, *Lower Canada*, 192.

146 Ouellet, *Lower Canada*, 206, 257.

147 According to newspaper reports in the latter half of August 1827, the candidates elected with English names were Thomas Young, Wolfred Nelson, Charles Ogden, John Neilson and Andrew Stuart.

148 *Vindicator*, 28 November 1834; Testimony of A. Norbert Morin before the Select Committee of 1834 on the Affairs of Lower Canada, in *British Parliamentary Papers* 1837 (96) VII. 644; reprint. *British Parliamentary Papers*, 1: 100.

149 *Vindicator*, 28 November 1834.

150 Janet Ajzenstat, 'Collectivity and Individual Right in "Mainstream" Liberalism: John Arthur Roebuck and the Patriots,' 99–111. Ajzenstat's assessment that the Canadien political élite was not preoccupied with cultural

self-preservation seems sound. The point might also be made, however, that they opposed anglicization orchestrated by state policy, as in the proposals for union. Ajzenstat's discussion of assimilation does not distinguish between assimilation accepted voluntarily, without state intervention in the cultural sphere, and assimilation prompted by state policies such as union, which intentionally sought to privilege a dominant way of life. Many among the elite of the Patriots probably accepted the first sort of assimilation, but understandably rejected the second sort.

151 Greer, *Patriots and the People*, 133.

152 Ibid.

153 Vallée, *Tocqueville*, 101; quoted in Ouellet, *Lower Canada*, 182.

154 *Le Patriote Canadien: Journal Historique, Biographique et Politique (Prospectus)*, December 1838. CIHM doc. 63323.

155 Testimony of Neilson, 136.

156 Clark, *Movements*, 275.

157 Ibid., 267.

158 Ibid., 278.

159 Manning, *Revolt*, 363; Ouellet, *Lower Canada*, 231.

160 Ouellet, *Lower Canada*, 275–80.

161 'Lord John Russell's Ten Resolutions,' 5 March 1837, *Documents*, 434.

162 Ouellet, *Lower Canada*, 284.

163 Ibid., 284, 290; Clark, *Movements*, 324.

164 Wade, *French Canadians*, 1: 152.

165 Ibid., 1: 167.

166 Clark, *Movements*, 305. The meeting passed resolutions in favour of popularly elected militia officers and magistrates. For a detailed account of the meeting, see Filteau, *Histoire des Patriotes*, 276–8. Cf. Fernand Ouellet, 'Papineau dans la révolution de 1837–1838,' in *Constitutionalism and Nationalism in Lower Canada*, ed. Ramsay Cook, Craig Brown, and Carl Berger, 75–94; Ouellet, *Lower Canada*, 295. See also Louis-Joseph Papineau, 'Adresse de la Confédération des Six Comtés au peuple du Canada,' 24 October 1837, in *Louis-Joseph Papineau, un Demi-Siècle de Combats: Interventions Publiques*, ed. Yvan Lamonde and Claude Larin, 501.

167 Ouellet, *Lower Canada*, 276; Wade, *French Canadians*, 1: 166–7.

168 Wade, *French Canadians*, 1: 173.

169 John Bumsted, *The Peoples of Canada: A Pre-Confederation History*, 253.

170 Archives Nationales du Québec (Ste Foy), Class E17; Événements 1837–8, depositions of Eloi Babin, no. 135, and Moise Marchessault, no. 496 (quoted); cited Ouellet, *Lower Canada*, 296; ; see also René Hardy, 'La

rébellion de 1837–38 et l' essor du protestantisme canadien-français,' 180–2.
See the contemporary account of these incidents by a Swiss missionary in
J.M. Cramp, *A Memoir of Madame Feller*, 110–13.

171 Dep. 496; trans. of Ouellet, *Lower Canada*, 296.
172 Ouellet, *Lower Canada*, 295.
173 'Stewart Derbishire's Report to Lord Durham,' 58.
174 Greet, *Patriots and the People*, 258–93.
175 Clark, *Movements*, 315.
176 Ouellet, *Lower Canada*, 317.
177 Wade, *French Canadians*, 1: 290.
178 Beverley Boissery, *A Deep Sense of Wrong: The Treason, Trials, and Trans-
     portation to New South Wales of Lower Canadian Rebels after the 1838
     Rebellion*, 107.
179 Stanley Ryerson, *Unequal Union: Confederation and the Roots of Conflict
     in the Canadas, 1815–1873*, 77–8.
180 Bumsted, *The Peoples of Canada*, 253.
181 Robert Christie, *A History of the Late Province of Lower Canada*, vol. 5, 271.
182 Charles Grey to Earl Grey, 11 November 1838, in *Crisis in the Canadas*,
     160.
183 *Le Patriote Canadien* (Prospectus).
184 Manning, *Revolt*, 368.
185 C.P. Lucas, ed., *Lord Durham's Report on the Affairs of British North
     America* (1839), 3 vols., 288–9. For the view that the Durham Report had
     little impact on the development of policy see Ged Martin, *The Durham
     Report and British Policy: A Critical Essay*; Martin, 'Attacking the Durham
     Myth: Seventeen Years On,' 39–59; and John Manning Ward, *Colonial Self-
     Government: The British Experience, 1759–1856*, 65, 79. Cf. Phillip A.
     Buckner, *The Transition to Responsible Government: British Policy in
     British North America, 1815–1850*, 250–90, 336; Chester New, *Lord Dur-
     ham's Mission to Canada*, An abridgement of *Lord Durham: A Biography of
     John George Lambton, First Earl of Durham* (1927), ed. H.W. McCready,
     186–93. For a view concerning the liberal ideological influences shaping
     Durham's outlook and a close textual analysis see Janet Ajzenstat, *The
     Political Thought of Lord Durham*. Ajzenstat argues that Durham intended
     to extend individual freedom and equality of opportunity to the French
     Canadians by eliminating their supposedly archaic institutions, as well as
     the associated ethnic system of stratification.
186 J.M.S. Careless, *The Union of the Canadas: The Growth of Canadian
     Institutions, 1841–1857*, 4.
187 Lucas, ed., *Report*, 294.

188 Ajzenstat, *Political Thought of Lord Durham*, 81–5. Note that 'way of life' is used in a different sense by Ajzenstat than in this work, to refer not specifically to the distinctive religious, linguistic, or cultural practices of real communities, but rather (also?) to the abstract ideological firmament of liberal democracy. Though there may be some conceivable connection between the referents of these two concepts, this is not at all obvious to me, given that a wide range of religions, languages, and cultural practices are presumably compatible with liberal government (and were so, even in Durham's era).

189 Ajzenstat cites the opposition of the Parti canadien to the initiatives relating to education and land tenures as evidence of quasi-feudal attitudes dominating the party elite. The impasse over education, however, was due not only to the lack of municipal government, but also to the English Party's historical promotion of aggressive anglification through education policy. (See the earlier discussion of the Royal Institution.) As for tenures, the Parti canadien had opposed the 1826 Canada Tenures Act not because it opposed freehold land tenure, but because it disputed whether the French version of *franc aleu*, or the English version of free and common soccage, would apply. This mattered because the French law, in contrast to the English version, provided for equal inheritance as opposed to primogeniture in the absence of a will, and for the rights of *communauté* and dower for widows. The 1826 Canada Tenures Act, affecting retroactively land tenures of the preceding five decades, had given rise to legal chaos (Testimony of Viger, 143). As for the commutation of land tenure, Papineau had endorsed the system legislated in the 1822 Canada Trade Act (Manning, *Revolt*, 174–5). Later, however, opposition arose because it was considered unjust that seigneurs, viewed as trustees, be permitted to convert ungranted lands into their personal private property (Testimony of Austin Cuvillier, 'Minutes,' 168) and because land registry offices in the townships had been notoriously corrupt and unfair (Testimony of Neilson, 86). Note, finally, that even the 92 Resolutions acknowledged that freehold tenures formed part of the legal status quo and that the Assembly was prepared to address 'this important subject' (see Resolutions 56–62, *Documents*, 380–4). Thus, the positions of many elite members of the Parti canadien on the complex land-tenures issue had little connection with either Whig or Tory conservatism. See also Greer, *Patriots and the People*, 131, 286, 293, 360.

190 Peter Burroughs, *British Attitudes towards Canada*, 57–8.

191 Norah Story, ed., 'Stewart Derbishire's Report to Lord Durham on Lower Canada, 1838,' *Canadian Historical Review* 18 (1937): 58.

192 Peter Burroughs, 'The Canadian Rebellions in British Politics,' in *Perspec-*

tives of Empire, eds. John Flint and Glyndwr Williams, 74–5, 82–5. See also Martin, *Durham Report and British Policy*, 49.

193 A federal union would have contained the cultural conflict and avoided compelling an unenthusiastic population of Upper Canada to join in a more intimate union with Lower Canada. A federal union, perhaps eventually encompassing all of British North America, would have also established a polity more able to resist the force of American annexationism (Ged Martin, 'Confederation Rejected: The British Debate on Canada, 1837–1840,' 44–6).

194 Lucas, ed., *Report*, 2: 292.

195 Martin, 'Confederation Rejected,' 49.

196 Lucas, ed., *Report*, 296; quoted in Ormsby, 'Lord Durham and the Assimilation of French Canada,' in *On Canada: Essays in Honour of Frank H. Underhill*, ed. Norman Penlington, 50.

197 Ormsby, 'Lord Durham and the Assimilation of French Canada,' 51.

198 Martin, 'Confederation Rejected,' 35, 45–51. See also Reginald Coupland, ed., introduction to *The Durham Report: An Abridged Version with an Introduction and Notes*, lvii–lix.

199 Buckner, *Transition to Responsible Government*, 335.

200 Lucas, ed., *Report*, 2: 48–50, 57.

201 Ormsby, 'Lord Durham and the Assimilation of French Canada,' 50; Lucas, ed., *Report*, 2: 296–7.

202 Quoted in Martin, 'Confederation Rejected,' 49. See also Ian Radforth, 'Sydenham and Utilitarian Reform,' in *Colonial Leviathan: State Formation in Mid-Nineteenth-Century Canada*, ed. Allan Greer and Ian Radforth (Toronto: University of Toronto Press, 1992), 71.

203 With respect to the analogous contemporary evolution of the British constitution and parliamentary practice, see Ward, *Colonial Self-Government*, 177–8; Terence Jenkins, *Parliament, Party and Politics in Victorian Britain*, 28–55; Ronald Butt, *The Power of Parliament*, 2d ed., 61–78.

204 Lucas, ed., *Report*, 2: 38.

205 Ibid., 2: 26–7.

206 Ibid., 2: 53.

207 Martin, 'Confederation Rejected,' 39. See also Ormsby, *Emergence of the Federal Concept in Canada, 1839–1845*, 76. Ormsby notes that the act encountered less opposition in the House of Commons than in the Lords, a pattern consistent with popular sentiments having lent support to the policy.

208 Greenwood, *Legacies of Fear*, 65–6, 79, 105, 177, 203. Greenwood's account draws on themes noted by Wade, who observed the 'shattering effect of the outbreak of the Terror upon British official opinion ... The tolerant attitude

earlier shown to the French Canadians was replaced after 1793 by a fear of everything French, whether Continental or Canadian ... an ethnic tension hitherto unknown in Canada was created, which left its mark on the French-Canadian mind' : Wade, *French Canadians*, 1: 93.

209 Osgoode to Burland, 27 October 1795; quoted in Greenwood, *Legacies of Fear*, 177.

210 Greenwood also observes that 'the perceived security threat provided a perfect vent for cultural prejudice' signifying that cultural prejudices were readily blended with prudent security concerns: *Legacies of Fear*, 110.

211 Manning, *Revolt*, 77. Cf. Sturgis, 'Anglicisation,' esp. 218, 220. Sturgis notes that Dalhousie believed the Canadien political elite should be bilingual and thus favoured the ban on French in the Assembly proposed in the 1822 Act of Union. However, Dalhousie's position on this matter does not amount to favour for 'direct anglicisation' of the Canadien people as a whole. The other evidence that Sturgis himself cites concerning Dalhousie – that, despite his own Scottish kirk background, Dalhousie was still prepared to propose a parallel Catholic Institution to the Royal Institution for the Advancement of Learning – seems more telling. As Dalhousie put it, 'The Catholic Religion in this Province is certainly the most sure Defence of it against our Neighbours; and every fair encouragement should be given to it in promoting Education and Learning': see Dalhousie to Bathurst, 10 June 1821, *Report*, 1899, 50–1.

Chapter 3: Triumphs and Failures of Affiliative Trusteeship, 1840–1896

1 *Le Canadien*, 20 November 1839; quoted in Jacques Monet, *The Last Cannon Shot: A Study of French-Canadian Nationalism*, 20.

2 *Le Canadien*, 8, 10 January 1840; quoted in ibid., 35. The quotation has been re-translated from a contemporary newspaper translation.

3 Monet, *1st Cannon Shot*, 25–6, 34–5.

4 Ian Radforth, 'Sydenham and Utilitarian Reform,' in *Colonial Leviathan: State Formation in Mid-Nineteenth-Century Canada*, ed. Allen Greer and Ian Radforth, 74, 95–6.

5 Bagot to Stanley, 26 September 1842; quoted in James Careless, *The Union of the Canadas: The Growth of Canadian Institutions, 1841–1857*, 66.

6 Bagot to Stanley, 12 June 1842; quoted in ibid., 65.

7 William Ormsby, *The Emergence of the Federal Concept in Canada, 1839–1845*, 85.

8 Careless, *Union of the Canadas*, 39–40, 47.

9 Monet, *Last Cannon Shot*, 42–57.

10 Ibid.; Careless, *Union of the Canadas*, 47–57.

11 Careless, *Union of the Canadas*, 55.

12 Harrison to Bagot, 11 July 1842; quoted in G.P. de T. Glazebrook, *Sir Charles Bagot in Canada: A Study in British Colonial Government*, 61.

13 John Manning Ward, *Colonial Self-Government: The British Experience, 1759–1856*, 260; Careless, *Union of the Canadas*, 67.

14 *Montreal Gazette* [Autumn 1842]; quoted in William Morrell, *British Colonial Policy in the Age of Peel and Russell*, 56.

15 Morrell, *British Colonial Policy*.

16 Monet, *Last Cannon Shot*, 96–7.

17 Careless, *Union of the Canadas*, 63. See also Monet, *Last Cannon Shot*, 97–8; Ormsby, *Emergence of the Federal Concept*, 108.

18 Metcalfe to Stanley, 29 April 1843; quoted in James Sturgis, 'Anglicisation as a Theme in Lower Canadian History, 1807–1843,' 224.

19 Ormsby, *Emergence of the Federal Concept*, 119.

20 Phillip A. Buckner, *The Transition to Responsible Government: British Policy in British North America, 1815–1850*, 267. See also Ormsby, *Emergence of the Federal Concept*, 108–15.

21 Ormsby, *Emergence of the Federal Concept*, 108–10.

22 Ibid., 118–19.

23 Ibid., 75.

24 Monet, *Last Cannon Shot*, 144.

25 Morin to Elgin, 27 February 1847; quoted in ibid., 258.

26 Careless, *Union of the Canadas*, 117–19; Monet, *Last Cannon Shot*, 263.

27 Elgin to Grey, 4 March 1848; quoted in Monet, *Last Cannon Shot*, 266.

28 Careless, *Union of the Canadas*, 117–19.

29 John Charles Dent, *The Last 40 Years*, 2: 176.

30 W.P.M. Kennedy, *The Constitution of Canada, 1534–1937: An Introduction to its Development, Law and Custom*, 2d ed., 270–1.

31 Jeffrey McNairn, 'Publius of the North: Tory Republicanism and the American Constitution in Upper Canada, 1848–54,' 504–37. Note that an elective legislative council was established in Canada in 1856, drawing support both from radical democrats and from Conservatives who sought a 'check on popular excess in the lower house': Careless, *Union of the Canadas*, 197; Careless, 'Mid-Century Victorian Liberalism in Central Canadian Newspapers, 1850–67,' 226–7.

32 Careless, *Union of the Canadas*, 167–9.

33 Thus, in the election of 1854 conservatives were divided on the issue of the clergy reserves: James Careless, *Brown of the* Globe, 1: 188; Careless, *Union of the Canadas*, 192.

34 Paul Cornell, *Alignment of Political Groups, 1841–1867*, 85.

35 Donald Creighton, *John A. Macdonald*, vol. 1: *The Young Politician*, 206; Cornell, *Alignment of Political Groups*, 39–40; William Morton, *Critical Years: The Union of British North America, 1857–1873*, 11.

36 Careless, *Brown of the* Globe, 1: 189; Careless, *Union of the Canadas*, 191–3.

37 Careless, *Union of the Canadas*, 171. Creighton refers tellingly to the 'many political arrangements and rearrangements of a troubled decade': Creighton, *John A. Macdonald*, 1: 208.

38 This point has been made clear to me by Jeffrey McNairn.

39 Careless, *Brown of the* Globe, 1: 117–18.

40 James Hervey Price, 18 June 1850, *Debates of the Legislative Assembly of United Canada, 1841–1867* [hereinafter cited as *Debates, 1841–1867*], vol. IX, pt. I, ed. Elizabeth Gibbs, 619, resolution no. 29. I am indebted to Jeffrey McNairn for referring me to this debate.

41 Robert Baldwin, 19 June 1850, *Debates, 1841–1867*, vol. IX, pt. I, 658–9. Baldwin had previously made his views on representation known to his constituents, declaring at a public meeting, 'I am not here to pledge myself on any question. I go to the House as a free man or not at all': quoted in Dent, *The Last 40 Years*, 2: 241. Cf. speeches in the same debate of Malcolm Cameron and John Scott, *Debates, 1841–1867*, vol. IX, pt. I, 696, 702. Scott, who nonetheless voted for the measure and acknowledged that he had previously voted for the Rebellion Losses bill 'to support his Lower Canadian friends,' noted that the 'wishes of the country' on the point were clear and that members ought to be 'guided' by the will of the people.

42 Baldwin, 19 June 1850, *Debates, 1841–1867*, 658. The resolution passed 48 to 19.

43 Careless, *Union of the Canadas*, 168. See also John Bumsted, *The Peoples of Canada: A Pre-Confederation History*, 322. But for an account of the hostility of many Canadian conservatives to Jacksonian democracy see Peter Smith, 'The Dream of Political Union: Loyalism, Toryism and the Federal Idea in Pre-Confederation Canada,' in *The Causes of Canadian Confederation*, ed. Ged Martin, 165.

44 Paul G. Cornell, *The Alignment of Political Groups in Canada, 1841–1867*, 25.

45 Careless, *Union of the Canadas*, 194.

46 Creighton, *John A. Macdonald*, 1: 188.

47 Franklin Walker, *Catholic Education and Politics in Upper Canada: A Study of the Documentation Relative to the Origin of Catholic Elementary Schools in the Ontario School System*, 76–180; John Moir, *Church and State in Canada West: Three Studies in the Relation of Denominationalism and Nationalism, 1841–1867*, 142–80.

48 Moir, *Church and State*, 180; Walker, *Catholic Education*, 310.
49 Walker, *Catholic Education*, 317. See also Careless, *Brown of the* Globe, 1: 171.
50 Careless, *Union of the Canadas*, 181. As for conservatives, Walker notes, 'Nor should the role of the Liberal-Conservative party in Upper Canada be forgotten; it is of amusing interest that many leaders in the Loyal Orange Order were Church of England Tories who frequently voted in favour of separate school measures': Walker, *Catholic Education*, 312.
51 Brown's position on popery is revealed in his editorials on the decision of Pope Pius IX to establish a full hierarchy with territorial titles in England, something that had long existed in Canada: see George Brown, 'Dr. Wiseman's Manifesto,' *The Globe*, 19 December 1850; cited in Careless, *Union of the Canadas*, 177, and Creighton, *John A. Macdonald*, 1: 163. The *Globe* expressed a hope, at least once, that common schools in Upper Canada would assimilate Catholics to Protestantism: see Walker, *Catholic Education*, 148. On sectionalism see the analysis of the representation by population campaign in Careless, *Brown of the* Globe, 1: 166–7. On Brown's voluntarism see ibid., 1: 122–6.
52 Peter Waite, *The Life and Times of Confederation, 1864–1867: Politics, Newspapers, and the Union of British North America*, 44.
53 *Globe*, 7 September 1852; quoted in Careless, *Brown of the* Globe, 1: 158.
54 Head to Labouchere, 16 June 1857; quoted in Morton, *Critical Years*, 20.
55 Creighton, *John A. Macdonald*, 1: 221.
56 Ibid., 1: 227.
57 Careless, *Union of the Canadas*, 208–10; Careless, *Brown of the* Globe, 1: 256, 1: 299.
58 Careless, *Union of the Canadas*, 99–100, 201, 210–11; Morton, *Critical Years*, 11–12.
59 Even Brown's hostile *Globe* acknowledged that the School bill, as amended, was as 'innocuous as a Papistical School Bill could well be' (*Globe*, 25 June 1855; quoted in Walker, *Catholic Education*, 175). Although Careless suggests that the measure was 'of major, of crucial, importance to Upper Canada,' Walker's closely reasoned verdict is that the measure 'actually made little difference': Careless, *Brown of the* Globe, 1: 204; Walker, *Catholic Education*, 171.
60 Bruce Hodgins, 'Democracy and the Ontario Fathers of Confederation,' in *Profiles of a Province: Studies in the History of Ontario*, Collection of Essays Commissioned by the Ontario History Society, 89; Hodgins, *John Sandfield Macdonald, 1812–1872*, 34–8, 56–74; Hodgins, 'John Sandfield Macdonald,' in *Dictionary of Canadian Biography*, 10: 464–9.
61 Bruce Hodgins, 'John Sandfield Macdonald and the Crisis of 1863,' *Cana-*

dian Historical Association Report of the Annual Meeting (1965): 37–9; Kennedy, *Constitution of Canada*, 281–2. Reformer Alexander Mackenzie referred in the Confederation debates to the principle having had a 'fair trial and a speedy death' in that instance: Peter Waite, ed., *The Confederation Debates in the Province of Canada, 1865: A Selection*, 103 [hereinafter cited as *Confederation Debates (Selection)*].

62 Hodgins, *John Sandfield Macdonald*, 64–5.
63 Cornell, *Alignment of Political Groups*, 84.
64 As discussed in the introduction, this minimum consensus has been noted by consociational theory to have proven indispensable for coalition government in segmented societies. Careless observes that the double-majority doctrine would at times, such as after the 1857 election, have meant 'rule by mixing fire and gunpowder': Careless, *Union of the Canadas*, 211.
65 Walker, *Catholic Education*, 148, n. 28; Careless, *Brown of the* Globe, 1: 235; Creighton, *John A. Macdonald*, 1: 225.
66 Ottawa *Citizen*, 7 October 1864; quoted in Waite, *Life of Times of Confederation*, 46.
67 Careless, *Union of the Canadas*, 210; Walker, *Catholic Education*, 145, n. 28.
68 Careless, *Union of the Canadas*, 210. Lafontaine 'counted seventeen divisions on Lower Canadians matters decided by Upper Canadian votes' (210).
69 The population of the West was 952,000 versus 890,000 for the East; the rate of growth in the West also appeared to be higher: Careless, *Brown of the* Globe, 1: 165–7.
70 Creighton, *John A. Macdonald*, 1: 225.
71 Careless, *Brown of the* Globe, 1: 252; 1: 262.
72 Ibid., 1: 253–4; 1: 262.
73 Ibid., 1: 254.
74 Ibid.
75 Speech at the Royal Exchange, 6 August 1858, *Globe*, 9 August 1858; cited in Careless, *Brown of the* Globe, 1: 346, n. 118. See also Jean-Claude Soulard, 'Sir Antoine-Aimé Dorion,' in *Dictionary of Canadian Biography*, vol. 12.
76 Speech at the Royal Exchange; emphasis mine.
77 Ibid.
78 Ibid.; Walker, *Catholic Education*, 230.
79 Toronto *Leader*, 31 August 1858; quoted in Walker, *Catholic Education*, 233. Brown's victory was otherwise narrow, 2,660 to 2,516.
80 Thibideau stated in the Assembly on 1 February 1859 that, although it had been falsely rumoured that 'he had joined the enemy of Catholicism, and sacrificed his principles,' in fact 'he had joined the Brown–Dorion Ministry because he thought them able and willing to settle the vexed questions of the

day upon equitable principles.' Dorion stated, 'It was agreed by himself and his colleagues that the question should be taken up at once and that an inquiry should, without delay, be made into the systems prevailing in such countries as Belgium, Ireland, and Prussia, where the same difficulties had arisen, and where they had more or less been satisfactorily settled, in order that the common school law might be so amended as to make it more in harmony with the feelings of the people in both sections of the Province, Protestants and Catholics, and until the inquiry was made the system would remain as at present': *Evening Colonist and Atlas*, 1 & 3 February 1859. The debate is cited in Creighton, *John A. Macdonald*, 1: 288.

81 Careless, *Brown of the* Globe, 1: 268.

82 Ibid., 1: 235.

83 Ibid., 1: 298; Walker, *Catholic Education*, 252.

84 Careless, *Brown of the* Globe, 1: 205.

85 Ibid., 1: 320.

86 George W. Brown, 'The Grit Party and the Great Reform Convention of 1859,' *Canadian Historical Review* 16 (1935): 245; Careless, *Brown of the* Globe, 1: 311–22.

87 Careless, *Brown of the* Globe, 1: 312.

88 Ibid., 1: 323.

89 Ibid.

90 See the essays published in *The Causes of Confederation*, ed. Ged Martin, including Ged Martin, 'The Case against Canadian Confederation, 1864–1867'; Phillip Buckner, 'The Maritimes and Confederation: A Reassessment'; and James Sturgis, 'The Opposition to Confederation in Nova Scotia, 1864–1868.' See also Ged Martin, *Britain and the Origins of Canadian Confederation, 1837–67*, 55–79. The term 'revisionist' is taken from the back cover of *Causes of Confederation*. Cf. Creighton, *John A. Macdonald*, 1: 354–465; Creighton, *The Road to Confederation, the Emergence of Canada: 1863–1867*; Careless, *Brown of the* Globe, 2: 103–46; William Whitelaw, *The Maritimes and Canada before Confederation*.

91 Creighton, *Road to Confederation*, 51–2; Waite, *Life and Times of Confederation*, 43.

92 Creighton, *Road to Confederation*, 44–7.

93 Ibid., 44–5.

94 According to the 1861 census, the population of Canada East stood at 1.11 million, that of Canada West at 1.40 million: Ralph C. Nelson, Walter C. Soderlund, Ronald H. Wagenberg, E. Donald Briggs, 'Canadian Confederation as a Case Study in Community Formation,' in *The Causes of Canadian Confederation*, ed. Ged Martin, 66.

95 Even at a relatively high point of Reform parliamentary influence during May 1863, Brown connected rep by pop with the federation plan of the 1859 Toronto convention, and with guarantees for Lower Canada. Later that month, before the election, Brown went so far as to tell Western Grits that no prospective coalition could commit itself to rep by pop as a 'cabinet question.' Brown was, however, apparently outflanked in the election by more junior Upper Canadian Reformers, who made rep by pop an election theme. After the Bleus won a strong majority in the election in Lower Canada, Brown could do no more than attempt to build a multipartisan consensus for constitutional change of some form: Careless, *Brown of the Globe*, 2: 92–101; Martin, *Origins of Canadian Confederation*, 48.
96 Martin, *Origins of Canadian Confederation*, 51.
97 Cornell, *Alignment of Political Groups*, 76; Martin, *Origins of Canadian Confederation*, 51.
98 Ged Martin, 'History as Science or Literature: Explaining Canadian Confederation, 1858–1867,' Canada House Lecture Series no. 41 (1989): 27; Martin, *Origins of Canadian Confederation*, 51.
99 Waite, ed., *Confederation Debates (Selection)*, 50. Cartier's demographic observations were not without basis. The populations and Roman Catholic proportions of the British colonies and provinces of Eastern North American in 1861 were: Upper Canada (1.4M, 18.5 per cent); Lower Canada (1.1M, 84.9 per cent); Nova Scotia (0.33M, 26.3 per cent [1871]); New Brunswick (0.25M, 33.6 per cent [1871]); P.E.I. (0.08M, 44.3 per cent); Newfoundland (0.15M, 46.4 per cent [1857]). This implies that the percentage of Catholics under the existing union was 47.9 per cent, and that for a federation including all of the Maritime provinces it would have declined only to 44.5 per cent. For the provinces that actually entered Confederation in 1867 it was also 44.5 per cent. (Data derived from Nelson et al., 'Canadian Confederation,' 66, 71.)
100 Careless, *Brown of the Globe*, 2: 136; Jean Charles Bonenfant, 'Sir George-Étienne Cartier,' in *Dictionary of Canadian Biography*, 10: 148. Cf. Martin, *Origins of British Confederation*, 51.
101 Waite, ed., *Confederation Debates (Selection)*, 49.
102 See for example ibid., 20, 26, 30–3, 39, 48, 50, 56, 60, 68–9, 107, 130; Careless, *Brown of the Globe*, 2: 23.
103 Waite, ed., *Confederation Debates (Selection)*, 30–3.
104 Bonenfant, 'Sir George-Étienne Cartier,' 149. Josephine Cartier wrote shortly after her father's death in May 1873 that 'almost his last words were to say how happy he was that the union with Prince Edward Island had been completed': William Morton, *The Critical Years: The Union of British North America, 1857–1873*, 275.

105 Ibid., 150.

106 Speech at Barrington, 8 June 1866; quoted in J. Murray Beck, *Joseph Howe*, vol. 2: *The Briton Becomes Canadian, 1848–1873*, 202.

107 George Johnson, biography of Howe, n. d.; quoted in Beck, *Joseph Howe*, 201.

108 Beck, *Joseph Howe*, 208.

109 Buckner, 'Maritimes and Confederation,' 107; J.S. Mill, *Considerations on Representative Government* (1861), ed. Currin V. Shields, 234.

110 Martin, *Origins of Canadian Confederation*, 237–90.

111 Ibid., 64, 134, 136, 173–81.

112 *The Times*, 3 September 1858; quoted in ibid., 160.

113 Lucas, ed., *Report*, 2: 312; quoted in Martin, *Origins of Canadian Confederation*, 150. See also Smith, 'Dream of Political Union,' 168–9.

114 Bonenfant, 'Sir George-Étienne Cartier,' 146.

115 Waite, *Life and Times of Confederation*, 89.

116 Ibid., 77–9, 81, 91, 97–8; William Annand, Halifax *Morning Chronicle*, 24 January 1866; quoted in Martin, 'Case Against Confederation,' 30.

117 Waite, *Life and Times of Confederation*, 185.

118 Ibid., 199.

119 Morton, *Critical Years*, 193.

120 Creighton, *John A. Macdonald*, 1: 271–9.

121 Confidential memorandum by T.F. Elliott, 4 November 1858; quoted in Martin, *Origins of Canadian Confederation*, 222–4. See also Bruce Knox, 'The British Government, Sir Edmund Head, and British North American Confederation, 1858,' 207–8.

122 Martin, *Origins of Canadian Confederation*, 224. This indeed became the basis of official policy after 1862. By July 1862 the British government no longer found it necessary to hinder British North American union: ibid., 230–5.

123 Careless, *Brown of the* Globe, 2: 100–1; 2: 120–1, 2: 126–7.

124 Ibid., 2: 135–43; Martin, *Origins of Canadian Confederation*, 52–5; Morton, *Critical Years*, 147–8.

125 Waite, *Life and Times of Confederation*, 48.

126 Ibid., 105; Creighton, *John A. Macdonald*, 1: 402.

127 Morton, *Critical Years*, 216. See also Bruce Knox, 'The Rise of Colonial Federation as an Object of British Policy, 1850–1870,' 108–9.

128 Toronto *Leader*, 22 November 1864; quoted in Waite, *Life and Times of Confederation*, 122.

129 Bruce Hodgins concludes that 'Confederation was basically the achievement of a pre-democratic elite at the very time when ideas of political democracy and concepts of local majoritarianism were growing, especially

in Upper Canada': Hodgins, 'The Canadian Political Elite's Attitudes to-ward the Nature of the Plan of Union,' in *Federalism in Canada and Australia: The Early Years*, ed. Bruce Hodgins, Don Wright, and W.H. Heick, 58.

130 Montreal *Gazette*, 2 November 1864; quoted in Waite, *Life and Times of Confederation*, 122.

131 Waite, *Life and Times of Confederation*, 122.

132 Morton, *Critical Years*, 177–8, 198.

133 Hodgins, 'Democracy and the Ontario Fathers,' 84.

134 Ibid, 85.

135 Waite, *Life and Times of Confederation*, 121. This was an interesting position, considering that so much of the media was in fact directly or indirectly controlled by political leaders themselves.

136 Based on total population figures reported in the 1861 Census, cited in Nelson et al., 'Canadian Confederation,' 66; Buckner, 'Maritimes and Confederation,' 107. Prince Edward Island and Newfoundland, which did not join Confederation until 1873 and 1949, respectively, were even more vastly outnumbered, possessing only 2.4 and 4.4 per cent of the total population of a prospective British North American union in the 1860s.

137 Joseph Howe, Speech at Dartmouth, 22 May 1867; quoted in Martin, 'Case against Confederation,' 44. See also Creighton, *Road to Confederation*, 251; Waite, *Life and Times of Confederation*, 293.

138 The Charlottetown *Examiner* asked, for example, why 'the awful and pompous air of mystery?' Quoted in Waite, *Life and Times of Confederation*, 76, 82 n. 39.

139 *Christian Guardian*, 23 September 1874; quoted in Sturgis, 'Opposition to Confederation,' 122. Premier John Gray of Prince Edward Island had a similar experience. He was forced to resign after he found his pro-Confederate stance at odds with those of the vast majority of Island residents as well as with that of his own attorney-general, Edward Palmer. As he put it in a letter to Nova Scotia premier Charles Tupper, 'When I returned from Canada after our happy intercourse, I found the whole community poisoned by [Attorney General] Mr. Palmer ... I *had sold* the Country.' Quoted in Waite, *Life and Times of Confederation*, 183.

140 Waite, *Life and Times of Confederation*, 124. Tilley had 'very hesitatingly' promised several months earlier that his government would not bring Confederation before the legislature without a popular mandate: ibid., 241.

141 Alfred Bailey, 'The Basis and Persistence of Opposition to Confederation in New Brunswick,' in *Confederation*, ed. Ramsay Cook, Craig Brown, and Carl Berger, 77–9. Waite, *Life and Times of Confederation*, 240–4.

142 Creighton, *Road to Confederation*, 248.

143 Although one, perhaps somewhat contrived, calculation suggested that the popular vote in the election had only narrowly favoured the antis, the sum of raw popular votes (leaving aside the effects of multi-member constituencies) had defeated the Confederates by 4,7000 to 29,000. Martin, *Origins of British Confederation*, 270; Waite, *Life and Times of Confederation*, 246.

144 Waite, *Life and Times of Confederation*, 247.

145 Ibid., 217, 220, 252–3, 258–62; William Baker, *Timothy Warren Anglin, 1822–1896: Irish Catholic Canadian*, 93–5; Bailey, 'Basis and Persistence of Opposition,' 85, 92–3; Morton, *Critical Years*, 188–90; Creighton, *Road to Confederation*, 353–73.

146 Morton, *Critical Years*, 190–2; Bailey, 'Basis and Persistence of Opposition,' 70.

147 Waite, *Life and Times of Confederation*, 213.

148 Ibid., 219.

149 Creighton, *Road to Confederation*, 364–6.

150 Waite, *Life and Times of Confederation*, 221–5, 269–70. In England during the summer of 1865, Annand had learned then of the British government's strong support for Confederation: see Martin, *Origins of Canadian Confederation*, 240, 258–65.

151 Waite, *Life and Times of Confederation*, 271. See also Martin, *Origins of Canadian Confederation*, 269–70.

152 Martin, *Origins of Canadian Confederation*, 265–8, 277.

153 Sturgis, 'Opposition to Confederation,' 117.

154 Ibid.

155 Beck, *Joseph Howe*, 2: 220; Waite, *Life and Times of Confederation*, 202. Note that the popular vote in the province as a whole was split 60 to 40 against Confederation. See Martin, *British Origins of Confederation*, 276.

156 Sturgis, 'Opposition to Confederation,' 120–1; Beck, *Joseph Howe*, 2: 197–218.

157 Howe to Isaac Buchanan, 20 June 1866, in *The Speeches and Public Letters of Joseph Howe*, rev. ed., ed. Joseph Chisholm, 464. Howe's rhetorical demand that the 'people' decide union rested in some tension with Howe's other views. Howe, 'never much of a democrat,' counselled Foreign Secretary Lord Stanley in 1866 against liberalizing the franchise in Britain, and himself revoked universal suffrage in Nova Scotia in 1863: Beck, *Joseph Howe*, 2: 204, 2: 169–70. The motif of cards being played is adapted from ibid., 2: 213, and Martin, *Origins of Canadian Confederation*, 64.

158 Sturgis, 'Opposition to Confederation,' 121.

159 'Confederation Considered in Relation to the Interests of the Empire'
    (1866), in Chisholm, ed., *Speeches and Public Letters of Joseph Howe*,
    2: 475, 2: 474, 2: 481, 2: 476.
160 Beck, *Joseph Howe*, 2: 288. Howe's words quoted in Martin, 'Case against
    Confederation,' 44, and Martin, *Origins of Canadian Confederation*, 32.
    See Waite, *Life and Times of Confederation*, 210; and Howe quoted in
    Creighton, *Road to Confederation*, 96.
161 J. Murray Beck, 'Joseph Howe,' in *Dictionary of Canadian Biography*,
    10: 367.
162 I am indebted to Ged Martin for this observation. Howe's party was de-
    feated in the May 1863 election and he was subsequently out of office (and
    apparently retired from politics) until the election of September 1867. His
    public leadership of the anti-Confederate cause lasted from May 1866 to
    December 1868, though he had also published the Botheration Letters
    anonymously in March 1865, and had all but given up hope of success by
    July 1868. Howe's most intense opposition was certainly during the extra-
    parliamentary phase.
163 William Grant, *The Tribune of Nova Scotia: A Chronicle of Joseph Howe*.
164 Martin, *Origins of Canadian Confederation*, 286.
165 Halifax *Evening Reporter*, 5 December 1865; quoted in Beck, *Joseph Howe*,
    2: 193.
166 G.M. Grant, *Joseph Howe* (1875), 75; quoted in Beck, 'Joseph Howe,' 369.
167 Beck, *Joseph Howe*, 2: 231–9.
168 Ibid., 2: 240.
169 Ibid., 2: 241.
170 Ibid., 2: 247; Morton, *Critical Years*, 231.
171 Morton, *Critical Years*, 232.
172 Kenneth G. Pryke, *Nova Scotia and Confederation*, 88, 94–7.
173 Beck, *Joseph Howe*, 2: 254.
174 Morton, *Critical Years*, 232; Sturgis, 'Opposition to Confederation,' 129.
175 Sturgis, ibid., 116.
176 William McConnell, *Commentary on the British North American Act*;
    Robert Vipond, *Liberty and Community: Canadian Federalism and the
    Failure of the Constitution*, 15–45; Morton, *Critical Years*, 204–8.
177 Vipond, *Liberty and Community*, 35–6.
178 McConnell, *British North America Act*, 382–3; Morton, *Critical Years*,
    204.
179 Waite, *Life and Times of Confederation*, 290.
180 McConnell, *British North America Act*, 288–9.
181 Ibid. 'Ingeniously' because the provision purported to institute parity,
    despite that the privileges enjoyed by dissentient schools in Upper Canada

were generally understood to be weaker and more tenuous than those in Lower Canada: Walker, *Catholic Education*, 307.

182 Morton, *Critical Years*, 208; Arthur Silver, *The French-Canadian Idea of Confederation, 1864–1900*, 88–110. However, Manoply Lupul notes that the 'spirit' of the BNA Act 'favoured' the earliest separate schools in the Northwest Territories: Lupul, *The Roman Catholic Church and the North-West School Question: A Study in Church–State Relations in Western Canada, 1875–1905*, 65.

183 Morton, *Critical Years*, 204; and Silver, *French-Canadian Idea of Confederation*, 55–66.

184 Silver, *French-Canadian Idea of Confederation*, 55–7.

185 Ibid., 57–9.

186 Ibid., 59.

187 Ibid., 58–60; Creighton, *John A. Macdonald*, 1: 400; Morton, *Critical Years*, 200.

188 Morton, *Critical Years*, 200. The substance of the Langevin bill was passed in March 1869 by the Quebec government of Premier P.-J.-O. Chauveau at the behest of anglophone cabinet members, who had accepted Alexander Galt's advice to refuse to serve otherwise: see Silver, *French-Canadian Idea of Confederation*, 63. Andrée Désilets, 'Joseph-Édouard Cauchon,' in *Dictionary of Canadian Biography*, 11: 162.

189 McConnell, *British North America Act*, 288.

190 Morton, *Critical Years*, 204.

191 Waite, *Life and Times of Confederation*, 290.

192 Hodgins, 'Democracy,' 88. Waite notes that few protested the reversion to Crown nomination for the Upper House, which had been made elective in 1856: Waite, *Life and Times of Confederation*, 129.

193 Waite, *Life and Times of Confederation*, 285.

194 Silver, *French-Canadian Idea of Confederation*, 55; Waite, *Life and Times of Confederation*, 286.

195 Speech of Macdonald at Quebec Conference, October 1864; quoted in Hodgins, 'Democracy,' 87. Recent scholarship would suggest that the connection between a 'powerful central government' and minority protection was a long-established conservative view in Upper Canada, although the protection contemplated in the earlier discourse was of political, not 'racial,' groups: see Jeffrey McNairn, 'Publius of the North: Tory Republicanism and the American Constitution in Upper Canada, 1848–54,' 526–9; Peter Smith, 'The Dream of Political Union: Loyalism, Toryism and the Federal Idea in Pre-Confederation Canada,' in *The Causes of Canadian Confederation*, ed. Ged Martin, 167.

196 Vipond, *Liberty and Community*, 24.

197 Waite, ed., *Confederation Debates (Selection)*, 44; Vipond, *Liberty and Community*, 22.
198 Waite, *Life and Times of Confederation*, 291.
199 Morton, *Critical Years*, 166.
200 Waite, *Life and Times of Confederation*, 142.
201 *La Minerve*, 15 October 1864; quoted in Silver, *French-Canadian Idea of Confederation*, 37.
202 Waite, *Life and Times of Confederation*, 142–3, 146–7. See also Silver, *French-Canadian Idea of Confederation*, for a more recent and well-documented presentation of Bleu constitutional rhetoric (34–50). Note also the outline of the somewhat tendentious retrospective constitutional interpretation of Oliver Mowat, Conservative premier of Ontario from 1872 to 1896, see Paul Romney, 'Sir Oliver Mowat,' in *Dictionary of Canadian Biography* 13: 728.
203 Waite, *Life and Times of Confederation*, 110, 114, 128; Morton, *Critical Years*, 165–6.
204 Morton, *Critical Years*, 165.
205 Silver, *French-Canadian Idea of Confederation*, 43; Vipond, *Liberty and Community*, 35, 24–5.
206 Walter Bagehot, *The English Constitution*, ed. R.H.S. Crossman, 59–3.
207 Vipond, *Liberty and Community*, 35–6. Quotation from Bagehot, *English Constitution*, 59.
208 Vipond, *Liberty and Community*, 24, 35; Waite, *Life and Times of Confederation*, 296.
209 Vipond, *Liberty and Community*, 30–3.
210 Ibid.
211 *Confederation Debates*, 690; cited in Vipond, *Liberty and Community*, 34.
212 McNairn, 'Publius of the North,' 528; Smith, 'Dream of Political Union,' 167.
213 Silver, *French-Canadian Idea of Confederation*, 51–5.
214 Ibid., 40.
215 Hodgins, 'Canadian Political Elite's Attitudes,' 59.
216 Silver, *French-Canadian Idea of Confederation*, 89–92; Vipond, *Liberty and Community*, 108–12; William Morton, 'Confederation, 1870–1896: The End of the Macdonaldian Constitution and the Return to Duality,' 11–24.
217 Silver, *French-Canadian Idea of Confederation*, 191, 204–9. Note, however, that the more junior ranks of the federal political elite, including MPs in Cartier's and Laurier's own parties, were far from united on this point. See discussions that follow.
218 Ramsay Cook, *Provincial Autonomy, Minority Rights, and the Compact*

Theory, 1867–1921, Studies of the Royal Commission on Bilingualism and Biculturalism (Ottawa: Queen's Printer, 1969), 53; quoted in Ralph Heintzman, 'The Spirit of Confederation: Professor Creighton, Biculturalism, and the Use of History,' 270.

219 Baker, *Timothy Warren Anglin*, 149; Thomas Acheson, 'George Edwin King,' in *Dictionary of Canadian Biography*, 5: 545.

220 Katherine MacNaughton, *The Development of the Theory and Practice of Education in New Brunswick, 1784–1900: A Study in Historical Background*, 189–95; Baker, *Timothy Warren Anglin*, 150.

221 MacNaughton, *Education in New Brunswick*, 191. About 35 per cent of the population of New Brunswick was Roman Catholic: Peter Waite, *Canada, 1874–1896: Arduous Destiny*, 7.

222 Acheson, 'George Edwin King,' 547.

223 MacNaughton, *Education in New Brunswick*, 191–2.

224 Ibid., 202; Peter Toner, 'New Brunswick Schools and the Rise of Provincial Rights,' in *Federalism in Canada and Australia*, ed. Bruce Hodgins et al., 130; Vipond, *Liberty and Community*, 120.

225 MacNaughton, *Education in New Brunswick*, 169.

226 Baker, *Timothy Warren Anglin*, 158.

227 Brian Young, 'The Defeat of George-Etienne Cartier in Montreal-East in 1872,' 395.

228 MacNaughton, *Education in New Brunswick*, 201–2.

229 Macdonald had proposed several criteria in 1868 for the use of disallowance, one of which referred to provincial legislation that 'affects the interest of the whole Dominion.' Quoted in Vipond, *Liberty and Community*, 117. Although the power of disallowance was wielded in only narrowly jurisdictional questions during the 1870s, the broader criterion just quoted provided the basis for the federal government's repeated disallowance in the 1880s of Ontario legislation judged to infringe individual property rights: ibid., 126–30. In the parliamentary debate of 1872, Costigan unsuccessfully cited the same criterion (as well as Section 93) in arguing against Macdonald that the Common Schools Act should be disallowed: MacNaughton, *Education in New Brunswick*, 202.

230 House of Commons, *Debates*, 20 May 1872, 706.

231 Young, 'Defeat of George-Etienne Cartier,' 391–406; Vipond, *Liberty and Community*, 123.

232 Cartier, who died a week later, and five French-Canadian members for Quebec ridings did not vote: House of Commons, *Debates* (Hansard Scrap Book), 14 May 1873. Debate cited in MacNaughton, *Education in New Brunswick*, 206. I am indebted to Teresa Riopelle of the Library of Parlia-

ment in Ottawa for making available a transcription of the debate and division, as well as a list of members and constituencies. Cf. Waite, *Canada*, 40; and Silver, *French-Canadian Idea of Confederation*, 91–2. Peter Toner emphasizes political considerations underlying Macdonald's decision in 'New Brunswick Schools,' 129–35. But cf. Vipond, *Liberty and Community*, 123.

233 MacNaughton, *Education in New Brunswick*, 212; Charles Sissons, *Church and State in Canadian Education: An Historical Study*, 240. See also George Stanley, 'The Caraquet Riots of 1875,' 37.

234 Acheson, 'George Edwin King,' 547.

235 Sissons, *Church and State*, 239–42; MacNaughton, *Education in New Brunswick*, 220.

236 Sissons, *Church and State*, 242.

237 MacNaughton, *Education in New Brunswick*, 222.

238 James Miller, *Equal Rights: the Jesuits' Estates Act Controversy*, 26–34, 175–99; Miller, 'Anti-Catholic Thought in Victorian Canada,' 474–8; John Saywell, Introduction to *The Canadian Journal of Lady Aberdeen, 1893–1898*, ed. John Saywell, xxiv. My thanks to Ged Martin for this reference. Larry Kulisek, 'D' Alton McCarthy,' in *Dictionary of Canadian Biography*, 12: 580–1; A. Margaret Evans, *Sir Oliver Mowat*, 224–77; Waite, *Canada*, 209–14.

239 Franklin Walker, *Catholic Education and Politics in Ontario: A Documentary Study*, vol. 2, 112; Miller, *Equal Rights*, 34.

240 The Jesuit order was restored in 1814: Miller, *Equal Rights*, 9.

241 Ibid., 9–10.

242 Ibid., 21.

243 Ibid., 18–20, 69.

244 Evans, *Sir Oliver Mowat*, 249. See also Walker, *Catholic Education and Politics in Ontario*, vol. 2, 126.

245 Miller, 'Anti-Catholic Thought,' 478, 487, 485. The third citation is quoted from *Canadian United Presbyterian Magazine*, 1 November 1856.

246 James Miller, 'The Jesuits' Estates Act Crisis: "An Incident in a Conspiracy of Several Years' Standing,"' 47.

247 Miller, *Equal Rights*, 66.

248 John Charlton, MP, House of Commons, *Debates*, 28 March 1889, 883–4; quoted in Miller, *Equal Rights*, 74.

249 Julius Scriver, MP, House of Commons, *Debates*, 28 March 1889, 894; quoted in Miller, *Equal Rights*, 69.

250 House of Commons, *Debates*, 26 March 1889, 811; quoted in Miller, *Equal Rights*, 68.

251 Waite, *Canada*, 213; Kulisek, 'D'Alton McCarthy,' 581.

252 Kulisek, 'D'Alton McCarthy,' 581; James Miller, 'D'Alton McCarthy, Jr.: A Protestant Irishman Abroad,' in *Boswell's Children: the Art of the Biographer*, ed. Ray Fleming, 195.

253 Walker, *Catholic Education and Politics in Ontario*, vol. 2, 113–16, 128, 148–67; Evans, *Sir Oliver Mowat*, 239–43, 260–2. In the 1886 and 1890 elections the Conservatives won 47.1 and 45.5 per cent, respectively, of the popular vote versus the Liberal's 48.4 and 48.8 per cent: Evans, *Sir Oliver Mowat*, 243, 273.

254 Walker, *Catholic Education and Politics in Ontario*, vol. 2, 150.

255 *Globe*, 9 March 1889; cited in Evans, *Sir Oliver Mowat*, 253.

256 Ibid.

257 Ibid. For ambivalent stance of contemporary Canadian imperialism, see Carl Berger, *The Sense of Power: Studies in the Ideas of Canadian Imperialism, 1867–1914*, 134–47.

258 Ibid.

259 Miller, *Equal Rights*, 96.

260 Waite, *Canada*, 214; Miller, *Equal Rights*, 99–100.

261 Equal Rights Association, *D'Alton McCarthy's Great Speech*, Ottawa, 12 December 1889; quoted in Miller, *Equal Rights*, 127, 108; Equal Rights Association, '"As A Politician He Is a Great Enigma": The Social and Political Ideas of D'Alton McCarthy,' 412–16.

262 Miller, *Equal Rights*, 111.

263 Miller, 'Protestant Irishman Abroad,' 197.

264 James Watt, 'Anti-Catholic Nativism in Canada: the Protestant Protective Association,' 54.

265 Watt, 'Protestant Protective Association,' 49.

266 Miller, *Equal Rights*, 163.

267 Watt, 'Protestant Protective Association,' 54; Evans, *Sir Oliver Mowat*, 315.

268 Walker, *Catholic Education and Politics in Ontario*, vol. 2, 163; Evans, *Sir Oliver Mowat*, 261–2; Miller, *Equal Rights*, 162.

269 Evans, *Sir Oliver Mowat*, 317.

270 Miller, *Equal Rights*, 165.

271 Evans, *Sir Oliver Mowat*, 276.

272 Ibid., 276, 312; Miller, *Equal Rights*, 33–4.

273 Note that in 1891 Roman Catholics constituted 41 per cent of the Canadian population, but only 17 per cent of the Ontarian population: *Census of Canada, 1890–91*, vol. 1, 224, 252.

274 William Morton, *Manitoba: A History*, 2d ed., 247.

275 Robert Clague, 'The Political Aspects of the Manitoba School Question, 1890–96' (MA thesis, University of Manitoba, 1939), 171. Clague also notes

that several Catholic fête days were abolished at this time as public holidays: ibid.

276 Morton, *Manitoba*, 245, 250; Clague, 'Political Aspects,' 89.

277 Winnipeg *Sun*, 1 August 1889; quoted in Clague, 'Political Aspects,' 144. See also James Miller, 'D'Alton McCarthy, Equal Rights, and the Origins of the Manitoba School Question,' 390. For a discussion of the Manitoba Act in relation to the separate schools issue, see Paul Crunican, *Priests and Politicians: Manitoba Schools and the Election of 1896*, 23–4, 35; Waite, *Canada*, 247–9.

278 Miller, 'Origins of the Manitoba School Question,' 379.

279 Brandon *Sun*, 17 October 1889; quoted in Clague, 'Political Aspects,' 139.

280 Crunican, *Priests and Politicians*, 10, n. 9.

281 Morton, *Manitoba*, 244.

282 Clague, 'Political Aspects,' 149.

283 Crunican, *Priests and Politicians*, 10; George Stanley, *The Birth of Western Canada: A History of the Riel Rebellions*, 48–58; Morton, *Manitoba*, 116; Gerald Friesen, *The Canadian Prairies: A History*, 117–25, 195–200, 227–35; Donald Swainson, 'Canada Annexes the West: Colonial Status Confirmed,' in *Federalism in Canada and Australia: The Early Years*, ed. Hodgins et al., 141–2, 153–7; Miller, *Equal Rights*, 33; Miller, 'McCarthy and the Manitoba School Question,' 384–5. Note that Riel's Provisional Government and the Red River Rebellion both presented appeals for support across ethnic lines and cannot be construed as exclusivist: see Stanley, *Birth of Western Canada*, 52, 62–3, 71–3; Friesen, *Canadian Prairies*, 116, 121–2; Howard Adams, 'Causes of the 1885 Struggle,' in *Riel to Reform: A History of Protest in Western Canada*, ed. George Melnyk, 78–85; and Douglas Owram, 'Disillusionment: Regional Discontent in the 1880s,' in *Riel to Reform*, ed. Melnyk, 90–4. Constraints of space prevent discussion of these episodes here.

284 Morton, *Manitoba*, 245, 247, 250.

285 Rev. George Bryce, 'The Manitoba School Question,' September 1893; quoted in *The Manitoba School Question: Majority Rule or Minority Rights?* ed. Lovell Clark, 64. Of course, not all subscribers to such views had always been so dispassionate. For the history of the various strains of ideas relating to empire, nationhood, and the aspiration to cultural uniformity, see Carl Berger's account of the Canada First group in *Sense of Power*, 58–77, 136–7; and Waite, *Canada*, 34–8.

286 John Ewart, 'Isms in the Schools,' July 1893; quoted in Clark, ed., *The Manitoba School Question*, 62.

287 Clague, 'Political Aspects,' 42, 108.

288 Ibid., 43.

289 Ibid., 113–28.

290 James Rea, 'Thomas Greenway,' in *Dictionary of Canadian Biography*, 13: 419.

291 Clague, 'Political Aspects,' 44.

292 Ibid., 132.

293 Rea, 'Thomas Greenway,' 418.

294 Clague, 'Political Aspects,' 79, 189.

295 Rea, 'Thomas Greenway,' 418. Cf. Clague, 'Political Aspects,' 136.

296 Clague, 'Political Aspects,' 79, 189.

297 Lupul, *North-West School Question*, 53–4.

298 Ibid.; Keith McLeod, 'Politics, Schools and the French Language, 1881–1931,' in *Shaping the Schools of the Canadian West*, ed. David Jones, Nancy Sheehan, and Robert Stamp, 60–1; Waite, *Canada*, 216.

299 Waite, *Canada*, 216–7; Lupul, *North-West School Question*, 61–2.

300 House of Commons, *Debates*, 14 February 1890, 674; quoted in Waite, *Canada*, 216.

301 Waite, *Canada*, 217. Note that the compromise amendment proposed by Thompson and accepted by the Commons granted the territorial legislative assembly the right to determine the language of debate and recorded proceedings. But the petition concerning separate schools was not granted: see Waite, *The Man from Halifax: Sir John Thompson Prime Minister*, 253–4; Lupul, *North-West School Question*, 64; Cook, *Provincial Autonomy*, 55–6.

302 House of Commons, *Debates*, 13 February 1890, 623; quoted in Heintzman, 'Spirit of Confederation,' 267.

303 House of Commons, *Debates*, 17 February 1890, 745; quoted in Waite, *Canada*, 216, and Cook, *Provincial Autonomy*, 55.

304 Lupul, *North-West School Question*, 65, 72, 80, 105, 111, 123, 134.

305 Waite, *Man from Halifax*, 254–5; Miller, *Equal Rights*, 119–20.

306 Crunican, *Priests and Politicians*, 23–36, 41–3; Waite, *Canada*, 246–51.'

307 Crunican, *Priests and Politicians*, 52; Waite, *Canada*, 256–9.

308 Kenneth McLaughlin, 'Race, Religion and Politics: The Election of 1896 in Canada,' 311; Crunican, *Priests and Politicians*, 203–4.

309 Paul Crunican discerns a shift in Laurier's position through 1895 as a direct result of his private debate with J.S. Willison, editor of the *Globe* and a strong proponent of provincial rights: Crunican, *Priests and Politicians*, 68–71. Waite, however, notices that as late as January 1896 Laurier and Mowat were both attempting (unsuccessfully) to obtain a shift in the *Globe*'s stance in favour of remedialism: Waite, *Canada*, 265. In weakly pressing at first for further investigation and then endorsing the provincial rights position for

the Ontario political market, Laurier seems to have been reduced to trailing rather than leading public opinion in Ontario.

310 Laurier, Public Address at La Salle Jacques Cartier, Quebec East, 7 May 1896; quoted in McLaughlin, 'Race Religion and Politics,' 323, 399.

311 Laurier, Address at Massey Hall, Toronto, 12 June 1896; quoted in McLaughlin, 'Race, Religion and Politics,' 401.

312 Ibid.

313 The three conscription-related crises of the following half-century would compromise these alliances much more openly. On divisions within the Conservative party, Ishbel Marjoribanks, Lady Aberdeen, the wife of the governor general, noted in January 1896 that the 'Conservative party is so divided amongst themselves that they dare not call a caucus': Saywell, ed., *The Canadian Journal of Lady Aberdeen 1893–1898*, 303.

314 Laurier's 'sunny ways' phrase is quoted in Waite, *Canada*, 260.

315 Crunican, *Priests and Politicians*, 274; Watt, 'Anti-Catholic Nativism in Canada,' 56. Crunican notes that more than fifteen Conservatives elected were pledged to anti-remedialism (314).

316 The terms of the settlement, here somewhat simplified, were: (i) a half hour of denominational teaching after regular schools hours upon request; (ii) the employment of at least one Roman Catholic teacher, where requested by sufficient parents; (iii) provision for bilingual teaching where sufficient numbers of students warranted; (iv) provision for Catholic personnel in the administration of the education system; and (v) an agreement to obtain mutually acceptable textbooks: Crunican, *Priests and Politicians*, 318 n. 4; William Morton, 'Manitoba Schools and Canadian Nationality, 1890–1923,' 53.

317 Pope Leo XIII, 'The Encyclical Letter of Pope Leo XIII [*Affari Vos*],' April, 1897; quoted in *The Manitoba School Question*, ed. Clark, 218.

318 Morton, *Manitoba*, 56–9. Bilingual education was terminated for reasons similar to the original 1890 policy.

319 Heintzman, 'Creighton and Biculturalism,' 272.

320 Head to Labouchere, 16 June 1857; quoted in Morton, *Critical Years*, 20.

Chapter 4: Ethnic Delegate Representation and the Rise of Official Exclusive Nationalism in Quebec

1 Howard Palmer, *Patterns of Prejudice: A History of Nativism in Alberta*, 9, 46, 78, 168; Peter Ward, *White Canada Forever: Popular Attitudes and Public Policy towards Orientals in British Columbia*, 22, 92–3, 169. See also

Ann Gomer Sunahara, *The Politics of Racism: The Uprooting of Japanese Canadians during the Second World War*, 47.

2 Irving Abella and Harold Troper, *None Is Too Many: Canada and the Jews of Europe*, 50–1, 161, 231–2. Abella and Troper cite a Gallup poll conducted in October 1946 in which 49 per cent of respondents cited Jews as a group of immigrants they 'would like to keep out' in response to an open-ended question.

3 Hubert Guindon, 'Social Unrest, Social Class, and Quebec's Bureaucratic Revolution,' in *Quebec Society: Tradition, Modernity, and Nationhood*, ed. Roberta Hamilton and John McMullan, 29–33; Kenneth McRoberts, *Quebec: Social Change and Political Crisis*, chap. 5. and 'The Sources of Neo-Nationalism in Quebec,' in *Quebec since 1945: Selected Readings*, ed. Michael Behiels, 80–107; Cf. William Coleman, *The Independence Movement in Quebec*, 7–16, 92–5; Marc Renaud, 'Quebec's New Middle Class in Search of Social Hegemony: Causes and Political Consequences,' in *Quebec State and Society*, ed. Alain Gagnon, 150–85.

4 See, for example, Marcel Rioux, *Quebec in Question*, trans. James Boake, 112–21; Pierre Godin, *La poudrière linguistique*, 155–9.

5 Michael Oliver, *The Passionate Debate: The Social and Political Ideas of Quebec Nationalism, 1920–1945*; Fernand Dumont, Jean Hamelin, and Jean-Paul Montminy, eds. *Idéologies au Canada Français, 1930–1939*; Fernand Dumont, Jean Hamelin, Jean-Paul Montminy, and Fernand Harvey, *Ideologies au Canada Français, 1900–1929*.

6 Oliver, *Passionate Debate*, 81, 148–62; Lionel Groulx, 'L'histoire, gardienne des traditions vivantes,' speech delivered 29 June 1937; reprinted in *Abbé Groulx: Variations on a Nationalist Theme*, trans. and ed. Susan Mann Trofimenkoff and Joanne L'Heureux, 146–62. See Lionel Groulx, 'Notre avenir politique: Conclusion,' 345; see also the series of articles in *L'Action française* during 1923 entitled 'Notre intégrité catholique,' including Antonio Perrault, 'Notre intégrité catholique: notre influence extérieure par le catholicisme,' 4–24; Joseph Ferland, 'Le Laïcisme,' 322–30; Paul Gouin, 'Problèmes de l' heure: refrancisation de la Province,' 195–205; Anatole Vanier, 'Problèmes de l' heure: les Juifs au Canada,' 5–24; Esdras Minville, 'L' éducation nationale: les chocs en retour de l' anglomanie,' 195–220; Dominique Beudin, 'A propos d' immigration,' 143–54; Victor Barbeau, 'Le français, langue inférieure,' 214–19.

7 Groulx, 'L'histoire,' 152.

8 André Raynauld, *Croissance et structure économique de la province de Québec*, 71; *Census of Canada* 1961, vol. 3, table 3.

9 Leroy Stone, *Urban Development in Canada: An Introduction to the Demographic Aspects*, 32, 39.

10 *Census of Canada* 1961, vol. 3, table 3.

11 Patricia Dirks, *The Failure of l' Action liberale nationale*; Bernard Vigod, *Quebec before Duplessis: The Political Career of Louis-Alexandre Taschereau*, 215–43.

12 Dirks, *Failure of L' Action libérale nationale*, 33.

13 Ibid., 13, 49–51; Vigod, *Quebec before Duplessis*, 189–99.

14 Herbert Quinn, 'The Bogey of Fascism in Quebec,' 304.

15 Pierre Trépanier, Interview by Gilles Gougeon in *A History of Québec Nationalism*, trans. Louis Blair et al., Lorimer 63. See also Oliver, *Passionate Debate*, 194.

16 Esther Delisle, *The Traitor and the Jew: Anti-Semitism and the Delirium of Extremist Right-Wing Nationalism in French Canada from 1929–1939*, trans. Madeleine Hébert, 32.

17 Vigod, *Quebec before Duplessis*, 160.

18 Oliver, *Passionate Debate*, 181, 189. As for the 'extremist fringe groups,' themselves, they were not as marginal as one might expect, at least measured in terms of passive popular interest. The circulation of *Le Goglu*, a publication dedicated to opposing the 'Jewish invasion,' reached 85,000 (or 3 per cent of the population of the province) in 1930. The active core was, of course, much smaller. The Nazi party of Adrien Arcand had only about 6,000 French-Canadian members in Quebec in 1938: Robert Lahaise, *La fin d'un Québec traditionnel, 1914–1939*, vol. 1, 155, 158, 190.

19 Oliver, *Passionate Debate*, 189–91.

20 Olivar Asselin, *Pensée française*, 195–6; quoted in Oliver, *Passionate Debate*, 190; *La Presse*, 19 June 1934.

21 *Le Devoir*, 16 June 1934.

22 *Le Devoir*, 19 June 1934.

23 Oliver, *Passionate Debate*, 158–9.

24 'Ste. Agathe met le ban sur les Juifs,' *Le Devoir*, 31 July 1939.

25 Oliver, *Passionate Debate*, 193.

26 Ibid.

27 Ibid., 192–3.

28 'Les incidents de Sainte-Agathe,' *Le Devoir*, 5 August 1939.

29 Oliver, *Passionate Debate*, 194.

30 See Oliver, *Passionate Debate*, 62; Dirks, *Failure of L'Action libérale nationale*, 34–5; Mason Wade, *The French Canadians, 1760–1967*, 2: 620, 2: 901–5; Oliver, *Passionate Debate*, 29, 68, 69, 81; Herbert Quinn, *The Union Nationale: Quebec Nationalism from Duplessis to Lévesque*, 2d ed., 37, 40–2, 57.

31 Oliver, *Passionate Debate*, 88–9.

32 In 1937 Groulx stated, 'I hope my political friends will forgive me if I ... say that party struggles – with all their stupid hatred and divisions, with the collective hysteria and distortion of conscience which they foment in French Canada – are as destructive for a nation as any class war ... for a tiny people, the substitution of party for country, party for nation, party mystique for national mystique may well mean death ...': Lionel Groulx, 'L'histoire,' 156. Cardinal Villeneuve attempted to reinforce the primacy of spiritual over temporal objectives for clerical youth movements, and proclaimed in late 1935 that 'no social, economic, nationalist action can be undertaken for itself by the groups in question, but only as a means to the ends of Catholic Action': quoted in Wade, *French Canadians*. 2: 906. See also Oliver, *Passionate Debate*, 100, 136–7; 87–93; 222; Susan Mann Trofimenkoff, *Action française: French Canadian Nationalism in the Twenties*, 84–5; Delisle, *Traitor and the Jew*, 52 n. 48.

33 André Laurendeau, a leading member of Jeune-Canada in 1935, later recalled their reasons for rejecting an affiliation with the party; 'We viewed the ALN with suspicion. Its reformist politicians weren't pure enough for our taste' (Laurendeau, 'Nationalism in 1936 and 1961,' 234; quoted in Donald Horton, *André Laurendeau: French Canadian Nationalist, 1912–1968*, 43).

34 One important exception, already mentioned, was the Program of Social Restoration developed under the auspices of the ESP. Still, it should be noted that Paul Gouin, who two years later adopted this program for the ALN, was not part of the group of lay-people called upon by the Jesuits to translate their own general philosophical outlook into concrete policy recommendations. The political movement thus operated at two degrees of separation from the Jesuits of the ESP: see Dirks, *Failure of L'Action libérale nationale*, 34–5.

35 Trofimenkoff, *Action française*, 60.

36 Omer Heroux, 'De quoi faire réfléchir,' *Le Devoir*, 22 September 1934.

37 Oliver, *Passionate Debate*, 81.

38 Paul Anger, '"Mme Blaschke,"' *Le Devoir*, 16 May 1933; cited by Delisle, *Traitor and the Jew*, 48.

39 André Laurendeau, *Notre Nationalism*, Tracts des Jeunes-Canada, no. 5, 1935, 50; quoted in Delisle, *Traitor and the Jew*, 112.

40 Delisle, *Traitor and the Jew*, 125.

41 See for example Lionel Groulx's novel, *Appel de la race* (1922), available in English translation as *The Iron Wedge*, trans. J.S. Wood.

42 Groulx, 'L'histoire,' 157–9.

43 Ibid.

44 Ibid.

45 Ibid.; Lionel Groulx, *Directives*, 13.

46 Trofimenkoff, *Action française*, 48, 57. Henri Bourassa also made a similar claim for the French language (which he later recanted) in a work published in 1918, *La Langue, gardienne de la foi*. See Oliver, *Passionate Debate*, 27, n. 27 234.

47 Trofimenkoff, *Action française*, 13–14.

48 Ibid., 50–6.

49 Groulx, 'L'histoire,' 159.

50 Joseph Bruchard, 'Le Canada français et les étrangers,' 201.

51 Groulx, *Directives*, 71.

52 Lionel Groulx, 'Le problème économique,' 558–65; reprinted in *Abbé Groulx*, ed. Trofimenkoff, 174.

53 Trofimenkoff, *Action française*, 65–6.

54 Groulx, 'Le problème économique,' 175.

55 'La petite secte' (editorial), *Le Soleil*, 21 October 1927; reprinted in *Abbé Groulx*, ed. Trofimenkoff, 234.

56 Fernand Dumont, 'Les années 30: la première Révolution tranquille,' in *Idéologies au Canada français, 1930–1939*, ed. Fernand Dumont, Jean Hamelin, and Jean-Paul Montminy, 1–20.

57 Note that under the agreement for the division of ridings between the Conservatives and the ALN, the ALN was allocated 60 to 65 ridings, and the Conservatives 25 to 30 ridings. All the same, the ALN won 29.6 per cent of the popular vote overall: Dirks, *Failure of L'Action libérale nationale*, 80–5.

58 Dirks, *Failure of L'Action libérale nationale*, 86.

59 Guy Lachapelle, Gérald Bernier, Daniel Salée, and Luc Bernier, *The Quebec Democracy: Structures, Processes and Policies*, 110.

60 Oliver, *Passionate Debate*, 137; Dirks, *Failure of L'Action libérale nationale*, 65.

61 Quinn, *Union Nationale*, 57; Dirks, *Failure of L'Action libérale nationale*, 35.

62 Dirks, *Failure of L'Action libérale nationale*, 49, 59–60.

63 'Le programme de l'Action libérale nationale,' *Le Devoir*, 13 August 1934.

64 Omer Bédard, 'Mobilisation générale, *La Province*, 7 November 1935.

65 Séraphin Vachon, 'Deliverance,' *La Province*, 31 October 1935. For a flavour of ALN pre-election rhetoric, see also Wheeler Dupont, 'Le Tocsin' in the same issue; Jean Gerin, 'Esclaves ou maîtres: c'est a nous de choisir,' *La Province*, 5 September 1935; 'Le Bras Venguer' (illustration), same issue, formally undertaking to imprison the *trustards*.

66 Dirks, *Failure of L'Action libérale nationale*, 152.

67 Note, however, that Gouin also sought to associate the ALN with a 'national education campaign,' distinct from its 'political campaign.' In spirit, such national education was linked to the prior refrancisation campaign ('to give our French-Canadian country a French-Canadian face'), which Gouin had himself advocated prior to founding the ALN. But in concrete terms, Gouin's carefully hedged proposal as of June 1935 extended only to the inculcation of a Groulxian national 'mystique' through the education system by means of 'contact ... with the realities and the lessons of their [French-Canadian] history and their land.' He also explicitly warned against 'chauvinism' and '"francophilia" pushed to the extreme': Paul Gouin, 'Politique Nationale, Education Nationale,' *La Province*, 20 June 1935. See also the nuanced account of national politics ('to favour our survival and not a struggle of races.' ... 'that can well accommodate the diversity of nationalities and religions') by Philippe Ferland: 'Une doctrine nationale: tel est la doctrine de Paul Gouin,' *La Province*, 22 August 1935.

68 Vigod, *Quebec before Duplessis*, 192.

69 Ibid., 254.

70 Dirks, *Failure of L'Action libérale nationale*, 80.

71 Quinn, *Union Nationale*, 58.

72 Dirks, *Failure of L'Action libérale nationale*, 100, 151.

73 Richard Desrosiers, Interview by Gougeon, *A History of Quebec Nationalism*, 72.

74 Dirks, *Failure of L'Action libérale nationale*, 94, 105.

75 Only five of twenty-six of ALN representatives followed Gouin out of the Union Nationale in June 1936. Nevertheless, Duplessis's first cabinet awarded just four former ALN members with cabinet seats, only one of these, Oscar Drouin, a former Liberal: ibid., 101, 117.

76 Conrad Black, *Duplessis*, 581–603; Vigod, *Quebec before Duplessis*, 32, 77, 253.

77 Dirks, *Failure of L'Action libérale nationale*, 112.

78 Lionel Groulx to René Chalout, 1 September 1936; in René Chalout, *Mémoires Politiques*, 91–2; cited in Black, *Duplessis*, 143.

79 Oliver, *Passionate Debate*, 128.

80 Ibid., 73.

81 Delisle, *Traitor and the Jew*, 89–91; Trofimenkoff, *Action française*, 84–98.

82 Trofimenkoff, *Action française*, 114–17.

83 Dirks, *Failure of L'Action libérale nationale*, 53, 148–9.

84 Ibid., 61.

85 Phillippe Ferland, *Paul Gouin*, 79. Ferland notes that the total circulation of *La Province* in 1936 was only 10,500.

86 Leslie Roberts, *The Chief: A Political Biography of Maurice Duplessis*, 1963), 116, 122–3, 126–36; 147–52; see also Quinn, *Union Nationale*, 137–45; Monière, *Ideologies in Quebec*, 239.

87 Quinn estimates that the Union Nationale after 1944 was able to spend some five to six times as much per election as the provincial Liberal party, their principal opponents. Quinn, *Union Nationale*, 143.

88 André Laurendeau likened the support of English newspapers in Montreal for Duplessis to the toleration of and tacit support for the 'Negro kings' by African colonialists. See his 'La théorie du roi nègre,' 'Bloc-Notes,' 'Théorie du roi nègre III.' On the peculiarities of election finance in Quebec, see his 'Une maladie de la démocratie.' 'Echec de la morale politique dans le Québec.' See also Pierre Elliott Trudeau, 'Some Obstacles to Democracy in Quebec,' 309–11.

89 Roberts, *The Chief*, 62–3, 179–82.

90 Black, *Duplessis*, 581–626.

91 Ibid., 583.

92 Vigod, *Quebec before Duplessis*, 253.

93 Mason Wade, *The French Canadians: 1760–1967*, rev. ed., 2: 1107.

94 Léon Dion, 'L'espirit démocratique chez les Canadiens de langue française,' 34–43.

95 Ibid., 39.

96 Ibid., 41.

97 Pierre Elliott Trudeau, 'Un manifeste démocratique,' 18.

98 See the debate captured in a recent collections of essays: Alain-G. Gagnon and Michel Sarra-Bournet, eds., *Duplessis: entre la grande noirceur et la société libérale*; and Gilles Bourque, Jules Duchastel, and Jacques Beauchemin, eds., *La société libérale duplessiste, 1944–1960*.

99 Raynauld, *Croissance et structure économique*, 44–5, 69. See also Gilles Paquet, 'Duplessis et la croissance économique: une analyse exploratoire,' in *Duplessis*, ed. Gagnon and Sarra-Bournet, 207–28.

100 Raynauld, *Croissance et structure économique*, 71. See also Paquet, 'Duplessis,' 213. For commentary on the postwar labour market economy in Quebec, see Paul-André Linteau, René Durocher, Jean-Claude Robert, and François Ricard, *Quebec since 1930*, trans. Robert Chodos and Ellen Garmaise, 219–27.

101 Raynauld, *Croissance et structure économique*, 62.

102 Linteau, *Quebec since 1930*, 599.

103 Jean-Louis Roy, *La Marche des québécois: le temps des ruptures (1945–1960)*, 363.

104 Ibid., 360.

105 Ibid.
106 Michael D. Behiels, *Prelude to Quebec's Quiet Revolution: Liberalism versus Neo-Nationalism, 1945–1960*, 122.
107 Ibid., 124, 128; Réginald Boisvert, 'The Strike and the Labour Movement,' in *The Asbestos Strike*, ed. Pierre Elliott Trudeau, trans. James Boake, 306–9.
108 Pierre Elliott Trudeau, 'Epilogue,' in *The Asbestos Strike*, 341.
109 Ibid., 346; also quoted in Behiels, *Prelude*, 127; see also Pierre Elliott Trudeau, 'Réflexions sur la politique au Canada français,' 65.
110 Coleman, *Independence Movement in Quebec*, 61.
111 Roy, *La Marche*, 114–22.
112 Behiels, *Prelude*, 168.
113 Coleman, *Independence Movement in Quebec*, 60.
114 Behiels, *Prelude*, 160, 168. The revolution in postsecondary education, it should be acknowledged, began well before 1960, with full-time undergraduate enrolment growing from 0.33 to 0.56 per cent of the Quebec population between 1931 and 1958. Much of the growth was in vocational education. Still, this progression (and endpoint) compares favourably with the increase in Ontario, from 0.33 to 0.42 per cent. Calculated from M.C. Urquhart ed., *Historical Statistics of Canada*, 14, 601. See also Raynauld, *Croissance et structure économique*, 267.
115 Roy, *La Marche*, 367.
116 Behiels, *Prelude*, 151.
117 Ibid., 154; Monière, *Ideologies in Quebec*, 230.
118 Behiels, *Prelude*, 233; Quinn, *Union Nationale*, 131–45.
119 Behiels, *Prelude*, 222.
120 Ibid.; see also Monière, *Ideologies in Quebec*, 252.
121 See, for example, Gérard Pelletier, 'Crise d'Autorité ou crise de liberté?,' 1–10; Trudeau, 'Réflexions sur la politique au Canada français,' 53–70; Trudeau, 'Un manifeste démocratique,' 1–31. See also Trudeau, 'Some Obstacles,' 297–304, and Behiels, *Prelude*, 247–68.
122 'Ou va le Canada français?,' *Le Devoir*, 4–21 December 1959.
123 Richard Arès, 'Ou va le Canada français? IV, '*Le Devoir*, 7 December 1959.
124 Paul Gérin-Lajoie, *Le Devoir*, 12 December 1959. Gérin-Lajoie's analysis foretold the mobilization of public opinion by leading reformers of the first Liberal government of Jean Lesage. Gérin-Lajoie, himself, advanced his agenda of education reform via the very Parent Commission named early in the first mandate; René Lévesque championed the cause of nationalizing hydro-electricity through direct public appeals: McRoberts, *Quebec*, 458 n. 21. See discussion below.

125 Behiels, *Prelude*, 37–120.
126 Ibid., 249–56.
127 Ibid., 120; Quinn, *Union Nationale*, 155–7; André Laurendeau, 'Ou va le Canada français? XIII.'
128 Marcel Faribault, 'Ou va le Canada français? X.' *Le Devoir*, 15 December 1959; Laurendeau, 'Ou va le Canada français? XIII.'
129 Jean-Louis Gagnon, 'Ou va le Canada français? I'; Michel Brunet, 'Ou va le Canada français? VIII'; see also Marcel Rioux, 'Idéologie et crise de conscience du Canada français,' 29.
130 Gérard Bergeron, 'Ou va le Canada français? IX.'
131 Jean-Marc Léger, 'Aspects of French-Canadian Nationalism,' 326.
132 Léger, 'Aspects,' 319. See also his 'Flagrance d'une injustice,' 60–5.
133 Léger, 'Aspects,' 319.
134 Jean-Marc Léger, 'Le salut de la langue française chez nous est lié à delui du Canada français comme tel,' 58–9.
135 Dominique Beaudin, 'La langue française est unilingue,' 206; see also the earlier article by Jean-Marc Léger, 'La langue française menacée au Québec,' 43–58, which is directed mainly at the linguistic proclivities of francophones, but does suggest a Secretariat of Tourism that would seek to give the province an 'exclusively French visage' (58).
136 William Coleman, *Independence Movement in Quebec*, 67.
137 Ibid., 75.
138 David Kwavnick, ed., *The Tremblay Report*, 29.
139 Ibid., 58.
140 Ibid., 19–20.
141 Ibid., 48.
142 Ibid., 20.
143 Ibid., 22.
144 Coleman, *Independence Movement in Quebec*, 77–9.
145 Ibid., 68.
146 Behiels, *Prelude*, 216.
147 Kwavnick, ed., *The Tremblay Report*, 18.
148 Rejean Pelletier, *Partis politiques et société québécoise: de Duplessis à Bourassa, 1944–1970*, 193.
149 For the origins of the term 'Quiet Revolution'see McRoberts, *Quebec*, 456, n. 1.
150 Ibid., 139.
151 Nicole Laurin-Frenette, *Production de l' Etat et Formes de la Nation*, 126.
152 Pelletier, *Partis politiques*, 214–27; Léon Dion, *Quebec: The Unfinished Revolution*, trans. Thérèse Romer, 117; Monière, *Ideologies in Quebec*,

288; Fernand Dumont, *Genèse de la société Québécoise*, 277, 331; Louis Balthazar, *Bilan du nationalisme au Québec*, 111; Marcel Rioux, 'The Development of Ideologies in Quebec,' in *Communities and Culture in French Canada*, ed. and trans. Gerald Gold and Marc Adélard Tremblay, 269–73; Rioux, *Quebec in Question*, 126–41.

153 Pelletier, *Partis politiques*, 194.

154 'Le gouvernement préservera le visage français au Québec.'

155 John Saywell, ed., *Canadian Annual Review for 1961*, 298. See also Gérard Bergeron, *Pratique de l'État au Québec*, 122; and Pelletier, *Partis politiques*, 234.

156 Coleman, *Independence Movement in Quebec*, 155.

157 Guy Frégault, *Chronique des années perdues*, 47–57, 250; Dale Thomson, *Jean Lesage and the Quiet Revolution*, 315.

158 *A Preliminary Report of the Royal Commission on Bilingualism and Biculturalism*, 113.

159 Evelyn Gagnon, 'Lesage: primauté du français sans l'unilingualisme.'

160 Quoted in Thomson, *Jean Lesage*, 320. For an extensive discussion of the content and politics surrounding the white paper, see the memoir of a key participant: Frégault, *Chronique des années perdues*, 159–92.

161 Monière, *Ideologies in Quebec*, 252; Rioux, 'Development of Ideologies in Quebec,' 111.

162 McRoberts, *Quebec*, 458, n. 21.

163 Léon Dion, *Le Bill 60 et la socièté québécoise*, 14–18; 107–25. See also 'Indispensable Collaboration between Public Authorities and Intermediate Organizations,' 124–9); see also Coleman, *Independence Movement in Quebec*, 164, 161–5.

164 Paul Gérin-Lajoie, *Pourquoi le Bill 60?*, 113–14; Pierre O' Neil, 'La bataille du Bill 60 est portée devant le peuple,' *La Presse*, 11 January 1964; quoted in Paul Gérin-Lajoie, *Combats d' un révolutionnaire tranquille*, 267; Gérald Dion, 'Corps intermédaires: groupes de pression ou organismes administratifs?,' 463–77. See also Coleman, *Independence Movement in Quebec*, 164–5; Coleman notes the presumption of a pluralistic society implicit in the Parent Commission and in the Lesage government's move to displace the church with the Ministry of Education.

165 Léon Dion, 'La foi profonde du ministre dans la démocratie,' *Maclean's*, October 1963; quoted in Gérin-Lajoie, *Combats*, 269.

166 McRoberts, *Quebec*, 92–8.

167 John Saywell, ed., *Canadian Annual Review for 1962*, 53.

168 Dion, *Quebec*, 136.

169 Monière, *Ideologies in Quebec*, 253.

170 Pelletier, *Partis politiques*, 212.
171 Royal Commission on Bilingualism and Biculturalism, *Report* (hereinafter cited as *B & B Report*), bk. 3: *The Work World*, 77.
172 Ibid.
173 *Report of the Commission of Inquiry on the Position of the French Language and on Language Rights in Quebec*, bk. 1: *The Language of Work*, 91; cited in Coleman, *The Independence Movement in Quebec*, 191.
174 McRoberts, *Quebec*, ch. 5; Renaud, 'Quebec's New Middle Class in Search of Social Hegemony,' 150–85.
175 *Census of Canada, 1961*, ser. 4.1, Table H9–3. See also Jacques Henripin, *Trends and Factors of Fertility in Canada*, 181–93. This development was observed in Jean-Marc Léger, 'Il faut créer dix, vingt, cinquante St-Léonard,' *Le Devoir*, 4 September 1968, for example.
176 Léger, 'Il faut créer dix, vingt, cinquante St-Léonard'; Bergeron, *Pratique de l'État*, 122–3.
177 Guy Ferland, 'Laporte: une lois reconnaîtra la priorité du français au Québec.'
178 Ibid.; Guy Ferland, 'Sur la priorité du français au Québec.'
179 'Lesage aura une discussion avec Laporte à son retour de voyage.'
180 Marcel Thivierge, 'Priorité au français dit R. Lévesque.' See also Don Murray and Věra Murray, *de Bourassa à Lévesque*, 81–3.
181 Thivierge, 'Priorité au français.'
182 See also Godin, *La Poudrière linguistique*, 13–23. Aquin, a founding member of the MSA, resigned in July 1968 in protest over Lévesque's stalwart opposition to unilingualism. Compare François Aquin, 'Pour un politique étrangère du Québec,' and Réné Lévesque, 'Le chemin de l'avenir (1968),' both reprinted in Andrée Ferretti and Gaston Miron, *Les grands textes indépendantistes: écrits, discours et manifestes québécois, 1774–1992*, 372–8 and 379–81.
183 Pierre Godin, *René Lévesque: héros malgré lui (1960–1976)*, 357.
184 Michel Roy, 'Au sein même du MSA, René Lévesque est contesté'; Godin, *René Lévesque*, 358–69.
185 Roy, 'Au sein même du MSA.'
186 Ibid.
187 Alain Touraine, *Post-Industrial Society, Tomorrow's Social History: Classes, Conflicts and Culture in the Programmed Society*, trans. Leonard Mayhew, 115.
188 Stephen Goode, *Affluent Revolutionaries: A Portrait of the New Left*, 2–5.
189 Touraine, *Post-Industrial Society*, 115–17.
190 Klaus Eder, *The New Politics of Class: Social Movements and Cultural*

Dynamics in Advanced Societies, 175. Eder posits that the new social movements, which he terms 'new middle-class radicalism' after their primary constituency, aim at differentiating themselves from other social groups in terms of interests and values. The movements tend to situate themselves in cultural arenas of conflict and transcend industrial relations. This arena is defined by terms such as 'identity, expressivity, and the good life' (174–5). The new social movements dichotomize social reality (i.e., distinguish themselves from their opposition) not on the basis of access to the means of production, but rather access to the 'social means of realizing identity' (175).

191 Pelletier, *Partis politiques*, 343.

192 See Andrée Fortin, *Passage de la Modernité: les Intellectuels québécois et leurs revues*, 167–233; Pierre St Germain, 'Un certain goût pour la violence,' in *Un certain révolution tranquille*, ed. Jean Sisto, 64–9.

193 Pierre Vallières, *White Niggers of America*, trans. Joan Pinkham, 278; originally published as *Nègres blancs d'amérique: autobiographie précoce d' un 'terroriste' québécois*.

194 Louis-Martin Tard, 'La panoplie du parfait étudiant protestataire.'

195 *Le Devoir*, 26 August 1968. The series on the 'Revolutionary student actions' was printed 3–5 September that year and carried such provocative subtitles as 'The end of the academic mandarinate and the sharing of cultural power.'

196 Fortin, *Passage de la modernité*, 184; Jean-Marc Léger, 'Il faut créer dix, vingt, cinquante St-Léonard.'

197 Godin, *Poudrière linguistique*, 65–86.

198 Donat Valois, 'Québec n'entend pas imposer une solution'; René Lévesque, Speech to Executive Committee of MSA, 11 September 1968; reprinted as 'Le MSA et la crise de Saint. Léonard.'

199 'Classes "bilingues": Québec ne bouge pas.'

200 'L'Affaire St. Léonard ne cesse de prendre de l'ampleur,' and 'Nous tiendrons jusqu'au bout, affirme t'on dans les deux camps.' The organization was the Federation of St Jean-Baptiste Societies.

201 Jean-Claude Leclerc, 'Un compromis à St Léonard.'

202 Godin, *René Lévesque*, 414.

203 Ibid., 416.

204 Ibid., 415–19.

205 McRoberts, *Quebec*, 216; John Saywell and Donald Forster, eds., *Canadian Annual Review for 1968*, 138.

206 Gilles Provost, 'Des milliers d'étudiants descendent dans la rue.' See also Godin, *La Poudrière linguistique*, 318–50; Marcel Rioux, *Quebec in Question*, trans. James Boake, 145–7.

207 On one occasion, 15,000 to 20,000 students converged before the parliament buildings in Quebec and police were forced to use tear gas to disperse a thousand or so militants that pelted police with rocks and molotov cocktails: see John Saywell and Donald Forster, eds., *Canadian Annual Review for 1969*, 58, 100–1; Godin, *René Lévesque*, 421.

208 Gilles Provost, 'Un sondage: mieux on connaît le bill 63, plus l' opposition est forte.

209 Quinn, *Union Nationale*, 251–3.

210 Claude Ryan, 'Une expérience épuisante mais instructive.'

211 Bergeron, *Pratique de l'État*, 122–3.

212 Quoted in Godin, *La Poudrière linguistique*, 320.

213 Gilles Lesage, 'M. Lesage révèle le programme du parti libéral.'

214 Saywell and Forster, eds., *Canadian Annual Review for 1968*, 95; François-Pierre Gingras, Neil Nevitte, 'The Evolution of Quebec Nationalism,' in *Quebec: State and Society*, ed. Alain Gagnon, 10.

215 Věra Murray, *Le Parti québécois: de la fondation à la prise du pouvoir*, 28, 125–8; Murray and Murray, *de Bourassa à Lévesque*, 89–90; Godin, *René Lévesque*, 392–3.

216 Saywell and Forster, eds., *Canadian Annual Review for 1968*, 95.

217 Věra Murray carefully documents the increasing penetration of unilingual policy within the PQ at the behest of the party's rank and file during the party's first five years: Murray, *Le Parti québécois*, 113 ns. 20 & 21, 114–16.

218 Official Language Act, Bill no. 22 (1974).

219 Ibid., secs. 29 and 39.

220 Ibid., secs. 18–23 and 35.

221 John Saywell, ed., *Canadian Annual Review of Politics and Public Affairs for 1974*, 132–3.

222 Quebec, Commission of Inquiry on the Position of the French Language and on Language Rights in Quebec (Gendron Commission), *The Position of the French Language in Québec*, vol. 2, 78. For example, while the commission recommended that both English and French be recognized as 'National Languages' of the province, the 'high public prestige' ostensibly attached to being an 'Official Language' was to be conferred on French alone (ibid.)

223 Ibid.

224 Gendron Commission, *Position of the French Language*, 1: 292. The commission left it to the (perhaps distant) future for French to become the common language of oral communication between French- and English-speaking people, and to become the 'language of written communication' (ibid.).

225 Ibid., 2: 79–81.

226 The report noted, for example that 67 per cent of French-speakers in an opinion sample cited by the report agreed that 'many laws protect the interests of English Canadians to the detriment of those of French Canadians' (ibid., 1: 139).

227 Graham Fraser, *PQ: René Lévesque and the Parti Québécois in Power*, 96; *Quebec's Policy on the French Language* (Quebec, 1977), 107.

228 *Quebec's Policy*, 52.

229 Fraser, *PQ*, 97; *Quebec's Policy*, 52.

230 McRoberts, *Quebec*, 182

231 Charter of the French Language in Quebec, Bill no. 1 (1977).

232 Fraser, *PQ*, 109.

233 McRoberts, *Quebec*, 276.

234 Charter of the French Language, ch. 5, secs. 35–40; MacMillan, *Practice of Language Rights*, 108.

235 Charter of the French Language, ch. 5, sec. 141(c). Emphasis added.

236 See C. Michael MacMillan, *The Practice of Language Rights in Canada*, 104.

237 René Lévesque, 'Pour un dialogue avec les anglophones: René Lévesque compte sur la bonne foi mutuelle,' *Le Devoir*, 26 March 1982; reprinted in *René Lévesque: Textes et entrevues, 1960–1987*, ed. Michel Lévesque and Rachel Casaubon, 315–20.

238 During the same period the total population of Quebec increased by 3 per cent: *Census of Canada, 1976*, ser. 5.1–7; *Census of Canada, 1981*, ser. 5.1–7.

239 McRoberts, *Quebec*, 477, n. 43; Coleman, *Independence Movement in Quebec*, 207.

240 McRoberts, *Quebec*, 389. McRoberts notes that, 'in a sense, it is ironic that Bill 101 should stand as perhaps the greatest accomplishment of the PQ government. As we have seen, René Lévesque and others in the cabinet had always been ill at ease with legislation to regulate language use in Quebec ...'

241 'Un engagement de René Lévesque: À condition de ne pas lâcher sur l'essentiel, Québec sera flexible au maximum dans l'application de la loi 101.' See also McRoberts, *Quebec*, 389.

242 Henri Bourassa, 'Le nationalisme et les partis.'

243 Henri Bourassa, Speech of 27 April 1902, *Le Patriotisme Canadien-Français*, 8.

244 Henri Bourassa, 'Lettre de M. Henri Bourassa à Sir Wilfrid Laurier,' October 1899, in Bourassa *Que devons-nous à l'Angleterre?*, 380–1.

245 Bourassa, *Le Patriotisme*, 13–14.

246 J.-P. Tardivel had suggested that the creation of a 'free, independent, and

autonomous French state' would be the logical culmination of French Canadians' efforts to preserve their language, institutions, and nationality. He had argued that the 'ideal' solution would be for Quebec to withdraw from Confederation, and to return to the status it enjoyed between 1791 and 1840 as a separate British colony. See his 'L'independance.'

247 Henri Bourassa, 'Reponse amicale a la 'Verité.'

248 Desmond Morton, 'French Canada and War, 1968–1917: The Military Background to the Conscription Crisis of 1917,' in *War and Society in North America*, ed. J.L. Granatstein and R.D. Cuff, 84–103; and, J.L. Granatstein and J.M. Hitsman, *Broken Promises: A History of Conscription in Canada*, 22–53.

249 Vigod, *Quebec before Duplessis*, 65.

250 Morton, 'French Canada and War,' 98.

251 Vigod, *Quebec before Duplessis*, 64.

252 Granatstein and Hitsman, *Broken Promises*, 82.

253 Vigod, *Quebec before Duplessis*, 65.

254 Henri Bourassa, 'Isolement des Canadiens-Français.'

255 Granatstein and Hitsman, *Broken Promises*, 82.

256 Oliver, *The Passionate Debate*, 69.

257 Groulx, 'Notre Avenir Politique: Conclusion,' 343, 347.

258 Ibid., 339; Bruchard, 'Le Canada français et les étrangers,' 194–209.

259 Bruchard, 'Le Canada français,' 207

260 Ibid., 171.

261 Antonio Perrault, 'Enquête sur le nationalisme.' 114–15.

262 Maurice Séguin, *L'idée d'indépendance au Québec: genèse et historique*, 60. Note that it was this turn towards French Catholic exclusivism during the late 1920s and early 1930s that alienated Bourassa, who had professed that his nationalism had always been a 'doctrine proper for English or Irish or for French electors' of Quebec, and who labelled the nationalism of the 1930s 'extremist.' The parting of ways culminated in Bourassa's ouster as editor of *Le Devoir* in 1932 and his denunciation in *L'Action nationale* in 1935: Oliver, *Passionate Debate*, 23, 71, 83.

263 Dostaler O'Leary, *Séparatisme, Doctrine Constructive*; see also Oliver, *Passionate Debate*, 142, 170, 203; Seguin, *L'idée d'indépendance*, 61–4.

264 O'Leary, *Séparatisme, Doctrine Constructive*, 17.

265 Ibid., 16.

266 Ibid., 182.

267 Ibid., 198.

268 Ibid., 206–7.

269 Granatstein and Hitsman, *Broken Promises*, 133, 171–2.

270 Paul-André Comeau, 'Le Bloc Populaire Canadien,' in *Idéologies au Canada Français, 1940–1976*, ed. Fernand Dumont, Jean Hamelin, and Jean-Paul Montminy, 122; Fernand Dumont, Jean Hamelin, and Jean-Paul Montminy, *Le Bloc Populaire, 1942–1948*, 85; André Laurendeau, *La crise de la conscription, 1942*, 115.

271 Comeau, *Le Bloc Populaire*, 153, 201; Behiels, *Prelude*, 494.

272 Maxime Raymond, *Programme provincial du Bloc*, 9; quoted in Comeau, 'Le Bloc Populaire Canadien,' 140; cf. Bourassa, *Patriotisme Canadien-Français*, 7.

273 Michael Behiels, 'The Bloc Populaire Canadien: Anatomy of Failure, 1942–1947,' 46.

274 Michael Behiels, 'The Bloc Populaire Canadien and the Origins of French-Canadian Neo-nationalism, 1942–8, 495–511.

275 Black, *Duplessis*, 447–6, 484.

276 Ibid., 447.

277 See Lévesque's speeches to the Quebec National Assembly, René Lévesque, 'Discours à l'ouverture du débat sur la question,' 4 March 1980, and 'Déclaration à la clôture du débat sur la question,' 20 March 1980; both reprinted in René Lévesque, *Oui*, ed. Pierre Turgeon, 267–92 and 293–305; Hubert Aquin, Michèle Lalonde, Gaston Miron, Pierre Vadeboncoeur, 'Réflexion à quatre voix sur l'émergence d'un pouvoir québécois' (1977), in *Les grands textes indépendantists: Ecrits, discours et manifestes québécois, 1774–1992*, ed. Andrée Ferretti and Gaston Miron, 189. See also François-Marie Monnet, *Le défi québécois*, 135; Murray and Murray, *De Bourassa à Lévesque*, 80–3; Godin, *René Lévesque*, 2: 465; and, McRoberts, *Quebec*, 435–6. McRoberts notes the 'clear commitment of the *indépendantiste* movement to cultural pluralism' (436), and that 'in the referendum campaign, the *indépendantiste* leadership projected not a preoccupation with the survival of the Québec nation but a determination that the nation be able to achieve its full potential ...' (435)

278 Rassemblement pour l'indépendance nationale, 'Manifeste,' reprinted in *Les grands textes indépendantistes: Écrits, discours et manifestes québécois, 1774–1992*, ed. Ferretti and Miron, 131–2; see also Réjean Pelletier, *Les militants du R.I.N.* (Ottawa: Editions de L'Université d'Ottawa, 1974), 10.

279 Godin, *René Lévesque*, 377; McRoberts, *Quebec*, 245.

280 Godin, *René Lévesque*, 380, 388–9.

281 Ibid., 389.

282 René Lévesque, *An Option for Quebec*, 14.

283 Godin, *René Lévesque*, 389.

284 Lévesque, *Option for Quebec*, 29.

285 Ibid., 17.
286 Parti Québécois, Conseil executif, *Prochaine étape: quand nous serons vraiment chez nous*, 15, 16–17.
287 Lévesque, *Option for Quebec*, 24.
288 Ibid., 18, 24; Parti Québécois. *Prochaine étape*, 41–6.
289 Lévesque, *Option for Quebec*, 18; Parti Québécois. *Prochaine étape*, 21, 22, 69–85; see also McRoberts, *Quebec*, 247–51.
290 Lévesque, *Option for Quebec*, 21; Parti Québécois. *Prochaine étape*, 15, 16–17.
291 Lévesque, *Option for Quebec*, 22–6, 30, 81–2.
292 Parti Québécois, *Prochaine étape*, 16, 20.
293 Quebec, Executive Council, *Québec–Canada: A New Deal, The Québec Government Proposal for a New Partnership between Equals: Sovereignty-Association*; Gertrude Robinson notes that the PQ's subsequent campaign was 'anchored' in this document: Gertrude Robinson, *Constructing the Quebec Referendum: French and English Media Voices*, 110.
294 Quebec, *A New Deal*, 33–42.
295 Ibid., 21–3.
296 Ibid., 3–12.
297 Ibid., 93, 56.
298 Ibid., 92–3.
299 Graham Fraser, 'Lévesque has changed little since 1967.'
300 François-Albert Angers, 'Notre référendum.'
301 Angers, 'Notre référendum.' Angers led the Front du Québec français, one of 200 active groups, in the struggle against Bill 63 in 1969. At the time of this writing in 1980 he was president of the Ligue d'action nationale and of the Mouvement Québec français, having been editor of *L'Action nationale* after 1956. See Godin, *René Lévesque*, 420, and Behiels, *Prelude*, 94. Angers's submission was quickly met with a sharp rebuttal by a separatist academic, René Durocher, who disposed of Angers's labelling of non-francophones in Quebec as 'foreigners.' Durocher espoused the conviction that one cannot found a modern nation on ethnic origin, any more than on the traditional ties in Quebec between Catholicism and nationalism: René Durocher, 'En reponse à François-Albert Angers.' Between these two extremes it is certainly possible to find rank-and-file exclusive nationalists who have participated in the discourse on sovereignty. Jean-Marc Léger's entreaty for a monolithic French Quebec (demanding that French be made 'officially and practically, the indispensable language, that is, the only language') was actually included (albeit in the midst of a long appendix) within Lévesque's *Option Québec* (Jean-Marc Léger, 'Sovereignty, Condi-

tion of Salvation,' appendix to *Option for Québec*, ed. René Lévesque, 113).
Léger's views have not subsequently softened: see his *Vers l'Indépendance?*
Le Pays à portée de main, a remarkably vociferous polemic for independence
expressing an exclusive nationalism that is 'at once territorial and ethnic'
(60), premised on French bloodlines, not language (60–1), and resistant to
multi-ethnic immigration (81) as well as to minority accommodation in
general (69). Denis Monière proposes a somewhat more voluntarist conception of the Québécois identity and prospective nationality. He associates an
over-preoccupation with language politics with the fact of continued minority status within Canada, implying that independence might present a rem-
edy: Denis Monière, *L'Indépendance*, 76–8, 106–9, 140–1. A relatively
moderate perspective is also articulated in the 1991 manifesto of the incipient
Bloc Québécois, which recommends building a broader consensus for
sovereignty: Bloc Québécois, 'Manifeste,' in *Les grands textes*, ed. Ferretti
and Miron, 307–10. See also Jacques Mackay, *Le courage de se choisir*.
302 McRoberts, *Quebec*, 333.
303 Roy, *La Marche*, 360. Emphasis added.

Chapter 5: Other Legacies of 1968

1 Richard Simeon and Ian Robinson, *State, Society, and the Development of
Canadian Federalism*, 186–9.
2 Ibid., 189.
3 *B & B Report*, bk. 3, 101.
4 Simeon and Robinson, *Development of Canadian Federalism*, 189.
5 Saywell and Forster, eds., *Canadian Annual Review for 1968*, 83.
6 Saywell and Forster, eds., *Canadian Annual Review for 1969*, 9.
7 Charles Taylor, *Reconciling the Solitudes: Essays on Canadian Federalism and
Nationalism*, 182.
8 Simeon and Robinson, *Development of Canadian Federalism*, 190.
9 House of Commons, *Debates*, 8 October 1971, 8580–1.
10 Ibid., 8581.
11 Cf. Evelyn Kallen, *Ethnicity and Human Rights in Canada*, 2d ed. 173–5.
12 Ibid., 172; John Saywell, ed., *Canadian Annual Review of Politics and Public
Affairs for 1971*, 98.
13 Saywell, ed., *Canadian Annual Review, 1971*, 98.
14 Ibid.
15 Ibid.
16 Stephen Clarkson and Christina McCall, *Trudeau and Our Times*, vol. 1: *The
Magnificent Obsession*, 89–90, 108–10.

17 Pierre Elliott Trudeau, *Federalism and the French Canadians*, 156.

18 Reginald Whitaker, 'Reason, Passion, and Interest: Pierre Trudeau's Eternal Liberal Triangle,' in *A Sovereign Idea: Essays on Canada as a Democratic Community*.

19 House of Commons, *Debates*, 8 October 1971, 8580.

20 Trudeau, *Federalism*, 11.

21 Ibid., 29.

22 Ibid., 35.

23 Randall Collins, *Conflict Sociology*, 74–6.

24 Guy Laforest, 'The Meaning and Centrality of Recognition,' in *Meech Lake and Canada: Perspectives from the West*, ed. Roger Gibbins, 81.

25 Trudeau, *Federalism*, 194–6.

26 Although Trudeau has been accused of nationalism (e.g., in Peter Russell, *Constitutional Odyssey: Can Canadians Become a Sovereign People*, 2d ed., 81), his views were clearly antithetical to the *exclusive* nationalism of concern here.

27 House of Commons, *Debates*, 8 October 1971, 8584.

28 Trudeau, *Federalism*, xxii.

29 Whitaker, 'Reason, Passion, and Interest,' 143.

30 Michel Roy, 'Saint-Léonard confirme l'urgence d'une charte des droits de l'homme.'

31 Department of Justice, Pierre Elliott Trudeau, Minister, *A Canadian Charter of Human Rights*, 14, 26–7.

32 Russell, *Constitutional Odyssey*, 73, 93.

33 Cynthia Williams, 'The Changing Nature of Citizen Rights,' in *Constitutionalism, Citizenship and Society in Canada*, ed. Alan Cairns and Cynthia Williams, 113–14.

34 Russell, *Constitutional Odyssey*, 92.

35 Ibid., 82, 92.

36 Ibid., 103–4.

37 Ibid., 98.

38 Ibid., 114; Rainer Knopff and F.L. Morton, 'Nation-Building and the Canadian Charter of Rights and Freedoms,' in *Constitutionalism, Citizenship and Society in Canada*, ed. Cairns and Williams, 152–4.

39 Robert Sheppard and Michael Valpy, *The National Deal*, 75; Whitaker, *A Sovereign Idea*, 224; Russell, *Constitutional Odyssey*, 111.

40 Russell, *Constitutional Odyssey*, 111.

41 Ibid., 112.

42 'Meeting of First Ministers on the Constitution 1987 Constitutional Accord, June 3, 1987,' reprinted in *The Meech Lake Primer: Conflicting Views of the*

1987 Constitutional Accord, ed. Michael Behiels 537–46; José Woehrling, 'The District Society Clause's Critics,' in *Meech Lake Primer*, ed. Behiels, 171–208; Raymond Breton, *Why Meech Failed: Lessons for Canadian Constitutionmaking*; Alan Cairns, *Disruptions: Constitutional Struggles, from the Charter to Meech Lake*, ed. Douglas Williams; Alan Cairns 'The Charter, Interest Groups, Executive Federalism, and Constitutional Reform,' in *After Meech Lake* (Conference held Nov. 1–3, 1990, Saskatoon, Saskatchewan), ed. David Smith, David MacKinnon, and John Courtney 13–32; Katherine Swinton, 'Competing Visions of Constitutionalism: of Federalism and Rights,' in *Competing Constitutional Visions: The Meech Lake Accord*, ed. Katherine Swinton and Carol Rogerson, 279–94; Patrick Monahan, *Meech Lake: The Inside Story*; Pierre Fournier, 'L'échec du Lac Meech: un point de vue québécois,' in *Canada: The State of the Federation 1990*, ed. Ronald Watts and Douglas Brown, 41–70; Richard Simeon, 'Why Did the Meech Lake Accord Fail,' in *Canada: The State of the Federation 1990*, ed. Watts and Brown, 15–40.

43 Russell, *Constitutional Odyssey*, 115.
44 Alain Noël, 'Deliberating a Constitution: The Meaning of the Canadian Referendum of 1992,' in *Constitutional Predicament: Canada after the Referendum of 1992*, ed. Curtis Cook, 74.
45 In addition to the limited language of education restrictions imposed by the Charter, the guarantees provided by the BNA Act with respect to religious education are maintained. However, in the Charter, the fundamental freedoms clause (encompassing freedom of religion) is subject to the override clause. One of the premiers who insisted upon it cited the laws concerning the observance of the Christian Sabbath as deserving of protection from the intrusion of constitutionally guaranteed rights: see Knopff and Morton, 'Nation-Building,' 170.
46 Edward McWhinney, *Canada and the Constitution, 1979–1982*, 102.
47 Quoted in Williams, 'Changing Nature of Citizen Rights,' 121. See also Cairns, *Disruptions*, 98.
48 Cairns, 'Charter,' 24.
49 McRoberts, *Quebec*, 356.
50 An early decision (*Devine* v *Quebec* [1982]) regarding article 3 of the Quebec Human Rights Act, which guarantees fundamental liberties, including freedom of conscience, of religion, of opinion, of expression, peaceful gathering and of association held that freedom of expression did not extend to choosing the *language* of expression. A later decision (*Ford* v *Quebec* [1985]), however, held that language of expression is protected, and it quashed article 58 of the Charter of the French Langue (Bill 101),

the French-only commercial sign provision: Commission des droits de la personne du Québec, Yves Dechênes, *Texte annoté de la Charte des droits et libertés de la personne du Québec*, 2d ed.

51 Jean Chrétien, *Straight from the Heart*, 174; see also Monahan, *Meech Lake*, 18–19.

52 In fact, it is useful to recall that Bill 101 included a provision for reciprocal agreements with other provinces to ensure official language minority education rights in all provinces. As the Charter dispensed with the need for such agreements in order to gain this assurance from other provinces, there was almost an exact correspondence between the altered Charter and the spirit of Bill 101 concerning official minority language rights in education: see Lévesque, *Memoirs*, 289. For a discussion of the shift in Liberal policy see the speech of Warren Allmand, MP, in House of Commons, *Debates*, 1 December 1981, 13589. It must be acknowledged, however, that the capacity of the Charter to intercede against exclusive nationalism in education policy is not *entirely* nil. In July 1984 the Supreme Court of Canada upheld the earlier rulings of two Quebec courts that Quebec must comply with the minority language guarantees of the Charter by opening English language education to the children of those educated in English in Canada (and not merely those educated in English in Quebec, as Bill 101 had had it). Still, this cannot be construed as a significant attack upon Bill 101, particularly given Bill 101's own assurance of reciprocal provision, as we have just seen. Furthermore, by the time of the Supreme Court's ruling, Quebec government had already initiated a measure in 1983, Bill 57, which moved toward the 'Canada clause': see R.B. Byers ed., *Canadian Annual Review for 1983*, 108.

53 Note, however, that Lévesque's position was unpopular in Quebec. In a poll in March 1982, of those expressing a preference, about 60 per cent disapproved of the PQ's unwillingness to sign the constitution: R.B. Byers, ed., *Canadian Annual Review* 1982, 233, 78. Still, it is possible that resistance to the Charter subsequently increased in Quebec as the exclusion of Quebec in the 'night of long knives' became the stuff of legend and a focus of discontent.

54 Sheppard and Valpy, *National Deal*, 144, 299.

55 Ibid., 299.

56 Quoted in Knopff and Morton, 'Nation-Building,' 169.

57 Sheppard and Valpy, *National Deal*, 299.

58 Monahan, *Meech Lake*, 58.

59 In immigration policy, in the selection of the judges of the Supreme Court of Canada, in the rules governing the establishment of new federal programs in areas of exclusive provincial jurisdiction, and in the amending procedures for constitutionally altering the Senate or admitting new provinces, provincial

governments were to gain slightly more weight overall under the new protocol.

60 Behiels, ed., *The Meech Lake Primer*, 541.

61 Woehrling, 'Distinct Society Clause's Critics,' 180.

62 Ibid., 175, 180.

63 According to Andrew Cohen's account, 'most of the premiers thought that it [the distinct society clause] posed no threat to the Charter of Rights' (*A Deal Undone*, 104). It is also worth noting that the Supreme Court of Canada in *Ford* v. *A.G. Quebec* [1988] accepted that the underlying objective of preserving the French visage of Quebec was 'of sufficient importance to warrant overriding a constitutionally protected right or freedom' (Woehrling, 'Distinct Society Clause's Critics,' 178–9). (The ruling confirmed an earlier decision of the Quebec Appeal Court that had struck down the French-only provision of the portion of Bill 101 regarding commercial signs.) Although the sign law was found to be disproportionate in its stringency to the objective in question, this judgment demonstrates that much of the rationale of the distinct society clause had already been promulgated in case law by the Supreme Court. See also the discussion in James Tully, 'Diversity's Gambit Declined,' in *Constitutional Predicament: Canada after the Referendum of 1992*, ed. Curtis Cook, 185. It is an interesting question whether the Supreme Court judgment in *Ford* tolerates official exclusive nationalism. The answer is clearly 'yes,' but in insisting that English be permitted to appear on signs, the judgment limits the extent to which French may be privileged *over* English, and thus at least lessens the exclusiveness of nationalist policies.

64 Michael Adams and Mary Jane Lennon, 'The Public's View of the Canadian Federation,' in *Canada: the State of the Federation 1990*, ed. Watts and Brown, 97–108.

65 *Globe and Mail*, 12 February 1990.

66 Paul Sniderman, Joseph Fletcher, Peter Russell, Philip Tetlock, 'Political Culture and the Problem of Double Standards: Mass and Elite Attitudes toward Language Rights in the Canadian Charter of Rights and Freedoms,' 267.

67 See Cairns, *Disruptions*, 243–4.

68 For other examples of 'anti-French sentiment' see ibid., 242.

69 Hugh Windsor, 'Anti-French Group Drawn to Wells: Poll Shows Many Backers of Premier Cool to Quebec,' *Globe and Mail*, 10 July 1990.

70 Ibid.

71 Breton, *Why Meech Failed*, 74.

72 Ibid., 16. See also Russell, *Constitutional Odyssey*, 143; Philip Resnick, *Toward a Canada–Quebec Union*, ch. 1; Alan Cairns, 'The Charlottetown

Accord: Multinational Canada v. Federalism,' in *Constitutional Predicament: Canada after the Referendum of 1992*, ed. Curtis Cook, 55.

73 Cairns, *Disruptions*, 247.
74 Stéphane Dion, 'Explaining Quebec Nationalism,' in *The Collapse of Canada?*, ed. R. Kent Weaver, 114. See also Fédération des femmes du Québec, 'Are Women's Rights Threatened by the Distinct Society Clause?,' in *The Meech Lake Primer: Conflicting Views of the 1987 Constitutional Accord*, ed. Behiels, 295–6; Woehrling, 'A Critique,' 180, 196; Pierre Fournier, 'L'échec du Lac Meech: un point de vue québécois,' in *Canada: the State of the Federation 1990*, ed. Watts and Brown, 42.
75 Cairns, 'Constitutional Minoritarianism in Canada,' in *Canada: the State of the Federation, 1990*, ed. Watts and Brown, 83.
76 Cairns, 'Political science, ethnicity and the Canadian constitution,' in *Federalism and Political Community: Essays in Honour of Donald Smiley*, ed. David Shugarman and Reg Whitaker, 122.
77 Cairns, *Disruptions*, 204–5.
78 Simeon, 'Why Did the Meech Lake Accord Fail?,' 30.
79 Ibid., 29.
80 Gerald Beaudoin and Jim Edwards, Joint Chairmen, Special Joint Committee of the Senate and the House of Commons), *The Process for Amending the Constitution of Canada*, 53.
81 Simeon, 'Why Did the Meech Lake Accord Fail?,' 31.
82 Cairns, *Disruptions*, 251.
83 Russell, *Constitutional Odyssey*, 163–84.
84 Ibid., 164.
85 Ibid., 176.
86 *Consensus Report on the Constitution*, 28 August 1992, Final Text, 1. See also Cairns, 'The Charlottetown Accord,' 37. Kenneth McRoberts, 'Disagreeing on Fundamentals: English Canada and Quebec,' in *The Charlottetown Accord, the Referendum, and the Future of Canada*, ed. Kenneth McRoberts and Patrick Monahan, 252.
87 Nationally only 10 per cent of respondents cited aboriginal self-government as something they 'particularly disliked' in response to an open-ended question. In Quebec, this rate was slightly greater, being 19 per cent. Omitting this aspect in response to an open-ended question is, of course, not the same as approval, and in November 1992 a majority of 62 per cent of those expressing a preference favoured the status quo. Still, the concessions to Quebec were rejected by a substantially larger proportion outside Quebec, and in most provinces by more than 40 per cent of respondents: Shawn Henry, *Public Opinion and the Charlottetown Accord*, 4–5.

88 Henry, 'Public Opinion,' 4.

89 Ontarians, particularly Torontonians, were somewhat more supportive: 50 per cent approved of recognizing the distinct society and 29 per cent accepted the guarantee of at least 25 per cent of the seats in the House of Commons: Hugh Windsor, 'Ontario, BC not Getting any Closer: Opinions on Charlottetown Accord Divided by Constitutional Faultline,' *Globe and Mail*, 23 October 1992.

90 Richard Johnston, André Blais, Elisabeth Gidengil, and Neil Nevitte, *The Challenge of Direct Democracy: The 1992 Canadian Referendum*, 170, 176–7, 267, 276. Johnston and colleagues report a regression coefficient of 0.67 ($R^2 = 0.16$) between feeling for Quebec and approval for the DSC, and of 0.45 (multivariate regression $R^2 = 0.08$) between feeling for Quebec and the vote. (170, 176, 313 n. 18).

91 Craig McInnes, 'The Invisible Angels of Yes,' *Globe and Mail*, 24 October 1992, D2.

92 Johnston and colleagues found only a very mild relationship between minority rights and the referendum vote. The relationship, moreover, was biased in the contrary direction. Concern for minority rights made one slightly more likely to vote *in favour* of the Accord: *Challenge of Direct Democracy*, 170.

93 Cairns, 'Charlottetown Accord,' 59.

94 Cairns, 'Constitutional Change and the Three Equalities,' in *Options for a New Canada*, ed. Ronald Watts and Douglas Brown, 77; Noël, 'Deliberating a Constitution,' 74.

95 Tully, 'Diversity's Gambit Declined,' 166.

96 Noël, 'Deliberating a Constitution,' 74–5.

97 Murray Dobbin, *Preston Manning and the Reform Party*, v.

98 Henry, 'Public Opinion,' 6.

99 Ibid. See also Johnston et al., *Challenge of Direct Democracy*, 277.

100 Dr Wong; quoted in McInnes, 'Invisible Angels;' Graham Fraser, 'What Does It Mean for Government? How to Decide What to Do Next?,' *Globe and Mail*, 27 October 1992, A1. See also Leslie Pal and F. Leslie Seidle, 'Constitutional Politics 1990–92: The Paradox of Participation,' in *How Ottawa Spends, 1993–94: A More Democratic Canada ...?*, ed. Susan Phillips. The authors observe the presence of a 'widespread mistrust of representational politics' at the time of the referendum (144).

101 Russell, *Constitutional Odyssey*, 219.

102 Resnick, *Toward a Quebec–Canada Union*, 93.

103 Neil Nevitte, *The Decline of Deference: Canadian Value Change in Cross-National Perspective*, 51–9, 77–83, 102–4; Neil Nevitte, 'New Politics, The

Charter and Political Participation,' in *Representation, Integration and Political Parties in Canada*, ed. Herman Bakvis, Royal Commission on Electoral Reform and Party Financing Study 14, 356–62, 371–90.

104 The World Values Survey data were collected in twenty-one and forty economically advanced countries, including Canada: Nevitte, *Decline of Deference*, 20. Both Rosenau and Nevitte cite, for example, Ronald Inglehart, *The Silent Revolution: Changing Values and Political Styles among Western Publics*, as well as the work of Samuel Huntington.

105 Nevitte, 'New Politics,' 375.

106 Ibid., 356–7, 404–5.

107 Citizens' Forum, *Report*, 101, 105.

108 Pal and Seidle, 'Constitutional Politics 1990–92,' 175.

109 Thomas Courchene, 'Death of a Political Era,' *Globe and Mail*, 27 October 1992, A1.

110 Major studies on the Reform Party include: Tom Flanagan, *Waiting for the Wave: The Reform Party and Preston Manning*; David Laycock, 'Reforming Canadian Democracy? Institutions and Ideology in the Reform Party Project,' 213–47; Keith Archer and Faron Ellis, 'Opinion Structure and Party Activists: the Reform Party of Canada,' 277–308; Trevor Harrison, *Of Passionate Intensity: Right-Wing Populism and the Reform Party of Canada*; Sydney Sharpe and Don Braid, *Storming Babylon: Preston Manning and the Rise of the Reform Party*; and Murray Dobbin, *Preston Manning and the Reform Party*. See also Preston Manning, *The New Canada*.

111 Laycock, 'Reform Party Project,' 213–47; Manning, *New Canada*, 6.

112 Sharpe and Braid, *Storming Babylon*, 31–3. For a description of post-materialism and its significance in the new politics see Nevitte, *Decline of Deference*, 12, 28–36.

113 Manning, *New Canada*, 324; Flanagan, *Waiting for the Wave*, 24–5; Laycock, 'Reforming Canadian Democracy?,' 240–1; Sharpe and Braid, *Storming Babylon*, 175–8.

114 See Dobbin, *Preston Manning and the Reform Project*, v–vi, 214–16.

115 Flanagan, *Waiting for the Wave*, 42.

116 Dobbin, *Preston Manning and the Reform Party*, v–vi.

117 For a review of early western populism see David Laycock, *Populism and Democratic Thought on the Canadian Prairies, 1910 to 1945*.

118 David Smith, 'Party Government, Representation and National Integration in Canada,' in *Party Government and Regional Representation in Canada*, ed. Peter Aucoin, 20–33.

119 Sharpe and Braid, *Storming Babylon*, 153; Flanagan, *Waiting for the Wave*, 44; Smith, 'Party Government,' 27.

120 Smith, 'Party Government,' 27.

121 Ibid., 31.

122 George Grant, *Lament for a Nation*.

123 Ibid., 33.

124 Ibid., 32.

125 The concept of political cartel is very loosely adapted from Heather MacIvor, 'Do Canadian Political Parties Form a Cartel?' 319–22. See also Laycock, 'Reform Party Project,' 220; and Flanagan, *Waiting for the Wave*, 40, 43.

126 Archer and Ellis, 'Opinion Structure and Party Activists,' 296.

127 Ibid.

128 Citizens' Forum on Canada's Future, *Report to the People and Government of Canada*, 162.

129 Note that the category 'decision makers' also includes individuals that are on the periphery of the political elite, including officials of two government departments and senior government lawyers. The gap might well have been greater had the category been restricted to cabinet ministers. The low figure of 9 per cent comes from collapsing the 'very important' and the 'somewhat important' categories in Table 1, p. 264. The high figure of 17 per cent comes from comparing levels of 'strong support' in Table 2, p. 267. Although attitudes concerning official language minority rights in education (in contrast with support for bilingual federal services) do not appear to be subject to a wide gap in nominal support, there is a significantly higher degree of 'pliability' among citizens: almost twice as many citizens would change their mind if guaranteeing rights were to 'substantially increase' taxes. See Sniderman et al., 'Political Culture and the Problem of Double Standards,' 276.

130 See Sniderman et al., 'Political Culture and the Problem of Double Standards,' 269.

131 Nevitte, *Decline of Deference*, 28.

132 Ibid., 226, 230–3.

133 Ibid., 234.

134 Sharpe and Braid, *Storming Babylon*, 15.

135 Flanagan, *Waiting for the Wave*, 178.

136 Flanagan, a party insider for several years, notes that Manning is 'frank about the danger that populism will degenerate into xenophobia or racism': ibid., 33.

137 Michael Atkinson, 'What Kind of Democracy Do Canadians Want?' 717–18.

138 Flanagan, *Waiting for the Wave*, 198.

139 Ibid., 196–7.

140 Rick Ogmundson and Lee Fisher, 'Beyond Lipset and His Critics: An Initial Reformulation,' 196–9. Emphasis in original.

141 See also Samuel LaSelva, *The Moral Foundations of Canadian Federalism: Paradoxes, Achievements, and Tragedies of Nationhood*, 193–5.

142 Alan Cairns and Cynthia Williams, 'Constitutionalism, Citizenship and Society in Canada: An Overview,' in *Constitutionalism*, ed. Cairns and Williams, 2.

143 Tully, 'Diversity's Gambit Declined,' 183–4; Noël, 'Deliberating a Constitution,' 74–5.

144 Tully, 'Diversity's Gambit Declined,' 184.

145 Ibid.

146 LaSelva, *Moral Foundations of Canadian Federalism*, 25–7.

147 Russell, *Constitutional Odyssey*, 147.

148 Johnston et al., 'Challenge of Direct Democracy,' 34, 166. The authors found much stronger support (two-thirds of those expressing a preference) for 'letting the majority decide' than for 'protecting the needs and rights of minorities' (one-third), although their question was loaded slightly by asking which of these is more important in a '*democratic* society' (166, 292).

149 Ibid., 230, 247, 281.

150 Ibid., 247.

151 Practically speaking, standing legislation in British Columbia, for example, requires any future constitutional amendment to be subjected to a provincial referendum.

152 A solid start has been provided by Michael Stein, 'Tensions in the Canadian Constitutional Process: Elite Negotiations, Referendums and Interest Group Consultations, 1980–1992,' in *Canada: The State of the Federation, 1993*, ed. Ronald Watts and Douglas Brown; Atkinson, 'What Kind of Democracy do Canadians Want?'; Richard Simeon, 'In Search of a Social Contract: Can We Make Hard Decisions as If Democracy Matters?,' C.D. Howe Institute Benefactors Lecture, 1994; David Cameron, 'Governing the European Community: Executive Federalism Rampant,' in *Toolkits and Building Blocks: Constructing a New Canada*, ed. Richard Simeon and Mary Janigan; 126; and Kathy Brock, 'The End of Executive Federalism?,' in *New Trends in Canadian Federalism*, ed. François Rocher, 91–106.

Bibliography

Primary Sources

Official and Parliamentary Sources

Canada. *Census of Canada*. Vol. 1, 1890–1; Vol. 3, 1961; Vol. 5.1–7. 1976 and 1981; Vol. 4.1, 1961.

Canada. Citizens' Forum on Canada's Future. *Report to the People and Government of Canada*. Ottawa, 1991.

– *Consensus Report on the Constitution*, 28 August 1992, Final Text.

– *Debates of the Legislative Assembly of United Canada, 1841–1867*, Vol. IX., pt. I. Edited by Elizabeth Gibbs. Centre d'Etude du Québec and Centre de recherche en histoire économique du Canada français, 1977.

– Department of Justice. Pierre Elliott Trudeau, Minister of Justice. *A Canadian Charter of Human Rights*. Ottawa, 1968.

– Dominion Bureau of Statistics. Leroy Stone. *Urban Development in Canada: An Introduction to the Demographic Aspects*. Ottawa, 1967.

– House of Commons. *Debates*. 20 May 1872; 14 May 1873; 8 October 1971; 1 December 1981.

– *Journals of the House of Commons of Canada*, 1st ser., vol. 6. (1873).

– 'Resolutions of Quebec Committee.' *Canadian Archives Report*. Ottawa, 1897.

– Royal Commission on Bilingualism and Biculturalism. A. Davidson Dunton, and André Laurendeau, Co-Chairmen. *Report*, various vols. Queen's Printer: Ottawa, 1965–1973.

– Special Joint Committee of the Senate and the House of Commons. Gerald Beaudoin, and Jim Edwards, Joint Chairmen. *The Process for Amending the Constitution of Canada*. Ottawa, 1991.

- Statistics Canada. *Historical Statistics of Canada*, 2d ed. edited by F.H. Leacy, Ottawa, 1983.
- Supreme Court of Canada. *Ford v A.G. Quebec.* 1988.
Parti Québécois. Conseil executif. *Prochaine étape: quand nous serons vraiment chez nous.* Quebec, 1972.
Quebec. Archives nationales de Québec (Ste Foy). *Événements de 1837–38.*
- Commission des droits de la personne du Québec. *Texte annoté de la Charte des droits et libertés de la personne du Québec*, 2d ed. Quebec: Société québécoise d'information juridique, 1989.
- Commission of Inquiry on the Position of the French Language and on Language Rights in Quebec. *The Position of the French Language in Québec*, 3 vols. Quebec, 1972.
- Executive Council. *Québec–Canada: A New Deal, The Québec Government Proposal for a New Partnership between Equals: Sovereignty-Association.* Quebec, 1979.
- Ministry of Industry and Commerce. André Raynauld. *Croissance et structure économique de la province de Québec.* Quebec, 1961.
- Ministry of State for Cultural Development. Camille Laurin, Minister. *Quebec's Policy on the French Language.* Quebec, 1977.
- National Assembly. Charter of the French Language in Quebec. Bill No. 1. 1977.
- National Assembly. Official Language Act. Bill No. 22. 1974.
United Kingdom. *British Parliamentary Papers* 1828 (569) VII. Reprinted in *British Parliamentary Papers: Colonies – Canada*, vol. 1. Shannon, Ireland: Irish University Press, 1968.
- *Hansard Parliamentary Debates*, 2d ser., vol. 7 (1822).
- House of Commons. *Debates of the House of Commons in the Year 1774 on the Bill for Making More Effectual Provision for the Government of the Province of Quebec, Drawn up from the Notes of the Right Honourable Sir Henry Cavendish Bart.* 1839. Reproduced as CIHM 48438
- *Parliamentary History of England*, Vol. 29, *1791–92.*
- *Proceedings and Debates of the British Parliaments Respecting North America, 1754–1783.* Edited by R.C. Simmons and P.D.G. Thomas. London: Kraus International Publications, 1982.

Magazines, Newspapers, and Newsletters

Le Canadien. November–December 1806; May 1831; May–October 1835;
Le Devoir. June 1934; December 1959; July 1960; March and October 1965; April 1966; April–May and August–October 1968; November 1969; August 1977.

Evening Colonist and Atlas. February 1859.
Globe and Mail. Various years.
Maclean's. 6 January 1992.
Le Minerve. September–December 1834.
Montreal Herald. October–November 1822.
La Province. May–October 1835.
Vindicator. November-December 1834.

Other Primary Documents

Angers, François-Albert. 'Notre référendum.' *Le Devoir.* 17, 18, 19, 22 September 1980.
Asselin, Olivar. *Pensée française.* Montreal: Editions de l'Action canadienne-française, 1937.
Barbeau, Victor. 'Le français, langue inférieure.' *L'Action Nationale* 9 (1937): 214–19.
Beaudin, Dominique. 'A propos d'immigration.' *L'Action Nationale* 4 (1934): 143–54.
Bergeron, Gérard. 'Ou va le Canada français? IX.' *Le Devoir.* 14 December 1959.
Bernard, Jean-Paul, ed. *Assemblées Publiques, Résolutions et Déclarations de 1837–1838.* Saint-Laurent: VLB Éditeur, 1988.
Bourassa, Henri. Speech of 27 April 1902. *Le Patriotisme Canadien-Français.* Montreal: Revue Canadienne, 1902.
– 'Isolement des Canadiens-Français,' *Le Devoir,* 26 December 1917.
– 'Le nationalisme et les partis.' *Le Devoir.* 14 May 1913.
– *Que devons-nous à l'Angleterre?* Montreal: n.p., 1915.
– 'Reponse amicale a la 'Verité.' *Le Nationaliste.* 3 April 1904.
Bruchard, Joseph. 'Le Canada français et les étrangers.' *L'Action Française* 8 (1922): 194–209.
Brunet, Michel. 'Ou va le Canada français? VIII.' *Le Devoir.* 13 December 1959.
Brymner, Douglas. *Report on Canadian Archives,* 1–15. Ottawa, 1886–1900.
Clark, Lovell. *Manitoba School Question: Majority Rule or Minority Rights?* Toronto: Copp Clark, 1968.
Cramp, J.M. *A Memoir of Madame Feller.* London: Elliot Stock, 1876.
Dion, Gérald. 'Corps intermédaires: groupes de pression ou organismes administratifs?' *Relations Industrielles* 19 (1964): 463–77.
Doughty, Arthur G., and Duncan A. McArthur, eds. *Documents Relating to the Constitutional History of Canada, 1791–1818.* Ottawa: King's Printer, 1914.
Durocher, René. 'En reponse à François-Albert Angers.' *Le Devoir.* 3 October 1980.

Faribault, Marcel. 'Ou va le Canada français? X.' *Le Devoir*. 15 December 1959.

Ferland, Guy. 'Laporte: une lois reconnaîtra la priorité du français au Québec.' *Le Devoir*. 25 October 1965.

– 'Sur la priorité du français au Québec.' *Le Devoir*. 27 October 1965.

Ferland, Joseph. 'Le Laïcisme.' *L'Action Française* 12 (1924): 322–30.

Ferretti, Andrée, and Gaston Miron. *Les grands textes indépendantistes: Écrits, discours et manifestes québécois, 1774–1992*. Montreal: L'Hexagone, 1992.

Gagnon, Jean-Louis. 'Ou va le Canada français? I.' *Le Devoir*. 4 December 1959.

Gouin, Paul. 'Problèmes de l'heure: refrancisation de la Province.' *L'Action Nationale* 1 (1933): 195–205.

Groulx, Lionel. *Abbé Groulx: Variations on a Nationalist Theme*. Translated and edited by Susan Mann Trofimenkoff and Joanne L'Heureux. Toronto: Copp Clark, 1973.

– *Appel de la race*. Translated by J.S. Wood as *The Iron Wedge*. 1922; Ottawa: Carleton University Press, 1986.

– 'Notre Avenir Politique: Conclusion.' *L'Action française* 8 (1922): 333–48.

– 'Le problème économique.' *L'Action française* 4 (1920): 558–65.

Heroux, Omer. 'De quoi faire réfléchir.' *Le Devoir*. 22 September 1934.

Kennedy, W.P.M., ed. *Documents of the Canadian Constitution, 1759–1915*. Toronto: Oxford University Press, 1918.

L.-J. Papineau and J. Neilson to His Majesty's Under Secretary of State on the Subject of the Proposed Union of the Provinces of Upper and Lower Canada. 1824. Reproduced as CIHM 38456.

Lamonde, Yvan, and Claude Larin, eds. *Louis-Joseph Papineau, un Demi-Siècle de Combats: Interventions Publiques*. Montreal: Fides, 1998.

Laurendeau, André. 'Bloc-Notes.' *Le Devoir*. 5 November 1958.

– *La crise de la conscription*. 1942; Montreal: Editions du jour, 1962.

– 'Echec de la morale politique dans le Québec.' *Le Devoir*. 11 July 1956.

– 'Une maladie de la démocratie.' *Le Devoir*. 13 July 1948.

– 'Ou va le Canada français? XIII.' *Le Devoir*. 21 December 1959.

– 'La théorie du roi nègre.' *Le Devoir*. 4 July 1958.

– 'Théorie du roi nègre III.' *Le Devoir*. 18 November 1958.

Léger, Jean-Marc. 'Aspects of French-Canadian Nationalism.' *University of Toronto Quarterly* 27 (1958): 310–29.

– 'Flagrance d'une injustice.' *Cité libre* 16 (Feb. 1957): 60–5.

– 'La langue française menacée au Québec.' *L'Action Nationale* 45 (1955): 43–58.

– 'Le salut de la langue française chez nous est lié à delui du Canada français comme tel.' *L'Action Nationale* 49 (1959): 56–63.

Lévesque, Michel, and Rachel Casaubon, eds. *René Lévesque: Textes et entrevues, 1960–1987*. Quebec, Presses de l'Université du Québec, 1991.

Lucas, Sir C.P., ed. *Lord Durham's Report on the Affairs of British North America* (1839), 3 vols. Oxford: Clarendon, 1912.

Minville, Esdras. 'L'éducation nationale: les chocs en retour de l'anglomanie.' *L'Action Nationale* 3 (1934): 195–220.

O'Leary, Dostaler. *Séparatisme, Doctrine Constructive*. Montreal: Editions des Jeunesses Patriotes, 1937.

Ormsby, William, ed. *Crisis in the Canadas: 1838–1839, The Grey Journals and Letters*. Toronto: Macmillan of Canada, 1964.

Ouellet, Fernand, ed. *Papineau: Textes choisis et présentés par Fernand Ouellet*, 2d ed. Laval: Les Presses de l'Université Laval, 1970.

Pelletier, Gérard. 'Crise d'autorité ou crise de liberté?' *Cité libre* 2 (1952): 1–10.

Perrault, Antonio. 'Notre intégrité catholique: notre influence extérieure par le catholicisme.' *L'Action française* 9 (1923): 4–24.

– 'Enquête sur le nationalisme.' *L'Action française* 11 (1924): 105–18.

Rioux, Marcel. 'Idéologie et crise de conscience du Canada français.' *Cité libre* 14 (Dec. 1955): 1–29.

Saywell, John, ed. *The Canadian Journal of Lady Aberdeen, 1893–1898*. Toronto: Champlain Society, 1960.

Shortt, Adam, and Arthur Doughty, *Documents Relating to the Constitutional History of Canada, 1719–1791*, 2d ed. Ottawa: King's Printer, 1918

Story, Norah, ed. 'Stewart Derbishire's Report to Lord Durham on Lower Canada, 1838.' *Canadian Historical Review* 18 (1937): 48–62.

Tardivel, J.-P. 'L'independance.' *La Verité*. 12 October 1901.

The Speeches and Public Letters of Joseph Howe, rev. ed. Edited by Joseph Chisholm. Halifax: Chronicle, 1909.

Trudeau, Pierre Elliott. 'Some Obstacles to Democracy in Quebec.' *Canadian Journal of Economics and Political Science* 24 (1958): 297–311.

– 'Un manifeste démocratique.' *Cité libre* 22 (Oct. 1958): 1–30.

– 'Réflexions sur la politique au Canada français.' *Cité libre* 6 (1952): 53–70.

Vallée, Jacques, ed. *Toqueville au Bas-Canada*. Montreal: Editions du Jour, 1973.

Vanier, Anatole. 'Problèmes de l'heure: les Juifs au Canada.' *L'Action Nationale* 2 (1933): 5–24.

Viger, D.B. *Analyse d'un entretien sur la conservation des établissemens du Bas-Canada des loix, des usages de ses habitans*. 1826. Reproduced as CIHM 21200.

Secondary Sources

Abella, Irving, and Harold Troper. *None Is Too Many: Canada and the Jews of Europe*. Toronto: Lester & Orpen Dennys, 1982.

Acheson, Thomas. 'George Edwin King.' In *Dictionary of Canadian Biography*, vol. 13, 544–8.

Acton, John Emerich Edward Dalberg, First Baron. 'Nationality' (1862). In *The History of Freedom and Other Essays*, edited by John Neville Figgis and Reginald Vere Laurence, 270–300. London: Macmillan, 1922.

Adams, Howard. 'Causes of the 1885 Struggle.' In *Riel to Reform: A History of Protest in Western Canada*, edited by George Melnyk, 78–85. Saskatoon: Fifth House, 1992.

Adams, Michael, and Mary Jane Lennon. 'The Public's View of the Canadian Federation.' In *Canada: The State of the Federation 1990*, edited by Ronald Watts and Douglas Brown, 97–108. Kingston: Institute of Intergovernmental Relations, Queen's University, 1990.

Addis, Adeno. 'On Human Diversity and the Limits of Toleration' In *Ethnicity and Group Rights*, edited by Will Kymlicka and Ian Shapiro, 112–53. New York: New York University Press, 1997.

Ajzenstat, Janet. 'Collectivity and Individual Right in "Mainstream" Liberalism: John Arthur Roebuck and the Patriotes.' *Journal of Canadian Studies* 19, no. 3 (1984): 99–111.

– *The Political Thought of Lord Durham*. Kingston and Montreal: McGill-Queen's University Press, 1988.

Almond, Gabriel A., and G. Bingham Powell, Jr. 'Political Systems and Political Change.' *American Behavioral Scientist* 6, no. 10 (1963): 3–10.

Alter, Peter. *Nationalism*, 2d ed. London: Edward Arnold, 1993.

Anderson, Benedict. *Imagined Communities: Reflections on the Origin and Spread of Nationalism*. London: Verso, 1983.

Archer, Keith, and Faron Ellis. 'Opinion Structure and Party Activists: The Reform Party of Canada.' *Canadian Journal of Political Science* 27 (1994): 277–308.

Audet, Louis-Philippe. *Le Système scolaire de la Province de Québec*, v. 3. Quebec: Les Presses Universitaires Laval, 1952.

Baer, Doug, Edward Grabb, and William Johnston. 'The Values of Canadians and Americans.' *Social Forces* 68 (1990): 693–713.

Bagehot, Walter. *The English Constitution* (1867), edited by R.H.S. Crossman. Ithaca, NY: Cornell University Press, 1966.

Bailey, Alfred 'The Basis and Persistence of Opposition to Confederation in New Brunswick.' In *Confederation*, edited by Ramsay Cook, Craig Brown, and Carl Berger, 70–93. Toronto: University of Toronto Press, 1967. First published in *Canadian Historical Review* 22 (1942): 374–97.

Baker, William. *Timothy Warren Anglin 1822–96: Irish Catholic Canadian*. Toronto: University of Toronto Press, 1977.

Balthazar, Louis. *Bilan du nationalisme au Québec*. Montreal: Hexagone, 1986.

Barry, Brian. *Justice as Impartiality*. Oxford: Clarendon Press, 1995.

Beaudin, Dominique. 'La langue française est unilingue.' *L'Action Nationale* 48 (1959): 206–11.

Beck, J. Murray. *Joseph Howe*, vol. 2: *The Briton Becomes Canadian, 1848–1873*. Montreal: McGill-Queen's, 1983.

– 'Joseph Howe.' In *Dictionary of Canadian Biography*, vol. 10, 362–70.

Behiels, Michael. 'The Bloc Populaire Canadien and the Origins of French-Canadian Neo-nationalism, 1942–8. *Canadian Historical Review* 53 (1982): 487–512.

– 'The Bloc Populaire Canadien: Anatomy of Failure, 1942–1947.' *Journal of Canadian Studies* 18 (1983–4): 45–74.

– *The Meech Lake Primer: Conflicting Views of the 1987 Constitutional Accord.* Ottawa: University of Ottawa Press, 1989.

– *Prelude to Quebec's Quiet Revolution: Liberalism Versus Neo-Nationalism, 1945–1960.* Montreal: McGill-Queen's University Press, 1985.

Bélanger, André-J. *L'apolitisme des idéologies québécoises: le grand tournant de 1934–1936.* Quebec: Les presses de l'université Laval, 1974.

Bentley, Arthur F. *The Process of Government: A Study of Social Pressures*, 2d ed. Evanston: Principia Press of Illinois, 1949.

Berger, Carl. *The Sense of Power: Studies in the Ideas of Canadian Imperialism, 1867–1914.* Toronto: University of Toronto Press, 1970.

Bergeron, Gérard. *Pratique de l'état au Québec.* Montreal: Editions Québec/Amérique, 1984.

Berlin, Sir Isaiah. *Four Essays on Liberty.* Oxford: Oxford University Press, 1969.

– 'Historical Inevitability.' In *Philosophy of History*, edited by Patrick Gardiner. London: Oxford University Press, 1974.

Black, Conrad. *Duplessis.* Toronto: McClelland & Stewart, 1977.

Boissery, Beverley. *A Deep Sense of Wrong: The Treason, Trials, and Transportation to New South Wales of Lower Canadian Rebels after the 1838 Rebellion.* Toronto: Dundurn, 1995.

Boisvert, Réginald. 'The Strike and the Labour Movement.' In *The Asbestos Strike*, edited by Pierre Elliott Trudeau. Translated by James Boake. Toronto: James Lewis & Samuel, 1974.

Bonenfant, Jean Charles. 'Sir George-Étienne Cartier.' In *Dictionary of Canadian Biography*, vol. 10, 142–52.

Bourque, Gilles. *Classes sociales et question nationale au Québec, 1760–1840.* Montreal: Parti Pris, 1970.

Bourque, Gilles, Jules Duchastel, and Jacques Beauchemin, eds. *La société libérale duplessiste, 1944–1960.* Montreal: Les Presses de Université de Montréal, 1994.

Breton, Raymond. *Why Meech Failed: Lessons for Canadian Constitution Making*. Toronto: C.D. Howe Institute, 1992.

Breuilly, John. *Nationalism and the State*, 2d ed. Manchester: Manchester University Press, 1993.

Briggs, Asa. *The Age of Improvement, 1783–1867*. London: Longmans, Green, 1959.

Brown, George W. 'The Grit Party and the Great Reform Convention of 1859.' *Canadian Historical Review* 16 (1935): 245–65.

– 'Guy Carleton.' In *Dictionary of Canadian Biography*, vol. 5, 141–55.

Browne, Gerald. 'James Murray.' In *Dictionary of Canadian Biography*, vol. 4, 569–78.

Brun, Henri. *La Formation des Institutions Parlementaires Québécoises, 1791–1838*. Quebec: Les presses de l'université Laval, 1970.

Brunet, M. 'La Conquête anglaise et la déchéance de la bourgeoisie canadienne (1760–1793).' In *La Présence anglaise et les Canadiens*. Montreal: Beauchemin, 1958.

– *Les Canadiens aprés la Conquête, 1759–1775. De la Révolution canadienne à la Révolution américaine*. Montreal: Fides, 1969.

Buckner, Phillip A. 'The Maritimes and Confederation: A Reassessment.' In *The Causes of Canadian Confederation*, edited by Ged Martin, 86–113. Fredericton, NB: Acadiensis, 1990. First published in *Canadian Historical Review* 71 (1990): 1–45.

– *The Transition to Responsible Government: British Policy in British North America, 1815–1850*. Westport, CN: Greenwood Press, 1985.

Bumsted, John. *The Peoples of Canada: A Pre-Confederation History*. Toronto: Oxford University Press, 1992.

Burleigh, Michael, and Wolfgang Wippermann. *The Racial State: Germany, 1933–1945*. Cambridge: Cambridge University Press, 1991.

Burroughs, Peter. *British Attitudes towards Canada*. Scarborough: Prentice-Hall of Canada, 1971.

– *The Canadian Crisis and British Colonial Policy, 1828–1841*. Toronto: Macmillan of Canada, 1972.

– 'The Canadian Rebellions in British Politics.' In *Perspectives of Empire*, edited by John E. Flint and Glyndwr Williams, 54–92. London: Longman Group, 1973.

Burt, Alfred L. *The Old Province of Quebec*. 2 vols. 1933. Reprint, Toronto: McClelland & Stewart, 1968.

Bury, J.B. 'The Science of History' (1902). Reprinted in *The Varieties of History: From Voltaire to the Present*, edited by Fritz Stern, 209–23. New York: World, 1956.

Bury, J.P.T. 'Nationalities and Nationalism.' In *The New Cambridge Modern History*. Vol. 10: *The Zenith of European Power, 1830–1870*, edited by J.P.T. Bury, 213–45. Cambridge: Cambridge University Press, 1960.

Butt, Ronald. *The Power of Parliament*, 2d ed. London: Constable, 1969.

Byers, R.B., ed. *Canadian Annual Review* 1982. Toronto: University of Toronto Press 1983.

– ed. *Canadian Annual Review* 1983. Toronto: University of Toronto Press 1985.

Cairns, Alan, and Cynthia Williams. 'Constitutionalism, Citizenship and Society in Canada: An Overview.' In *Constitutionalism, Citizenship and Society in Canada*, edited by Alan Cairns and Cynthia Williams, 1–50. Toronto: University of Toronto Press, 1985.

Cairns, Alan C. 'The Charlottetown Accord: Multinational Canada *v* Federalism.' In *Constitutional Predicament: Canada after the Referendum of 1992*, edited by Curtis Cook, 25–63. Montreal: McGill-Queen's University Press, 1994.

– 'The Charter, Interest Groups, Executive Federalism, and Constitutional Reform.' In *After Meech Lake*, edited by David E. Smith, David MacKinnon, and John C. Courtney, 13–32. Saskatoon: Fifth House, 1991.

– 'Constitutional Minoritarianism in Canada.' In *Canada: the State of the Federation 1990*, edited by Ronald Watts and Douglas Brown, 71–96. Kingston: Institute of Intergovernmental Relations, Queen's University, 1990.

– 'Constitutional Change and the Three Equalities.' In *Options for a New Canada*, edited by Ronald Watts and Douglas Brown, 77–100. Toronto: University of Toronto Press, 1991.

– 'Political Science, Ethnicity and the Canadian Constitution.' In *Federalism and Political Community: Essays in Honour of Donald Smiley*, edited by David P. Shugarman and Reg Whitaker, 113–40. Peterborough: Broadview, 1989.

– *Disruptions: Constitutional Struggles, from the Charter to Meech Lake*, edited by Douglas E. Williams. Toronto: McClelland & Stewart, 1991.

Careless, James. *Brown of the Globe*, 2 vols. Toronto: Macmillan, 1959–63.

– 'Mid-Century Victorian Liberalism in Central Canadian Newspapers, 1850–67.' *Canadian Historical Review* 31 (1950): 221–36.

– *The Union of the Canadas: The Growth of Canadian Institutions, 1841–1857*. Toronto: McClelland & Stewart, 1967.

Carrard, Philippe. 'Theory of a Practice: Historical Enunciation and the *Annales* School.' In *A New Philosophy of History*, edited by Frank Ankersmit and Hans Kellner, 108–26. London: Reaktion, 1995.

Chalout, René. *Mémoires politiques*. Montreal: Editions du Jour, 1969.

Chrétien, Jean. *Straight from the Heart*. Toronto: Key Porter, 1985.

Christie, Robert. *History of Lower Canada*, vol. 5 and 6. Montreal: John Lovell, 1855.

Clague, Robert. 'The Political Aspects of the Manitoba School Question, 1890–96.' MA thesis, University of Manitoba, 1939.

Clark, Samuel. *Movements of Political Protest in Canada, 1640–1840*. Toronto: University of Toronto Press, 1959.

Clarkson, Stephen, and Christina McCall. *The Magnificent Obsession*. Vol. 1, *Trudeau and Our Times*. Toronto: McClelland & Stewart, 1990.

Coakley, John. 'The Resolution of Ethnic Conflict: Towards a Typology.' *International Political Science Review* 13 (1992): 343–58.

Cohen, Andrew. *A Deal Undone*. Vancouver: Douglas & McIntyre, 1990.

Coleman, William. *Independence Movement in Quebec*. Toronto: University of Toronto Press, 1984.

Colley, Linda. *Britons: Forging the Nation, 1707–1837*. New Haven: Yale University Press, 1992.

Collingwood, R.G. *An Autobiography*. London: Oxford University Press, 1939.

– *Essays in the Philosophy of History*, edited by William Debbins. Austin: University of Texas Press, 1965.

– *The Idea of History*, rev. ed., edited by Jan Van Der Dussen. 1946; Oxford: Clarendon Press, 1993.

Collins, Randall. *Conflict Sociology*. New York: Academic, 1975.

Comeau, Paul-André. 'Le Bloc Populaire Canadien.' In *Idéologies au Canada Français, 1940–1976*, edited by Fernand Dumont, Jean Hamelin, and Jean-Paul Montminy, 121–52. Quebec: Laval, 1981.

Comeau, Paul-André. *Le Bloc Populaire, 1942–1948*. Montreal: Québec/Amérique, 1982.

Connor, Walker. 'Nation-Building or Nation-Destroying.' *World Politics* 24 (1972): 319–54.

– 'A Nation Is a Nation, Is a State, Is an Ethnic Group, Is a ...' In *Ethnonationalism: The Quest for Understanding*, 90–117. Princeton: Princeton University Press, 1994. First published in *Ethnic and Racial Studies* 1 (1978): 377–400.

Cook, Albert. *History Writing*. Cambridge: Cambridge University Press, 1988.

Cook, Ramsay. *Canada and the French-Canadian Question*. Toronto: Macmillan, 1966.

– *Canada, Québec and the Uses of Nationalism*, 2d ed. Toronto: McClelland & Stewart, 1995.

– *The Maple Leaf Forever: Essays on Nationalism and Politics in Canada*. Toronto: Macmillan, 1971.

– *Provincial Autonomy, Minority Rights and the Compact Theory*. Studies of the

Royal Commission on Bilingualism and Biculturalism. Ottawa: Queen's Printer, 1969.

Cornell, Paul G. *The Alignment of Political Groups in Canada, 1841–1867.* Toronto: University of Toronto Press, 1962.

Coupland, Sir Reginald. *The Quebec Act: A Study in Statesmanship.* Oxford: Clarendon Press, 1925.

– Introduction to *The Durham Report: An Abridged Version with an Introduction and Notes.* Oxford: Clarendon Press, 1945.

Craddock, Patricia. *Edward Gibbon, Luminous Historian, 1772–1794.* Baltimore: Johns Hopkins University Press, 1989.

Craig, Gordon. 'The System of Alliances and the Balance of Power.' In *The Zenith of European Power, 1830–1870,* edited by J.P.T. Bury, 246–73. Vol. 10 of *The New Cambridge Modern History.* Cambridge: Cambridge University Press, 1960.

Creighton, Donald Grant. *The Commercial Empire of the St. Lawrence, 1760–1850.* Toronto: Ryerson, 1937.

– *Dominion of the North: A History of Canada.* London: Robert Hale, 1947.

– *John A. Macdonald,* 2 vols. Toronto: Macmillan, 1952–5.

– *The Road to Confederation, the Emergence of Canada: 1863–1867.* Toronto: Macmillan, 1964.

Crunican, Paul. *Priests and Politicians: Manitoba Schools and the Election of 1896.* Toronto: University of Toronto Press, 1974.

Danto, Arthur. 'The Decline and Fall of the Analytical Philosophy of History.' In *A New Philosophy of History,* edited by Frank Ankersmit and Hans Kellner, 70–85. London: Reaktion, 1995.

Delisle, Esther. *The Traitor and the Jew: Anti-Semitism and the Delirium of Extremist Right-Wing Nationalism in French Canada from 1929 to 1939.* Translated by Madeleine Hébert. Montreal: Robert Davies, 1993.

Dent, John Charles. *The Last 40 Years.* Vol. 2. Toronto: George Virtue, 1881.

Derry, John Wesley. *English Politics and the American Revolution.* New York: St Martin's, 1977.

Désilets, Andrée. 'Joseph-Édouard Cauchon.' In *Dictionary of Canadian Biography,* vol. 11, 159–65.

Desrosiers, Richard. Interview by Gilles Gougeon. In *A History of Québec Nationalism.* Translated by Louis Blair et al., 55–65. Toronto: Lorimer, 1994.

Deutsch, Karl. *Nationalism and Social Communication: An Inquiry Into the Foundations of Nationality.* Cambridge, MA: MIT Press, 1953.

– 'Nation-Building and National Development: Some Issues for Political Research.' In *Nation-Building,* edited by Karl Deutsch and William Foltz, 1–16. New York: Atherton, 1963.

Dion, Léon. 'L'espirit démocratique chez les Canadiens de langue française.' *Cahiers d'information et de documentation* (Institut canadien d'éducation des adultes) 2 (Nov. 1958): 34–43.

– *Nationalismes et politiques au Québec*. Montreal: Hurtubise, 1975.

– *Quebec: The Unfinished Revolution*. Translated by Thérèse Romer. Montreal: McGill-Queen's University Press, 1976.

Dion, Stéphane. 'Explaining Quebec Nationalism.' In *The Collapse of Canada?* edited by R. Kent Weaver, 77–122. Washington: Brookings Institution, 1992.

Dirks, Patricia. *The Failure of l'Action liberale nationale*. Kingston and Montreal: McGill-Queen's University Press, 1986.

Dobbin, Murray. *Preston Manning and the Reform Party*. Toronto: Lorimer, 1991.

Doyle, Arthur T. *The Premiers of New Brunswick*. Fredericton: Brunswick Press, 1983.

Dumont, Fernand. 'Les années 30: la première Révolution tranquille.' In *Idéologies au Canada français, 1930–1939*, edited by Fernand Dumont, Jean Hamelin, and Jean-Paul Montminy, 1–20. Quebec: Les Presses de l'Université Laval, 1978.

– *Genèse de la société québécoise*. Montreal: Boréal, 1993.

– *The Vigil of Quebec*. Translated by Sheila Fischman and Richard Howard. 1971; Toronto: University of Toronto Press, 1974.

Dumont, Fernand, Jean Hamelin, Jean-Paul Montminy, and Fernand Harvey, eds. *Ideologies au Canada Français 1900–1929*. Quebec: Les Presses de l'Université Laval, 1974.

Dunn, John. *Western Political Theory in the Face of the Future*. Cambridge: Cambridge University Press, 1979.

Dworkin, Ronald 'Comment on Narveson,' *Social Philosophy and Policy* 1 (1983): 24–40.

Eder, Klaus. *The New Politics of Class: Social Movements and Cultural Dynamics in Advanced Societies*. London: Sage, 1993.

Evans, A. Margaret. *Sir Oliver Mowat*. Toronto: University of Toronto Press, 1992.

Ewart, John S. *The Manitoba School Question*. Toronto: Copp, Clark Company, 1894.

Faucher, Albert. '*Le Canadien* Upon the Defensive, 1806–1810.' *Canadian Historical Review* 28 (1947): 249–65.

Fédération des femmes du Québec. 'Are Women's Rights Threatened by the Distinct Society Clause?' In *The Meech Lake Primer: Conflicting Views of the 1987 Constitutional Accord*, edited by Michael D. Behiels, 295–301. Ottawa: University of Ottawa Press, 1989.

Ferland, Phillippe. *Paul Gouin*. Montreal: Guérin, 1991.

Filteau, Gérard. *Histoire des Patriotes*. 1938–42. Reprint. Montreal: L'Aurore Univers, 1980.

Fortin, Andrée. *Passage de la Modernité: les Intellectuels québécois et leurs revues*. Quebec: Les Presses de l'Université Laval, 1993.

Fournier, Pierre. 'L'échec du Lac Meech: un point de vue québécois.' In *Canada: The State of the Federation 1990*, edited by Ronald Watts and Douglas Brown, 41–70. Kingston: Institute of Intergovernmental Relations, Queen's University, 1990.

Fraser, Graham. *PQ: René Lévesque & the Parti Québécois in Power*. Toronto: Macmillan, 1984.

Frégault, Guy. *Canada: The War of the Conquest*. Translated by Margaret Cameron. Toronto: Oxford University Press, 1969.

– *Chronique des années perdues*. Montreal: Leméac, 1976.

– 'La colonisation du Canada au XVIIIe siècle.' *Cahiers de l'Académie canadienne-française* 2 (1957): 53–81.

Friedman, Milton. *Capitalism and Freedom*. Chicago: University of Chicago Press, 1962.

Friesen, Gerald. *The Canadian Prairies: A History*. Toronto: University of Toronto Press, 1987.

Gagnon, Alain G., ed. *Quebec: State and Society*. Toronto: Methuen, 1984.

Gagnon, Alain-G. and Michel Sarra-Bournet, eds. *Duplessis: entre la grande noirceur et la société libérale*. Montreal: Éditions Québec Amérique, 1997.

Gardiner, Patrick. ed. *The Philosophy of History*. London: Oxford University Press, 1974.

Garneau, F.-X. *History of Canada, from the Time of Its Discovery till the Union Year (1840–1)*. Translated by Andrew Bell. Montreal: J. Lovell, 1860.

Gellner, Ernest. *Nationalism: Five Roads to Modernity*. Cambridge, MA: Harvard University Press, 1992.

– *Nations and Nationalism*. Oxford: Blackwell Publishers, 1983.

Gérin-Lajoie, Paul. *Combats d'un révolutionnaire tranquille*. Montreal: Centre Educatif, 1989.

– *Pourquoi le Bill 60?* Montreal: Editions du Jour, 1963.

Ghosh, Peter. 'The Conception of Gibbon's *History*.' In *Edward Gibbon and Empire*, edited by Rosamond McKitterick and Roland Quinault, 271–316. Cambridge: Cambridge University Press, 1997.

Gibbon, Edward. *A Vindication of Some Passages in the Fifteenth and Sixteenth Chapters of the History of the Decline and Fall of the Roman Empire* (1779). Reprinted as *Gibbon's Vindication*. Edited by H.R. Trevor-Roper. London: Oxford University Press, 1961.

Giddens, Anthony. *The Nation-State and Violence*. Vol. 2 of *A Contemporary Critique of Historical Materialism*. Cambridge: Polity Press, 1985.

Gingras, François-Pierre, and Neil Nevitte. 'The Evolution of Quebec Nationalism.' In *Quebec: State and Society*, edited by Alain Gagnon, 2–14. Toronto: Methuen, 1984.

Glazebrook, G.P. de T. *Sir Charles Bagot in Canada: A Study in British Colonial Government*. Oxford: Oxford University Press, 1929.

Godin, Pierre. *La Poudrière linguistique*. Montreal: Boréal, 1990.

Godin, Pierre. *René Lévesque: héros malgré lui (1960–1976)*. Montreal: Boréal, 1997.

Goode, Stephen. *Affluent Revolutionaries: A Portrait of the New Left*. New York: Franklin Watts 1974.

Granatstein, J.L., and J.M. Hitsman. *Broken Promises: A History of Conscription in Canada*. Toronto: Oxford University Press, 1977.

Grant, George. *Lament for a Nation*. Princeton, NJ: D. Van Nostrand, 1965.

Grant, William. *The Tribune of Nova Scotia: A Chronicle of Joseph Howe*. Toronto: Glasgow, Brook, 1915.

Green, Leslie. 'Internal Minorities and Their Rights.' In *The Rights of Minority Cultures*, edited by Will Kymlicka, 257–72. New York: Oxford University Press, 1995.

Greenfeld, Liah. *Nationalism: Five Roads to Modernity*. Cambridge, MA: Harvard University Press, 1992.

Greenwood, F. Murray. *Legacies of Fear: Law and Politics in Quebec in the Era of the French Revolution*. Toronto: The Osgoode Society, 1993.

Greer, Allan. *The Patriots and the People: The Rebellion of 1837 in Rural Lower Canada*. Toronto: University of Toronto Press, 1993.

Groulx, Lionel. *Directives*. Montreal: Les Editions du Zodiaque, 1937.

– *Histoire du Canada français depuis la Découverte*, vol. 1. 4th ed. Montreal: Fides, 1960.

– *Lendemains de conquête*. Montreal: Bibliothéque action français, 1920.

Guibernau, Montserrat. *Nationalisms: The Nation-State and Nationalism in the Twentieth Century*. Cambridge: Polity Press, 1996.

Guindon, Hubert. 'Social Unrest, Social Class, and Quebec's Bureaucratic Revolution.' In *Quebec Society: Tradition, Modernity, and Nationhood*, edited by Roberta Hamilton and John L. McMullan, 27–37. Toronto: University of Toronto Press, 1988.

Gurr, Ted Robert. *Minorities at Risk: A Global View of Ethnopolitical Conflicts*. Washington, DC: United States Institute of Peace Press, 1993.

Hall, John A. 'Nationalisms, Classified and Explained.' In *Notions of Nationalism*, ed. Sukumar Periwal, 8–33. London: Central European University Press, 1995.

Halpenny, Francess, ed. *Dictionary of Canadian Biography*, vols. 4–7. Toronto: University of Toronto Press, 1979–88.

Hamelin, Jean. 'Le comportement de la paysannerie rurale et urbaine de la région de Québec pendant l'occupation américaine 1775–1776.' *Mélanges d'histoire du Canada français offerts au professeur Marcel Trudel*, 145–50. Ottawa: Éditions de l'Université d'Ottawa, 1978. First published in *Revue de l'Université d'Ottawa* 47 (1977): 145–50.

– 'Conclusion.' In *Économie et société en Nouvelle-France*, edited by Jean Hamelin. Quebec: Les Presses Universitaires Laval, 1960.

Hardy, René. 'La rébellion de 1837–38 et l'essor du protestantisme canadien-français.' *Revue d'Histoire de l'Amérique Française* 29 (1975): 163–89.

Hare, John. 'L'assemblée législative du Bas-Canada, 1792–1814: députation et polarisation politique.' *Revue d'Histoire de l'Amérique Française* 27 (1973): 361–95.

– *Aux Origines du Parlementarisme Québécois, 1791–1793.* Sillery: Septentrion, 1993.

Harlow, Vincent. *The Founding of the Second British Empire.* Vol. 1: *New Continents and Changing Values.* With portions by A.F. Madden. London: Longmans, 1964.

Hartney, Michael. 'Some Confusions Concerning Collective Rights.' In *The Rights of Minority Cultures.* Edited by Will Kymlicka, 202–27. New York: Oxford University Press, 1995.

Hayek, Friedrich. *Law Legislation and Liberty.* Vol. 3. London: Routledge and Kegan Paul, 1979.

Hayes, Carlton. *The Historical Evolution of Modern Nationalism.* New York: Macmillan, 1931.

Hechter, Michael. *Internal Colonialism: The Celtic Fringe in British National Development, 1536–1966.* Berkeley: University of California Press, 1975.

Heintzman, Ralph. 'The Spirit of Confederation: Professor Creighton, Biculturalism, and the Use of History.' *Canadian Historical Review* 52 (1971): 245–75.

Henripin, Jacques. *Trends and Factors of Fertility in Canada.* Ottawa: Statistics Canada, 1972.

Henry, Shawn. *Public Opinion and the Charlottetown Accord.* Calgary: Canada West Foundation, 1993.

Herb, Guntram, and David Kaplan, eds. *Nested Identities: Nationalism, Territory, and Scale.* Lanham, ML: Rowman & Littlefield, 1999.

Hinkhouse, Fred. *The Preliminaries of the American Revolution as Seen in the English Press, 1763–1775.* New York: Columbia University Press, 1926.

Hobsbawm, Eric. *Nations and Nationalism since 1780: Programme, Myth, Reality.* New York: Cambridge University Press, 1990.

Hodgins, Bruce. 'The Canadian Political Elite's Attitudes Toward the Nature of the Plan of Union.' In *Federalism in Canada and Australia: The Early Years*, edited by Bruce Hodgins, Don Wright, and Welf Heick, 43–60. Waterloo: Wildrid Laurier University Press, 1978.

– 'Democracy and the Ontario Fathers of Confederation.' In *Profiles of a Province: Studies in the History of Ontario*, Collection of Essays Commissioned by the Ontario History Society, 83–91. Toronto: Ontario Historical Society, 1967.

– *John Sandfield Macdonald, 1812–1872*. Toronto: University of Toronto Press, 1971.

– 'John Sandfield Macdonald.' In *Dictionary of Canadian Biography*, vol. 10, 462–9.

Honey, Rex. 'Nested Identities in Nigeria.' In *Nested Identities: Nationalism, Territory, and Scale*. Edited by Guntram Herb and David Kaplan, 175–97. Lanham, ML: Rowman & Littlefield, 1999.

Horowitz, Donald L. 'Ethnic Conflict Management for Policymakers.' In *Conflict and Peacemaking in Multiethnic Societies*, edited by Joseph V. Montville. Lexington, MA: Lexington Books, 1990.

– *Ethnic Groups in Conflict*. Berkeley: University of California Press, 1985.

Horton, Donald. *André Laurendeau: French Canadian Nationalist, 1912–1968*. Toronto: Oxford University Press, 1992.

Horton, John, and Susan Mendus, eds. *Toleration, Identity and Difference*. London: Macmillan, 1999.

Hroch, Miroslav. 'National Self-determination from a Historical Perspective.' In *Notions of Nationalism*, edited by Sukumar Periwal, 65–82. London: Central European University Press, 1995.

Humphreys, R.A., and S. Morley Scott. 'Lord Northington and the Laws of Canada.' *Canadian Historical Review* 14 (1933): 42–61.

Huntington, Samuel P., Michel Crozier, and Joji Watanuki. *The Crisis of Democracy: Report on the Governability of Democracies to the Trilateral Commission*. New York: New York University Press, 1975.

Hutchinson, John. *Modern Nationalism*. London: Fontana, 1994.

Jenkins, Terence. *Parliament, Party and Politics in Victorian Britain*. Manchester: Manchester University Press, 1996.

Johnston, Richard, André Blais, Elisabeth Gidengil, and Neil Nevitte. *The Challenge of Direct Democracy: The 1992 Canadian Referendum*. Montreal: McGill-Queen's University Press, 1996.

Joseph, Femia, 'An Historicist Critique of "Revisionist" Methods for Studying the History of Ideas' (1981). Reprinted in *Meaning and Context: Quentin Skinner and His Critics*, edited by James Tully, 156–75. Cambridge: Polity, 1988.

Kallen, Evelyn. *Ethnicity and Human Rights in Canada*, 2d ed. Toronto: Oxford University Press, 1995.

Kant, Immanuel. *Critique of Pure Reason*. Translated by Norman Kemp Smith. 1781; New York: St Martin', 1965.

Kaplan, David. 'Territorial Identities and Geographic Scale.' In *Nested Identities: Nationalism, Territory, and Scale*, edited by Guntram Herb and David Kaplan, 31–49. Lanham, MD: Rowman & Littlefield, 1999.

Keating, Michael. *Nations against the State: The New Politics of Nationalism in Quebec, Catalonia, and Scotland*. New York: St Martin's, 1996.

Kedourie, Elie. *Nationalism*, 4th ed. Oxford: Blackwell, 1993.

Kellner, Hans. 'Introduction: Describing Redescriptions.' In *A New Philosophy of History*, edited by Frank Ankersmit and Hans Kellner, 1–18. London: Reaktion, 1995.

Kennedy, W.P.M. *The Constitution of Canada, 1534–1937, An Introduction to Its Development, Law and Custom*. 2d ed. London: Oxford University Press, 1938.

Kingsford, William. *The History of Canada*, vols. 4 and 5. Toronto: Rowsell & Hutchison, 1890–92.

Knopff, Rainer, and F.L. Morton. 'Nation-building and the Canadian Charter of Rights and Freedoms.' In *Constitutionalism, Citizenship and Society in Canada*, edited by Alan C. Cairns and Cynthia Williams, 133–82. Toronto: University of Toronto Press, 1985.

Knox, Bruce. 'The British Government, Sir Edmund Head, and British North American Confederation, 1858.' *Journal of Imperial and Commonwealth History* 4 (1976): 206–17.

– 'The Rise of Colonial Federation as an Object of British Policy, 1850–1870.' *The Journal of British Studies* 11 (1971): 92–112.

Kohn, Hans. *The Idea of Nationalism: A Study in Its Origins and Background*. New York: Macmillan, 1961.

Kukathas, Chandran. 'Are there Any Cultural Rights?' In *The Rights of Minority Cultures*, edited by Will Kymlicka, 228–56. New York: Oxford University Press, 1995.

– 'Cultural Toleration.' In *Ethnicity and Group Rights*, edited by Will Kymlicka and Ian Shapiro, 69–104. New York: New York University Press, 1997.

Kulisek, Larry. 'D'Alton McCarthy.' In *Dictionary of Canadian Biography*, vol. 12, 578–88.

Kwavnick, David, ed. *The Tremblay Report*. Toronto: McClelland & Stewart, 1973.

Kymlicka, Will. *Finding Our Way: Rethinking Ethnocultural Relations in Canada*. Toronto: Oxford University Press, 1998.

– *Liberalism, Community, and Culture*. Oxford, Clarendon Press, 1989.
– *Multicultural Citizenship: A Liberal Theory of Minority Rights*. Oxford: Clarendon Press, 1995.
Lachapelle, Guy, Gérald Bernier, Daniel Salée, and Luc Bernier. *The Quebec Democracy: Structures, Processes and Policies*. Toronto: McGraw-Hill Ryerson, 1993.
Laforest, Guy. 'The Meaning and Centrality of Recognition.' In *Meech Lake and Canada: Perspectives from the West*, edited by Roger Gibbins, 73–90. Edmonton: Academic, 1988.
Lahaise, Robert. *La fin d'un Québec traditionnel, 1914–1939*, vol. 1. Montreal: Hexagone, 1994.
Langford, Paul. *A Polite and Commercial People, England, 1727–1783*. Oxford: Clarendon Press, 1989.
Laqueur, Walter. *Fascism: Past, Present, Future*. New York: Oxford University Press, 1996.
Laselva, Samuel. *The Moral Foundations of Canadian Federalism: Paradoxes, Achievements, and Tragedies of Nationhood*. Montreal: McGill-Queen's University Press, 1996.
Laurin-Frenette, Nicole. *Production de l'État et Formes de la Nation*. Montreal: Nouvelle Optique, 1978.
Lawson, Philip. *The Imperial Challenge: Quebec and Britain in the Age of the American Revolution*. Montreal: McGill-Queen's University Press, 1989.
Léger, Jean-Marc. 'Sovereignty, Condition of Salvation.' Appendix to *An Option for Québec* by René Lévesque, 108–117. Toronto: McClelland & Stewart, 1968.
– *Vers l'Indépendance? Le Pays à Portée de Main*. Montreal: Leméac Éditeur, 1993.
Lévesque, René. *Memoirs*. Translated by Philip Stratford. Toronto: McClelland & Stewart, 1986.
– *My Québec*. Translated by Gaynor Fitzpatrick. Toronto: Methuen, 1979.
– *Oui*. Edited by Pierre Turgeon. Montreal: Éditions de l'homme, 1980.
– *An Option for Quebec*. Translator unknown. Toronto: McClelland & Stewart, 1968.
Lijphart, Arend. *Democracy in Plural Societies*. New Haven, CT: Yale University Press, 1977.
– *The Politics of Accommodation: Pluralism and Democracy in the Netherlands*. Berkeley: University of California Press, 1968.
– *Power-Sharing in South Africa*. Berkeley: Institute of International Studies, University of California, 1985.
Linteau, Paul-André, René Durocher, Jean-Claude Robert, and François Ricard.

Quebec since 1930. Translated by Robert Chodos and Ellen Garmaise. Toronto: Lorimer, 1991.

Lipset, Seymour Martin. *Political Man: The Social Bases of Politics.* Garden City: Anchor Books, 1960.

– *Continental Divide: The Values and Institutions of the United States and Canada.* Toronto: Canadian–American Committee, 1989.

Lowe, John. *The Concert of Europe: International Relations 1814–70.* London: Hodder & Stoughton, 1990.

Lupul, Manoly. *The Roman Catholic Church and the North-West School Question: A Study in Church-State Relations in Western Canada, 1875–1905.* Toronto: University of Toronto Press, 1974.

Lustick, Ian. 'Stability in Deeply Divided Societies: Consociationalism versus Control.' *World Politics* 31 (1979): 325–44

Mackay, Jacques. *Le courage de se choisir.* Montreal: L'Hexagone, 1983.

MacMillan, C. Michael. *The Practice of Language Rights in Canada.* Toronto: University of Toronto Press, 1998.

MacNaughton, Katherine. *The Development of the Theory and Practice of Education in New Brunswick, 1784–1900: A Study in Historical Background.* Fredericton: University of New Brunswick, 1947.

Manning, Helen Taft. *The Revolt of French Canada, 1800–1835: A Chapter in the History of the British Commonwealth.* London: Macmillan, 1962.

Manning, Preston. *The New Canada.* Toronto: Macmillan Canada, 1992.

Martin, Ged. 'Attacking the Durham Myth: Seventeen Years On.' *Journal of Canadian Studies* 25 (1990): 39–59.

– *Britain and the Origins of Canadian Confederation, 1837–67.* Vancouver: UBC Press, 1995; London: Macmillan, 1995.

– 'The Case against Canadian Confederation 1864–1867.' In *The Causes of Canadian Confederation*, edited by Ged Martin, 19–49. Fredericton, NB: Acadiensis, 1990.

– 'Confederation Rejected: The British Debate on Canada, 1837–1840.' *Journal of Imperial and Commonwealth History* 11 (1982): 44–6.

– *The Durham Report and British Policy: A Critical Essay.* Cambridge: Cambridge University Press, 1972.

– 'History as Science or Literature: Explaining Canadian Confederation, 1858–1867.' Canada House Lecture Series no. 41 (1989).

Martin, K.L.P. 'The Union Bill of 1822.' *Canadian Historical Review* 5 (1924): 42–51.

Matthews, John. 'Gibbon and the Later Roman Empire: Causes and Circumstances.' In *Edward Gibbon and Empire*, edited by Rosamond McKitterick and Roland Quinault, 12–33. Cambridge: Cambridge University Press, 1997.

McConnell, William. *Commentary on the* British North American Act. Toronto: Macmillan, 1977.

McLaughlin, Kenneth. 'Race, Religion and Politics: the Election of 1896 in Canada.' PhD diss., University of Toronto, 1974.

McLeod, Keith. 'Politics, Schools and the French Language, 1881–1931.' In *Shaping the Schools of the Canadian West*, edited by David Jones, Nancy Sheehan, and Robert Stamp. Calgary: Detselig Enterprises, 1979.

McNairn, Jeffrey. 'Publius of the North: Tory Republicanism and the American Constitution in Upper Canada, 1848–54.' *Canadian Historical Review* 77 (1996): 504–37.

McRae, Kenneth. 'Canada: Reflections on Two Conflicts.' In *Conflict and Peacemaking*, edited by Joseph V. Montville. Lexington, MA: Lexington Books, 1990.

McRoberts, Kenneth. 'Disagreeing on Fundamentals: English Canada and Quebec.' In *The Charlottetown Accord, the Referendum, and the Future of Canada*, edited by Kenneth McRoberts and Patrick Monahan. Toronto: University of Toronto Press, 1993.

– *Quebec: Social Change and Political Crisis*. Toronto: McClelland & Stewart, 1988.

– 'The Sources of Neo-Nationalism in Quebec.' In *Quebec since 1945: Selected Readings*, edited by Michael D. Behiels, 80–107. Toronto: Copp Clark Pitman, 1987.

McWhinney, Edward. *Canada and the Constitution, 1979–1982*. Toronto: University of Toronto Press, 1982.

Meadwell, Hudson. 'Breaking the Mould? Quebec Independence and Secession in the Developed West.' In *Notions of Nationalism*, edited by Sukumur Periwal. London: Central European University Press, 1995.

Megill, Allan. '"Grand Narrative" and the Discipline of History.' In *A New Philosophy of History*, edited by Frank Ankersmit and Hans Kellner, 151–73. London: Reaktion, 1995.

Mill, J.S. *Considerations on Representative Government* (1861). Edited by Currin V. Shields. Indianapolis: Bobbs-Merrill, 1958.

– *On Liberty* (1859). Edited by David Spitz. New York: W.W. Norton, 1975.

Miller, David. 'Group Identities, National Identities and Democratic Politics.' In *Toleration, Identity and Difference*, edited by John Horton and Susan Mendus, 103–25. London: Macmillan, 1999.

Miller, James. 'Anti-Catholic Thought in Victorian Canada.' *Canadian Historical Review* 66 (1985): 474–94.

– 'D'Alton McCarthy, Equal Rights, and the Origins of the Manitoba School Question.' *Canadian Historical Review* 54 (1973): 369–92.

- 'D'Alton McCarthy, Jr.: A Protestant Irishman Abroad.' In *Boswell's Children: The Art of the Biographer*, ed. Ray Fleming, 191–203. Toronto: Dundurn, 1992.
- *Equal Rights: The Jesuits' Estates Act Controversy*. Montreal: McGill-Queen's University Press, 1979.
- 'The Jesuits' Estates Act Crisis: "An Incident in a Conspiracy of Several Years' Standing,"' *Journal of Canadian Studies* 9 (1974): 36–50.
- '"As a Politician He Is a Great Enigma": The Social and Political Ideas of D'Alton McCarthy.' *Canadian Historical Review* 58 (1977): 399–422.
Milobar, David. 'Conservative Ideology, Metropolitan Government, and the Reform of Quebec, 1782–1791.' *International History Review* 12 (1990): 45–64.
Minogue, Kenneth. 'Method in Intellectual History: Quentin Skinner's *Foundations*' (1981). Reprinted in *Meaning and Context: Quentin Skinner and His Critics*, edited by James Tully, 176–93. Cambridge: Polity, 1988.
Moir, John. *Church and State in Canada West: Three Studies in the Relation of Denominationalism and Nationalism, 1841–1867*. Toronto: University of Toronto Press, 1959.
Monahan, Patrick. *Meech Lake: The Inside Story*. Toronto: University of Toronto Press, 1991.
Monet, Jacques. *The Last Cannon Shot: A Study of French-Canadian Nationalism, 1837–1850*. Toronto: University of Toronto Press, 1969.
Monière, Denis. *Ideologies in Quebec: The Historical Development*. Translated by Richard Howard. Toronto: University of Toronto Press, 1981.
- *L'Indépendance*. Montreal: Éditions Québec, 1992.
Monnet, François-Marie. *Le défi québécois.* Paris: Éditions Robert Laffont, 1977.
Montcalm, Mary Beth. 'Quebec Nationalism in Comparative Perspective.' In *Quebec: State and Society*, edited by Alain Gagnon, 45–58. Toronto: Methuen, 1984.
Morrell, William. *British Colonial Policy in the Age of Peel and Russell*. Oxford: Oxford University Press, 1930.
Morton, Desmond. 'French Canada and War, 1968–1917: the Military Background to the Conscription Crisis of 1917.' In *War and Society in North America*, edited by J.L. Granatstein and R.D. Cuff, 84–103. Toronto: Thomas Nelson, 1971.
Morton, William. 'Confederation, 1870–1896: the End of the Macdonaldian Constitution and the Return to Duality.' *Journal of Canadian Studies* 1 (1966): 11–24.
- *The Critical Years: The Union of British North America, 1857–1873*. Toronto: McClelland & Stewart, 1964.
- *Manitoba: A History*, 2d ed. Toronto: University of Toronto Press, 1967.

– 'Manitoba Schools and Canadian Nationality 1890–1923.' *Report of the Annual Meeting*, Canadian Historical Association (1951): 51–9.

Murphy, Alexander. 'Rethinking the Concept of European Identity.' In *Nested Identities: Nationalism, Territory, and Scale*, edited by Guntram Herb and David Kaplan, 53–73. Lanham, ML: Rowman & Littlefield, 1999.

Murray, Don, and Vera Murray. *de Bourassa à Levesque*. Montreal: Quinze, 1978.

Murray, Vera. *Le Parti québécois: de la fondation à la prise du pouvoir*. Montreal: Hurtubise, 1976.

Nagel, Thomas. 'Moral Conflict and Political Legitimacy.' *Philosophy and Public Affairs* 16 (1987): 215–40.

Nairn, Tom. *The Break-Up of Britain: Crisis and Neo-Nationalism*. London: NLB, 1977.

Neatby, Hilda. *Quebec: The Revolutionary Age*. Toronto: McClelland & Stewart, 1966.

– *The Quebec Act: Protest and Policy*. Scarborough: Prentice-Hall, 1972.

Nelson, Ralph, Walter Soderlund, Ronald Wagenberg, and Donald Briggs. 'Canadian Confederation as a Case Study in Community Formation.' In *The Causes of Canadian Confederation*, ed. Ged Martin, 50–85. Fredericton, NB: Acadiensis, 1990.

New, Chester. *Lord Durham's Mission to Canada*. An abridgement of *Lord Durham: A Biography of John George Lambton, First Earl of Durham*, edited by H.W. McCready. Toronto: McClelland & Stewart, 1963.

Newman, Gerald. *The Rise of English Nationalism: A Cultural History, 1740–1830*. New York: St Martin's, 1987.

Nicholls, A.J. 'Germany.' In *European Fascism*, edited by S.J. Woolf, 61–87. London: Weidenfeld & Nicolson, 1968.

Nodia, Ghia. 'Nationalism and Democracy.' In *Nationalism, Ethnic Conflict, and Democracy*, edited by Larry Diamond and Marc F. Plattner, 3–22. Baltimore: Johns Hopkins University Press, 1994.

Noël, Alain. 'Deliberating a Constitution: The Meaning of the Canadian Referendum of 1992.' In *Constitutional Predicament: Canada after the Referendum of 1992*, edited by Curtis Cook, 64–80. Montreal: McGill-Queen's University Press, 1994.

Nordlinger, Eric A. *Conflict Regulation in Divided Societies*. Occasional Papers in International Affairs, no. 29. Cambridge, MA: Center for International Affairs, Harvard University, 1972.

Ogmundson, Rick, and Lee Fisher. 'Beyond Lipset and His Critics: An Initial Reformulation.' *Canadian Review of Sociology and Anthropology* 31 (1994): 196–9.

Oliver, Michael. *The Passionate Debate: The Social and Political Ideas of Quebec Nationalism, 1920–1945.* Montreal: Véhicule Press, 1991.

Ormsby, William. 'Lord Durham and the Assimilation of French Canada.' In *On Canada: Essays in Honour of Frank H. Underhill*, edited by Norman Penlington, 37–53. Toronto: University of Toronto Press, 1971.

– *The Emergence of the Federal Concept in Canada, 1839–1845.* Toronto: University of Toronto Press, 1969.

O'Sullivan, Katherine. *First World Nationalisms: Class and Ethnic Politics in Northern Ireland and Quebec.* Chicago, University of Chicago Press, 1986.

Ouellet, Fernand. *Economic and Social History of Quebec, 1760–1850: Structures and Conjonctures.* Translated by Institute of Canadian Studies. Ottawa: Gage, 1980. Originally published as *Histoire économique et sociale du Québec, 1760–1850: Structures et conjuncture.* Ottawa: Fides, 1966.

– *Lower Canada, 1791–1840: Social Change and Nationalism.* Translated by Patricia Claxton. Toronto: McClelland & Stewart, 1980.

– 'Papineau dans la révolution de 1837–1838.' In *Constitutionalism and Nationalism in Lower Canada*, edited by Ramsay Cook, Craig Brown, and Carl Berger, 75–94. Toronto: University of Toronto Press, 1969.

Oury, Guy-Marie. *Mgr Briand: Évêque de Québec et les problèmes de son Époque.* Sablé-sur-Sarthe, France: Les Éditions de Solesmes, 1985.

Owram, Douglas, ed. *Confederation to the Present.* Vol. 2 of *Canadian History: A Reader's Guide.* Toronto: University of Toronto Press, 1994.

– 'Disillusionment: Regional Discontent in the 1880s.' In *Riel to Reform: A History of Protest in Western Canada*, edited by George Melnyk, 86–105. Saskatoon: Fifth House, 1992.

Pacquet, Gilles. 'Duplessis et la croissance économique: une analyse exploratoire.' In *Duplessis: entre la grande noirceur et la société libérale*, edited by Alain-G. Gagnon and Michel Sarra-Bournet. Montreal: Éditions Québec Amérique, 1997.

Palmer, Howard. *Patterns of Prejudice: A History of Nativism in Alberta.* Toronto: McClelland & Stewart, 1982.

Pappalardo, Adriano. 'The Conditions for Consociational Democracy: A Logical and Empirical Critique.' *European Journal of Political Research* 9 (1981): 365–90.

Paquet, Gilles, and Wallot, J.P. *Lower Canada at the Turn of the Nineteenth Century.* Ottawa: Canadian Historical Association, 1988.

Parker, W.H. 'A New Look at the Unrest in Lower Canada in the 1830's,' *Canadian Historial Review* 40 (1959). Reprinted in *Constitutionalism and Nationalism in Lower Canada*, edited by Ramsay Cook, Craig Brown, and Carl Berger, 58–66. Toronto: University of Toronto Press, 1969.

Parkman, Francis. *The Old Régime in Canada*. Boston: Little Brown, 1874.

Pešić, Vesna. 'The Cruel Face of Nationalism.' In *Nationalism, Ethnic Conflict, and Democracy*, edited by Larry Diamond and Marc F. Plattner, 132–6. Baltimore: Johns Hopkins University Press, 1994.

Pelletier, Réjean. *Les militants du R.I.N.* Ottawa: Editions de L'Université d'Ottawa, 1974.

– *Partis politiques et société québécoise: de Duplessis à Bourassa, 1944–1970*. Montreal: Éditions Québec/Amérique, 1989.

Perkin, Harold. *The Origins of Modern English Society, 1780–1880*. London: Routledge & Kegan Paul, 1969.

Pfaff, William. *Civilization and the Furies of Nationalism*. New York: Simon & Schuster, 1993.

Plamenatz, John. 'Two Types of Nationalism.' In *Nationalism: The Nature and Evolution of an Idea*, edited by Eugene Kamenka. Canberra: Australian National University Press, 1973.

Pogge, Thomas. 'Group Rights and Ethnicity.' In *Ethnicity and Group Rights*, edited by Will Kymlicka and Ian Shapiro, 187–221. New York: New York University Press, 1997.

Popper, Karl. *The Poverty of Historicism*. London: Routledge & Kegan Paul, 1957.

Pryke, Kenneth G. *Nova Scotia and Confederation*. Toronto: University of Toronto Press, 1979. Quinn, Herbert. 'The Bogey of Fascism in Quebec.' *Dalhousie Review* 18 (1938): 301–8.

– *The Union Nationale: Quebec Nationalism from Duplessis to Lévesque*, 2d ed. Toronto: University of Toronto Press, 1979.

Radforth, Ian. 'Sydenham and Utilitarian Reform.' In *Colonial Leviathan: State Formation in Mid-Nineteenth-Century Canada*, edited by Allan Greer and Ian Radforth, 64–102. Toronto: University of Toronto Press, 1989.

Rawls, John. 'Justice as Fairness: Political Not Metaphysical.' *Philosophy and Public Affairs* 14 (1985): 223–51.

– *Political Liberalism*. New York: Columbia University Press, 1993.

Raz, Joseph. *The Morality of Freedom*. Oxford: Clarendon Press, 1986.

Rea, James. 'Thomas Greenway.' In *Dictionary of Canadian Biography*, vol. 13, 416–23.

Renaud, Marc. 'Quebec's New Middle Class in Search of Social Hegemony: Causes and Political Consequences.' In *Quebec State and Society*, edited by Alain G. Gagnon, 150–85. Toronto: Methuen, 1984. First published in *International Review of Community Development* 39–40 (1978): 1–37.

Resnick, Philip. *Toward a Canada-Quebec Union*. Montreal: McGill-Queen's University Press, 1991.

Rioux, Marcel. 'The Development of Ideologies in Quebec.' Translated by
Gerald Gold. In *Communities and Culture in French Canada*, edited by
Gerald Gold and Marc Adélard Tremblay, 260–79. Toronto: Holt, Rinehart &
Winston of Canada, 1973. Originally published as 'Sur l'evolution des
idéologies au Québec.' *Revue de l'Institut de Sociologie* 41 (1968): 95–124.
- *Quebec in Question*. Translated by James Boake. Toronto: James Lewis &
Samuel, 1971.
Roberts, Leslie. *The Chief: A Political Biography of Maurice Duplessis*. Toronto:
Clarke, Irwin, 1963.
Robinson, Gertrude. *Constructing the Quebec Referendum: French and English
Media Voices*. Toronto: University of Toronto Press, 1998.
Rogers, Nicholas. 'Crowd and People in the Gordon Riots.' In *The Transforma-
tion of Political Culture: England and Germany in the Late Eighteenth Cen-
tury*, edited by Eckhart Hellmuth. London: German Historical Institute, 1986.
- *Whigs and Cities: Popular Politics in the Age of Walpole and Pitt*. Oxford:
Clarendon Press, 1989.
Romney, Paul. 'Sir Oliver Mowat.' In *Dictionary of Canadian Biography*, vol. 13,
724–42.
Rosenau, James N. *Turbulence in World Politics: A Theory of Change and
Continuity*. Princeton: Princeton University Press, 1990.
Roy, Jean-Louis. *La Marche des québécois: le temps des ruptures (1945–1960)*.
Montreal, Leméac, 1976.
Russell, Peter. *Constitutional Odyssey: Can Canadians Become a Sovereign
People?* 2d ed. Toronto: University of Toronto Press, 1993.
Ryerson, Stanley. *Unequal Union: Confederation and the Roots of Conflict in
the Canadas, 1815–1873*. Toronto: Progress, 1968.
Sandel, Michael. *Liberalism and the Limits of Justice*. Cambridge: Cambridge
University Press, 1982.
- 'The Procedural Republic and the Unencumbered Self.' *Political Theory* 12
(1984): 93.
Saywell, John. Introduction to *The Canadian Journal of Lady Aberdeen, 1893–
1898*. Edited by John Saywell. Toronto: Champlain Society, 1960.
- ed. *Canadian Annual Review for 1971*. Toronto: University of Toronto Press,
1972.
- ed. *Canadian Annual Review for 1974*. Toronto: University of Toronto Press,
1975.
Saywell, John, and Donald Forster, eds. *Canadian Annual Review for 1961*.
Toronto: University of Toronto Press, 1962.
- eds. *Canadian Annual Review for 1962*. Toronto: University of Toronto Press,
1963.

– eds. *Canadian Annual Review for 1968*. Toronto: University of Toronto Press, 1969.

Séguin, Maurice. 'La Conquête et la vie économique des Canadiens.' *Action nationale* 28 (1947): 308–26

– *L'idée d'indépendance au Québec: genèse et historique*. Trois-Rivières: Boréal Express, 1968.

Senior, Elinor Kyte. *Redcoats and Patriotes: The Rebellions in Lower Canada, 1837–38*. Stittsville: National Museums of Canada, 1985.

Senior, Hereward. *Orangeism: The Canadian Phase*. Toronto: McGraw-Hill Ryerson, 1972.

Seton-Watson, Hugh. *Nations and States: An Enquiry into the Origins of Nations and the Politics of Nationalism*. London: Methuen, 1977.

Sheppard, Robert, and Michael Valpy. *The National Deal*. Scarborough: Fleet, 1982.

Silver, Arthur. *The French-Canadian Idea of Confederation, 1864–1900*. Toronto: University of Toronto Press, 1982.

Simeon, Richard, and Ian Robinson. *State, Society, and the Development of Canadian Federalism*. Toronto: University of Toronto Press, 1990.

Simeon, Richard. 'Why Did the Meech Lake Accord Fail?' In *Canada: The State of the Federation 1990*, edited by Ronald Watts and Douglas Brown, 15–40. Kingston: Institute of Intergovernmental Relations, Queen's University, 1990.

Sissons, Charles. *Church and State in Canadian Education: An Historical Study*. Toronto: Ryerson, 1959.

Sked, Alan. *Europe's Balance of Power, 1815–1848*. London: Macmillan, 1979.

Skinner, Quentin. 'Meaning and Understanding in the History of Ideas' (1969). Reprinted in *Meaning and Context: Quentin Skinner and His Critics*, edited by James Tully, 29–67. Cambridge: Polity, 1988.

– 'A Reply to My Critics.' In *Meaning and Context: Quentin Skinner and His Critics*, edited by James Tully, 231–88. Cambridge: Polity, 1988.

– '"Social Meaning" and the Explanation of Social Action' (1972). Reprinted in *Meaning and Context: Quentin Skinner and His Critics*. Edited by James Tully, 79–96. Cambridge: Polity, 1988.

Skocpol, Theda. *States and Social Revolutions: A Comparative Analysis of France, Russia, and China*. Cambridge: Cambridge University Press, 1979.

Smith, Anthony. *The Ethnic Origins of Nations*. Oxford: Blackwell, 1986.

– *The Ethnic Revival in the Modern World*. Cambridge: Cambridge University Press, 1981.

– *National Identity*. London: Penguin, 1991.

– *Theories of Nationalism*, 2d ed. London: Duckworth, 1983.

Smith, Lawrence. '*Le Canadien* and the British Constitution, 1806–1810.' *Canadian Historical Review* 38 no. 2 (1957): 93–108.

Smith, Peter. 'The Dream of Political Union: Loyalism, Toryism and the Federal Idea in Pre-Confederation Canada.' In *The Causes of Canadian Confederation*, edited by Ged Martin, 148–71. Fredericton, NB: Acadiensis, 1990.

Smooha, Sammy, and Theodor Hanf. 'The Diverse Modes of Conflict Regulation in Deeply Divided Societies.' *International Journal of Comparative Sociology* 33 (1992): 26–47.

Sniderman, Paul M., Joseph F. Fletcher, Peter H. Russell, and Philip E. Tetlock. 'Political Culture and the Problem of Double Standards: Mass and Élite Attitudes toward Language Rights in the Canadian Charter of Rights and Freedoms.' *Canadian Journal of Political Science* 22 (1989): 259–84.

Snyder, Louis. *The Meaning of Nationalism.* New York: Greenwood, 1968.

Soulard, Jean-Claude. 'Sir Antoine-Aimé Dorion.' In *Dictionary of Canadian Biography*, vol. 12, 260–5.

Spira, Thomas. 'Nationalism: Recent Research and New Opportunities.' In *Nationalism: Essays in Honor of Louis L. Snyder*, edited by Michael Palumbo and William Shanahan, 33–52. Westport, CT: Greenwood, 1981.

St Germain, Pierre. 'Un certain goût pour la violence.' In *Un certain révolution tranquille*, edited by Jean Sisto, 61–77. Montreal: La presse, 1975.

– *The Birth of Western Canada: A History of the Riel Rebellions.* 1936; Toronto: University of Toronto Press, 1961.

Stanley, George. 'The Caraquet Riots of 1875.' *Acadiensis* 2 (1972–3): 21–38.

Stevenson, John. *Popular Disturbances in England*, 2d ed. London: Longman, 1992.

Strauss, Leo. *Liberalism Ancient and Modern.* (1968). Ithaca: Cornell University Press, 1989.

Sturgis, James. 'Anglicisation as a Theme in Lower Canadian History, 1807–1843.' *British Journal of Canadian Studies* 3 (1988): 210–29. First published in *Bulletin of Canadian Studies* 3 (1979): 29–54.

– 'The Opposition to Confederation in Nova Scotia, 1864–1868.' In *The Causes of Canadian Confederation*, edited by Ged Martin, 114–29. Fredericton, NB: Acadiensis, 1990.

Sunahara, Ann Gomer. *The Politics of Racism: the Uprooting of Japanese Canadians during the Second World War.* Toronto: James Lorimer, 1981.

Swainson, Donald. 'Canada Annexes the West: Colonial Status Confirmed.' In *Federalism in Canada and Australia: the Early Years*, edited by Bruce Hodgins, Don Wright, and Welf Heick, 137–58. Waterloo: Wilfrid Laurier University Press, 1978.

Swinton, Katherine. 'Competing Visions of Constitutionalism: of Federalism and Rights.' In *Competing Constitutional Visions: The Meech Lake Accord*, edited by Katherine Swinton and Carol Rogerson. Toronto: Carswell, 1988.

Taylor, Brook, ed. *Beginnings to Confederation*. Vol. 1 of *Canadian History: A Reader's Guide*. Toronto: University of Toronto Press, 1994.

Taylor, Charles. 'Atomism.' *Philosophy and the Human Sciences*, vol. 2., 187–210. Cambridge: Cambridge University Press, 1985.

– *Reconciling the Solitudes: Essays on Canadian Federalism and Nationalism*. Montreal: McGill-Queen's University Press, 1993.

– 'Shared and Divergent Values,' in *Reconciling the Solitudes: Essays on Canadian Federalism and Nationalism*. Montreal: McGill-Queen's University Press, 1993.

Thomson, Dale. *Jean Lesage and the Quiet Revolution*. Toronto: Macmillan, 1984.

Toner, Peter. 'New Brunswick Schools and the Rise of Provincial Rights.' In *Federalism in Canada and Australia: the Early Years*, ed. Bruce Hodgins, Don Wright, and Welf Heick, 125–36. Waterloo: Wiltrid Laurier University Press, 1978.

Touraine, Alain. *Post-Industrial Society; Tomorrow's Social History: Classes, Conflicts and Culture in the Programmed Society*. Translated by Leonard F.X. Mayhew. New York: Random House, 1971.

Tousignant, Pierre. 'The Integration of the Province of Quebec into the British Empire, 1763–91.' In *Dictionary of Canadian Biography*. Vol. 4, xxxii–xlix. Toronto: University of Toronto Press, 1979.

– 'La première campagne électorale des Canadiens en 1792.' *Histoire sociale* 8 (1975): 120–148.

– 'Problématique pour un nouvelle approche de la constitution de 1791.' *Revue d'histoire de L'Amerique française* 27 (1973): 181–234.

Trépanier, Pierre. Interview by Gilles Gougeon. In *A History of Québec Nationalism*. Translated by Louis Blair et al., 55–65. Toronto: Lorimer, 1994.

Trofimenkoff, Susan Mann. *Action Française: French-Canadian Nationalism in the Twenties*. Toronto: University of Toronto Press, 1975.

– *The Dream of Nation: A Social and Intellectual History of Quebec*. Toronto: Macmillan, 1982.

Trudeau, Pierre Elliott. *The Asbestos Strike*. Translated by James Boake. Toronto: James Lewis and Samuel, 1974.

– *Federalism and the French Canadians*. Toronto: Macmillan, 1967.

– 'Un manifeste démocratique.' *Cité Libre* 22 (1958): 1–31.

Truman, David. *The Governmental Process: Political Interests and Public Opinion*. New York: Knopf, 1951.

Tully, James. 'Diversity's Gambit Declined.' In *Constitutional Predicament:*

Canada after the Referendum of 1992, edited by Curtis Cook, 149–98. Montreal: McGill-Queen's University Press, 1994.

Urquhart, M.C., ed. *Historical Statistics of Canada*. Cambridge: Cambridge University Press, 1965.

Vallières, Pierre. *White Niggers of America*. Translated by Joan Pinkham. Toronto: McClelland & Stewart, 1971. Originally published as *Négres blancs d'amérique: autobiographie précoce d'un 'terroriste' québécois*. Montreal: Parti Pris, 1968.

Van Evera, Stephen. 'Hypotheses on Nationalism and War.' In *Nationalism and Ethnic Conflict*, edited by Michael Brown, Owen Coté, Jr, Sean Lynn-Jones, and Steven Miller, 26–60. Cambridge, MA: MIT Press, 1997.

Viger, D.B. *Analyse d'un entretien sur la conservation des établissemens du Bas-Canada des loix, des usages de ses habitans*. Montreal: James Lane, 1826.

Vigod, Bernard. *Quebec before Duplessis: The Political Career of Louis-Alexandre Taschereau*. Kingston and Montreal: McGill-Queen's University Press, 1986.

Vipond, Robert. 'Constitutional Politics and the Legacy of the Provincial Rights Movement in Canada.' *Canadian Journal of Political Science* 28 (1985): 267–94.

– *Liberty and Community: Canadian Federalism and the Failure of the Constitution*. Albany, NY: State University of New York Press, 1991.

Wade, Mason. *The French Canadians, 1760–1967*. Vol. 1: *1760–1911*, 2d ed. Toronto: Macmillan, 1975.

Waite, Peter, ed. *The Confederation Debates in the Province of Canada, 1865: A Selection*. Toronto: McClelland & Stewart, 1963.

Waite, Peter. *Canada 1874–1896: Arduous Destiny*. Toronto: McClelland & Stewart, 1971.

– *The Life and Times of Confederation, 1864–1867: Politics, Newspapers, and the Union of British North America*. Toronto: University of Toronto Press, 1962.

– *The Man from Halifax: Sir John Thompson, Prime Minister*. Toronto: University of Toronto Press, 1985.

Waldron, Jeremy. 'Minority Cultures and the Cosmopolitan Alternative.' In *The Rights of Minority Cultures*, edited by Will Kymlicka, 93–119. New York: Oxford University Press, 1995.

Walker, Franklin. *Catholic Education and Politics in Ontario: A Documentary Study*, vol. 2. Toronto: Federation of Catholic Education Associations, 1976.

– *Catholic Education and Politics in Upper Canada: A Study of the Documentation Relative to the Origin of Catholic Elementary Schools in the Ontario School System*. Toronto: J.M. Dent & Sons, 1955.

Wallot, Jean-Pierre. *Intrigues françaises et américaines au Canada, 1800–1802*.

Montreal: Editions Leméac, 1965.

– *Un Québec qui bougeait: trame socio-politique du Québec au tournant du XIXe siècle*. Montreal: Boréal Express, 1973.

– 'Sir Robert Milnes.' In *Dictionary of Canadian Biography*, vol. 7, 613–16.

Walzer, Michael. 'Pluralism: a Political Perspective.' In *The Rights of Minority Cultures*, edited by Will Kymlicka, 139–54. New York: Oxford University Press, 1995.

Ward, John Manning. *Colonial Self-Government: The British Experience, 1759–1856*. Toronto: University of Toronto Press, 1976.

Ward, Peter. *White Canada Forever: Popular Attitudes and Public Policy towards Orientals in British Columbia*. Montreal: McGill-Queen's University Press, 1978.

Watt, James. 'Anti-Catholic Nativism in Canada: The Protestant Protective Association.' *Canadian Historical Review* 48 (1967): 45–58.

Weaver, R. Kent. 'Political Institutions and Canada's Constitutional Crisis.' In *The Collapse of Canada?* edited by R. Kent Weaver, 7–76. Washington, DC: Brookings Institution, 1992.

Whitaker, Reginald. 'Reason, Passion, and Interest: Pierre Trudeau's Eternal Liberal Triangle.' In *A Sovereign Idea: Essays on Canada as a Democratic Community*. Montreal: McGill-Queen's University Press 1992. First published in *Canadian Journal of Political and Social Theory* 4 (1980): 5–31.

Whitelaw, William. *The Maritimes and Canada/Before Confederation*. Toronto: Oxford University Press, 1934.

Williams, Cynthia. 'The Changing Nature of Citizen Rights.' In *Constitutionalism, Citizenship and Society in Canada*, edited by Alan Cairns and Cynthia Williams, 99–132. Toronto: University of Toronto Press, 1985.

Woehrling, José. 'The Distinct Society Clause's Critics.' In *The Meech Lake Primer: Conflicting Views of the 1987 Constitutional Accord*, edited by Michael D. Behiels, 171–208. Ottawa: University of Ottawa Press, 1989.

Yonge, Charles Duke, ed., *The Life and Administration of Lord Liverpool*. Vol. 1. London: Macmillan, 1868.

Young, Brian. 'The Defeat of George-Etienne Cartier in Montreal-East in 1872.' *Canadian Historical Review* 51 (1970): 386–406.

Index